CIMA
STUDY TEXT

Final Paper 13

Management Accounting:
Financial Strategy

BPP'S STUDY TEXTS FOR CIMA'S NEW SYLLABUS

- Targeted to the **syllabus** and **learning outcomes**

- **Quizzes** and **questions** to check your understanding

- Incorporates CIMA's new Official Terminology

- Clear layout and style designed to save you time

- Plenty of **exam-style questions**

- **Chapter Roundups** and summaries to help revision

- **Mind Maps** to integrate the key points

New in this July 2001 edition

- More **case examples**

- More detailed coverage of topical areas

BPP Publishing
July 2001

First edition July 2000

Second edition July 2001

ISBN 0 7517 3169 2 (Previous edition 0 7517 3144 7)

British Library Cataloguing-in-Publication Data
A catalogue record for this book
is available from the British Library

Published by

BPP Publishing Ltd
Aldine House, Aldine Place
London W12 8AW

www.bpp.com

Printed in Great Britain by Ashford Colour Press

We are grateful to the Chartered Institute of Management Accountants for permission to reproduce past examination questions and questions from the pilot paper. The suggested solutions to the illustrative questions have been prepared by BPP Publishing Limited.

Page

THE BPP STUDY TEXT (v)

HELP YOURSELF STUDY FOR YOUR CIMA EXAMS (vii)
The right approach - suggested study sequence - developing your
personal Study Plan

SYLLABUS AND LEARNING OUTCOMES (xii)

THE EXAM PAPER (xix)

WHAT THE EXAMINER MEANS (xx)

REVIEW FORM & FREE PRIZE DRAW

ORDER FORM

THE BPP STUDY TEXT

Aims of this Study Text

To provide you with the knowledge and understanding, skills and application techniques that you need if you are to be successful in your exams

This Study Text has been written around the **Management Accounting: Financial Strategy** syllabus.

- It is **comprehensive**. It covers the syllabus content. No more, no less.

- It is written at the **right level**. Each chapter is written with CIMA's precise learning outcomes in mind.

- It is targeted to the **exam**. We have taken account of the Pilot Paper, questions put to the examiners at the recent CIMA conference and the assessment methodology.

To allow you to study in the way that best suits your learning style and the time you have available, by following your personal Study Plan (see page (ix))

You may be studying at home on your own until the date of the exam, or you may be attending a full-time course. You may like to (and have time to) read every word, or you may prefer to (or only have time to) skim-read and devote the remainder of your time to question practice. Wherever you fall in the spectrum, you will find the BPP Study Text meets your needs in designing and following your personal Study Plan.

To tie in with the other components of the BPP Effective Study Package to ensure you have the best possible chance of passing the exam (see page (vi))

BPP PUBLISHING

Recommended period of use	Elements of the BPP Effective Study Package
Three to twelve months before the exam	**Study Text** Use the Study Text to acquire knowledge, understanding, skills and the ability to use application techniques.
One to six months before the exam	**Practice & Revision Kit** Try the numerous examination-format questions, for which there are realistic suggested solutions prepared by BPP's own authors. Then attempt the two mock exams.
From three months before the exam until the last minute	**Passcards** Work through these short, memorable notes which are focused on what is most likely to come up in the exam you will be sitting.
One to six months before the exam	**Success Tapes** These audio tapes cover the vital elements of your syllabus in less than 90 minutes per subject. Each tape also contains exam hints to help you fine tune your strategy.
Three to twelve months before the exam	**Breakthrough Videos** Use a Breakthrough Video to supplement your Study Text. They give you clear tuition on key exam subjects and allow you the luxury of being able to pause or repeat sections until you have fully grasped the topic.

HELP YOURSELF STUDY FOR YOUR CIMA EXAMS

Exams for professional bodies such as CIMA are very different from those you have taken at college or university. You will be under **greater time pressure before** the exam - as you may be combining your study with work. There are many different ways of learning and so the BPP Study Text offers you a number of different tools to help you through. Here are some hints and tips: they are not plucked out of the air, but **based on research and experience**. (You don't need to know that long-term memory is in the same part of the brain as emotions and feelings - but it's a fact anyway.)

The right approach

1 The right attitude

Believe in yourself	Yes, there is a lot to learn. Yes, it is a challenge. But thousands have succeeded before and you can too.
Remember why you're doing it	Studying might seem a grind at times, but you are doing it for a reason: to advance your career.

2 The right focus

Read through the Syllabus and learning outcomes	These tell you what you are expected to know and are supplemented by Exam Focus Points in the text.
Study the Exam Paper section	Past papers are a reasonable guide of what you should expect in the exam.

3 The right method

The big picture	You need to grasp the detail - but keeping in mind how everything fits into the big picture will help you understand better. • The **Introduction** of each chapter puts the material in context. • The **Syllabus content, learning outcomes** and **Exam focus points** show you what you need to **grasp**. • **Mind Maps** show the links and key issues in key topics.
In your own words	To absorb the information (and to practise your written communication skills), it helps to **put it into your own words.** • **Take notes.** • Answer the **questions** in each chapter. As well as helping you absorb the information, you will practise the assessment formats used in the exam and your written communication skills, which become increasingly important as you progress through your CIMA exams. • Draw **mind maps**. We have some examples. • Try 'teaching' a subject to a colleague or friend.

Give yourself cues to jog your memory	The BPP Study Text uses **bold** to **highlight key points** and **icons** to identify key features, such as **Exam focus points** and **Key terms.** • Try **colour coding** with a highlighter pen. • Write **key points** on cards.

4 The right review

Review, review, review	It is a **fact** that regularly reviewing a topic in summary form can **fix it in your memory**. Because **review** is so important, the BPP Study Text helps you to do so in many ways. • **Chapter roundups** summarise the key points in each chapter. Use them to recap each study session. • The **Quick quiz** is another review technique to ensure that you have grasped the essentials. • Use the **Key terms** as a quiz. • Go through the **Examples** in each chapter a second or third time.

Suggested study sequence

Tackle the chapters in the order you find them in the Study Text. Taking into account your individual learning style, you could follow this sequence.

Key study steps	Activity
Step 1 **Topic list**	Each numbered topic is a numbered section in the chapter.
Step 2 **Introduction**	This gives you the **big picture** in terms of the **context** of the chapter, the **content** you will cover, and the **learning outcomes** the chapter assesses - in other words, it sets your **objectives for study.**
Step 3 **Knowledge brought forward boxes**	In these we highlight information and techniques that it is assumed you have 'brought forward' with you from your earlier studies. If there are topics which have changed recently due to legislation for example, these topics are explained in more detail.
Step 4 **Explanations**	Proceed methodically through the chapter, reading each section thoroughly and making sure you understand.
Step 5 **Key terms and Exam focus points**	• **Key terms** can often earn you *easy marks* if you state them clearly and correctly in an appropriate exam answer (and they are highlighted in the index at the back of the text). • **Exam focus points** give you a good idea of how we think the examiner intends to examine certain topics.
Step 6 **Note taking**	Take brief notes if you wish, avoiding the temptation to copy out too much.

Key study steps	Activity
Step 7 **Examples**	Follow each through to its solution very carefully.
Step 8 **Case examples**	Study each one, and try to add flesh to them from your own experience – they are designed to show how the topics you are studying come alive (and often come unstuck) in the real world.
Step 9 **Questions**	Make a very good attempt at each one.
Step 10 **Answers**	Check yours against ours, and make sure you understand any discrepancies.
Step 11 **Chapter roundup**	Work through it very carefully, to make sure you have grasped the major points it is highlighting.
Step 12 **Quick quiz**	When you are happy that you have covered the chapter, use the **Quick quiz** to check how much you have remembered of the topics covered and to practise questions in a variety of formats.
Step 13 **Question(s) in the Question bank**	Either at this point, or later when you are thinking about revising, make a full attempt at the **Question(s)** suggested at the very end of the chapter. You can find these at the end of the Study Text, along with the **Answers** so you can see how you did. We highlight those that are introductory, and those which are of the standard you would expect to find in an exam.
Step 14 **Multiple choice questions**	Use the bank of MCQs at the back of this Study Text to practise this important assessment format and to determine how much of the Study Text you have absorbed. If you have bought the MCQ cards, use these too.

BPP PUBLISHING

Developing your personal Study Plan

Preparing a Study Plan (and sticking closely to it) is one of the key elements in learning success.

Step 1. How do you learn?

First you need to be aware of your style of learning. There are four typical learning styles. Consider yourself in the light of the following descriptions and work out which you fit most closely. You can then plan to follow the key study steps in the sequence suggested.

Learning styles	Characteristics	Sequence of key study steps in the BPP Study Text
Theorist	Seeks to understand principles before applying them in practice	1, 2, 3, 4, 7, 8, 5, 9/10, 11, 12, 13 (6 continuous)
Reflector	Seeks to observe phenomena, thinks about them and then chooses to act	
Activist	Prefers to deal with practical, active problems; does not have much patience with theory	1, 2, 9/10 (read through), 7, 8, 5, 11, 3, 4, 9/10 (full attempt), 12, 13 (6 continuous)
Pragmatist	Prefers to study only if a direct link to practical problems can be seen; not interested in theory for its own sake	9/10 (read through), 2, 5, 7, 8, 11, 1, 3, 4, 9/10 (full attempt), 12, 13 (6 continuous)

Step 2. How much time do you have?

Work out the time you have available per week, given the following.

- The standard you have set yourself
- The time you need to set aside later for work on the Practice & Revision Kit and Passcards
- The other exam(s) you are sitting
- Very importantly, practical matters such as work, travel, exercise, sleep and social life

Note your time available in box A.   A [Hours]

Step 3. Allocate your time

- Take the time you have available per week for this Study Text shown in box A, multiply it by the number of weeks available and insert the result in box B.   B [   ]

- Divide the figure in Box B by the number of chapters in this text and insert the result in box C.   C [   ]

Step 4. Implement

Set about studying each chapter in the time shown in box C, following the key study steps in the order suggested by your particular learning style.

This is your personal **Study Plan**.

(x)

Short of time: Skim study technique?

You may find you simply do not have the time available to follow all the key study steps for each chapter, however you adapt them for your particular learning style. If this is the case, follow the **skim study** technique below (the icons in the Study Text will help you to do this).

- Study the chapters in the order you find them in the Study Text.

- For each chapter, follow the key study steps 1-3, and then skim-read through step 4. Jump to step 11, and then go back to step 5. Follow through steps 7 and 8, and prepare outline answers to questions (steps 9/10). Try the Quick quiz (step 12), following up any items you can't answer, then do a plan for the Question (step 13), comparing it against our answers. You should probably still follow step 6 (note-taking), although you may decide simply to rely on the BPP Passcards for this.

Moving on...

However you study, when you are ready to embark on the practice and revision phase of the BPP Effective Study Package, you should still refer back to this Study Text, both as a source of **reference** (you should find the index particularly helpful for this) and as a **refresher** (the Chapter roundups and Quick quizzes help you here).

And remember to keep careful hold of this Study Text – you will find it invaluable in your work.

BPP PUBLISHING

SYLLABUS MIND MAP

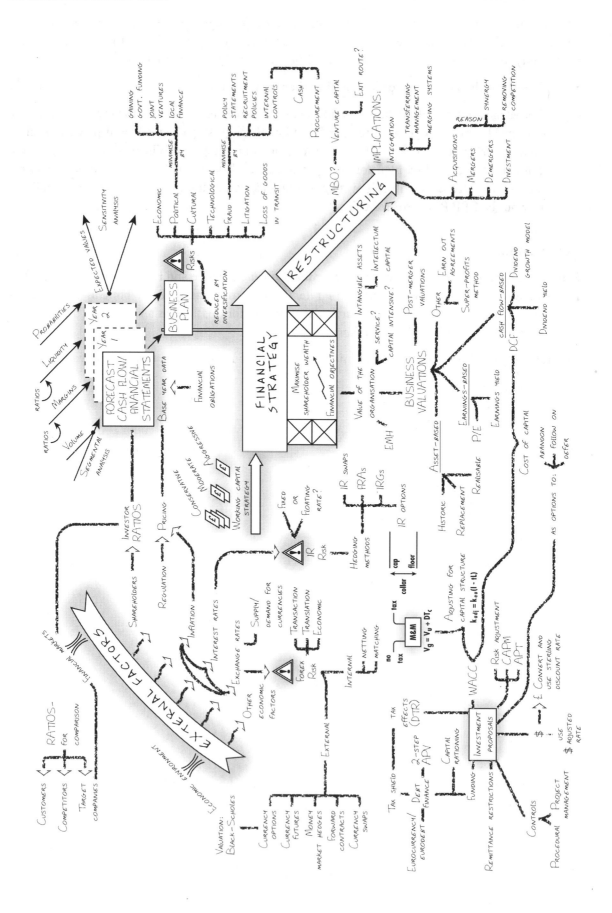

SYLLABUS AND LEARNING OUTCOMES

Syllabus overview

This syllabus explores financial management from a domestic and international perspective. It builds on material covered in the *Finance* and *Management Accounting Decision Making* papers at Intermediate level.

The risk management section of the paper introduces entirely new material not seen in previous papers whereas the other three sections of the syllabus represent developments on material introduced in earlier papers.

Aims

This syllabus aims to test the student's ability to:

- Evaluate and interpret the financial implications of strategies
- Calculate, evaluate and recommend the value of an organisation
- Interpret the risks facing an organisation and recommend risk management strategies
- Evaluate advanced investment proposals

Assessment

There will be a written paper of 3 hours. Section A will contain a compulsory question up to a maximum of 50 marks, based upon a scenario. Section B will contain a choice of questions, normally two from four.

All learning outcomes may be tested in each section.

Formulae will be given as required.

Learning outcomes and syllabus content

13(i) Financial strategy formulation - 25%

Learning outcomes

On completion of their studies students should be able to:

- Identify appropriate actions for improving financial performance

- Evaluate the attainment of financial objectives

- Analyse and interpret the risk implications of business plans

- Analyse and interpret company accounts of customers, competitors and target companies

- Identify and interpret the impact of internal and external constraints on financial strategy (eg funding, regulatory bodies, investor relations, strategy, and economic factors)

BPP
PUBLISHING

Syllabus and learning outcomes

Syllabus content

	Covered in chapter
• Modelling annual cash flow forecasts and other financial statements based on expected changes in values over a number of years (eg inflation, volume, margins and probabilities, expected values and sensitivity analysis). No detailed testing of cash management models will be set since these were covered in the Finance paper	4
• Constructing forecast financial statements based upon base year data. (Note: these will not need to be presented in published accounts formats)	4
• Working capital management strategies, ie aggressive, moderate and conservative strategies. No detailed testing of stock management models will be set since these were covered in the Finance paper	4
• Interpreting the segmental analysis section of published accounts	3
• Financial objectives of an organisation	1
• Financial obligations indicated in financial accounts, eg redeemable debt, earn out arrangements, potential liabilities, long-term commitments (a UK example would be the Private Finance Initiative)	3
• Ratio analysis (liquidity, profitability, shareholder investment, gearing)	3
• Impact of regulation on developing strategy, eg competition authorities, pricing and services regulation, eg OFTEL, OFWAT	2
• Major economic forces affecting an organisation's financial plans (eg interest rates, inflation, exchange rates)	2
• Policies for distribution of earnings, eg dividends, share repurchase. (Note: theory of dividend relevance will not be tested)	5

(ii) Business valuations - 25%

Learning outcomes

On completion of their studies students should be able to:

• Calculate values of organisations of different types, eg service, capital intensive

• Identify and calculate the value of intangible assets in an organisation (including intellectual capital)

• Identify and evaluate the financial and strategic implications of proposals for mergers, acquisitions, demergers and divestments

• Compare, contrast and recommend settlement methods and terms

• Calculate post merger values of companies

- Identify post acquisition value enhancement strategies

- Illustrate and explain the impact of regulation on take-overs

- Evaluate exit strategies

Syllabus content

	Covered in chapter
• Asset valuation bases (eg historic, replacement, realisable)	6
• Earnings valuation bases (eg price/earnings (P/E) multiples, earnings yield)	6
• Cash flow valuation bases (ie DCF, dividend yield, dividend growth model using the formula $P_0 = D_1/r - g$)	6
• Other valuation bases (eg earn out arrangements, super profits method)	6
• The strengths and weaknesses of each valuation method and when each method is most suitable	6
• Application of the efficient market hypothesis (EMH) to business valuations	7
• Application of valuation bases to new issues	6, 7
• Selection of an appropriate cost of capital if using discounted cash flow to value a business (see section (iv) of this syllabus)	6, 17
• The impact of changing capital structures on the market value of a company will be tested using the formula $V_g = V_u + DT_c$. An understanding of the principles of Modigliani and Miller's theory of gearing with and without tax will be expected, but no proof of their theory will be examined (ie arbitrage)	8
• The different forms of intellectual capital	6
• The methods of valuing intellectual capital	6
• The reasons for acquisitions (eg synergistic benefits, removing competition)	9
• Different payment methods (eg cash, shares, convertibles, earn out arrangements)	9
• The integration process following a take-over, eg transferring management, merging systems	9
• The implications of regulation in take-over situations (detailed knowledge of the City Code will not be tested)	9
• The priorities of different stakeholders in terms of business valuations	9
• The function/role of management buyouts, venture capitalists, including appropriate exit strategies	9

BPP PUBLISHING

(iii) Risk management - 25%

Learning outcomes

On completion of their studies students should be able to:

- Interpret the risks facing an organisation

- Evaluate risk management strategies

- Identify appropriate methods for managing interest rate risk

- Demonstrate how and when to convert fixed to floating rate interest

- Interpret the impact of currency risk

- Calculate the impact of different national inflation rates on forecasting exchange rates

- Explain exchange rate theory

- Recommend foreign exchange risk management strategies

Syllabus content

	Covered in chapter
• Management of risk: cultural, economic, political, technological and fraud	10
• Minimisation of political risk (eg gaining government funding, joint ventures, obtaining local finance)	10, 16
• Minimising the risk of fraud (eg fraud policy statements, effective recruitment policies and good internal controls especially over procurement and cash)	10
• The principle of diversifying risk (no numerical calculations required)	10
• The risk of loss while goods are in transit and the risk of litigation in different countries (no specific country will be tested)	10
• Management of interest rate risk including the use of interest rate swaps (simple calculations to illustrate an interest rate swap may be required)	11
• Forward rate agreements and interest rate guarantees (numerical questions will not be set on these topics)	11
• Illustration and interpretation of interest options using simple graphs to show caps, floors and collars (numerical questions will not be set)	11
• Transaction, translation and economic risk	12
• Interest rate parity, purchasing power parity and the Fisher effect	12
• Forward contracts and money market hedges (numerical questions will be set including the need to be able to use cross rates)	12

Covered in chapter

- Currency futures and options including tick values (numerical questions including tick values but ignoring basis risk will be set: the Black Scholes option pricing model will not be tested numerically, however, an understanding of the variables which will influence the value of an option should be appreciated) — 13

- Internal hedging techniques, eg netting and matching — 12

- Currency swaps (calculations to illustrate a currency swap may be set) — 13

(iv) Advanced investment appraisal - 25%

Learning outcomes

On completion of their studies students should be able to:

- Evaluate investment proposals (domestic and international)

- Recommend methods of funding investments

- Interpret the impact of changing exchange rates and inflation rates on the investment

- Calculate and interpret real options (abandonment, follow-on, deferment)

- Calculate the tax shield of debt finance on an investment

- Identify and describe procedures for the control of international investments

- Recommend investment decisions when capital is rationed

Syllabus content

Covered in chapter

- Calculate the net present value and internal rate of return by either converting the foreign currency cash flows into sterling and discounting at a sterling discount rate, or discounting the cash flows in the host country's currency using an adjusted discount rate — 14, 16

- The effect of taxation, including differential tax rates and double tax relief — 14, 16

- The effects of restrictions on remittances — 16

- Predict changing exchange rates using the purchasing power parity method or interest rate parity — 12

- The benefits of finance drawn from the foreign environment (ie matching the characteristics of the investment with that of the financing) — 16

- The sources of long-term finance including Euro currency and Eurodebt markets — 16

- Capital investment real options (ie the option to make follow-on investment, the option to abandon and the option to wait) — 15

- Weighted Average Cost of Capital (WACC) and when it is appropriate to use WACC — 6, 8, 16, 17

Covered in chapter

- Adjusting the WACC for changes in capital structure. Knowledge of the use of $r^\star = r(1 - T^\star L)$ will be expected — 17

- Single period capital rationing for divisible and non-divisible projects (multi-period capital rationing will not be tested) — 15

- Adjusted present value (APV). The two step method of APV will be tested for debt introduced permanently and debt in place for the duration of the project — 17

- Capital Asset Pricing Model (CAPM). The ability to gear and ungear betas will be tested (candidates will not be asked to calculate a beta value from raw data using regression or other methods) — 17

- Arbitrage pricing theory. The main principles of this theory will be tested and its advantages and disadvantages compared with the CAPM. — 17

- Risk adjustment using the certainty equivalent method when given a risk free rate and certainty equivalent values — 17

- Investment controls in practice (eg procedural controls, project management) — 14

THE EXAM PAPER

Format of the paper

		Number of marks
Section A:	One compulsory scenario-based question	50
Section B:	Two questions from four (normally)	50
		100

Time allowed: 3 hours

May 2001

Section A

1   Company valuation; sources of finance; loss of staff

Section B

2   Financial objectives of listed company and health care trust; Private Finance Initiative

3   Adjusted present value; capital rationing

4   NPV of overseas project; purchase arrangement; effect of inflation

5   Currency swaps

Pilot paper

Section A

1   Evaluation of whether company with expansion plans is meeting financial objectives: prepare forecast financial statements; report on suitability of objectives, methods of financing, inflation and forecasts

Section B

2   Manufacturer considering expansion into another country: evaluation of foreign income cash flows; management of risks involved; funding the investment

3   Foreign currency receipts and payments schedule of an importer/ exporter; methods of hedging risks; comparison of use of currency options with fixed forward contracts

4   Private company operating in area dominated by the public sector: links between private and public sectors; valuation of private companies with substantial intellectual capital

5   Treasury department of company with diversified international interests: use of interest rate swap, financial derivatives and other forms of interest rate risk management

WHAT THE EXAMINER MEANS

The table below has been prepared by CIMA to help you interpret exam questions.

Learning objective	Verbs used	Definition
1 Knowledge What you are expected to know	• List • State • Define	• Make a list of • Express, fully or clearly, the details of/facts of • Give the exact meaning of
2 Comprehension What you are expected to understand	• Describe • Distinguish • Explain • Identify • Illustrate	• Communicate the key features of • Highlight the differences between • Make clear or intelligible/state the meaning of • Recognise, establish or select after consideration • Use an example to describe or explain something
3 Application Can you apply your knowledge?	• Apply • Calculate/ compute • Demonstrate • Prepare • Reconcile • Solve • Tabulate	• To put to practical use • To ascertain or reckon mathematically • To prove with certainty or to exhibit by practical means • To make or get ready for use • To make or prove consistent/compatible • Find an answer to • Arrange in a table
4 Analysis Can you analyse the detail of what you have learned?	• Analyse • Categorise • Compare and contrast • Construct • Discuss • Interpret • Produce	• Examine in detail the structure of • Place into a defined class or division • Show the similarities and/or differences between • To build up or compile • To examine in detail by argument • To translate into intelligible or familiar terms • To create or bring into existence
5 Evaluation Can you use your learning to evaluate, make decisions or recommendations?	• Advise • Evaluate • Recommend	• To counsel, inform or notify • To appraise or assess the value of • To advise on a course of action

Part A
Financial strategy formulation

Chapter 1

FINANCIAL OBJECTIVES OF ORGANISATIONS

Topic list	Syllabus reference	Ability required
1 Objectives of companies	(i)	Evaluation
2 Stakeholders and objectives	(i)	Analysis
3 Objectives of publicly owned and non-commercial bodies	(i)	Analysis
4 Financial management decisions	(i)	Analysis

Introduction

In Part A of this Study Text, we are concerned with how **financial objectives** of different types of organisation are identified and formulated; the **constraints** on formulating financial strategy; **non-financial objectives** and non-financial information; and also the analysis of the **performance of organisations**. The topics in Part A are most likely to be examined along with the syllabus areas covered later in the Study Text, but are no less important because of this.

Learning outcomes covered in this chapter

- Identify appropriate actions for improving financial performance
- Evaluate the attainment of financial objectives
- Analyse and interpret the risk implications of business plans

Syllabus content covered in this chapter

- Financial objectives of an organisation

1   OBJECTIVES OF COMPANIES

Pilot paper, 5/01

Strategic financial management

> **KEY TERM**
>
> **Strategic financial management** is defined in the *CIMA Official Terminology 2000 edition (OT 2000)* as 'the identification of the possible strategies capable of maximising an organisation's net present value, the allocation of scarce capital resources among the competing opportunities and the implementation and monitoring of the chosen strategy so as to achieve stated objectives'.

BPP PUBLISHING

1.1　The above definition given indicates that **strategy** depends on stated **objectives** or **targets**. Therefore, an obvious starting point is the identification and formulation of these objectives.

> ## KEY TERM
>
> **Strategy** is a course of action, including the specification of resources required, to achieve a specific objective. *(OT 2000)*

Case examples

The following statements of objectives, both formally and informally presented, were taken from 1999/2000 Annual Report and Accounts.

Tate & Lyle ('a global leader in carbohydrate processing')

The board of Tate & Lyle is totally committed to a strategy that will achieve a substantial improvement in profitability and return on capital and therefore in shareholder value. To that end we will:

- continue to develop higher margin, higher value-added and higher growth carbohydrate-based products, building on the Group's technology strengths in our world-wide starch business

- ensure that all retained assets produce acceptable returns

- divest businesses which do not contribute to value creation, and/or are no longer core to the Group's strategy

- conclude as rapidly as practicable our review of the strategic alternatives available to us in our US sugar operations

- continue to improve efficiency and reduce costs through our business improvement projects which include employee development and training programmes.

Kingfisher ('one of Europe's leading retailers concentrating on markets serving the home and family')

Customers are our primary focus. We are determined to provide them with an unbeatable shopping experience built on great value, service and choice, whilst rapidly identifying and serving their ever-changing needs.

This goal is pursued through some of Europe's best known retail brands and increasingly through innovative e-commerce channels which harness our traditional retailing expertise.

By combining global scale and local marketing we aim to continue to grow our business, deliver superior returns to our shareholders and provide unique and satisfying opportunities for our people.

Hilton Group ('A global company operating in the hospitality and gaming markets with the leading brand names of Hilton and Ladbroke')

The group intends to enhance shareholder value by exploiting its prime position in these international markets both of which are expected to experience significant long-term growth.

Financial objectives of a company

1.2　The theory of company finance is based on the assumption that **the objective of management is to maximise the market value of the enterprise**. Specifically, the main objective of a company should be to maximise the wealth of its ordinary shareholders.

1.3　A company is financed by ordinary shareholders, preference shareholders, loan stock holders and other long-term and short-term creditors. All surplus funds, however, belong to the legal owners of the company, its ordinary shareholders. Any retained profits are undistributed wealth of these equity shareholders.

How are the wealth of shareholders and the value of a company measured?

1.4 If the financial objective of a company is to maximise the value of the company, and in particular the value of its ordinary shares, we need to be able to put values on a company and its shares. How do we do it?

1.5 Three possible methods of valuation of a company might occur to us.

(a) **A balance sheet valuation, with assets valued on a going concern basis**. Certainly, investors will look at a company's balance sheet. If retained profits rise every year, the company will be a profitable one. Balance sheet values are not a measure of 'market value', although retained profits might give some indication of what the company could pay as dividends to shareholders.

(b) **The valuation of a company's assets on a break-up basis**. This method of valuing a business is only of interest when the business is threatened with liquidation, or when its management is thinking about selling off individual assets (rather than a complete business) to raise cash.

(c) **Market values**. The market value is the price at which buyers and sellers will trade stocks and shares in a company. This is the method of valuation which is most relevant to the financial objectives of a company.

(i) When shares are traded on a recognised stock market, such as the Stock Exchange, the market value of a company can be measured by the price at which shares are currently being traded.

(ii) When shares are in a private company, and are not traded on any stock market, there is no easy way to measure their market value. Even so, the financial objective of these companies should be to maximise the wealth of their ordinary shareholders.

1.6 The **wealth of the shareholders** in a company comes from dividends received and the market value of the shares. A **shareholder's return** on investment is obtained in the form of **dividends received** and **capital gains** from increases in the market value of his or her shares.

1.7 **Dividends** are generally paid just twice a year (interim and final dividends), whereas a current market value is (for quoted shares) always known from share prices. There is also a theory, supported by empirical evidence and common sense, that market prices are influenced strongly by expectations of what future dividends will be. So we might conclude that **the wealth of shareholders in quoted companies can be measured by the market value of the shares.**

How is the value of a business increased?

1.8 If a company's shares are **traded on a stock market,** the wealth of shareholders is increased when the share price goes up. Ignoring day-to-day fluctuations in price caused by patterns of supply and demand, and ignoring fluctuations caused by 'environmental' factors such as changes in interest rates, **the price of a company's shares will go up when the company is expected to make attractive profits,** which it will pay out as dividends or re-invest in the business to achieve future profit growth and dividend growth. However, to increase the share price the company should achieve its profits without taking **business risks** and **financial risks** which worry shareholders.

How does this influence the setting of financial targets?

1.9 If there is an increase in earnings and dividends, management can hope for an increase in the share price too, so that shareholders benefit from both higher revenue (dividends) and also capital gains (higher share prices).

1.10 Management should set **primary financial targets** for factors which they can influence directly, such as cash flows, profits and dividend growth. And so a financial objective might be expressed as the aim of increasing profits, earnings per share and dividend per share by, say, 10% a year for each of the next five years.

Other financial targets

1.11 In addition to targets for earnings, EPS, and dividend per share, a company might set **other financial** targets, such as:

(a) A restriction on the company's **level of gearing**, or debt. For example, a company's management might decide that:

    (i) The ratio of long-term debt capital to equity capital should never exceed, say, 1:1

    (ii) The cost of interest payments should never be higher than, say, 25% of total profits before interest and tax

(b) A target for **profit retentions**. For example, management might set a target that dividend cover (the ratio of distributable profits to dividends actually distributed) should not be less than, say, 2.5 times.

(c) A target for **operating profitability**. For example, management might set a target for the profit/sales ratio (say, a minimum of 10%) or for a return on capital employed (say, a minimum ROCE of 20%).

Case example

In their annual report 2000, Tate & Lyle identified the '**signposts to shareholder value**' as being:

- *Focus* – we focus on adding value to carbohydrates within a group that has clear objectives

- *Efficiency* – we initiate programmes to maximise efficiency, reduce costs and enhance the value on investment

- *Markets* – our extensive market knowledge and geographic reach enable us to serve global customers and maintain our leading market positions

- *Growth* – new products, innovative manufacturing processes and our strong brand portfolio deliver growth by adding value to consumer products

- *Investment* – selective investment, combined with volume manufacturing skills, enable us to grow our business and become a low-cost processor

---

1.12 These financial targets are not primary financial objectives, but they can act as **subsidiary targets** or constraints which should help a company to achieve its main financial objective without incurring excessive risks.

1.13 Some **recently privatised companies** act within regulatory financial constraints imposed by 'consumer watchdog' bodies set up by government. For example, BT (British Telecom) is overseen by the telecommunications regulator (OFTEL), which restricts price rises to protect consumers.

Short-term and long-term objectives

1.14 Targets such as those mentioned above are usually measured over a year rather than over the long term, and it is the maximisation of shareholder wealth in the long term that ought to be the corporate objective.

1.15 **Short-term measures of return can encourage a company to pursue short-term objectives at the expense of long-term ones**, for example by deferring new capital investments, or spending only small amounts on research and development and on training.

Multiple financial targets

1.16 A major problem with setting a number of different financial targets, either primary targets or supporting secondary targets, is that they might not all be consistent with each other, and so might not all be achievable at the same time. When this happens, some compromises will have to be accepted.

1.17 EXAMPLE: EVALUATION OF THE ATTAINMENT OF FINANCIAL OBJECTIVES

Lion Grange Ltd has recently introduced a formal scheme of long range planning. At a meeting called to discuss the first draft plans, the following estimates emerged.

(a) Sales in the current year reached £10,000,000, and forecasts for the next five years are £10,600,000, £11,400,000, £12,400,000, £13,600,000 and £15,000,000.

(b) The ratio of net profit after tax to sales is 10%, and this is expected to continue throughout the planning period.

(c) Net asset turnover, currently 0.8 times, will remain more or less constant.

It was also suggested that:

(d) If profits rise, dividends should rise by at least the same percentage

(e) An earnings retention rate of 50% should be maintained

(f) The ratio of long-term borrowing to long-term funds (debt plus equity) is limited (by the market) to 30%, which happens also to be the current gearing level of the company

Prepare a financial analysis of the draft long range plan and suggested policies for dividends, retained earnings and gearing.

1.18 SOLUTION

The draft financial plan, for profits, dividends, assets required and funding, can be drawn up in a table, as follows.

	Current year £m	Year 1 £m	Year 2 £m	Year 3 £m	Year 4 £m	Year 5 £m
Sales	10.0	10.6	11.4	12.4	13.6	15.0
Net profit after tax	1.0	1.06	1.14	1.24	1.36	1.5
Dividends (50% of profit after tax)	0.5	0.53	0.57	0.62	0.68	0.75
Net assets (125% of sales)	12.5	13.25	14.25	15.5	17.0	18.75

	Current year £m	Year 1 £m	Year 2 £m	Year 3 £m	Year 4 £m	Year 5 £m
Equity (increased by retained earnings)	8.75*	9.28	9.85	10.47	11.15	11.9
Maximum debt (30% of assets)	3.75	3.97	4.27	4.65	5.10	5.62
	12.50	13.25	14.12	15.12	16.25	17.52
Funds available/ (Shortfalls in funds), given maximum gearing of 30% and no new issue of shares = funds available minus net assets required	0	0	(0.13)	(0.38)	(0.75)	(1.23)

* The current year equity figure is a balancing figure, equal to the difference between net assets and long-term debt, which is currently at the maximum level of 30% of net assets.

1.19 These figures show that the financial objectives of the company are not compatible with each other, and adjustments will have to be made.

(a) Given the assumptions about sales, profits, dividends and net assets required, there will be an increasing shortfall of funds from year 2 onwards, unless new shares are issued or the gearing level rises above 30%.

(b) In years 2 and 3, the shortfall can be eliminated by retaining a greater percentage of profits, but this may have a serious adverse effect on the share price. In year 4 and year 5, the shortfall in funds cannot be removed even if dividend payments are reduced to nothing.

(c) The net asset turnover appears to be low. The situation would be eased if investments were able to generate a higher volume of sales, so that fewer fixed assets and less working capital would be required to support the projected level of sales.

(d) If net asset turnover cannot be improved, it may be possible to increase the profit to sales ratio by reducing costs or increasing selling prices.

(e) If a new issue of shares is proposed to make up the shortfall in funds, the amount of funds required must be considered very carefully. Total dividends would have to be increased in order to pay dividends on the new shares. The company seems unable to offer prospects of suitable dividend payments, and so raising new equity might be difficult.

(f) It is conceivable that extra funds could be raised by issuing new debt capital, so that the level of gearing would be over 30%. It is uncertain whether investors would be prepared to lend money so as to increase gearing. If more funds were borrowed, profits after interest and tax would fall so that the share price might also be reduced.

Non-financial objectives

1.20 A company may have important **non-financial objectives** relating to the following.

(a) **The welfare of employees.** A company may try to provide good wages and salaries, comfortable and safe working conditions, good training and career development, and good pensions.

(b) **The welfare of management.** Managers may seek to improve their own circumstances, eg with high salaries, company cars and other perks, even though their decisions will incur expenditure and so reduce profits.

(c) **The welfare of society as a whole**. Some managements are aware of the role that their company has to play in providing for the well-being of society, eg oil companies' awareness of their role as providers of energy for society, faced with the problems of protecting the environment and preserving the Earth's dwindling energy resources

(d) **The provision of a service.** The objectives of some companies include the provision to a particular standard of a service to the public, eg for many privatised utility companies such as British Telecom (BT) and British Gas and the regional electricity distribution companies, the regulatory regime imposed by government specifies certain service standards

(e) **The fulfilment of responsibilities towards customers and suppliers.**

(i) Responsibilities towards customers include providing a product or service of a quality that customers expect, and dealing honestly and fairly with customers.

(ii) Responsibilities towards suppliers are expressed mainly in terms of trading relationships. A company's size could give it considerable power as a buyer. The company should not use its power unscrupulously.

(f) **Leadership in research and development.**

The relationship between financial and non-financial objectives

1.21 Non-financial objectives do not negate financial objectives, but they do mean that the simple theory of company finance, that the objective of a firm is to maximise the wealth of ordinary shareholders, is too simplistic. Financial objectives may have to be compromised in order to satisfy non-financial objectives.

2 STAKEHOLDERS AND OBJECTIVES

> **KEY TERM**
>
> **Stakeholders** are groups or individuals having a legitimate interest in the activities of an organisation, generally comprising customers, employees, the community, shareholders, suppliers and lenders. *(OT 2000)*

Stakeholder groups

2.1 There is a variety of different groups or individuals whose interests are directly affected by the activities of a firm: the **stakeholders** in the firms:

- Common (equity) shareholders
- Preferred shareholders
- Trade creditors
- Holders of unsecured debt securities
- Holders of secured debt securities
- Intermediate (business) customers
- Final (consumer) customers
- Suppliers
- Employees
- Past employees
- Retirees

- Competitors
- Neighbours
- The immediate community
- The national society
- The world society
- Corporate management
- Organisational strategists
- The chief executive
- The board of directors
- Government
- Special interest groups

(Sharplin, *Strategic Management*)

Objectives of stakeholder groups

2.2   The various groups of stakeholders in a firm will have different goals which will depend in part on the particular situation of the enterprise. Some of the more important aspects of these different goals are as follows.

(a)   **Ordinary (equity) shareholders** are the providers of the risk capital of a company and usually their goal will be to **maximise the wealth which they have** as a result of the ownership of the shares in the company.

(b)   **Trade creditors** have supplied goods or services to the firm. Trade creditors will generally be profit-maximising firms themselves and have the objective of **being paid the full amount due by the date agreed**. On the other hand, they usually wish to ensure that they continue their trading relationship with the firm and may sometimes be prepared to accept later payment to avoid jeopardising that relationship.

(c)   **Long-term creditors,** which will often be banks, have the objective of **receiving payments of interest and capital on the loan by the due date for the repayments.** Where the loan is secured on assets of the company, the creditor will be able to appoint a receiver to dispose of the company's assets if the company defaults on the repayments.

(d)   **Employees** will usually want to **maximise their rewards** paid to them in salaries and benefits, according to the particular skills and the rewards available in alternative employment. Most employees will also want **continuity of employment**.

(e)   **Government** has objectives which can be formulated in political terms. Government agencies impinge on the firm's activities in different ways including through taxation of the firm's profits, the provision of grants, health and safety legislation, training initiatives and so on. Government policies will often be related to macroeconomic objectives such as **sustained economic growth** and **high levels of employment**.

(f)   **Management** has, like other employees (and managers who are not directors will normally be employees), the objective of maximising their own rewards. It is the duty of the directors and the managers to whom they delegate responsibilities to manage the company for the benefit of shareholders. The objective of reward maximisation might conflict with the exercise of this duty, in ways which we shall examine a little later.

Stakeholder groups and strategy

2.3   The actions of stakeholder groups in pursuit of their various goals can exert influence on strategy. The greater the power of the stakeholder, the greater his influence will be. Each stakeholder group will have different expectations about what it wants, and the **expectations of the various groups will conflict**. Each group, however, will influence strategic decision-making.

Shareholders and management

2.4   Although ordinary shareholders (equity shareholders) are the owners of the company to whom the board of directors are accountable, the actual powers of shareholders tend to be restricted, except in companies where the shareholders are also the directors.

2.5   The day-to-day running of a company is the responsibility of the management, and although the company's results are submitted for shareholders' approval at the annual general meeting (AGM), there is often apathy and acquiescence in directors' recommendations. AGMs are often very poorly attended.

2.6   Shareholders have no right to inspect the books of account, and their forecasts of future prospects generally need to be gleaned from the annual report and accounts, stockbrokers, investment journals and daily newspapers.

The agency problem

> **KEY TERM**
>
> **Agency theory** is the hypothesis that attempts to explain elements of organisational behaviour through an understanding of the relationships between **principals** (such as shareholders) and **agents** (such as **company managers and accountants**).
>
> A **conflict** may exist between the actions undertaken by agents in furtherance of their own self-interest, and those required to promote the interests of the principals. *(OT 2000)*

2.7   The relationship between management and shareholders is sometimes referred to as an **agency relationship**, in which managers act as agents for the shareholders, using delegated powers to run the affairs of the company in the shareholders' best interests.

2.8   The agency relationship arising from the separation of ownership from management is sometimes characterised as the **agency problem**. For example, if managers hold none or very little of the equity shares of the company they work for, what is to stop them from:

- Working inefficiently?
- Not bothering to look for profitable new investment opportunities?
- Giving themselves high salaries and perks?

2.9   One power that shareholders possess is **the right to remove the directors from office**. But shareholders have to take the initiative to do this, and in many companies, the shareholders lack the energy and organisation to take such a step. Even so, directors will want the company's report and accounts, and the proposed final dividend, to **meet with shareholders' approval at the AGM.**

2.10   Another reason why managers might do their best to improve the financial performance of their company is that **managers' pay is often related to the size or profitability of the company**. Managers in very big companies, or in very profitable companies, will normally expect to earn higher salaries than managers in smaller or less successful companies.

Goal congruence

2.11   **Agency theory** sees employees of businesses, including managers, as individuals, each with his or her own objectives. Within a department of a business, there are departmental objectives. If achieving these various objectives leads also to the achievement of the objectives of the organisation as a whole, there is said to be **goal congruence**.

> **KEY TERM**
>
> In a control system, **goal congruence** is the state which leads individuals or groups to take actions which are in their self-interest and also in the best interest of the entity.
>
> *(OT 2000)*

How can goal congruence be achieved?

2.12 Goal congruence may be better achieved, and the 'agency problem' better dealt with, by providing managers with incentives which are related to profits or share price, such as:

(a) Pay or bonuses related to the size of profits (**profit-related pay**).

(b) Rewarding managers with **shares**, eg when a private company 'goes public' and managers are invited to subscribe for shares in the company at an attractive offer price.

(c) Rewarding managers with **share options**. In a share option scheme, selected employees are given a number of share options, each of which gives the holder the right after a certain date to subscribe for shares in the company at a fixed price. The value of an option will increase if the company is successful and its share price goes up. For example, an employee might be given 10,000 options to subscribe for shares in the company at a price of £2.00 per share. If the share price goes up to, say, £5 per share by the time that the exercise date for the options arrives, the employee will be able to profit by £30,000 (by buying £50,000 worth of shares for £20,000).

2.13 Such measures might encourage management to adopt '**creative accounting**' methods which will distort the reported performance of the company in the service of the managers' own ends. However, creative accounting methods such as off-balance sheet finance present a temptation to management at all times given that they allow a more favourable picture of the state of the company to be presented than otherwise, to shareholders, potential investors, potential lenders and others.

2.14 An alternative approach is to attempt to monitor managers' behaviour, for example by establishing '**management audit**' procedures, to introduce additional reporting requirements, or to seek assurances from managers that shareholders' interests will be foremost in their priorities.

Shareholder value analysis

2.15 **Shareholder value analysis** (SVA) was developed during the 1980s from the work of Rappaport and focuses on value creation using the net present value (NPV) approach. Thus, SVA assumes that **the value of a business is the net present value of its future cash flows, discounted at the appropriate cost of capital.** Many leading companies (including, for example, Pepsi, Quaker and Disney) have used SVA as a way of linking management strategy and decisions to the creation of value for shareholders. We cover SVA in more detail in Chapter 6 but a brief introduction now emphasises important considerations that are relevant through this text.

> **KEY TERM**
>
> **Shareholder value analysis** is an approach to financial management which focuses on total return to shareholders in terms of both dividends and price growth, calculated as the present value of future free cash flows of the business discounted at the weighted average cost of capital of the business less the market value of its debt. *(OT 2000)*

2.16 SVA takes the following approach.

(a) Key decisions with implications for cash flow and risk are specified. These may be **strategic, operational, related to investment** or **financial**.

(b) **Value drivers** are identified as the factors having the greatest impact on shareholder value, and management attention is focused on the decisions which influence the value drivers. Value drivers include:

    (i)   Sales growth and margin

    (ii)   Working capital and fixed capital investment

    (iii) The cost of capital

2.17   SVA may help managers to concentrate on **activities which create value** rather than on short-term profitability. A problem with the approach is that of specifying a terminal value at the end of the planning horizon, which will extend for perhaps five or ten years.

Why should managers bother to know who their shareholders are?

2.18   A company's senior management should remain aware of who its major shareholders are, and it will often help to retain shareholders' support if the chairman or the managing director meets occasionally with the major shareholders, to exchange views.

(a) The company's management might learn about **shareholders' preferences** for either high dividends or high retained earnings for profit growth and capital gain.

(b) For public companies, changes in shareholdings might help to **explain recent share price movements**.

(c) The company's management should be able to learn about **shareholders' attitudes to both risk and gearing**. If a company is planning a new investment, its management might have to consider the relative merits of seeking equity finance or debt finance, and shareholders' attitudes would be worth knowing about before the decision is taken.

(d) Management might need to know its shareholders in the event of an **unwelcome takeover bid** from another company, to identify key shareholders whose views on the takeover bid might be crucial to the final outcome.

2.19   Having a **wide range of shareholders** has advantages.

(a) Likelihood of greater activity in the market in the firm's shares, ie greater 'market liquidity'

(b) Less likelihood of one shareholder having a controlling interest

(c) Since shareholdings are smaller on average, likelihood of less effect on the share price if one shareholder sells his holding

(d) Greater likelihood of a takeover bid being frustrated

Question

Before looking at what follows below, see if you can think of some **disadvantages** of a company having a large number of shareholders.

2.20   A large number of shareholders also has disadvantages.

(a) **High administrative costs** eg the costs of sending out copies of the annual report and accounts, counting proxy votes, registering new shareholders and paying dividends

(b) The **varying tax rates and objectives** of shareholder clientele groups, which make a dividend/retention policy more difficult for the management to decide upon

Shareholders, managers and the company's long-term creditors

2.21 The relationship between **long-term creditors** of a company, the **management** and the **shareholders** of a company encompasses the following factors.

(a) Management may decide to raise finance for a company by taking out long-term or medium term loans. They might well be taking risky investment decisions using outsiders' money to finance them.

(b) Investors who provide debt finance will rely on the company's management to generate enough net cash inflows to make interest payments on time, and eventually to repay loans.

However, long-term creditors will often take security for their loan, perhaps in the form of a fixed charge over an asset (such as a mortgage on a building). Debentures are also often subject to certain restrictive covenants, which restrict the company's rights to borrow more money until the debentures have been repaid.

If a company is unable to pay what it owes its creditors, the creditors may decide:

(i) To exercise their security, or
(ii) To apply for the company to be wound up

(c) The money that is provided by long-term creditors will be invested to earn profits, and the profits (in excess of what is needed to pay interest on the borrowing) will provide extra dividends or retained profits for the shareholders of the company. In other words, shareholders will expect to increase their wealth using creditors' money.

3   OBJECTIVES OF PUBLICLY OWNED AND NON-COMMERCIAL BODIES
5/01

Nationalised industries

3.1 The framework of financial management in **state-owned** (or **nationalised**) **industries** consists of:

- Strategic objectives
- Rules about investment plans and their appraisal
- Corporate plans, targets and aims
- External financing limits

Following the privatisation programme of the 1980s and early 1990s, the UK's nationalised industries are much fewer in number than they were. The largest nationalised industry remaining in the UK is the **Post Office**. Some other countries have more extensive state ownership of industries.

3.2 Nationalised industries are generally financed by **government loans**, and some **borrowing from the capital markets**. They do not have equity capital, and there is no stock exchange to give a day-by-day valuation of the business. The financial objective cannot be to maximise the wealth of its owners, the government or the general public, because this is not a concept which can be applied in practice. Nevertheless, there will be a financial objective, to contribute in a certain way to the national economy, possibly according to the political views of the government.

(a) There may be an objective to earn enough profits for the industry to **provide for a certain proportion of its investment needs from its own resources.**

(b) A very profitable state-owned industry may be expected to **transfer surplus funds to the government.**

3.3   Even so, the principal objective of a nationalised industry will in most cases not be a financial one at all. Financial objectives will be subordinated to a number of political and social considerations.

(a)   A nationalised industry may be expected to provide a **certain standard of service** to all customers, regardless of the fact that some individuals will receive a service at a charge well below its cost. For example, the postal service must deliver letters to remote locations at standard prices.

(b)   The need to provide a service may be of such overriding social and political importance that the government is prepared to **subsidise** the industry. There is a strong body of opinion, for example, which argues that public transport is a social necessity and a certain level of service must be provided, with losses made up by government subsidies.

3.4   **Financial targets** vary from industry to industry, depending on how profitable or unprofitable it is expected to be. Nationalised industries in the UK are generally expected to aim at a **rate of return** (before interest and tax) on their new investment programmes of **5% in real terms**. The return is measured as a current cost operating profit on the net replacement cost of assets employed.

3.5   Such a target is applied so that the industries do not divert resources away from those areas where they could be used to best effect.

3.6   **Performance aims** back up the financial targets, and may be expressed in terms of target cost reductions or efficiency improvements. Achieving cost reduction through efficiency improvements has been a prime target of nationalised industries in the UK in recent years. The Post Office, for example, has in the past had a target to reduce real unit costs in its mail business and in its counters business.

3.7   **External financing limits (EFLs)** control the flow of finance to and from nationalised industries. They set a limit on the amount of finance the industry can obtain from the government, and in the case of very profitable industries, they set requirements for the net repayment of finance to the government.

Not-for-profit organisations

3.8   Some organisations are set up with a prime objective which is not related to making profits. Charities and government organisations are examples. These organisations exist to pursue **non-financial aims,** such as providing a service to the community. However, there will be **financial constraints** which limit what any such organisation can do.

(a)   A not-for-profit organisation needs finance to pay for its operations, and the major financial constraint is **the amount of funds that it can obtain**.

(b)   Having obtained funds, a not-for-profit organisation should seek to use the funds:

(i)   **Economically**: not spending £2 when the same thing can be bought for £1
(ii)   **Efficiently**: getting the best use out of what money is spent on
(iii)   **Effectively**: spending funds so as to achieve the organisation's objectives

3.9   The nature of financial objectives in a not-for-profit organisation can be explained in more detail, using government organisations in the UK as an illustration.

Government departments

3.10   Financial management in **government departments** is different from financial management in an industrial or commercial company for some fairly obvious reasons.

(a) Government departments **do not operate to make a profit,** and the objectives of a department or of a programme of spending cannot be expressed in terms of maximising the return on capital employed.

(b) Government services are provided **without the commercial pressure of competition.** There are no competitive reasons for controlling costs, being efficient or, when services are charged for (such as medical prescriptions), keeping prices down.

(c) Government departments have full-time professional civil servants as their **managers,** but decisions are also taken by **politicians.**

(d) The government gets its money for spending from **taxes, other sources of income and borrowing** (such as issuing gilts) and the nature of its fund-raising differs substantially from fund-raising by companies.

3.11 Since managing government is different from managing a company, a different framework is needed for planning and control. This is achieved by:

(a) **Setting objectives** for each department
(b) **Careful planning** of public expenditure proposals
(c) Emphasis on getting **value for money**

Executive agencies

3.12 A development in recent years has been the creation of agencies to carry out specific functions (such as vehicle licensing and hospitals). These **executive agencies** are answerable to the government for providing a certain level of service, but are independently managed on business principles.

3.13 In 1992 the Treasury published a guide entitled *Executive Agencies - A guide to setting targets and measuring performance.* The following are some of the salient points.

(a) The targets will usually fall under one or other of the following broad headings.

- Financial performance
- Volume and output
- Quality of service (embracing timeliness, quality of 'product', and availability)
- Efficiency

(b) No agency should set more than a handful of key targets.

(c) It is important that an explicit balance should be decided between the targets set for quality of service and those covering volume of output and efficiency.

(d) Consistent terminology should be used to avoid confusion when different terms are used to describe the same phenomenon.

3.14 Regarding point (d) the annex to the guide includes the following table.

Term	Definition	Example
Effectiveness	An effectiveness measure reveals the extent to which objectives have been met: it makes no reference to cost.	Total hip replacement operations are associated with a mortality rate of less than 2 per cent.
Efficiency	An efficiency measure describes the relationship between the output of an agency and the associated inputs.	Average total hip replacement costs (unit cost of output) is £5,000.

Term	Definition	Example
Quality	A quality measure describes the usefulness or value of a service. Relates to the delivery of that service to the recipient.	The average waiting time for a total hip replacement operation is 4 months.
Target	A target is a quantified objective set by management to be attained at a specified date.	Output target: Average number of total hip replacement operations per week next year to be 10.5 or above. Quality target: Waiting time for a first appointment next year to be no more than 2 weeks.

4 FINANCIAL MANAGEMENT DECISIONS

4.1 **Maximising the wealth of shareholders** generally implies maximising profits consistent with long-term stability. It is often found that short-term gains must be sacrificed in the interests of the company's long-term prospects. In the context of this overall objective of financial management, there are three main types of decisions facing financial managers: **investment decisions, financing decisions** and **dividend decisions**.

In practice, these three areas are interconnected and should not be viewed in isolation.

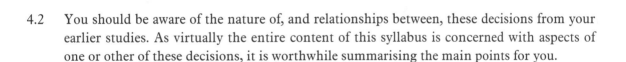

Exam focus point

Be aware that topics covered in detail in Paper 4 may also be examined in Paper 13. A good example was the compulsory question in May 2001, asking about the merits of different was of financing expansion.

4.2 You should be aware of the nature of, and relationships between, these decisions from your earlier studies. As virtually the entire content of this syllabus is concerned with aspects of one or other of these decisions, it is worthwhile summarising the main points for you.

Knowledge brought forward from Paper 4 (IFIN)

Financial management decisions

- The three key decisions of financial management are those concerning **investment, financing** and **dividends.**

- **Investment decisions** may be on the undertaking of new **projects** within the existing business, the **takeover** of, or the **merger** with, another company or the **selling off** of a part of the business.

- The financial manager will need to **identify** investment opportunities, **evaluate** them and decide on the **optimum allocation of funds** available between investments.

- **Financial decisions** include those for both the long term **(capital structure)** and the short term **(working capital management)**.

- The financial manager will need to determine the **source, cost** and effect on **risk** of the possible sources of long-term finance. A balance between **profitability** and **liquidity** must be taken into account when deciding on the optimal level of short-term finance.

- **Dividend decisions** may affect the view that shareholders have of the long-term prospects of the company, and thus the **market value of the shares.**

- The amount of surplus cash paid out as **dividends** will have a direct impact on **finance** available for **investment**, illustrating one way in which these decisions are interconnected.

BPP
PUBLISHING

CASE STUDY LINK

In the case study you might be asked to assess various strategies in the light of stated objectives, for example maintaining a strong profit margin and avoiding financial risk.

Chapter roundup

- This chapter has set the scene for the study of strategic financial management. We have identified the **objectives of companies and other organisations**, and we will now go on to study both the **financial resources available** to achieve these objectives and the **methods** for doing so.

- We have also set out the **types of decision** a financial manager has to make, in seeking to attain the financial objectives of the organisation or enterprise.

Quick quiz

1   On what management objective is the theory of company finance primarily based?

2   To which areas might non-financial objectives of a company relate?

3   List six types of stakeholder group.

4   **Fill in the blanks**

    .... theory sees employees as individuals, each with their own objectives, the relationship between managers and shareholders being an .... relationship. If achieving individual and departmental objectives leads to achievement of the organisations objectives, there is ....

5   Where external financing limits apply government-owned industries are not usually set financial targets.

    True ☐

    False ☐

6   To obtain value for money, a not-for-profit organisation should aim for the '**Three Es**', which are (**fill in the blanks**):

    E ....

    E ....

    E ....

7   **Fill in the blanks**

```
              ┌─────────────────────────────────────┐
              │  Decisions of the financial manager │
              └─────────────────────────────────────┘
        ┌────────────┼────────────┐
┌──────────────┐ ┌──────────────┐ ┌──────────────┐
│ .......... decisions │ │ .......... decisions │ │ .......... decisions │
└──────────────┘ └──────────────┘ └──────────────┘
```

Answers to quick quiz

1   The objective of management is to **maximise the market value** of the enterprise.

2   (1) Welfare of employees   (2) Welfare of management
    (3) Welfare of society   (4) Quality of service provision
    (5) Responsibilities to customers and suppliers   (5) Leadership in research and development

3   See the list in Section 2.

4   Agency; agency; goal congruence.

5   False.

6   Economy; efficiency; effectiveness.

7   Investment; financing; dividend.

Now try the question below from the Exam Question Bank

Number	Level	Marks	Time
1	Introductory	n/a	20 mins

Chapter 2

EXTERNAL CONSTRAINTS ON FINANCIAL STRATEGY

Topic list	Syllabus reference	Ability required
1 Government and regulatory constraints	(i)	Analysis
2 Economic influences	(i)	Analysis
3 Published information	(i)	Analysis

Introduction

We now examine the range of **external factors** which may influence the formulation of financial strategy.

It is important to see how changes or differences in these factors may influence strategy. For example, a **change in government legislation** may open up (or close up) opportunities. In seeking **investment opportunities in other countries**, the particular external factors which operate there will need to be considered.

Learning outcomes covered in this chapter

* Analyse and interpret the risk implications of business plans

* Identify and interpret the impact of internal and external constraints on financial strategy (eg funding, regulatory bodies, investor relations, strategy, and economic factors)

Syllabus content covered in this chapter

* Impact of regulation on developing strategy eg competition authorities, pricing and services regulations, eg OFTEL, OFWAT

* Major economic forces affecting an organisation's financial plans (eg interest rates, inflation, exchange rates)

Exam focus point

In *Financial Strategy*, the focus with regard to external constraints is likely to be on constraints to maximisation of shareholder wealth.

1   GOVERNMENT AND REGULATORY CONSTRAINTS

The influence of government

1.1   The government does not have a direct interest in companies (except for those in which it actually holds shares). However, the government does often have a strong indirect interest in companies' affairs.

(a) **Taxation.** The government raises taxes on sales and profits and on shareholders' dividends. It also expects companies to act as tax collectors for income tax and VAT. The tax structure might influence investors' preferences for either dividends or capital growth.

(b) **Encouraging new investments.** The government might provide funds towards the cost of some investment projects. It might also encourage private investment by offering tax incentives.

(c) **Encouraging a wider spread of share ownership.** In the UK, the government has made some attempts to encourage more private individuals to become company shareholders, by means of attractive privatisation issues (such as in the electricity, gas and telecommunications industries) and tax incentives, such as ISAs (Individual Savings Accounts), to encourage individuals to invest in shares.

(d) **Legislation.** The government also influences companies, and the relationships between shareholders, creditors, management, employees and the general public, through legislation, including the Companies Acts, legislation on employment, health and safety regulations, legislation on consumer protection and consumer rights and environmental legislation.

(e) **Economic policy.** A government's economic policy will affect business activity. For example, exchange rate policy will have implications for the revenues of exporting firms and for the purchase costs of importing firms. Policies on economic growth, inflation, employment, interest rates and so on are all relevant to business activities.

The encouragement of free market forces

1.2 Throughout the industrialised world, governments have tried to stimulate their economies by giving **encouragement to free market forces** through:

(a) Greater liberalisation of markets, by removing regulations and legislative restrictions on them (deregulation)

(b) A reduction in the role of the government in industry and commerce

(c) A simplified tax system, which encourages firms to take commercial decisions which are not influenced by tax advantages or disadvantages

(d) The privatisation of state-owned assets (such as British Gas, British Telecom and the electricity industry in the UK)

(e) Opening up state-controlled activities to competition from private firms

(f) Encouraging competition, by a judicious regulation of monopolies and mergers, and by giving encouragement to small firms

(g) The removal or reduction of import restrictions, to open up domestic markets to greater foreign competition

Financial reporting and accounting concepts

1.3 As you will be aware, limited companies and their directors are bound by the provisions of the Companies Act 1985 (CA 1985). This legislation governs the preparation and publication of the annual financial statements of companies.

1.4 The form and content of a company's accounts are regulated primarily by CA 1985, but must also comply with the FRSs (Financial Reporting Standards) published by the Accounting Standards Board (ASB) and by the Accounting Standards Committee, which the ASB has now replaced.

1.5 The shorter term financial objectives of companies include targets for **profitability**. The measurement of profit under historical cost accounting follows the principles of the generally accepted fundamental accounting concepts (going concern, accruals, consistency and prudence) set out in the accounting standard SSAP 2. Although profits do matter, they are not necessarily the best measure of a company's achievements.

(a) Accounting profits are not the same as 'economic' profits. **Accounting profits can be manipulated** to some extent by choices of accounting policies.

Question 1

Can you give three examples of how accounting profits might be so manipulated?

Answer

Here are some examples you might have chosen.

(i) Provisions, such as provisions for depreciation or anticipated losses
(ii) The capitalisation of various expenses, such as development costs
(iii) Adding overhead costs to stock valuations

(b) A company might make an accounting profit **without having used its resources in the most profitable way possible.** There is a difference between the accounting concept of 'historical cost' and the economic concept of 'opportunity cost', which is the value that could have been obtained by using resources in their most profitable alternative way.

(c) Profits on their own take no account of the **volume of investment that it has taken to earn the profit.** Profits must be related to the volume of investment to have any real meaning. Hence measures of financial achievement include:

(i) Accounting return on capital employed

(ii) Earnings per share

(iii) Yields on investment, for example dividend yield as a percentage of stock market value

(d) Profits are reported every year (with half-year interim results for quoted companies). They are measures of **short-term** performance, whereas a company's performance should ideally be judged over a longer term.

KEY TERM

Corporate governance is the system by which companies are directed and controlled. **Boards of directors** are responsible for the governance of their companies. The **shareholders'** role in governance is to appoint the directors and the **auditors** and to satisfy themselves that an appropriate governance structure is in place.

The responsibilities of the board include:

- setting the company's **strategic aims**
- providing the **leadership** to put them into effect
- supervising the **management** of the business
- **reporting** to shareholders on their stewardship

The board's actions are subject to laws, regulations and the shareholders in general meeting. *(OT 2000)*

Corporate governance and the Cadbury Report

1.6 Issues of **corporate governance** in the UK were originally addressed in the report of the Cadbury Committee, which was formed in 1991. The terms of reference of the committee were to consider, along with any other relevant matters, the following issues:

   (a) Responsibilities of executive and non-executive directors for **reviewing and reporting on performance to shareholders** and other financially interested parties, and the frequency, clarity and form in which information should be provided

   (b) The case for **audit committees** of the board, including their composition and role

   (c) Principal responsibilities of **auditors** and the extent and value of the audit

   (d) **Links** between shareholders, boards, and auditors

1.7 The **Cadbury Report** defines corporate governance as 'the system by which companies are directed and controlled'. The roles of those concerned with the financial statements are described.

   (a) The **directors** are responsible for the corporate governance of the company.

   (b) **Shareholders** are linked to the directors via the financial reporting system.

   (c) The **auditors** provide the shareholders with an external objective check on the directors' financial statements.

   (d) Other concerned **users**, particularly employees (to whom the directors owe some responsibility) are indirectly addressed by the financial statements.

1.8 The Cadbury Committee was set up because of the lack of confidence which was perceived in financial reporting and in the ability of auditors to provide the assurances required by the users of financial statements.

   (a) The main difficulties were considered to be in the **relationship between auditors and boards of directors**. In particular, the commercial pressures on both directors and auditors caused pressure to be brought to bear on auditors by the board and the auditors often capitulated.

   (b) Problems were also perceived in the **ability of the board of directors to control their organisations**.

BPP PUBLISHING

1.9 These problems have been debated for some time, but company collapses in the late 1980s, often sudden and unexpected, intensified the worries of regulating bodies, the Stock Exchange and the government. The lack of board accountability in many of these company collapses intensified the perceived need for action.

1.10 The Committee aimed to set out the responsibilities of each group involved in the reporting process and to make recommendations on good practice.

Code of Best Practice

1.11 The **Code of Best Practice** included in the Cadbury Report is aimed at the directors of all UK public companies, but the directors of all companies are encouraged to use the Code for guidance. Pressure should be brought by all the relevant parties on the directors to ensure compliance with the Code. In particular, institutional investors will have a lot of power to influence the directors. Directors should state in the annual report and accounts whether they comply with the Code and give reasons for any non-compliance.

1.12 Some of the key points in the Code are summarised in the following paragraphs.

The board of directors

1.13 The board must **meet on a regular basis**, retain full **control** over the company and **monitor** the executive management. A clearly accepted division of responsibilities is necessary at the head of the company, so no one person has complete power, answerable to no-one. (Compare this to the Robert Maxwell situation.) The report thus encourages the separation of the posts of chairman and chief executive.

Non-executive directors

1.14 The following points are made about **non-executive directors**, who are those directors not running the day-to-day operations of the company.

(a) They should bring **independent judgement** to bear on important issues, including key appointments and standards of conduct.

(b) There should be **no business, financial or other connection** between the non-executive directors and the company, apart from fees and shareholdings.

(c) **Fees should reflect the time they spend** on the business of the company, so extra duties could earn extra pay.

(d) **They should not take part in share option schemes** and their service should not be pensionable, to maintain their independent status.

(e) Appointments should be for a specified term and **reappointment should not be automatic**. The board as a whole should decide on their nomination and selection.

(f) Procedures should exist whereby non-executive directors may **take independent advice**, at the company's expense if necessary.

Executive directors

1.15 In relation to the directors who run companies on a day to day basis, the main points in the Code relate to **service contracts** (contracts of employment) and **pay**. The length of such contracts should be three years at most, unless the shareholders approve a longer contract. A remuneration committee of non-executive directors should decide on the level of executive pay.

The audit committee

1.16 A major recommendation in the Code is that all listed companies must establish effective **audit committees** if they have not already done so. The Code takes its example from countries such as Canada and the USA where audit committees for listed companies are compulsory.

1.17 The audit committees should have formal terms of reference dealing with their membership, authority and duties. They should meet at least three times every year and membership of the committee should be shown in the annual report.

The Greenbury Report

1.18 The controversy surrounding the pay of directors and managers in the former utilities - the 'fat cat' debate, led to the government appointing the **Greenbury Committee** to look at the issues involved and make various recommendations. The main recommendations, which went further than Cadbury, are as follows and **compliance has been made a Stock Exchange listing requirement.**

   (a) The **remuneration committee** (already part of the Cadbury Code) should consist entirely of non-executive directors 'with no personal financial interest other than as shareholders in the matter to be decided' and no potential conflict of interest from cross-directorships.

   (b) There should be an **annual report** to shareholders, which should be approved by the shareholders in annual general meeting.

   Greenbury has also extended the Cadbury disclosure of directors' remuneration to '**full transparency**' giving full details of each director's pay package.

Question 2

If you were on the main board of a large plc, would you be very happy about the **Greenbury** proposals?

1.19 There is a variety of problems to be faced with these recommendations, including the difficulty of assessing executive remuneration in what is acknowledged to be an imperfect market for executive skills.

1.20 As well as assessing this market, the remuneration committee would have to consider:

   (a) Differentials at management/director level (difficult with many layers of management)

   (b) The ability of managers to leave, taking clients and knowledge to a competitor or their own new business

   (c) Individual performance and additional work/effort

   (d) The company's overall performance

   The problem here, particularly with (c) and (d), is that it places the non-executive directors of the remuneration committee in charge of the executive directors, ie it goes further than simply providing 'transparency' as regards executive pay.

1.21 In view of scandals in other areas, it has been suggested that the **Greenbury** proposals should be extended to all types of quango and also to charities, building societies etc.

The Hampel Report

1.22 The **Hampel Committee on Corporate Governance** produced a final report in January 1998. The committee followed up matters raised in the Cadbury and Greenbury reports, aiming to restrict the regulatory burden on companies and **substituting principles for detail** whenever possible. The introduction to the report also states that whilst the Cadbury and Greenbury reports concentrated on the **prevention of abuses**, Hampel was equally concerned with the **positive contribution** good corporate governance can make.

1.23 Hampel proposed combining the various best practices, principles and codes of **Cadbury, Greenbury** and **Hampel** into one single 'supercode'. The London Stock Exchange has now issued a **Combined Code** on corporate governance, which was derived from the recommendations of the Cadbury, Greenbury and Hampel reports. In June 1998 the Stock Exchange Listing Rules were amended to make compliance with the new code obligatory for listed companies.

1.24 The introduction to the report points out that the **primary duty of directors is to shareholders,** to enhance the value of shareholders' investment over time. Relationships with other stakeholders are important, but making the directors responsible to other stakeholders would mean there was no clear yardstick for judging directors' performance.

1.25 The Hampel Committee is also **against treating the corporate governance codes as sets of prescriptive rules**, and judging companies by whether they have complied. The report states that there can be guidelines which will normally be appropriate but the differing circumstances of companies mean that sometimes there are valid reasons for exceptions.

1.26 The major recommendations of the report were as follows.

Directors

1.27 **Executive** and **non-executive directors** should continue to have the same duties under the law.

(a) The majority of **non-executive directors** should be independent, and boards should disclose in the annual report which of the non-executive directors are considered to be independent. Non-executive directors should comprise at least one third of the membership of the board.

(b) The roles of **chairman** and **chief executive** should generally be separate. Whether or not the roles of chairman and chief executive are combined, a **senior non-executive director** should be identified.

(c) All directors should submit themselves for **re-election** at least once every three years.

(d) Boards should assess the **performance** of individual directors and collective board performance.

Directors' remuneration

1.28 (a) Boards should establish a **remuneration committee,** made up of independent non-executive directors, to develop policy on remuneration and devise remuneration packages for individual executive directors. Remuneration committees should use their judgement in devising schemes appropriate for the specific circumstances of the company. Total rewards from such schemes should not be excessive.

(b) Boards should try and **reduce directors' contract periods** to one year or less, but this cannot be achieved immediately.

(c) The accounts should include a **general statement on remuneration policy,** but this should not be the subject of an AGM vote.

Shareholders and the AGM

1.29 (a) Companies should consider providing a business presentation at the **AGM,** with a question and answer session.

(b) Shareholders should be able to vote separately on each substantially separate issue; and that the practice of 'bundling' unrelated proposals in a single resolution should cease.

(c) Companies should propose a resolution at the AGM relating to the report and accounts.

(d) Notice of the AGM and related papers should be sent to shareholders at least 20 working days before the meeting.

Accountability and audit

1.30 (a) Each company should establish an **audit committee** of at least three non-executive directors, at least two of them independent. The audit committee should keep under review the overall financial relationship between the company and its auditors, to ensure a balance between the maintenance of objectivity and value for money.

(b) Directors should report on **internal control,** but should not be required to report on effectiveness of controls.

(c) Auditors should report privately on internal controls to directors.

(d) Companies which do not already have a **separate internal audit function** should consider the need for one.

Reporting

1.31 The accounts should contain a **statement** of how the company applies the corporate governance principles, and should **explain their policies,** including any circumstances justifying departure from best practice.

Criticisms of the Hampel report

1.32 Some commentators have criticised the Hampel report for stating that the debate on accountability has **obscured the first responsibility of a board,** to enhance the prosperity of a company over time. Critics have argued that accountability and prosperity should be seen as compatible. In addition, Hampel has been criticised for dropping the requirement for the board to report publicly on the effectiveness of internal controls and for the auditors to report publicly on the statement made by the board.

1.33 The government is contemplating certain **statutory changes** to reinforce the work of the corporate governance committees, but will otherwise leave the approach of **voluntary compliance** alone for now. However Margaret Beckett, the Trade and Industry Secretary, has stated that there should be an emphasis on **growth, investment, accountability** and **transparency**.

Legislation and governments

1.34 As you have seen in your earlier studies, business need to be aware of the whole range of legislation that affects their operations. This includes company, tax, health and safety and consumer legislation. An important role of the government is the **regulation of private markets** where these fail to bring about an efficient use of resources. As you should be aware from your earlier studies in economics, **market failure** is said to occur when the market mechanism fails to result in economic efficiency, and therefore the outcome is **sub-optimal**.

1.35 In response to the existence of market failure, and as an alternative to taxation and public provision of production, the state often resorts to regulating economic activity in a variety of ways. Of the various forms of market failure, the following are the cases where regulation of markets can often be the most appropriate policy response.

(a) **Imperfect competition** - where monopoly power is leading to inefficiency, the state will intervene through controls on, **say**, prices or profits in order to try to reduce the effects of the monopoly.

(b) **Externalities** - a possible means of dealing with the problem of external costs and benefits is via some form of regulation. Regulations might include, **for example,** controls on emissions of pollutants, restrictions on car use in urban areas, the banning of smoking in public buildings, compulsory car insurance and compulsory education.

(c) **Imperfect information** - regulation is often the best form of government action whenever informational inadequacies are undermining the efficient operation of private markets. This is particularly so when **consumer choice is being distorted. Examples** here would include legally enforced product quality/safety standards, consumer protection legislation, the provision of job centres and other means of improving information flows in the labour market and so on.

(d) **Equity** - the government may also resort to regulation to improve social justice. **For example**, legislation to prevent racial and/or sexual discrimination in the labour market; regulation to ensure equal access to goods such as health care, education and housing; minimum wage regulations and equal pay legislation.

Rôles of regulatory bodies

KEY TERM

Regulation can be defined as any form of state interference with the operation of the free market. This could involve regulating demand, supply, price, profit, quantity, quality, entry, exit, information, technology, or any other aspect of production and consumption in the market.

1.36 Where privatisation has perpetuated natural monopolies, in the UK the regulatory authorities specific to each industry such as OFTEL (telecommunications), OFGEM (gas and electricity) and OFWAT (water), have the role of ensuring that consumers' interests are not subordinated to those of other stakeholders, such as employees, shareholders and tax authorities. The regulator's role is generally 'advisory' rather than statutory, and may extend only to a part of a company's business, necessitating a correct allocation of costs across different activities of the company. The activities of these regulatory bodies are discussed in more detail below.

1.37 The two main methods used to regulate monopoly industries are as follows.

(a) **Price control**: the regulator agreeing the output prices with the industry. Typically, the price is progressively reduced in real terms each year by setting price increases at a rate below that of inflation as measured by the Retail Prices Index (RPI). This has been used with success by regulators in the UK but can be confrontational.

(b) **Profit control**: the regulator agreeing the maximum profit which the industry can make. A typical method is to fix maximum profit at x% of capital employed, but this does not provide any incentive to making more efficient use of assets: the higher the capital employed, the higher the profit.

1.38 In addition the regulator will be concerned with:

(a) Actively **promoting competition** by encouraging new firms in the industry and preventing unreasonable barriers to entry

(b) Addressing **quality** and **safety** issues and considering the **social implications** of service provision and pricing

OFTEL

1.39 To illustrate the objectives and role of the UK regulatory authorities mentioned above, we shall take a brief look at OFTEL – the Office of Telecommunications. This was set up under the Telecommunications Act 1984.

1.40 The stated goal of OFTEL is to '**obtain the best deal for the consumer in terms of quality, choice and value for money**'.

1.41 All telecommunications operators, such as BT and the increasing number of competing operators, local cable companies, mobile network operators etc must have an **operating licence**. These set out what the operators can (or must) do or not do. For example BT's licence contains the formula which controls the prices of its main network services (currently RPI – 4.5%), and the licences of local cable companies contain targets for the number of premises that must be reached by certain dates.

1.42 The main functions of OFTEL are to:

(a) Ensure that licensees comply with the licence conditions

(b) Initiate the modification of licence conditions either by agreement with the licensee, or, failing that, by reference to the Monopolies and Mergers Commission (MMC) together with the Director General of Fair Trading to enforce competition legislation in relation to telecommunications

(c) Advise the Secretary of State for Trade and Industry on telecommunications matters and new licenses

(d) Obtain information and arrange for publication where this would help users

(e) Consider complaints and enquiries made about telecommunications services or apparatus

BPP PUBLISHING

1.43 OFTEL was originally set up to **manage the transition** from a market dominated by a former state-owned monopoly (British Telecom) towards a competitive market. Since then, the telecommunications industry in the UK has been through rapid change in terms of **competition** and **technological advances,** not least with the increasingly widespread use of **mobile phones** and the **Internet,** both by business and individuals.

1.44 In January 2000, OFTEL announced a **new strategy** in light of the rapidly developing telecoms market. At the heart of the strategy was the rolling back of formal regulation where competition is effective and already protects consumers, resulting in **greater self-regulation** by the industry.

1.45 In a press release, David Edmonds, Director General of Telecommunications said:

> 'As telecoms markets become more competitive OFTEL needs to review its approach to regulation.
>
> Up to now regulation has focussed on opening up a previously monopoly market, to promote competition and protect consumers. OFTEL's new approach is to **focus on effective competition**, which gives the customer the best deal. **Over-regulation** distorts markets and disadvantages consumers. Regulation should be appropriate to the level of competition.
>
> OFTEL's new strategy is therefore one of '**competition-plus**'... consumers will have the same protection but with less formal regulation. OFTEL will no longer promote competition in competitive markets, but will continue to act to prevent anti-competitive practices...'

1.46 Four new underlying **objectives** were thus set out as:

- Effective competition – benefiting customers
- Well informed consumers
- Adequately protected consumers
- Prevention of significant anti-competitive practice

1.47 One of the principles laid out in the new strategy, under the objective of **adequately protected consumers** was that, where competition cannot provide agreed services to all at affordable prices, OFTEL would regulate to ensure there is such provision in a way that minimises distorting effects.

1.48 An example of such regulation came about in March 2000, where it was determined by OFTEL that **Vodafone** and **BTCellnet continue to have market influence** in the UK **mobile market**. This meant that Vodafone and BTCellnet had to continue to provide Service Providers with access to their networks on non-discriminatory terms and publish charges, terms and conditions for their services. This was to ensure, in David Edmonds' words 'that consumers continue to get the best deal'.

OFWAT and OFGEM

1.49 Another example of industry regulation was in the matter of the bid for **Hyder plc**, the holding company for Welsh Water (Dwr Cymru) and South Wales Electricity (Swalec), by **Nomura** (a European subsidiary of a Japanese investment bank) in April 2000.

1.50 Hyder is a multi-utility company, one of the largest private sector employers in Wales, and its subsidiary water and electricity companies serve a large part of Wales. The division of Nomura responsible for the bid has a record of acquiring and developing businesses in the UK and the US.

1.51 The bid involved the take-over of two UK regulated businesses by a financial institution that had no track record of management of a regulated utility either in the UK or abroad. This was the first example of an acquisition of a multi-utility by such a company.

1.52 The bid gave rise to a merger situation. The Secretary of State for Trade and Industry referred it to the Competition Commission to determine whether it was likely to have effects adverse to the public interest. In this situation the Secretary of State is advised by the Director General of Fair Trading, and where a merger proposal involves a regulated business, he, in turn, is advised by the appropriate regulators – in this case, OFWAT and OFGEM.

1.53 The issues for consideration by the regulators included:

   (a) Whether Nomura had the operational and financial capacity to deliver the capital programmes and improvements to which the utility companies were committed

   (b) That the change in ownership would not negatively impact on the development of competition in the water or electricity markets

   (c) The effects of the loss of market information available to the public, City analysts and shareholders caused by the cessation of Hyder's listing on the London Stock Exchange if the bid were successful

   (d) The requirement for the 'ring fencing' of assets and resources attributable to the utility companies once under Nomura's control, to avoid the possibility of their financial viability being prejudiced by financial constraints experienced by Nomura in its other investment ventures

   (e) That the effective and independent management of the utility companies under regulatory control should not be compromised

1.54 Since then, there have been further bids, including one by Western Power Distribution Ltd and Gals Cymru (for Welsh Water); as a result of the issues raised by such bids, OFWAT issued a consultative document on new forms of ownership for water companies in June 2000.

Self-regulation

1.55 In many areas, the participants may decide to maintain a system of voluntary self-regulation, possibly in order to try to avert the imposition of government controls. Areas where self-regulation often exists are the professions (eg the Law Society, the British Medical Association and other professional bodies), and financial markets (eg the Council of the Stock Exchange, the Take-over Panel and the Securities and Investments Board).

Costs of regulation

1.56 The potential costs of regulation include the following.

   (a) **Enforcement costs.** Regulation can, manifestly, only be effective if it is properly monitored and enforced. **Direct costs** of enforcement include the setting up and running of the regulatory agencies - employing specialist staff, monitoring behaviour, prosecuting offenders (or otherwise ensuring actions are modified in line with regulations). **Indirect costs** are those incurred by the regulated (eg the firms in the industry) in conforming to the restrictions.

BPP PUBLISHING

(b) **Regulatory capture.** This refers to the process by which the regulator becomes dominated and controlled by the regulated firms, such that it acts increasingly in the latter's interests, rather than those of consumers. This is a phenomenon which has been observed in the USA (where economic regulation has always been more widespread).

(c) **Unintended consequences of regulation.** An example is the so-called 'Aversch-Johnson effect'. This refers to the tendency of rate-of-return (profit) regulation to encourage firms to become too capital-intensive. In other words, firms regulated in this way (which is a common method of economic regulation in the USA) have an incentive to choose a method of production which is not least-cost, because it involves too high a ratio of capital to labour.

Deregulation

1.57 **Deregulation** is, in general, the opposite of regulation. Deregulation can be defined as the removal or weakening of any form of statutory (or voluntary) regulation of free market activity. Deregulation allows free market forces more scope to determine the outcome. There was a shift in policy in the 1980s in the UK and in the USA towards greater deregulation of markets, in the belief that this would improve efficiency. Indeed, many politicians and commentators believed that it was state over-regulation of British industry that was largely responsible for Britain's comparatively uncompetitive and inefficient performance. Whether or not this was, or remains, true is an open question.

1.58 As with the appraisal of regulation, a rational assessment of a deregulatory measure or a programme of such measures should weigh up the potential **social benefits** against the **social costs**. If there will be a net gain to society, we can say that the deregulation should proceed. It would be simplistic to contend that **all** regulation is detrimental to the economy. As we have seen, where there is a clear case of market failure, then state regulation may be the most appropriate way of achieving a more socially efficient or equitable outcome.

1.59 More competition is however not always desirable and in some industries it could have certain disadvantages, including the following.

(a) **Loss of economies of scale.** If increased competition means that each firm produces less output on a smaller scale, unit costs will be higher. Liberalising a 'natural monopoly', for instance, is undesirable, and often not feasible.

(b) **Lower quality or quantity of service.** The need to reduce costs may lead firms to reduce quality or eliminate unprofitable but socially valuable services.

2 ECONOMIC INFLUENCES

Aggregate demand and inflation

2.1 **Aggregate demand** is the total expenditure in a national economy on goods and services. A growth in aggregate demand can have either or both of the following consequences.

(a) Firms will **produce more** to meet the demand. These firms could be either domestic firms or foreign suppliers.

(b) Firms will be unable to produce more to meet the demand, because of capacity limitations, and so **prices will go up** because of the strength of demand.

2.2 The rate of **price inflation** in the economy is important because it affects:

(a) Costs of production and selling prices

(b) Interest rates

(c) Foreign exchange rates

(d) Demand in the economy (high rates of inflation seem to put a brake on real economic growth.)

2.3 Companies faced with higher costs of production and higher interest rates will try to pass on their extra costs to customers by raising their selling prices. Some companies will be able to raise prices more easily than others, depending on the nature of demand in the industry's markets.

Expectations of inflation and the effects of inflation

2.4 When managers evaluate a particular project, or when shareholders evaluate their investments, they can only guess at what the rate of inflation is going to be. Their expectations will probably be wrong, at least to some extent, because it is extremely difficult to forecast the rate of inflation accurately. The only way in which uncertainty about inflation can be allowed for in project evaluation is by **risk and uncertainty analysis.**

2.5 Inflation affects **asset values, costs and revenues** in the following ways.

(a) Since fixed assets and stocks will increase in money value, the **same quantities of assets** must be financed by **increasing amounts of capital.**

   (i) If the future rate of inflation can be predicted, management can work out how much extra finance the company will need, and take steps to obtain it (for example by increasing retentions of earnings, or borrowing).

   (ii) If the future rate of inflation cannot be predicted with accuracy, management should guess at what it will be and plan to obtain extra finance accordingly. However, plans should also be made to obtain 'contingency funds' if the rate of inflation exceeds expectations. For example, a higher bank overdraft facility might be negotiated, or a provisional arrangement made with a bank for a loan.

(b) Inflation means higher costs and higher selling prices. The effect of higher prices on demand is not necessarily easy to predict. A company that raises its prices by 10% because the general rate of inflation is running at 10% might suffer a serious fall in demand.

Interest rates

2.6 **Interest rates** are an important element in the economic environment, and are of particular relevance for financial managers. Under the rules introduced by the new UK Labour Government in 1997, short-term interest rates are set by an independent Monetary Policy Committee of the Bank of England, the UK's central bank, to be consistent with the inflation target set by the Government.

(a) Interest rates **measure the cost of borrowing**. If a company wants to raise money, it must pay interest on its borrowing, and the rate of interest payable will be one which is 'current' at the time the borrowing takes place. When interest rates go up, companies will pay more interest on some of their borrowing (for example on bank overdrafts).

(b) Interest rates in a country **influence the foreign exchange value** of the country's currency.

(c) Interest rates act as a **guide to the sort of return** that a company's shareholders might want, and changes in market interest rates will affect share prices.

2.7 The interest rates in the UK financial markets which are most commonly quoted are as follows.

(a) The clearing banks' **base rates.** Banks will lend money to small companies and individual customers at certain margins above their base rate, which acts as a reference point. The base rate is set independently by each clearing bank, although in practice, an increase in the base rate of one bank will be followed by similar changes by other banks.

(b) The **inter-bank lending rate** on the London inter-bank money market. This interest rate is referred to as **LIBOR,** short for the London Inter-Bank Offered Rate. For large loans to big companies, banks will set interest rates at a margin above LIBOR rather than at a margin above base rate.

(c) The **Treasury bill rate.** This is the rate at which the Bank of England sells Treasury bills to the money market. It is an average rate, since institutions tender for bills and tender prices vary.

(d) The **yield on long-dated gilt-edged securities** (20 years to maturity). Gilt-edged securities are securities issued by the government.

2.8 There are many other different interest rates you might see quoted, for example:

(a) The yield on bank deposit accounts or building society accounts

(b) Bank overdraft rates, for personal customers

(c) Various money market rates, such as the yield on deposits with discount houses, the rate of discount on bank bills or 'fine' trade bills, the yield on sterling certificates of deposit, and the yield on local authority deposits

(d) The rate of discount offered by the Bank of England for its purchase of different types of eligible bills from financial institutions

2.9 There are several reasons why interest rates differ in **different markets** and **market segments**.

(a) **Risk.** Higher risk borrowers must pay higher rates on their borrowing, to compensate lenders for the greater risk involved.

(b) **The need to make a profit on re-lending.** Financial intermediaries make their profits from re-lending at a higher rate of interest than the cost of their borrowing.

(c) **The duration of the lending.** Normally, long-term loans will earn a higher yield than short-term loans. You should be familiar with the reasons for this term structure of interest rates as illustrated by the **yield curve**, from your previous studies; the main points are summarised below.

(d) **The size of the loan.** Deposits above a certain amount with a bank or building society might attract higher rates of interest than smaller deposits.

(e) **International interest rates.** The level of interest rates varies from country to country. The reasons for these variations are:

(i) Differing rates of inflation from country to country

(ii) Government policies on interest rates and foreign currency exchange rates

(f) **Different types of financial asset**. Different types of financial asset attract different rates of interest. This reflects the competition for deposits between different types of financial institution.

Knowledge brought forward from Paper 4 (IFIN)

The term structure of interest rates: the yield curve

- **Interest rates depend on the term to** maturity **of the asset.** For example, Treasury Stock might be short-dated, medium-dated, or long-dated.

- The term **structure of interest rates** refers to the way in which the yield on a security varies according to the term of the borrowing, as shown by the **yield curve**.

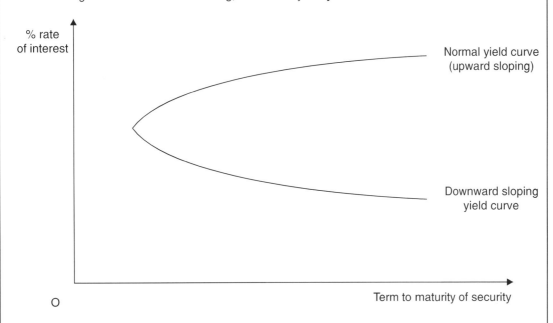

Yield curves

- The reasons why, in theory, the yield curve will normally be **upward sloping,** so that long-term financial assets offer a higher yield than short-term assets, are as follows.

  (a) **The investor must be compensated for tying up his money in the asset for a longer period of time.** The only way to overcome this **liquidity preference** of investors is to compensate them for the loss of liquidity; in other words, to offer a higher rate of interest on longer dated stock.

  (b) **There is a greater risk in lending long-term than in lending short-term.** To compensate investors for this risk, they might require a higher yield on longer dated investments.

- A yield curve might **slope downwards**, with short-term rates higher than longer term rates for the following reasons.

  (a) **Expectations.** When interest rates are expected to fall, short-term rates might be higher than long-term rates, and the yield curve would be downward sloping.

  (b) **Government policy.** A policy of keeping interest rates relatively high might therefore have the effect of forcing short-term interest rates higher than long-term rates.

  (c) The **market segmentation theory.** The slope of the yield curve will reflect conditions in different segments of the market. This theory holds that the major investors are confined to a particular segment of the market and will not switch segment even if the forecast of likely future interests rates changes.

BPP PUBLISHING

Nominal rates and real rates of interest

2.10 **Nominal rates of interest** are the actual rates of interest paid. **Real rates of interest** are rates of interest adjusted for the rate of inflation. The real rate is therefore a measure of the increase in the real wealth, expressed in terms of **buying power,** of the investor or lender.

(a) The real rate of interest can be calculated as:

$$\text{Real rate of interest} = \frac{1 + \text{nominal rate of interest}}{1 + \text{rate of inflation}} - 1$$

If the nominal rate of interest is 12% and the rate of inflation is 8%, the real rate of interest would be 1.12/1.08 – 1 = 0.037 = 3.7%.

(b) The real rate of interest is sometimes estimated (for arithmetical simplicity) as the difference between the nominal rate of interest and the rate of inflation. In our example, this would be 12% – 8% = 4%.

2.11 The real rate of interest will usually be **positive,** although when the rate of inflation is very high, the real rate of interest might become negative (the rate of inflation exceeding the nominal interest rate). Nominal rates of interest will tend to rise when the rate of inflation increases, because lenders will want to earn a real return and will therefore want nominal rates to exceed the inflation rate.

Interest rates, inflation and capital gains or losses

2.12 A positive real rate of interest adds to an investor's real wealth from the income he earns from his investments. However, when interest rates go up or down, perhaps due to a rise or fall in the rate of inflation, there will also be a potential capital loss or gain for the investor. In other words, the market value of interest-bearing securities will alter. **Market values will fall when interest rates go up and vice versa.**

2.13 For example, when the Government issues long-term gilts at a coupon interest rate of, say, 10% and the market rate of interest is also 10%, the market value of the securities will be £100 per £100 face value of the stock (or '£100 per cent').

(a) Now if nominal interest rates in the market subsequently rise to, say, 14% the re-sale value of the gilts will fall to:

$$£100 \times \frac{10\%}{14\%} = £71.43 \text{ per £100 face value of the stock.}$$

An investor in the gilts will make a capital loss of £28.57 per cent (plus selling costs) if he decides to sell the securities.

(b) If nominal interest rates subsequently fall to, say, 8%, the re-sale value of the gilts will rise to:

$$£100 \times \frac{10\%}{8\%} = £125 \text{ per cent.}$$

An investor could then sell his asset for a capital gain of £25 per cent (less selling costs).

Interest rates and share prices

2.14 **When interest rates change, the return expected by investors from shares will also change.** For example, if interest rates fell from 14% to 12% on government securities, and from 15% to 13% on company debentures, the return expected from shares (dividends and capital growth) would also fall. This is because shares and debt are alternative ways of investing money. **If interest rates fall, shares become more attractive to buy**. As demand for shares increases, their prices rise too, and so the dividend return gained from them falls in percentage terms.

2.15 You should be familiar with the fundamental theory of share values from your earlier studies. Basically, it is predicted that if a shareholder expects a 15% return on his investment in equities, and the annual dividend on one of his shares is 21p, then the market value of the share should be 21p/15% = £1.40 (ignoring any prospect of capital growth).

2.16 However, if interest rates fell, the shareholder would probably be satisfied with a lower return from his shares, say 14%, and the price of a share offering an annual dividend of 21p should then rise to 21p/14% = £1.50.

2.17 Equally, if interest rates went up, the shareholder would probably want a higher return from his shares, and share prices would fall. If, in our example, the investor wanted a 16% return, the predicted share price would fall to 21p/16% = £1.31.

Changes in interest rates and financing decisions

2.18 Interest rates are important for financial decisions by companies.

(a) **When interest rates are low**, it might be financially prudent:

(i) To **borrow more**, preferably at a fixed rate of interest, and so increase the company's gearing

(ii) To **borrow for long periods** rather than for short periods

(iii) To **pay back loans which incur a high interest rate**, if it is within the company's power to do so, and take out new loans at a lower interest rate

(b) **When interest rates are higher:**

(i) A company might decide to **reduce the amount of its debt finance**, and to substitute equity finance, such as retained earnings

(ii) A company which has a large surplus of cash and liquid funds to invest might **switch some of its short-term investments out of equities and into interest-bearing securities**

(iii) A company might opt to raise new finance by **borrowing short-term funds and debt at a variable interest rate** (for example on overdraft) rather than long-term funds at fixed rates of interest, in the hope that interest rates will soon come down again

Interest rates and new capital investments

2.19 When interest rates go up, and so the cost of finance to a company goes up, **the minimum return that a company will require on its own new capital investments will go up too**. Some new capital projects might be in the pipeline, with purchase contracts already signed with suppliers, and so there will often be a time lag before higher interest rates result in fewer new investments.

2.20 A company's management should give close consideration, when interest rates are high, to keeping investments in assets, particularly unwanted or inefficient fixed assets, stocks and debtors, down to a minimum, in order to reduce the company's need to borrow.

Management also need to bear in mind the deflationary effect of high interest rates in deterring spending by raising the cost of borrowing.

Exchange rates

> ### KEY TERM
>
> **Exchange rate** is the rate at which the national currency exchanges for other national currencies, being set by the interaction of demand and supply of the various currencies in the foreign exchange markets (**floating** exchange rate) or by government intervention in order to maintain a constant rate of exchange (**fixed** exchange rate). *(OT 2000)*

2.21 An **exchange rate** is the rate at which money in one currency can be exchanged for money in another currency. Exchange rates between different currencies on the world's foreign exchange markets are continually changing, and often by large amounts.

2.22 Foreign exchange rates are important for a business and its financial management because they affect:

- The cost of imports
- The value of exports
- The costs and benefits of international borrowing and lending

2.23 Changes in the value of sterling will affect the cost of goods from abroad. For example, if a consignment of goods is shipped from the USA to the UK, and the invoice price is US$420,000:

(a) If the sterling-dollar exchange rate is £1 = $1.75, the cost of the imports would be £240,000

(b) If sterling fell in value to £1 = $1.50, the cost of the imports would be higher, at £280,000

2.24 Changes in the value of sterling affect buying costs for everyone in the UK, companies and households alike, because a large proportion of the raw materials, components and finished goods that we consume is imported.

2.25 Exchange rates affect **exporting companies**, for similar reasons, because changes in exchange rates affect the price of exported goods to foreign buyers.

(a) **When sterling goes up in value,** goods sold abroad by a UK exporter, and invoiced in sterling, will cost more to the foreign buyer (who must purchase sterling with his own currency in order to pay).

(b) **When sterling falls in value,** goods sold abroad by a UK exporter and invoiced in sterling will become cheaper to foreign buyers.

To the extent that demand is influenced by price, the demand for exports will therefore vary with changes in the exchange rate.

Exchange rate policies

2.26 Governments may choose to let currencies fluctuate completely freely (a 'free float'), or they can attempt to regulate the values of their national currencies. Under a system of **fixed or**

semi-fixed exchange rates, a government acts to ensure that its currency keeps its value. This may be accomplished by market operations, or by legislation forbidding transactions at other than the official rate.

2.27 Under **managed floating**, a government will buy or sell its currency to prevent sharp fluctuations in its value, but will set no particular limits to the currency's value.

Exchange rate policies: the view of business

2.28 Businesses want both **certainty** and an exchange rate which will make them **competitive**. Fixed exchange rates offer the greatest certainty, followed by a managed float. However, rigidity of exchange rates can rapidly damage the competitiveness of exporting businesses in a country. While importers might benefit in the short term from fixed exchange rates if domestic inflation remained comparatively high, they could in the longer term find that foreign currency was simply not available.

International capital investments

2.29 Exchange rates can affect **international capital investments** significantly. Suppose that a UK company issues some shares. What is the likelihood that overseas investors will buy some of the shares? Obviously, prospects for capital growth and dividends will influence the investors' decision, but prospects of changes in the value of sterling will be important too. A 20% increase in the market value of UK company shares is worthless to a US investor if in the same period of time the value of sterling falls by a corresponding amount against the dollar, leaving no capital gain in dollars.

2.30 When a UK company wishes to **finance operations overseas**, there may be advantages in borrowing in the same currency as an investment. Assets and liabilities in the same currency can be 'matched' with one another, thus avoiding exchange losses on conversion in the group's annual accounts. Revenues in the foreign currency can be used to repay borrowings in the same currency, thus eliminating losses due to fluctuating exchange rates.

The Treasury economic model

2.31 The Treasury first developed an economic forecasting model in the late 1940s, and this came to be used by government as an aid to demand management policies. The forecasts are now published in the Financial Statement and Budget Report which accompanies the Budget. The model is run on desk-top computers and is used to simulate how a set of policy actions such as interest rate changes affect variables such as consumer spending or job vacancies. It consists of over 1,000 mathematical equations linking variables such as unemployment, the rate of inflation and the budget deficit.

2.32 A significant problem with constructing an economic forecast is that of making estimates of economic output (GDP) for the period from the last known figures to the month in which the forecast is made. For example, for a forecast prepared in February, only the GDP figures up to the previous September are known. The GDP estimate for the intervening period must be estimated from various indicators, including exports, imports, retail sales, industrial production and employment. Difficulties arise when these indicators give conflicting messages.

2.33 Once the base period figures have been established, the part of the forecast relating to the future can be built up. This task is assisted by the existence of a number of forward indicators which provide information on the prospects in particular sectors of the economy. For example, the Department of Trade and Industry compiles figures based on enquiries to businesses asking for estimates of percentage changes in expected investment. The Confederation of British Industry (CBI) also makes enquiries about its members' investment intentions. Figures for new orders received, wage settlements and government expenditure forecasts are also incorporated into the model. These various forms of data provide a fairly direct means of forecasting for the forthcoming 6 to 12 months. For the longer term, the Treasury's integrated econometric model must be employed.

2.34 The main product of the Treasury model is a detailed table of Gross Domestic Product (GDP) and its components, given on a quarterly basis for a period of two to three years.

2.35 An article published in the *Financial Times* in May 1993 drew attention to some of the problems involved in modelling the economy.

> 'Dozens, if not hundreds, of models are used worldwide to simulate activities in specific economies. They differ from each other largely in the way their equations link up variables and how easy they are to use.'

2.36 The performance of the UK economy itself acts as a **control** upon the validity of the model.

> 'The Treasury model has entered the spotlight partly because of the inadequacies of the Treasury's recent forecasts, which in common with many private-sector projections failed to spot either the 1986-88 boom or the seriousness of the recession before it was too late.

> Although the model can hardly take the full blame for the poor predictions - other important factors include the judgements made by Treasury economists and the political "spin" imparted to projections - by ministers - Treasury officials conceded the software in the model has not been kept sufficiently up to date.'

2.37 The Treasury publishes average errors for its calendar year forecasts; for example, these showed a mean absolute error of 1% for GDP for the ten year period to 1988. The errors in the forecasts for component expenditures tend to be greater than for the GDP itself.

2.38 The Treasury model is in a state of constant revision, and there must necessarily be some room left for judgement, for example when events of which the model does not take account, such as strikes and fuel shortages, occur.

3 PUBLISHED INFORMATION

3.1 Published sources provide financial and non-financial data which, in the process of formulating financial strategy, can supplement the information that management obtains from internal sources or from trade contacts.

Exam focus point

You should be broadly aware of the information sources outlined in this section, but you do not need to learn them in detail.

3.2 **Planning and decision-making rely on accurate and complete information.** Financial managers often rely on externally provided information systems as the source of much current information about other companies (which might be targets for takeover bids), certain markets (such as commodity and foreign exchange markets), share prices, or business and economic matters.

3.3 There are various sources of environmental data.

(a) **Newspapers and periodicals** contain relevant environmental information.

(b) Sometimes more detailed country information is needed than that supplied by the press. **Export consultants** might specialise in dealing with particular countries, and so can be a valuable source of information.

(c) **Trade journals** might give information about a wide variety of relevant issues to a particular industry. **Trade associations**, also, are good at spreading news.

(d) **The government** is a source of statistical data relating to the economy and society. Also, the government can be a source of specific advice to businesses. The Business in Europe programme of the DTI includes the following.

- Single European Market information
- Advice on overcoming trade barriers
- Information on individual markets and opportunities
- Expertise from private sector advisors
- Where to get further advice
- A telephone hotline

(e) Sources of **technological** information include the **Patent Office, trade journals** and **universities**.

(f) A firm's **sales and marketing staff** are aware of competitive data.

(g) Various **databases** can be accessed (see below).

3.4 Some companies specialise in providing an external 'electronic reference library' or **on-line information retrieval system** (OLIRS) to make this information available to subscribers. This is an externally supplied database. Subscribers can gain access to the supplier's information from a terminal in their office and pay a fee for access to the data.

3.5 A number of firms provide on line information systems on commercial and tax matters, such as Datastream, Data-Star, Extel and Butterworths. Reuters provides an OLIRS about money market interest rates and foreign exchange rates to firms involved in money and foreign exchange markets, and to the treasury departments of a large number of companies.

3.6 Large volumes of information are available through **databases held by public bodies**. Some newspapers offer computerised access to old editions, with search facilities looking for information on particular companies or issues. FT PROFILE, for example, provides on-line business information. Public databases are also available for inspection.

3.7 An example of a public database is *Spearhead*, run by the Department for Trade and Industry (DTI). This is an on-line database of information relating to the single European market programme of the European Union (EU).

3.8 The **government** provides a wealth of **statistical information**, which often provides the best indicators of the economic environment within which businesses must operate.

Question 3

Interpret the following indices of output in a country.

Standard Industrial Classification	20X1	20X2	20X3	20X4	20X5	20X6	20X7	20X8	20X9
Rubber products	107.8	111.4	113.8	113.1	100.0	86.4	79.2	81.3	79.1
Processing of plastics	95.2	102.3	106.5	110.6	100.0	94.7	99.0	110.1	121.0

Answer

These figures show that over the decade the plastics processing industry had expanded strongly, with a temporary setback in the years 20X5-20X7. In contrast, the rubber products industry fell into serious recession in 20X5-20X7 and by 20X9 had failed to recover. These figures would have implications for firms planning investment in these industries.

Price indices

3.9   Statistics about **prices** are presented in the form of price indices, including the following.

(a)   **General Index of Retail Prices or Retail Prices Index (RPI).** This measures monthly changes in retail prices of goods and services bought by UK households. Separate indices are published for groups, and sub-groups of goods and services.

(b)   **Tax and Price Index (TPI).** This index measures the change in gross taxable income needed to compensate taxpayers for any increase in retail prices, taking into account both changes in retail prices and also changes in individuals' liability to income tax and National Insurance contributions.

(c)   **Producer price indices.** Index numbers are calculated for:

(i)   Groups of commodities

(1)   Produced in the UK
(2)   Imported into the UK

(ii)   Materials purchased by certain sectors of industry

(iii)   Output of certain sectors of industry

3.10   (a)   If the Retail Prices Index is rising, a company's own costs may be rising at a comparable rate, and we should expect:

(i)   The workforce to demand wage increases that are at least in line with increases in the RPI

(ii)   Unit costs of output to rise

(iii)   Interest rates to be somewhat higher than the rate of increase in the RPI

(iv)   That a company will have some scope for putting up its own prices in line with increases in the RPI, without provoking adverse customer reaction

(b)   Sometimes, increases in a specific producer price index or commodity price index might help to explain a company's particular problems. For example, if a company uses timber as a major raw material, and the price index for timber rises at an exceptionally high rate, the company will expect:

(i)   The rate of inflation in its own industry to be particularly high

(ii)   Unit costs to rise substantially, so that selling prices have to be raised by a large amount too

(iii)   Customer demand to fall in response to exceptionally high price increases

Interest rates and yields on securities

3.11   Statistics on **interest rates and other security yields** are available from a variety of sources, not just the government. The *Financial Times* provides daily information on dividend yields and interest rates, for example, but the best historical record of interest rates and yields is probably provided in the *Bank of England Quarterly Bulletin*. The most important statistics are also published in the government's monthly Financial Statistics booklet.

Exchange rates

3.12 The main government sources of **exchange rate statistics** are the monthly Financial Statistics and the Bank of England Quarterly Bulletin. Exchange rates are also published daily in the Financial Times. Exchange rates between currencies are continually changing. Statistics are available giving monthly closing 'spot' and 'three month forward' rates. There is also a sterling index, which expresses the value of sterling against a basket of other currencies.

Sources of published statistics

3.13 Here is a summary list of some of the important sources of published statistics.

(a) **Government sources**

(i) The *Monthly Digest of Statistics* is a collection of various statistics from all government departments.

(ii) *Financial Statistics* is a monthly series of financial statistics, many supplied by the Bank of England.

(iii) The *Annual Abstract of Statistics* is similar to the *Monthly Digest*, except published annually and containing more statistics.

(iv) *Business Monitors* are produced for each industry every quarter (sometimes monthly) and includes statistics on sales figures, production, exports and imports.

(v) *Overseas Trade Statistics* is published monthly. There is also the annual 'Pink Book' on the UK balance of payments which was mentioned above.

(b) **Non-government sources**

(i) The London Business School, which produces regular economic reports.

(ii) Stockbroking companies, which provide regular financial forecasting services, with particular emphasis on investment-related topics.

(iii) The National Institute of Economic and Social Research, the Confederation of British Industry (CBI) and other bodies, which produce occasional reports.

(iv) Daily newspapers, such as the Financial Times; also weekly and monthly specialist magazines.

(v) Banks, which can provide customers with some business information, particularly about economic conditions and customers in overseas countries.

(vi) Occasional reports of trade associations or local Chambers of Commerce.

Exam focus point

As with the previous Chapter, topics in this chapter may well feature in questions in conjunction with topics from the rest of the syllabus.

BPP
PUBLISHING

Chapter roundup

- This chapter has covered the environment within which businesses must operate. **Environmental factors** can be very significant for businesses, but are outside their control.

- The environment can **change** unexpectedly, with serious consequences for many businesses. It is therefore essential both to allow for such possible changes when making plans and to monitor the relevant economic statistics, so that changes can be anticipated as far as possible and responded to with minimal disruption.

- The **Cadbury Report** has clarified many of the contentious issues of corporate governance and sets standards of best practice in relation to financial reporting and accountability, while the **Greenbury Code** has made recommendations on directors' pay. The **Hampel Report** has reviewed the Cadbury and Greenbury recommendations.

- Further **regulation** is provided by bodies such as OFWAT and OFTEL, in the areas of pricing and competition.

- **Economic constraints** on strategy will be imposed by **inflation, interest rates** and **exchange rates**.

Quick quiz

1   **Fill in the blanks**

The .... Report defines .... as 'the system by which companies are directed and controlled'.

2   Which three Reports have led to the combined corporate governance code?

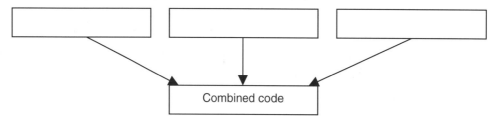

3   List two principal methods of regulating a monopoly industry.

4   Draw a 'normal' yield curve, labelling axes.

5   Fill in the following at (A), (B) and (C) in the equation below

- Nominal rate of interest
- Real rate of interest
- Rate of inflation

$$\frac{1 + (A)}{1 + (B)} - 1 = (C)$$

Answers to quick quiz

1   Cadbury; corporate governance.

2   Cadbury; Greenbury; Hampel.

3   Price control; profit control.

4

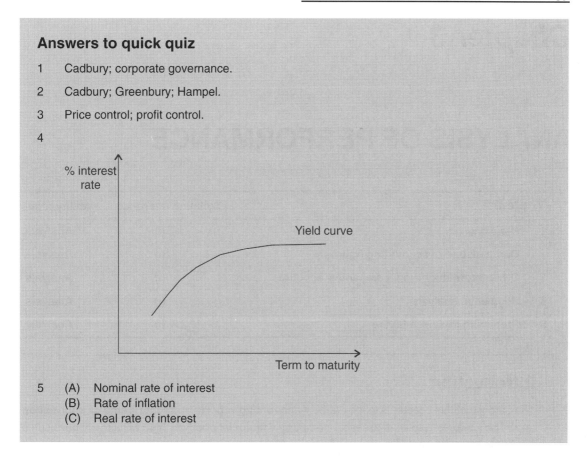

5   (A)   Nominal rate of interest
      (B)   Rate of inflation
      (C)   Real rate of interest

Now try the question below from the Exam Question Bank

Number	Level	Marks	Time
2	Introductory	n/a	20 mins

Chapter 3

ANALYSIS OF PERFORMANCE

Topic list	Syllabus reference	Ability required
1 Ratio analysis	(i)	Analysis
2 Comparisons of accounting figures	(i)	Analysis
3 Other information from companies' accounts	(i)	Analysis
4 Segmental analysis	(i)	Analysis
5 Predicting business failure	(i)	Analysis

Introduction

The purpose of this chapter is to look at how **accounting reports** and **other items of information** should be interpreted so as to assess a **company's financial position**. You will already have some familiarity with **ratio analysis**.

Learning outcomes covered in this chapter

- Analyse and interpret company accounts of customers, competitors and target companies

Syllabus content covered in this chapter

- Ratio analysis (liquidity, profitability, shareholder investment, gearing)

- Financial obligations indicated in financial accounts, eg redeemable debt, earn out arrangements, potential liabilities, long-term commitments (a UK example would be the Private Finance Initiative)

- Interpreting the segmental analysis section of published accounts

1   RATIO ANALYSIS

1.1   As part of the system of financial control in an organisation, it will be necessary to have ways of measuring the progress of the enterprise and of individual subsidiaries, so that managers know how well the company concerned is doing. The financial situation of a company will also obviously affect its share price. Is the company profitable? Is it growing? Does it have satisfactory liquidity? Is its gearing level acceptable? What is its dividend policy?

1.2   The answers to some of these questions can be obtained from accounting reports produced by the company. The usual way of interpreting accounting reports is to calculate and then to analyse certain ratios (**ratio analysis**).

Broad categories of ratios

1.3   Ratios can be grouped into the following four categories:

(a) Profitability and return
(b) Debt and gearing
(c) Liquidity: control of cash and other working capital items
(d) Shareholders' investment ratios (or 'stock market ratios')

1.4   Within each heading we will identify a number of standard measures or ratios that are normally calculated and generally accepted as meaningful indicators. It must be stressed however that **each individual business must be considered separately,** and a ratio that is meaningful for a manufacturing company may be completely meaningless for a financial institution. Also, **ratios need to be compared** over a number of periods if the analysis is to be of value.

1.5   Try not to be too mechanical when working out ratios, and think constantly about what you are trying to achieve.

1.6   The Du Pont system of ratio analysis involves constructing a pyramid of interrelated ratios like that below.

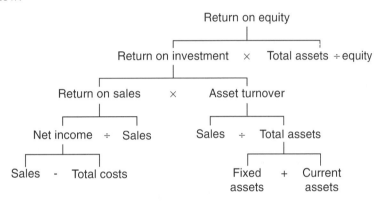

1.7   Such **ratio pyramids** help in providing for an overall management plan to achieve profitability, and allow the interrelationships between ratios to be checked.

1.8   The key to obtaining meaningful information from ratio analysis is **comparison**: comparing ratios over time within the same business to establish whether the business is improving or declining, and comparing ratios between similar businesses to see whether the company you are analysing is better or worse than average within its own business sector.

1.9   **Ratio analysis on its own is not sufficient** for interpreting company accounts, and there are other items of information which should be looked at. These include the following.

(a) Comments in the Chairman's report and the directors' report

(b) The age and nature of the company's assets

(c) Current and future developments in the company's markets, at home and overseas

(d) Recent acquisitions or disposals of a subsidiary by the company

(e) The nature and level of financial obligations

(f) The cash flow statement (where required by FRS 1)

(g) Other features of the report and accounts, such as post balance sheet events, contingencies a qualified auditors' report, the company's taxation position, and so on

Several of these areas are discussed further later in this chapter or in the next.

Profitability

1.10 A company ought of course to be profitable, and obvious checks on **profitability** are:

- Whether the company has made a profit or a loss on its ordinary activities
- By how much this year's profit or loss is bigger or smaller than last year's profit or loss

1.11 It is probably better to consider separately the profits or losses on extraordinary items if there are any. An extraordinary gain would obviously be a good bonus and an extraordinary loss might cause concern. However, such gains or losses should not be expected to occur again, unlike profits or losses on normal trading.

1.12 **Profit on ordinary activities before taxation** is generally thought to be a better figure to use than profit after taxation, because there might be unusual variations in the tax charge from year to year which would not affect the underlying profitability of the company's operations.

1.13 Another profit figure that should be calculated is **PBIT**: profit before interest and tax. This is the amount of profit which the company earned before having to pay interest to the providers of loan capital. By providers of loan capital, we usually mean longer term loan capital, such as debentures and medium-term bank loans, which will be shown in the balance sheet as 'Creditors: amounts falling due after more than one year.' This figure is of particular importance to bankers and lenders.

1.14 Profit before interest and tax is therefore:

- The profit on ordinary activities before taxation, **add back**
- Interest charges on long term loan capital.

1.15 To calculate PBIT, in theory, all we have to do is to look at the interest payments in the relevant note to the accounts. Do not take the net interest figure in the profit and loss account itself, because this represents interest payments less interest received, and PBIT is profit **including** interest received but **before** interest payments.

1.16 The note to the accounts on interest charges, unfortunately, does not give us the exact figure we want, and we have to take the most suitable figure available. Company law requires companies to show the amount of interest in respect of:

- Bank loans and bank overdrafts, and other loans which are repayable within five years
- Loans repayable by instalments (for example finance leases) beyond five years
- All other loans (for example long-term debentures)

1.17 The interest cost we want is (c) plus (b) and probably a part of (a) (for interest on loans repayable within one to five years which are 'Creditors: amounts falling due after more than one year'). Unless a company gives clear details of its interest costs, it is probably simplest to approximate the interest for PBIT as the total of (a), (b) and (c).

Profitability and return: the return on capital employed (ROCE)

1.18 It is impossible to assess profits or profit growth properly without relating them to the amount of funds (the capital) employed in making the profits. An important profitability ratio is therefore **return on capital employed (ROCE)**, which states the profit as a percentage of the amount of capital employed.

1.19 **Profit** is usually taken as PBIT, and **capital employed** is shareholders' capital plus long-term liabilities and debt capital. This is the same as total assets less current liabilities. The underlying principle is that we must compare like with like, and so if capital means share capital and reserves plus long-term liabilities and debt capital, profit must mean the profit earned by all this capital together. This is PBIT, since interest is the return for loan capital.

$$\text{Thus ROCE} = \frac{\text{Profit on ordinary activities before interest and taxation (PBIT)}}{\text{Capital employed}}$$

Capital employed = Shareholders' funds plus 'creditors: amounts falling due after more than one year' plus any long-term provisions for liabilities and charges.

Evaluating the ROCE

1.20 What does a company's ROCE tell us? What should we be looking for? There are three comparisons that can be made.

(a) The change in ROCE from one year to the next

(b) The ROCE being earned by other companies, if this information is available

(c) A comparison of the ROCE with current market borrowing rates

(i) What would be the cost of extra borrowing to the company if it needed more loans, and is it earning an ROCE that suggests it could make high enough profits to make such borrowing worthwhile?

(ii) Is the company making an ROCE which suggests that it is making profitable use of its current borrowing?

Analysing profitability and return in more detail: the secondary ratios

1.21 We may analyse the ROCE, to find out why it is high or low, or better or worse than last year. There are two factors that contribute towards a return on capital employed, both related to turnover.

(a) **Profit margin**. A company might make a high or a low profit margin on its sales. For example, a company that makes a profit of 25p per £1 of sales is making a bigger return on its turnover than another company making a profit of only 10p per £1 of sales.

(b) **Asset turnover**. Asset turnover is a measure of how well the assets of a business are being used to generate sales. For example, if two companies each have capital employed of £100,000, and company A makes sales of £400,000 a year whereas company B makes sales of only £200,000 a year, company A is making a higher turnover from the same amount of assets and this will help company A to make a higher return on capital employed than company B. Asset turnover is expressed as 'x times' so that assets generate x times their value in annual turnover. Here, company A's asset turnover is 4 times and company B's is 2 times.

1.22 Profit margin and asset turnover together explain the ROCE, and if the ROCE is the primary profitability ratio, these other two are the secondary ratios. The relationship between the three ratios is as follows.

Profit margin × Asset turnover = ROCE

$$\frac{\text{PBIT}}{\text{Sales}} \times \frac{\text{Sales}}{\text{Capital employed}} = \frac{\text{PBIT}}{\text{Capital employed}}$$

1.23 It is also worth commenting on the **change in turnover** from one year to the next. Strong sales growth will usually indicate volume growth as well as turnover increases due to price rises, and volume growth is one sign of a prosperous company.

The gross profit margin, the net profit margin and profit analysis

1.24 Depending on the format of the profit and loss account, you may be able to calculate the gross profit margin as well as the net profit margin. Looking at the two together can be quite informative.

1.25 EXAMPLE: PROFITABILITY

A company has the following summarised profit and loss accounts for two consecutive years.

	Year 1	Year 2
	£	£
Turnover	70,000	100,000
Less cost of sales	42,000	55,000
Gross profit	28,000	45,000
Less expenses	21,000	35,000
Net profit	7,000	10,000

Although the net profit margin is the same for both years at 10%, the gross profit margin is not.

In year 1 it is: $\dfrac{28,000}{70,000} = 40\%$

and in year 2 it is: $\dfrac{45,000}{100,000} = 45\%$

1.26 Is this good or bad for the business? An increased profit margin must be good because this indicates a wider gap between selling price and cost of sales. However, given that the net profit ratio has stayed the same in the second year, expenses must be rising. In year 1 expenses were 30% of turnover, whereas in year 2 they were 35% of turnover. This indicates that administration, selling and distribution expenses or interest costs require tight control.

1.27 A percentage analysis of profit between year 1 and year 2 is as follows.

	Year 1	Year 2
	%	%
Cost of sales as a % of sales	60	55
Gross profit as a % of sales	40	45
	100	100
Expenses as a % of sales	30	35
Net profit as a % of sales	10	10
Gross profit as a % of sales	40	45

Debt and gearing ratios

1.28 **Debt ratios** are concerned with how much the company owes in relation to its size and whether it is getting into heavier debt or improving its situation.

(a) When a company is heavily in debt, and seems to be getting even more heavily into debt, the thought that should occur to you is that this cannot continue. If the company carries on wanting to borrow more, banks and other would-be lenders are very soon likely to refuse further borrowing and the company might well find itself in trouble.

(b)   When a company is earning only a modest profit before interest and tax, and has a heavy debt burden, there will be very little profit left over for shareholders after the interest charges have been paid. And so if interest rates were to go up or the company were to borrow even more, it might soon be incurring interest charges in excess of PBIT. This might eventually lead to the liquidation of the company.

1.29   These are the two main reasons why companies should keep their debt burden under control. Four ratios that are particularly worth looking at are the **debt ratio**, **gearing**, **interest cover** and the **cash flow ratio**.

1.30   The **debt ratio** is the ratio of a company's total debts to its total assets.

(a)   **Assets** consist of fixed assets at their balance sheet value, plus current assets.

(b)   **Debts** consist of all creditors, whether amounts falling due within one year or after more than one year.

You can ignore long-term provisions and liabilities, such as deferred taxation.

1.31   There is no absolute rule on the **maximum safe debt ratio**, but as a very general guide, you might regard 50% as a safe limit to debt. In practice, many companies operate successfully with a higher debt ratio than this, but 50% is nonetheless a helpful benchmark. In addition, if the debt ratio is over 50% and getting worse, the company's debt position will be worth looking at more carefully.

> **KEY TERM**
>
> **Financial leverage/gearing:** The use of debt finance to increase the return on equity by deploying borrowed funds in such a way that the return generated is greater than the cost of servicing the debt. If the reverse is true, and the return on deployed funds is less than the cost of servicing the debt, the effect of gearing is to reduce the return on equity.
>
> *(OT 2000)*

1.32   **Capital gearing** is concerned with the amount of debt in a company's **long-term** capital structure. **Gearing ratios** provide a long-term measure of liquidity.

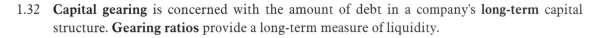

$$\text{Gearing ratio} = \frac{\text{Prior charge capital (long-term debt)}}{\text{Long-term debt} + \text{equity (shareholders' funds)}}$$

1.33   **Operating gearing** is concerned with the relationship in a company between its **variable/fixed cost operating structure** and its profitability. It can be calculated as the ratio of **contribution** (sales minus variable costs of sales) **to PBIT**. The possibility of rises or falls in sales revenue and volumes means that operating gearing has possible implications for a company's business risk.

1.34   The **interest cover** ratio shows whether a company is earning enough profits before interest and tax to pay its interest costs comfortably, or whether its interest costs are high in relation to the size of its profits, so that a fall in profit before interest and tax (PBIT) would then have a significant effect on profits available for ordinary shareholders.

$$\text{Interest cover} = \frac{\text{PBIT}}{\text{Interest charges}}$$

1.35 **An interest cover of 2 times or less would be low**, and it should really exceed 3 times before the company's interest costs can be considered to be within acceptable limits. Note that although preference share capital is included as prior charge capital for the gearing ratio, it is usual to exclude preference dividends from 'interest' charges. We also look at all interest payments, even interest charges on short-term debt, and so interest cover and gearing do not quite look at the same thing.

1.36 The **cash flow ratio** is the ratio of a company's net annual cash inflow to its total debts:

$$\frac{\text{Net annual cash inflow}}{\text{Total debts}}$$

   (a) **Net annual cash inflow** is the amount of cash which the company has coming into the business each year from its operations. This will be shown in a company's cash flow statement for the year.

   (b) **Total debts** are short-term and long-term creditors, together with provisions for liabilities and charges.

1.37 Obviously, a company needs to earn enough cash from operations to be able to meet its foreseeable debts and future commitments, and the cash flow ratio, and changes in the cash flow ratio from one year to the next, provides a useful indicator of a company's cash position.

Liquidity ratios: cash and working capital

1.38 Profitability is of course an important aspect of a company's performance, and debt or gearing is another. Neither, however, addresses directly the key issue of liquidity. **A company needs liquid assets so that it can meet its debts when they fall due.**

1.39 **Liquidity** is the amount of cash a company can obtain quickly to settle its debts (and possibly to meet other unforeseen demands for cash payments too). **Liquid funds** consist of:

   (a) **Cash**

   (b) **Short-term investments for which there is a ready market,** such as investments in shares of other companies. (Short-term investments are distinct from investments in shares in subsidiaries or associated companies.)

   (c) **Fixed term deposits** with a bank or building society, for example six month deposits with a bank

   (d) **Trade debtors.** (These are not cash, but ought to be expected to pay what they owe within a reasonably short time.)

   (e) **Bills of exchange receivable.** (Like ordinary trade debtors, these represent amounts of cash due to be received soon.)

1.40 Some assets are more liquid than others. **Stocks** of goods are fairly liquid in some businesses. Stocks of finished production goods might be sold quickly, and a **supermarket** will hold consumer goods for resale that could well be sold for cash very soon. Raw materials and components in a **manufacturing company** have to be used to make a finished product before they can be sold to realise cash, and so they are less liquid than finished goods. Just how liquid they are depends on the **speed of stock turnover** and the **length of the production cycle.**

1.41 **Fixed assets are not liquid assets**. A company can sell off fixed assets, but unless they are no longer needed, or are worn out and about to be replaced, they are necessary to continue the company's operations. Selling fixed assets is certainly not a solution to a company's cash needs, and so although there may be an occasional fixed asset item which is about to be sold off, probably because it is going to be replaced, it is safe to disregard fixed assets when measuring a company's liquidity.

1.42 In summary, liquid assets are current asset items that will or could soon be converted into cash, and cash itself. Two common definitions of liquid assets are **all current assets** or **all current assets with the exception of stocks.**

1.43 The main source of liquid assets for a trading company is **sales**. A company can obtain cash from sources other than sales, such as the issue of shares for cash, a new loan or the sale of fixed assets. But a company cannot rely on these at all times, and in general, obtaining liquid funds depends on making sales and profits.

1.44 A company must be able to pay its debts when they fall due, and in the balance sheet, foreseeable creditors to be paid are represented by **current liabilities**, that is, amounts falling due within one year. There are of course other payments that a company might want to make as well, such as the purchase of new fixed assets for cash.

Why does profit not provide an indication of liquidity?

1.45 If a company makes profits, it should earn money, and if it earns money, it might seem that it should receive more cash than it pays out. In fact, profits are not always a good guide to liquidity. Two examples will show why this is so.

(a) Suppose that company X makes all its sales for cash, and pays all its running costs in cash without taking any credit. Its profit for the year just ended was as follows.

	£	£
Sales		400,000
Less costs: running costs	200,000	
depreciation	50,000	
		250,000
Profit		150,000
Less dividends (all paid)		80,000
Retained profits		70,000

During the year, the company purchased a fixed asset for £180,000 and paid for it in full.

Depreciation is not a cash outlay, and so the company's 'cash profits' less dividends were sales less running costs less dividends = £120,000. However, the fixed asset purchase required £180,000, and so the company's cash position worsened in the year by £60,000, in spite of the profit.

(b) Suppose that company Y buys three items for cash, each costing £5,000, and resells them for £7,000 each. The buyers of the units take credit, and by the end of the company's accounting year, they were all still debtors.

   (i) The profit on the transactions is £2,000 per unit and £6,000 in total.

   (ii) The company has paid £15,000 to buy the goods, but so far it has received no cash back from selling them, and so its cash position is so far £15,000 worse off from the transactions.

(iii)   The effect so far of the transactions is:

Reduction in cash	£15,000
Increase in debtors	£21,000
Increase in profit	£6,000

The increase in assets is £6,000 in total, to match the £6,000 increase in profit, but the increase in assets is the net change in cash (reduced balance) and debtors (increased balance).

Exam focus point

You could be expected to reconcile profit statements to cash flow statements, a skill you should have acquired in earlier studies.

1.46   Both of the examples above show ways in which **a company can be profitable but at the same time get into cash flow problems**. If an analysis of a company's published accounts is to give us some idea of the company's liquidity, profitability ratios are not going to be appropriate for doing this. Instead, we look at **liquidity ratios** and **working capital turnover ratios**.

Knowledge brought forward from Paper 4 (IFIN)

Liquidity ratios

- The **current ratio** is defined as:

$$\frac{\text{Current assets}}{\text{Current liabilities}}$$

- In practice, a current ratio comfortably in excess of 1 should be expected, but what is 'comfortable' varies between different types of businesses.

- In some businesses where stock turnover is slow, such as manufacturing companies, most stocks are not very liquid assets, because the cash cycle is so long. For these reasons, we calculate an additional liquidity ratio, known as the **quick ratio** or **acid test** ratio.

- The **quick ratio**, or **acid test ratio**, is:

$$\frac{\text{Current assets less stocks}}{\text{Current liabilities}}$$

- This ratio should ideally be at least 1 for companies with a slow stock turnover. For companies with a fast stock turnover, a quick ratio can be less than 1 without suggesting that the company is in cash flow difficulties.

- An excessively large current/quick ratio may indicate a company that is **over-investing in working capital**, suggesting poor management of debtors or stocks by the company.

- We can calculate **turnover periods** for stock, debtors and creditors (debtor and creditor days). If we add together the stock days and the debtor days, this should give us an indication of how soon stock is convertible into cash. Both debtor days and stock days therefore give us a further indication of the company's liquidity.

Question 1

Calculate liquidity and working capital ratios from the accounts of a manufacturer of products for the construction industry, and comment on the ratios.

	20X8	20X7
	£m	£m
Turnover	2,065.0	1,788.7
Cost of sales	1,478.6	1,304.0
Gross profit	586.4	484.7
Current assets		
Stocks	119.0	109.0
Debtors (note 1)	400.9	347.4
Short-term investments	4.2	18.8
Cash at bank and in hand	48.2	48.0
	572.3	523.2
Creditors: amounts falling due within one year		
Loans and overdrafts	49.1	35.3
Corporation taxes	62.0	46.7
Dividend	19.2	14.3
Creditors (note 2)	370.7	324.0
	501.0	420.3
Net current assets	71.3	102.9

Notes

	20X8	20X7
	£m	£m
1 Trade debtors	329.8	285.4
2 Trade creditors	236.2	210.8

Answer

	20X8		20X7	
Current ratio	$\dfrac{572.3}{501.0}$	= 1.14	$\dfrac{523.2}{420.3}$	= 1.24
Quick ratio	$\dfrac{453.3}{501.0}$	= 0.90	$\dfrac{414.2}{420.3}$	= 0.99
Debtors' payment period	$\dfrac{329.8}{2,065.0} \times 365$	= 58 days	$\dfrac{285.4}{1,788.7} \times 365$	= 58 days
Stock turnover period	$\dfrac{119.0}{1,478.6} \times 365$	= 29 days	$\dfrac{109.0}{1,304.0} \times 365$	= 31 days
Creditors' turnover period	$\dfrac{236.2}{1,478.6} \times 365$	= 58 days	$\dfrac{210.8}{1,304.0} \times 365$	= 59 days

As a manufacturing group serving the construction industry, the company would be expected to have a comparatively lengthy debtors' turnover period, because of the relatively poor cash flow in the construction industry. It is clear that the company compensates for this by ensuring that they do not pay for raw materials and other costs before they have sold their stocks of finished goods (hence the similarity of debtors' and creditors' turnover periods).

The company's current ratio is a little lower than average but its quick ratio is better than average and very little less than the current ratio. This suggests that stock levels are strictly controlled, which is reinforced by the low stock turnover period. It would seem that working capital is tightly managed, to avoid the poor liquidity which could be caused by a high debtors' turnover period and comparatively high creditors.

Creditors' turnover is ideally calculated by the formula:

$$\frac{\text{Average stock}}{\text{Purchases}} \times 365$$

However, it is rare to find purchases disclosed in published accounts and so cost of sales serves as an approximation. The creditors' turnover ratio often helps to assess a company's liquidity; an increase in creditor days is often a sign of lack of long-term finance or poor management of current assets, resulting in the use of extended credit from suppliers, increased bank overdraft and so on.

Exam focus point

In allocating marks, the examiner will give at least as much weighting to the ability to choose and to interpret appropriate indicators as to the ability to calculate ratios correctly.

Stock market ratios

1.47 The final set of ratios to consider are the ratios which help equity shareholders and other investors to assess the value and quality of an investment in the ordinary shares of a company.

1.48 You have covered the computations of stock market ratios in your previous studies, and the formulae for the main ones are summarised below. We shall then consider their significance in the analysis of performance.

Knowledge brought forward from Paper 4 (IFIN)

Stock market ratios

- **Dividend yield** $= \dfrac{\text{Dividend per share}}{\text{Market price per share}}$

- **Interest yield** $= \dfrac{\text{Interest payable}}{\text{Market value of loan stock}}$

- **Earnings per share** $= \dfrac{\text{Profit after tax, extraordinary items and preference dividends}}{\text{Number of equity shares in issue and ranking for dividend}}$

- **P/E ratio** $= \dfrac{\text{Market value per share}}{\text{Earnings per share}}$

- **Dividend cover** $= \dfrac{\text{Earnings available for distribution to ordinary shareholders}}{\text{Actual dividend for ordinary shareholders}}$

1.49 Investors are interested in:

- The value (market price) of the securities that they hold
- The return that the security has obtained in the past
- Expected future returns
- Whether their investment is reasonably secure

Dividend yield and interest yield

1.50 In practice, we usually find with quoted companies that the dividend yield on shares is less than the interest yield on debentures and loan stock (and also less than the yield paid on gilt-edged securities). The share price generally rises in most years, giving shareholders capital gains. In the long run, shareholders will want the return on their shares, in terms of dividends received plus capital gains, to exceed the return that investors get from fixed interest securities.

Exam focus point

Note that the interest yield, which is the **investor's** rate of return, is different from the **coupon** rate payable by the company as the nominal value of the loan stock. (Many students confuse these.)

Earnings per share (EPS)

Exam focus point

The Examiner has commented that many candidates do not know how to calculate earnings per share correctly. Make sure that you do.

1.51 EPS is widely used as a measure of a company's performance and is of particular importance in comparing results over a period of several years. A company must be able to sustain its earnings in order to pay dividends and re-invest in the business so as to achieve future growth. Investors also look for **growth** in the EPS from one year to the next.

Question 2

Walter Wall Carpets plc made profits before tax in 20X8 of £9,320,000. Tax amounted to £2,800,000.

The company's share capital is as follows.

	£
Ordinary share (10,000,000 shares of £1)	10,000,000
8% preference shares	2,000,000
	12,000,000

Required

Calculate the EPS for 20X8.

Answer

	£
Profits before tax	9,320,000
Less tax	2,880,000
Profits after tax	6,520,000
Less preference dividend (8% of £2,000,000)	160,000
Earnings	6,360,000
Number of ordinary shares	10,000,000
EPS	63.6p

1.52 EPS on its own does not really tell us anything. It must be seen in the context of several other matters.

(a) EPS is used for comparing the results of a company over time. Is its EPS growing? What is the rate of growth? Is the rate of growth increasing or decreasing?

(b) Is there likely to be a significant dilution of EPS in the future, perhaps due to the exercise of share options or warrants, or the conversion of convertible loan stock into equity?

BPP PUBLISHING

(c) EPS should not be used blindly to compare the earnings of one company with another. For example, if A plc has an EPS of 12p for its 10,000,000 10p shares and B plc has an EPS of 24p for its 50,000,000 25p shares, we must take account of the numbers of shares. When earnings are used to compare one company's shares with another, this is done using the P/E ratio or perhaps the earnings yield.

(d) If EPS is to be a reliable basis for comparing results, it must be calculated consistently. The EPS of one company must be directly comparable with the EPS of others, and the EPS of a company in one year must be directly comparable with its published EPS figures for previous years. Changes in the share capital of a company during the course of a year cause problems of comparability.

1.53 Note that EPS is a figure based on **past data**, and it is easily manipulated by changes in accounting policies and by mergers or acquisitions. The use of the measure in calculating management bonuses makes it particularly liable to manipulation. The attention given to EPS as a performance measure by City analysts is arguably disproportionate to its true worth. Investors should be more concerned with future earnings, but of course estimates of these are more difficult to reach than the readily available figure.

1.54 The value of the P/E ratio reflects the market's appraisal of the shares' future prospects. In other words, if one company has a higher P/E ratio than another it is because investors either expect its earnings to **increase faster** than the other's or consider that it is a **less risky** company or in a more 'secure' industry. The P/E ratio is, simply, a measure of the relationship between the market value of a company's shares and the earnings from those shares.

1.55 It is an important ratio because it relates two key considerations for investors, the market price of a share and its earnings capacity. It is significant only as a **measure of this relationship between earnings and value.**

1.56 As we shall see later in the text, one approach to assessing what share prices ought to be, which is often used in practice, is a P/E ratio approach. It is a common-sense approach to share price assessment (although not as well founded in theory as the dividend valuation model), which is that:

(a) The relationship between the EPS and the share price is measured by the P/E ratio

(b) There is no reason to suppose, in normal circumstances, that the P/E ratio will vary much over time

(c) So if the EPS goes up or down, the share price should be expected to move up or down too, and the new share price will be the new EPS multiplied by the constant P/E ratio

1.57 For example, if a company had an EPS last year of 30p and a share price of £3.60, its P/E ratio would have been 12. If the current year's EPS is 33p, we might expect that the P/E ratio would remain the same, 12, and so the share price ought to go up to $12 \times 33p = £3.96$.

1.58 **Changes** in the P/E ratios of companies over time will depend on several factors.

(a) If interest rates go up, investors will be attracted away from shares and into debt capital. Share prices will fall, and so P/E ratios will fall.

Similarly, if interest rates go down, shares will become relatively more attractive to invest in, so share prices and P/E ratios will go up.

(b) If prospects for company profits improve, share prices will go up, and P/E ratios will rise. Share prices depend on expectations of future earnings, not historical earnings, and so a change in prospects, perhaps caused by a substantial rise in international trade, or an economic recession, will affect prices and P/E ratios.

(c) Investors' confidence might be changed by a variety of circumstances, such as:

    (i) The prospect of a change in government

    (ii) The prospects for greater exchange rate stability between currencies

The dividend cover

1.59 The dividend cover is the number of times the actual dividend could be paid out of current profits and indicates:

(a) The **proportion** of distributable profits for the year that is being **retained** by the company

(b) The level of **risk** that the company will **not be able to maintain the same dividend** payments in future years, should earnings fall

1.60 A high dividend cover means that a high proportion of profits are being retained, which might indicate that the company is investing to achieve earnings growth in the future.

Theoretical ex-rights price

1.61   This is calculated to take account of a rights issue being made at discount prices.

EXAM FORMULAE

Theoretical ex-rights price

$$\text{TERP} = \frac{1}{N+1}[(N \times \text{rights on price}) + \text{Issue price}]$$

Value of a right

$$\text{Value of a right} = \frac{\text{Rights on price} - \text{Issue price}}{N+1}$$

$$\text{or} = \frac{\text{Theoretical ex rights price} - \text{Issue price}}{N+1}$$

where N = number of rights required to buy one share

2 COMPARISONS OF ACCOUNTING FIGURES

2.1 Useful information is obtained from ratio analysis largely by means of comparisons.

Results of the same company over successive accounting periods

2.2 Although a company might present useful information in its five year or ten year summary, it is quite likely that the only detailed comparison you will be able to make is between the current year's and the previous year's results. The comparison should give you some idea of whether the company's situation has improved, worsened or stayed much the same between one year and the next.

2.3 Useful comparisons over time include:

(a) Percentage growth in profit (before and after tax) and percentage growth in turnover

(b) Increases or decreases in the debt ratio and the gearing ratio

(c) Changes in the current ratio, the stock turnover period and the debtors' payment period

(d) Increases in the EPS, the dividend per share, and the market price

2.4 The principal advantage of making comparisons over time is that they give some indication of progress: are things getting better or worse? However, there are some weaknesses in such comparisons.

(a) The effect of **inflation** should not be forgotten.

(b) The progress a company has made needs to be set in the context of **what other companies have done**, and whether there have been any **special environmental or economic influences** on the company's performance.

Allowing for inflation

2.5 Ratio analysis is not usually affected by **price inflation**, except as follows.

(a) **Return on capital employed** (ROCE) can be misleading if fixed assets, especially property, are valued at historical cost net of depreciation rather than at current value. As time goes by and if property prices go up, the fixed assets would be seriously undervalued if they were still recorded at their historical cost, and so the return on capital employed would be misleadingly high.

(b) Some growth trends can be misleading, in particular the **growth in sales turnover**, and the **growth in profits or earnings**.

2.6 For example, suppose that a company achieved the following results.

	20X8	20X7	% growth
	£m	£m	
Turnover	46	43	7.0
Profit	12	11	9.1

If price inflation from 20X7 to 20X8 was 10%, the performance of the company would show a drop in turnover and profit in real terms, of about 3% in turnover and of about 0.9% in profit.

Putting a company's results into context

2.7 The financial and accounting ratios of one company should be looked at in the context of what other companies have been achieving, and also any special influences on the industry or the economy as a whole. Here are two examples.

(a) If a company achieves a 10% increase in profits, this performance taken in isolation might seem commendable, but if it is then compared with the results of rival companies, which might have been achieving profit growth of 30% the performance might in comparison seem very disappointing.

(b) An improvement in ROCE and profits might be attributable to a temporary economic boom, and an increase in profits after tax might be attributable to a cut in the rate of corporation tax. When improved results are attributable to factors outside the control of the company's management, such as changes in the economic climate and tax rates other companies might be expected to benefit in the same way.

Comparisons between different companies in the same industry

2.8 Making comparisons between the results of different companies in the same industry is a way of assessing which companies are outperforming others.

(a) Even if two companies are in the **same broad industry** (for example, retailing) they might not be direct competitors. For example, in the UK, the Kingfisher group (including Woolworths/B&Q/Comet) does not compete directly with the Burton/Debenhams group. Even so, they might still be expected to show broadly similar performance, in terms of growth, because a boom or a depression in retail markets will affect all retailers. The results of two such companies can be compared, and the company with the better growth and accounting ratios might be considered more successful than the other.

(b) If two companies are **direct competitors**, a comparison between them would be particularly interesting. Which has achieved the better ROCE, sales growth, or profit growth? Does one have a better debt or gearing position, a better liquidity position or better working capital ratios? How do their P/E ratios, dividend cover and dividend yields compare? And so on.

2.9 Comparisons between companies in the same industry can help investors to rank them in order of desirability as investments, and to judge relative share prices or future prospects. It is important, however, to make comparisons with caution: **a large company and a small company in the same industry might be expected to show different results**, not just in terms of size, but in terms of:

(a) Percentage rates of growth in sales and profits

(b) Percentages of profits re-invested (Dividend cover will be higher in a company that needs to retain profits to finance investment and growth.)

(c) Fixed assets (Large companies are more likely to have freehold property in their balance sheet than small companies.)

Comparisons between companies in different industries

2.10 Useful information can also be obtained by comparing the financial and accounting ratios of companies in different industries. An investor ought to be aware of how companies in one industrial sector are performing in comparisons with companies in other sectors. For example, it is important to know:

(a) Whether sales growth and profit growth is higher in some industries than in others (For example, how does growth in the financial services industry compare with growth in heavy engineering, electronics or leisure?)

(b) How the return on capital employed and return on shareholder capital compare between different industries

(c) How the P/E ratios and dividend yields vary between industries (For example, if a publishing company has a P/E ratio of, say, 20, which is average for its industry, whereas an electronics company has a P/E ratio of, say, 14, do the better growth performance and prospects of the publishing company justify its higher P/E ratio?)

3 OTHER INFORMATION FROM COMPANIES' ACCOUNTS

3.1 Two features of a company's fixed assets which can be looked at are:

61

(a) How the company has accounted for the **revaluation** of fixed assets

(b) The amount of **intangible** fixed assets in the balance sheet

The revaluation of fixed assets

3.2 Fixed assets may be stated in the balance sheet at cost less accumulated depreciation. They may also be revalued from time to time to a current market value. When this happens:

(a) The increase in the balance sheet value of the fixed asset is matched by an increase in the **revaluation reserve**

(b) **Depreciation** in subsequent years is based on the revalued amount of the asset, its estimated residual value and its estimated remaining useful life

3.3 It has been usual for companies to revalue their land and buildings periodically, but not their other fixed assets such as plant and machinery. There has been nothing to stop companies revaluing all their fixed assets regularly, but land and buildings have been an obvious example of fixed assets that can increase substantially in value. To avoid a serious understatement of their balance sheet value, companies have therefore revalued their land and buildings from time to time, typically every two or three years.

Intangible fixed assets

3.4 **Intangible fixed assets** are assets which do not have any physical substance, but are of use to a business over a number of years in helping to provide goods or services. Intangible assets include trademarks, patents, copyrights, development expenditure and goodwill, some of which may also be identified as **intellectual capital**.

3.5 Companies are allowed to include intangible fixed assets in their balance sheet, but if they do, they must depreciate them over their estimated useful lives. Instead of having intangible fixed assets, many companies write off the cost of intangible items in the year of acquisition.

3.6 An important area of debate over the last ten years or so is the extent to which companies should be allowed to include the values of **brand names** in their balance sheets. Valuations of such assets are likely to be highly subjective.

Share capital and reserves

3.7 The **capital and reserves** section of a company's accounts contains information which appears to be mainly the concern of the various classes of shareholder. However, because the shareholders' interest in the business acts as a **buffer for the creditors** in the event of any financial problems, this section is also of some importance to creditors.

3.8 The nature of any increase in reserves will be of some interest. For example, if a company has increased its total share capital and reserves in the year:

(a) Did it do so by **issuing new shares** resulting in a higher allotted share capital and share premium account?

(b) Did it do so by **revaluing some fixed assets**, resulting in a higher revaluation reserve?

(c) Did it make a substantial profit and **retain a good proportion of this profit** in the business resulting in a higher profit and loss account balance?

3.9 A **scrip issue** might also be of some interest. It will result in a fall in the market price per share. If it has been funded from a company's profit and loss account reserves, a scrip issue could indicate that the company recognised and formalised its long-term capital needs by now making some previously distributable reserves non-distributable.

3.10 If a company has **issued shares in the form of a dividend**, are there obvious reasons why this should be so? For example, does the company need to retain capital within the business because of poor trading in the previous year, making the directors reluctant to pay out more cash dividend than necessary?

3.11 **Financial obligations** of a company may also be significant, and the timescale over which these become or could become repayable should be considered

3.12 Examples are:

- Levels of **redeemable debt**
- **Earn out arrangements**
- **Potential or contingent liabilities,** such as liabilities under unresolved legal cases
- **Long-term commitments** (eg the Private Finance Initiative in the UK)

Debentures, loans and other liabilities

3.13 Two points of interest about debentures, loans and other liabilities are:

- Whether or not loans are **secured**
- The **redemption dates** of loans

3.14 For debentures and loan stock which are **secured**, the details of the security are usually included in the terms of a trust deed. Details of any **fixed or floating charges against assets** must be disclosed in a note to the accounts.

3.15 In analysing a set of accounts, particular attention should be paid to some significant features concerning **debenture or loan stock redemption**. These are:

(a) The closeness of the redemption date, which would indicate how much finance the company has to find in the immediate future to repay its loans. It is not unusual, however, to repay one loan by taking out another, and so a company does not necessarily have to find the money to repay a loan from its own resources.

(b) The percentage interest rate on the loans being redeemed, compared with the current market rate of interest. This would give some idea, if a company decides to replace loans by taking out new loans, of the likely increase (or reduction) in interest costs that it might face, and how easily it might accommodate any interest cost increase.

3.16 There are classes of debentures which do not have a redemption date attached. This does not mean that they will never be redeemed because a company can always buy back its own debentures in the market. The holder of an **irredeemable debenture** does not, however, have a date by which redemption must take place, so he cannot demand repayment. Consequently, not being very attractive to investors, this is a rare form of finance.

Earn-out arrangements

KEY TERM

An **earn-out arrangement** is a procedure whereby owner/managers selling an organisation receive a portion of their consideration linked to the financial performance of the business during a specified period after the sale. The arrangement gives a measure of security to the new owners, who pass some of the financial risk associated with the purchase of a new enterprise to the sellers. *(OT 2000)*

3.17 FRS 7 *Fair values in acquisition accounting,* deals specifically with the treatment of **deferred consideration,** where the amount payable is uncertain because it is contingent on the outcome of future events. Obligations arising out of earn-out arrangements are one of the most common examples. The standard requires 'a reasonable estimate of the fair value of amounts expected to be payable in the future' to be included in the cost of acquisition (and thus goodwill) and recognised as a liability in the accounts.

3.18 In the case of an earn-out arrangement, it is likely to be **very difficult to make reliable estimates** of the future amounts payable, where they will depend upon future profits of the acquired company, particularly if that company is in a development state. In these circumstances, at least those amounts that are reasonably expected to be payable would be recognised.

3.19 Thus any **minimum amount guaranteed** to be payable as part of deferred consideration must be initially provided. As information upon which any further obligations may be reasonably estimated becomes available (for example, short-term profit forecasts for the acquired company), **further provisions** must be made.

Case example

An extract from the 1999 accounts of company, **Logica plc,** the IT company, which provided for contingent consideration arising from an earn-out arrangement, is shown below.

Notes to the financial statements

Acquisitions (continued)

DDV Telecommunications & Media Consultants BV

The acquisition of DDV Telecommunications & Media consultants (DDV), a company registered in the Netherlands, was completed on 30 December 1999.

The consideration paid or payable is as follows.

(i)   an initial consideration of NLG 27.0 million (£8.7 million) was paid in December 1998,

(ii) further consideration of up to NLG 10.0 million (£3.2 million) is payable in December 1999 as earn-out targets are met,

(iii) a final amount of NLG 10.0 million (£3.2 million) will be payable in June 2000 subject to the continued employment with Logica of the vendors.

In the last financial year, prior to acquisition, to 31 December 1997, DDV made a profit after tax of NLG 1.9 million.

For the period since that date to the date of acquisition, DDV made a profit after tax of NLG 1.7 million.

The provisional fair value to the group is shown below:

Satisfied by:	Book value of assets acquired £'000	Revaluation adjustments £'000	Accounting policy adjustments £'000	Provisional fair value to the group £'000
Tangible fixed assets	1,293	–	–	1,293
Debtors	5,289	(120)	(605)	4,564
Cash	414	(414)	–	–
Creditors	(5,603)	406	(240)	(5,437)
Net assets required	1,393	(128)	(845)	420
Goodwill				14,351
				14,771

Satisfied by:	
Initial cash consideration (including costs of the acquisition of £83,000)	8,737
Contingent cash consideration	6,279
Discount on contingent consideration	(245)
	14,771

In their **2000 accounts,** it was noted that '...the contingent consideration payment has been revised from £6.3 million to £4.9 million due to performance targets not being met. As a result, goodwill has been revised from £14.4 million to £13.1 million'.

3.20 Clearly, when reviewing the financial statements of a company that includes such a provisions, the **underlying uncertainty** surrounding the amount of the ultimate liability must be taken into account.

Contingencies

3.21 **Contingencies** are conditions which exist at the balance sheet date where the outcome will be confirmed only on the occurrence or non-occurrence of one or more uncertain future events.

3.22 Contingencies can result in contingent gains or contingent losses. The fact that the condition **exists at the balance sheet date** distinguishes a contingency from a post balance sheet event.

3.23 Some of the **typical types of contingencies** disclosed by companies are as follows.

- Guarantees given by the company
- Discounted bills of exchange
- Uncalled liabilities on shares or loan stock
- Lawsuits or claims pending
- Tax on profits where the basis on which the tax should be computed is unclear

Again, knowledge of such contingencies will enhance the quality of the information used in analysis.

Private finance initiative (PFI) **5/01**

3.24 FRS 5 *Reporting the substance of transactions*, requires that the commercial **effect** of an entity's transactions and any resulting assets, liabilities, gains or losses should be faithfully represented in its financial statements. One area to which this principle may be applied is in private finance initiative (PFI) transactions.

3.25 Under PFI contracts, the private sector provides a service to the public sector, eg the government, in return for a payment that covers both the use of any assets involved, and the cost of any ancillary services provided. Examples would include research and development, prison security, road maintenance and catering contracts.

3.26 In general, the private sector company has the responsibility for the upfront investment in the capital assets required, and then sells a service using those assets to the public sector. The three main types of PFI transaction are:

(a) **Services sold to the public sector** where the public sector pays only on delivery of specified services to specified quality standards

(b) **Financial free standing projects** where the private sector recovers its costs through direct charges on the private use of the asset (eg tolling) rather than from payments by the public sector

(c) **Joint ventures,** where the costs of the project are not met entirely through charges on the end users, but are subsidised from public funds

3.27 Thus under PFI contracts, private firms become long term providers of services rather than simply upfront asset builders, combining the responsibilities of designing, building, financing and operating assets in order to deliver the required services to the public sector. By March 1999 £11.9 billion of PFI projects were signed.

Case example

Jarvis, a quoted facilities management company, has a subsidiary that specialises in building and running schools under PFI deals with local authorities, and has so far signed 11 such contracts. This subsidiary accounts for 27% of the total group profits. For example Barnhill Community School, in West London, cost £20m to build and the local council has contracted to make 25 annual payments of £1.6m to cover both building and operating costs. Jarvis takes both the asset and liability into its balance sheet for the 25-year contract. The company feels such deals are 20% cheaper than traditional funding, taking account of the higher value of the school at the end of the PFI contract.

3.28 Where a company enters into a PFI contract it will be generally taking on **long-term obligations,** with compensation payable if the company cancels the contact. There may also be the possibility of **penalties** if the service is not provided at the required level or quality. This will affect the analyst's view of the **risks and rewards** associated with the related assets.

3.29 For example, in the case of the schools built by Jarvis (see case example above):

(a) If lessons cannot take place because of equipment failure or building maintenance problems, Jarvis pays a penalty.

(b) If services – catering, IT, cleaning etc – are not provided to the standard promised, penalties also apply.

(c) Jarvis also has responsibility to generate a certain level of third-party income at the schools – for example, by hiring out facilities for sports and leisure – and if this is not achieved, the shortfall is made up by Jarvis.

Post balance sheet events

KEY TERM

Post balance sheet events are favourable and unfavourable events which occur between the balance sheet date and the date on which the financial statements are approved by the board of directors. *(OT 2000)*

3.30 The following are examples of post balance sheet events which should normally be disclosed.

- Mergers and acquisitions
- The issue of new shares and debentures
- The purchase and sales of major fixed assets and investments
- Losses of fixed assets or stocks as a result of a catastrophe such as fire or flood
- The opening of new trading activities
- The closure of a significant part of the trading activities
- A decline in the value of property and investments held as fixed assets
- Changes in exchange rates (if there are significant overseas interests)
- Government action, such as nationalisation
- Strikes and other labour disputes
- The augmentation of pension benefits to employees

Knowledge of such events allows the analyst to 'update' the latest published figures by taking account of their potential impact.

4   SEGMENTAL ANALYSIS

4.1   The Companies Act 1985 and the Stock Exchange both require the disclosure of **segmental information** in published accounts. The company's directors decide on the classification used in presenting this information. The classification methods should be applied consistently. **Geographical analysis** must be by destination of **sale**.

4.2   An example of segmental information, from the 1999 Report and Accounts of National Power plc, the UK power generator, is shown below.

National Power
Report and Accounts 1999

Notes to the accounts

1   Group segmental analysis

(a)   By class of business

	1999		1998 (restated)	
		Operating		Operating
	Turnover	profit	Turnover	profit
	£m	£m	£m	£m
Electricity sales – wholesale	2,110	593	2,291	681
Electricity sales – retail	425	12	448	(7)
Electricity sales – cogeneration and renewables	87	18	72	14
Eastern lease	224	209	436	215
Other income	136	35	91	37
Corporate and development	27	(206)	16	(157)
	3,009	661	3,354	783
Share of profit before taxation of associates and joint ventures (including interest)		24		72
Profit before interest and tax		685		855

(b)   By geographical area

	1999			1998 (restated)		
		Operating	Profit for		Operating	Profit for
	Turnover	profit	the year*	Turnover	profit	the year*
	£m	£m	£m	£m	£m	£m
Europe (excluding UK)	59	13	14	1	1	13
Australia	119	42	42	130	45	45
USA	24	7	11	26	11	13
Rest of world	47	13	15	45	15	˙59
International	249	75	82	202	72	130
UK operations	2,733	792	599	3,136	868	661
UK corporate and development	27	(206)	(208)	16	(157)	(201)
	3,009	661	473	3,354	783	590

* Profit for the year is profit after taxation and minority interests but before exceptional items.

(c)   Analysis of operating costs

	1999	1998
	£m	£m
Cost of sales	1,376	1,639
Other operating costs	972	943
Exceptional item	–	(11)
	2,348	2,571

Notes to accounts

continued

1 Group segmental analysis (continued)

(d) Net assets employed by division

1999	Europe £m	Australia £m	USA £m	Rest of world £m	International business £m	UK business £m	Corporate and development £m	Total £m
Investment in associates	137	–	–	366	503	–	–	503
Investment in joint ventures	17	–	52	–	69	34	–	103
All other net operating assets	36	875	168	50	1,129	2,794	1,123	5,046
Total assets less current liabilities	190	875	220	416	1,701	2,828	1,123	**5,652**
Net assets employed	162	376	215	416	1,169	2,265	(805)	**2,629**

1998	Europe £m	Australia £m	USA £m	Rest of world £m	International business £m	UK business £m	Corporate and development £m	Total £m
Investment in associates	163	–	–	302	465	1	–	466
Investment in joint ventures	–	–	56	–	56	32	–	88
All other net operating assets	7	930	83	21	1,041	2,861	960	4,862
Total assets less current liabilities	170	930	139	323	1,562	2,894	960	**5,416**
Net assets employed	170	400	136	323	1,029	2,360	(970)	**2,419**

The presentation of the Group segmental analysis has been changed this year to better reflect the nature of our business. All the activities of the Group relate to one class of business, electricity generation. For the purposes of note 1(a) the subsets of that class of business have been analysed.

The contribution of acquisitions in the international business to turnover and operating profit in the year ended 31 March 1999 was £52 million and £9 million respectively. The contribution of acquisitions to turnover and operating profit/(loss) in the UK business was £10 million and £(2) million respectively.

Assets and liabilities, including project-specific debt, have been allocated to the two main business divisions in accordance with their geographic source. Certain assets and liabilities that are not directly attributable to those divisions are shown under Corporate and development.

4.3 Segmental information can be useful in the following ways.

(a) Segmental information can **explain** factors which gave **contributed to company results.**

(b) Users can **compare the results of different products from year to year.**

(c) Users can **compare performance** with companies **within the same market.**

(d) Users can **assess the future risks and rewards** associated with the business.

4.4 As explained in its annual report, National Power is engaged in one class of business – electricity generation. In section 1(a) of the analysis the company has shown the split of the turnover and operating profit from this activity into **sub-classes.**

4.5 Section 1(b) shows the division of activities by **geographical area.** This can help to show the degree of exposure of a company to the risks and opportunities of international diversification. The section indicates the extent to which the company is a multinational enterprise.

4.6 In the case of National Power, the **analysis of operating costs** (section 1 (c)) shows only limited information, giving only a split between cost of sales, other operating costs and exceptional items.

4.7 Section 1(d) of National Power's analysis shows the split of **net assets employed by division**.

Question 3

Using the segmental analysis shown above, calculate the return on capital employed by geographical area for National Power plc in 1998 and 1999. Exclude 'corporate and development' activities.

Answer

	1999		*1998*	
UK	(792/2,265)	35.0%	(868/2,360)	36.8%
Rest of Europe	(13/162)	8.0%	(1/170)	0.6%
Australia	(42/376)	11.2%	(45/400)	11.3%
USA	(7/215)	3.3%	(11/136)	8.1%
Rest of World	(13/416)	3.1%	(15/323)	4.6%

Note: The 1998 figures for Rest of Europe is of limited accuracy, due to rounding to the nearest £ million.

---

5 PREDICTING BUSINESS FAILURE

5.1 The analysis of financial ratios is largely concerned with the efficiency and effectiveness of the use of resources by a company's management, and also with the financial stability of the company. Investors will wish to know:

- Whether additional funds could be lent to the company with reasonable safety
- Whether the company would fail without additional funds

5.2 One method of predicting business failure is the use of **liquidity ratios** (the current ratio and the quick ratio). A company with a current ratio well below 2:1 or a quick ratio well below 1:1 might be considered illiquid and in danger of failure. Research seems to indicate, however, that the current ratio and the quick ratio and trends in the variations of these ratios for a company, are poor indicators of eventual business failure.

Z scores

5.3 E I Altman researched into the simultaneous analysis of several financial ratios as a combined **predictor of business failure**. Altman analysed 22 accounting and non-accounting variables for a selection of failed and non-failed firms in the USA and from these, five key indicators emerged. These five indicators were then used to derive a **Z score**. Firms with a Z score above a certain level would be predicted to be financially sound, and firms with a Z score below a certain level would be categorised as probable failures. Altman also identified a range of Z scores in between the non-failure and failure categories in which eventual failure or non-failure was uncertain.

> **KEY TERM**
>
> **Z-score** is a single figure, produced by a financial model, which combines a number of variables (generally financial statements ratios), whose magnitude is intended to aid the prediction of failure (*OT 2000*)

5.4 Altman's Z score model (derived in 1968) emerged as:

$$Z = 1.2X_1 + 1.4X_2 + 3.3X_3 + 0.6X_4 + 1.0X_5$$

where

$X_1 =$ working capital/total assets
$X_2 =$ retained earnings/total assets
$X_3 =$ earnings before interest and tax/total assets
$X_4 =$ market value of equity/book value of total debt (a form of gearing ratio)
$X_5 =$ sales/total assets

Exam focus point

It is not necessary for you to memorise this formula, which would be given in the exam if needed.

5.5 In Altman's model, a Z score of 2.7 or more indicated non-failure, and a Z score of 1.8 or less indicated failure.

5.6 Altman's sample size was small, and related to US firms in a particular industry. Subsequent research based on the similar principle of identifying a Z score predictor of business failure has produced different prediction models, using a variety of financial ratios and different Z score values as predictors of failure. It would be argued, for example, that different ratios and Z score values would be appropriate for conditions in the UK.

The value of Z scores

5.7 A current view of the link between financial ratios and business failure would appear to be as follows.

(a) The financial ratios of firms which fail can be seen in retrospect to have **deteriorated significantly** prior to failure, and to be worse than the ratios of non-failed firms. In retrospect, financial ratios can be used to suggest why a firm has failed.

(b) No fully accepted **model for predicting** future business failures has yet been established, although some form of Z score analysis would appear to be the most promising avenue for progress. In the UK, several Z score-type failure prediction models exist.

(c) Because of the use of X_4: market value of equity/book value of debt, Z score models cannot be used for unquoted companies which lack a market value of equity.

5.8 Z score models are used widely in the banking sector, in risk assessment, loan grading and corporate finance activities. They are also used by accountancy firms, fund management houses, stockbrokers and credit insurers (such as Trade Indemnity).

Other corporate failure models

5.9 **Beaver** conducted a study which found the following.

(a) The **worst predictor** of failure is the current ratio (current assets/current liabilities).
(b) The **best predictor** of failure is cash flow borrowings.

5.10 Other writers have put forward alternative models designed to predict whether a business will fail. From historical data on a wide range of actual cases, **Argenti** developed a model which is intended to predict the likelihood of company failure. The model is based on calculating scores for a company based on (a) defects of the company; (b) management mistakes and (c) the symptoms of failure. For each of the scores (a), (b) and (c) there is a 'danger mark'.

5.11 Among the most important factors in the model are:

(a) **Defects**

- Autocratic Chief Executive (Robert Maxwell is an example here)
- Passive board
- Lack of budgetary control

(b) **Mistakes**

- Over-trading (expanding faster than cash funding)
- Gearing - high bank overdrafts/loans
- Failure of large project jeopardises the company (eg Laker Airways)

(c) **Symptoms**

- Deteriorating ratios
- Creative accounting - signs of window-dressing
- Declining morale and declining quality

Weaknesses of corporate failure models and prediction methods

5.12 Weaknesses of corporate failure models include the following.

(a) In common with all correlation models, they relate to the past, without taking into account the current state of the macroeconomic environment (the level of inflation and interest rates, and so on).

(b) The models share the limitations of the accounting model (including the accounting concepts and conventions) on which they are based.

(c) The publication of accounting data by companies is subject to a delay. Failure might occur before the data becomes available.

(d) If the measures incorporated in the models become used as objectives, as some suggest, then the model is likely to become less useful as a predictive tool, as the measures will be subject to manipulation.

(e) The definition of corporate failure is not clear, given that various forms of rescue or restructuring are possible, short of liquidation, for a company which is in trouble.

5.13 There are the following problems in using available **financial information** to predict failure.

(a) **Significant events** can take place between the end of the financial year and the publication of the accounts. An extreme example of this would be the collapse of the Barings merchant bank. A further feature of the Barings case that is worthy of comment is the fact that the factors that led up to the collapse were essentially internal to the business and would never have become apparent in the published accounts.

(b) The information is essentially **backward looking** and takes no account of current and future situations. An extreme example would be the Central American banana producers. There would be nothing in their published accounts to predict the effect on their businesses of Hurricane Mitch.

5.14 The use of **creative, or even fraudulent, accounting** can be significant in situations of corporate failure. **Polly Peck** was the fastest growing company in the UK at one time, but eventually and catastrophically it failed when accounting manipulation could no longer conceal its true financial position.

5.15 Similarly, the **pressure to deliver earnings growth** may result in companies making poor decisions that eventually lead to their downfall. It is arguable that a recent deterioration in the performance of BTR (now Invensys) is attributable to its policy of aggressive acquisition followed by price increases and stringent cost reduction. Although this delivered growth in earnings for a while and made it a highly regarded company in which to invest, the effects of this policy are now being felt in a shrinking customer base and the consequences of a lack of investment in the underlying businesses.

5.16 Business is not an exact science, and the use of apparently objective models can foster the illusion that it can be reduced to a set of numerical ratios. Businesses must always operate under conditions of inadequate and imperfect information. It is thus not surprising that deterministic models of failure prediction only ever appear to meet with partial success.

Other indicators of financial difficulties

5.17 You should not think that **ratio analysis of published accounts** and **Z score analysis** are the only ways of spotting that a company might be running into financial difficulties. There are other possible indicators too.

(a) **Other information in the published accounts**

Some information in the published accounts might not lend itself readily to ratio analysis, but still be an indicator of financial difficulties, for example:

(i) Very large increases in intangible fixed assets
(ii) A worsening net liquid funds position, as shown by the funds flow statement
(iii) Very large **potential or contingent liabilities**
(iv) Important post balance sheet events

(b) **Information in the chairman's report and the directors' report**

The report of the chairman or chief executive that accompanies the published accounts might be very revealing. Although this report is not audited, and will no doubt try to paint a rosy picture of the company's affairs, any difficulties the company has had and not yet overcome will probably be discussed in it. There might also be warnings of problems to come in the future.

The directors' report is usually restricted to the minimum information required by law, but it might be interesting to check whether there have been any changes in the composition of the board since last year. Have many of last year's directors gone? Are there many new directors, and if so, what are their qualifications?

(c) **Information in the press**

Newspapers and financial journals are a source of information about companies, and the difficulties or successes they are having. There may be reports of strikes, redundancies and closures.

There are often articles in newspapers which focus on particular companies. If a company is in financial difficulty, adverse comments might well appear in one of these articles.

(d) **Published information about environmental or external matters**

There will also be published information about matters that will have a direct influence on a company's future, although the connection may not be obvious. Examples of external matters that may affect a company adversely are:

(i) New legislation, for example on product safety standards or pollution controls, which affect a company's main products

(ii) International events, for example political disagreements with a foreign country, leading to a restriction on trade between the countries (The foreign country concerned might be a major importer of a company's products.)

(iii) New and better products being launched on to the market by a competitor

(iv) A big rise in interest rates, which might affect a highly-geared company seriously

(v) A big change in foreign exchange rates, which might affect a major importer or exporter seriously

---

Chapter roundup

- The **ratios** covered in this chapter provide various tools with which you can analyse financial statements. Comments on a company based on such ratios are far more likely to be right than comments based on a casual read through a set of accounts. However, you should also make use of whatever other information can be gleaned from a company's accounts.

- It is important to bear in mind that **historical (past) data** has limitations for the purpose of **forecasting** what will happen in future periods. A firm's profitability may have risen steadily over the past five years, but we cannot simply extrapolate this trend into the future.

- You should also be aware of **other information** from financial statements that can be used to analyse the company's performance and to identify possible problem areas. This will include information relating to **fixed assets** and **financial obligations.**

Quick quiz

1 Identify terms (A) to (F) to complete the equation.

Profit margin × Asset turnover = ROCE

$$\frac{(A)}{(B)} \times \frac{(C)}{(D)} = \frac{(E)}{(F)}$$

2 Complete the following in respect of capital gearing.

$$\text{Gearing ratio} = \frac{(A)}{(B)+(C)}$$

3 Complete the following.

$$\text{Interest cover} = \frac{(A)}{(B)}$$

4 $$\frac{\text{Current assets less stock}}{\text{Current liabilities}} = ?$$

5   **Fill in the blanks**, using the terms in the box

Dividend yield $= \dfrac{(1)}{(2)} \times 100\%$

Interest yield $= \dfrac{(3)}{(4)} \times 100\%$

EPS $= \dfrac{(5)}{(6)}$

P/E ratio $= \dfrac{(7)}{(8)}$

Dividend cover $= \dfrac{(9)}{(10)}$

• Gross dividend per share	• Net dividend per share	• Profit after tax
• Loan stock market value	• Share price	• Gross interest
• Number of shares	• Earnings attributable to one share	

Answers to quick quiz

1   (A) PBIT
    (B) Sales
    (C) Sales
    (D) Capital employed
    (E) PBIT
    (F) Capital employed

2   (A) Prior charge capital
    (B) Long-term debt
    (C) Equity

3   (A) PBIT
    (B) Interest charges

4   Quick or acid test ratio

5   (1) Gross dividend per share
    (2) Share price
    (3) Gross interest
    (4) Loan stock market value
    (5) Profit after tax
    (6) Number of shares
    (7) Share price
    (8) Earnings attributable to one share
    (9) Earnings attributable to one share
    (10) Net dividend per share

Now try the question below from the Exam Question Bank

Number	Level	Marks	Time
3	Examination	25	45 mins

Chapter 4

CASH FLOW PLANNING AND FORECASTING FINANCIAL STATEMENTS

Topic list	Syllabus reference	Ability required
1 Cash flow planning	(i)	Evaluation
2 Cash forecasts	(i)	Analysis
3 Modelling cash flow forecasts	(i)	Analysis
4 Forecast financial statements: example	(i)	Analysis

Introduction

Cash forecasting is vital to ensure that sufficient funds will be available when they are needed to sustain the activities of an enterprise, at an acceptable cost.

Learning outcomes covered in this chapter

- Analyse and interpret the risk implications of business plans

Syllabus content covered in this chapter

- Working capital management strategies, ie aggressive, moderate and conservative strategies

- Modelling annual cash flow forecasts and other financial statements based on expected changes in values over a number of years (eg inflation, volume, margins and probabilities, expected values and sensitivity analysis).

- Constructing forecast financial statements based upon base year data. (Note: These will not need to be presented in published accounts formats.)

1 CASH FLOW PLANNING

Strategic fund management

1.1 A business must maintain an adequate inflow of cash in order to survive. If a business owes money and cannot pay its debts when they fall due, it can be put into liquidation by its creditors, even if it is making profits. Since a company must have adequate cash inflows to survive, **management should plan and control cash flows as well as profitability.**

1.2 **Cash budgeting** is an important element in short-term cash flow planning. Cash budget periods might be for one year, or less (for example monthly budgets). The purpose of cash budgets is to make sure that the organisation will have enough cash inflows to meet its cash outflows. If a budget reveals that a short-term cash shortage can be expected, steps will be taken to meet the problem and avoid the cash crisis (perhaps by arranging a bigger bank overdraft facility).

1.3 Cash budgets and cash flow forecasts on their own do not give full protection against a cash shortage and enforced liquidation of the business by creditors. There may be **unexpected changes in cash flow patterns**. When unforeseen events have an adverse effect on cash inflows, a company will only survive if it can maintain adequate cash inflows despite the setbacks. **Strategic fund management** is an extension of cash flow planning, which takes into consideration the ability of a business to overcome unforeseen problems with cash flows.

Exam focus point

No detailed testing of stock management models will be set since these were covered in the *Finance* paper.

1.4 Strategic fund management recognises that the assets of a business can be divided into three categories.

(a) Assets which are **needed to carry out the 'core' activities of the business.** A group of companies will often have one or several main activities, and in addition will carry on several peripheral activities. The group's strategy should be primarily to develop its main activities, and so there has to be enough cash to maintain those activities and to finance their growth.

(b) Assets which are not essential for carrying out the main activities of the business, and which **could be sold off at fairly short notice**. These assets will consist mainly of short-term marketable investments.

(c) Assets which are not essential for carrying out the main activities of the business, and which **could be sold off** to raise cash, although it would probably take time to arrange the sale, and the amount of cash obtainable from the sale might be uncertain. These assets would include:

   (i) Long-term investments (for example, substantial shareholdings in other companies)

   (ii) Subsidiary companies engaged in 'peripheral' activities, which might be sold off to another company or in a management buyout

   (iii) Land and buildings

1.5 If an unexpected event takes place which threatens a company's cash position, the company could meet the threat by:

(a) Working capital management to improve cash flows by reducing stocks and debtors, taking more credit, or negotiating a higher bank overdraft facility

(b) Changes to dividend policy

(c) Arranging to sell off non-essential assets (The assets in category (b) above would be saleable at short notice, and arrangements could also be made to dispose of the assets in category (c), should the need arise and provided that there is enough time to arrange the sale.)

Strategic cash flow planning

1.6 It is essential for the survival of any business to have an adequate inflow of cash. Cash flow planning at a strategic level is similar to normal cash budgeting, with the following exceptions.

(a) The **planning horizon** is longer.

(b) The **uncertainties about future cash inflows and cash outflows** are much greater.

(c) The business should be able to respond, if necessary, to an unexpected need for cash. Where could extra cash be raised, and in what amounts?

(d) A company should have planned cash flows which are consistent with:

    (i) Its dividend payment policy, and

    (ii) Its policy for financial structuring, debt and gearing

---

Question

Suppose that WXY plc had the following balance sheet as at 31 December 20X8.

	£
Fixed assets	3,500,000
Current assets less current liabilities	500,000
	4,000,000
Share capital	500,000
Reserves	1,600,000
Long-term 10% debt	1,900,000
	4,000,000

The company's strategic planners have formulated the following policies.

(a) By the end of the next year (31 December 20X9), gearing should not exceed 100% - ie long term debt should not exceed the total of share capital and reserves.

(b) The company shall pay out 50% of its profits as dividend to shareholders.

The following estimates have been made.

(a) Each £10,000 of assets generates profits of £2,000 pa, before interest.
(b) The current market cost of debt capital is 10% pa.

The company would like to invest a further £500,000 but does not intend to make a share issue to raise the finance. Advise its management. Could it borrow the money and still achieve its strategic targets by the end of 20X9?

Ignore taxation and fixed asset depreciation.

Answer

The company's strategic aims *can* all be achieved, without a new share issue, even though it is already near the gearing limit it has set itself, of 100%.

A further £500,000 investment in capital would yield extra annual profits of £100,000 p.a. before interest.

Without a share issue, the £500,000 would have to be raised as a loan at 10%, raising the total company debt to £2,400,000 and total assets at the beginning of the year to £4,500,000.

	£
Profits before interest in 20X9 (£4,500,000 × 20%)	900,000
Interest (10% of £2,400,000)	240,000
Profits before dividend	660,000
Dividend (NB: taxation ignored)	330,000
Retained profits	330,000

Balance sheet at 31 December 20X9

	£
Total assets (depreciation ignored)	
At 31.12.X8	4,000,000
New investment	500,000
Retained profits	330,000
	4,830,000

	£
Financed by	
Share capital	500,000
Reserves	1,930,000
Debt capital	2,400,000
	4,830,000

The company's gearing would just about remain below the maximum target limit of 100%.

Working capital management strategies

1.7   There are different ways in which the funding of the current and fixed assets of a business can be achieved by employing long and short-term sources of funding. The diagram below illustrates three alternative types of policy A, B and C. The dotted lines A, B and C are the cut-off levels between short-term and long-term financing for each of the policies A, B and C respectively: assets above the relevant dotted line are financed by short-term funding while assets below the dotted line are financed by long-term funding.

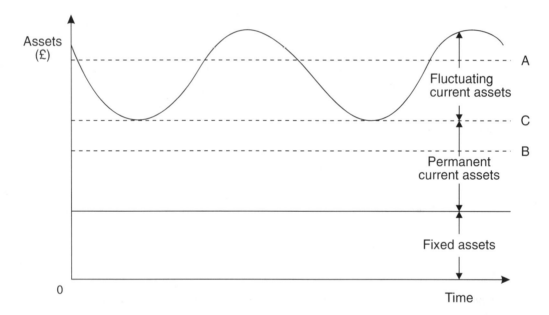

1.8   Fluctuating current assets together with permanent current assets form part of the working capital of the business, which may be financed by either long-term funding (including equity capital) or by current liabilities (short-term funding). This can be seen in terms of policies A, B and C.

   (a)   Policy A can be characterised as a **conservative approach** to financing working capital. All fixed assets and permanent current assets, as well as part of the fluctuating current assets, are financed by long-term funding. There is only a need to call upon short-term financing at times when fluctuations in current assets push total assets above the level of dotted line A. At times when fluctuating current assets are low and total assets fall below line A, there will be **surplus cash** which the company will be able to invest in marketable securities.

(b) Policy B is a more **aggressive approach** to financing working capital. Not only are fluctuating current assets all financed out of short-term sources, but so are some of the permanent current assets. This policy represents an **increased risk of liquidity and cash flow problems**, although potential returns will be increased if short-term financing can be obtained more cheaply than long-term finance.

(c) A **balance** between risk and return might be best achieved by the **moderate approach** of policy C, a policy of maturity matching in which long-term funds finance permanent assets while short-term funds finance non-permanent assets.

2 CASH FORECASTS   Pilot paper

> **KEY TERM**
>
> A **cash budget** (or **forecast**) is a detailed budget of estimated cash inflows and outflows incorporating both revenue and capital items.   *(OT 2000)*

2.1 Cash forecasts (or budgets) provide an early warning of liquidity problems, by estimating:

- How much cash is required
- When it is required
- How long it is required for
- Whether it will be available from anticipated sources

A company must know **when** it might need to borrow and **for how long**, not just **what amount** of funding could be required.

> **Exam focus point**
>
> No detailed testing of cash management models will be set since these were covered in the *Finance* paper.

Deficiencies

2.2 Any forecast **deficiency** of cash will have to be funded.

(a) **Borrowing**. If borrowing arrangements are not already secured, a source of funds will have to be found. If a company cannot fund its cash deficits it could be wound up.

(b) The firm can make arrangements to **sell any short-term financial investments** to raise cash.

(c) The firm can delay payments to creditors, or pull in payments from debtors. This is sometimes known as **leading and lagging**.

2.3 Because cash forecasts cannot be entirely accurate, companies should have **contingency funding,** available from a surplus cash balance and liquid investments, or from a bank facility. The approximate size of contingency margin will vary from company to company, according to the cyclical nature of the business and the approach of its cash planners.

2.4 Forecasting gives management time to arrange its funding. If planned in advance, instead of a panic measure to avert a cash crisis, a company can more easily choose when to borrow, and will probably obtain a lower interest rate.

Forecasting a cash surplus

2.5 Many cash-generative businesses are less reliant on high quality cash forecasts. If a **cash surplus** is forecast, having an idea of both its size and how long it will exist could help decide how best to invest it.

2.6 In some cases, the amount of **interest** earned from surplus cash could be significant for the company's earnings. The company might then need a forecast of its interest earnings in order to indicate its prospective **earnings per share** to stock market analysts and institutional investors.

Cash forecasts based on the balance sheet

2.7 The balance sheet based forecast is produced for **management accounting purposes** and so not for external publication or statutory financial reporting. **It is not an estimate of cash inflows and outflows.** A number of sequential forecasts can be produced, for example, a forecast of the balance sheet at the end of each year for the next five years.

2.8 As an estimate of the company's balance sheet at a future date, a balance sheet based forecast is used to identify either the **cash surplus** or the **funding shortfall** in the company's balance sheet **at the forecast date**.

Estimating a future balance sheet

2.9 A balance sheet estimate calls for some prediction of the amount/value of each item in the company's balance sheet, **excluding cash and short-term investments**, as these are what we are trying to predict. A forecast is prepared by taking each item in the balance sheet, and estimating what its value might be at the future date. The assumptions used are critical, and the following guidelines are suggested.

(a) Intangible **fixed assets** (gross book value) and long term investments, if there are any, should be taken at their current value unless there is good reason for another treatment.

(b) Some estimate of **fixed asset purchases** (and disposals) will be required. Revaluations can be ignored as they are not cash flows.

(c) **Current assets.** Balance sheet estimates of **stocks** and **debtors** can be based on fairly simple assumptions, and can be made in any of the following ways.

    (i) Same as current amounts. This is unlikely if business has boomed.

    (ii) Increase by a certain percentage, to allow for growth in business volume. For example, the volume of debtors might be expected to increase by a similar amount.

    (iii) Decrease by a certain percentage, to allow for tighter management control over working capital.

    (iv) Assume to be a certain percentage of the company's estimated annual turnover for the year.

    (v) The firm can assume that the operating cycle will more or less remain the same. In other words, if a firm's debtors take two months to pay, this relationship can be expected to continue. Therefore, if total annual sales are £12m and debtors take two months to pay, debtors at the year end will be $^2/_{12} \times £12m = £2m$. If turnover increases to £18m, and the collection period stays at two months, debtors will amount to $^2/_{12} \times £18m = £3m$. Similar relationships might be plotted for stocks and hence purchases and creditors.

(d) **Current liabilities**. Some itemising of current liabilities will be necessary, because no single set of assumptions can accurately estimate them collectively.

    (i) **Trade creditors and accruals** can be estimated in a similar way to current assets, as indicated above.

    (ii) Current liabilities include **bank loans** due for repayment within 12 months. These can be identified individually.

    (iii) **Bank overdraft facilities** might be in place. It could be appropriate to assume that there will be no overdraft in the forecast balance sheet. Any available overdraft facility can be considered later when the company's overall cash requirements are identified.

    (iv) **Taxation**. Any corporation tax payable should be estimated from anticipated profits and based on an estimated percentage of those profits.

    (v) **Dividends payable**. Any ordinary dividend payable should be estimated from anticipated profits, and any preference dividend payable can be predicted from the coupon rate of dividend for the company's preference shares.

    (vi) **Other creditors** can be included if required and are of significant value.

(e) **Long-term creditors**. Long-term creditors are likely to consist of long-term loans, bond issues, debenture stock and any other long-term finance debt. Unless the company has already arranged further long-term borrowing, this item should include just existing long-term debts, minus debts that will be repaid before the balance sheet date (or debts transferred from long-term to short-term creditors).

(f) **Share capital and reserves**. With the exception of the profit and loss account reserves (retained profits), the estimated balance sheet figures for share capital and other reserves should be the same as their current amount, unless it is expected or known that a new issue of shares will take place before the balance sheet date, the total amount raised (net of issue expenses) should be added to the share capital/other reserves total.

(g) An estimate is required of the change in the company's **retained profits** in the period up to the balance sheet date. This reserve should be calculated as:

    (i) The existing value of the profit and loss reserve

    (ii) **Plus** further retained profits anticipated in the period to the balance sheet date (ie post tax profits minus estimated dividends)

2.10 The various estimates should now be brought together into a balance sheet. The figures on each side of the balance sheet will not be equal, and there will be one of the following.

(a) A surplus of share capital and reserves over net assets (total assets minus total creditors). If this occurs, the company will be forecasting a **cash surplus**.

(b) A surplus of net assets over share capital and reserves. If this occurs, the company will be forecasting a **funding deficit**.

2.11 Alpha Limited has an existing balance sheet and an estimated balance sheet in one year's time before the necessary extra funding is taken into account, as follows.

	Existing £	Existing £	Forecast after one year £	Forecast after one year £
Fixed assets		100,000		180,000
Current assets	90,000		100,000	
Short-term creditors	(60,000)		(90,000)	
Net current assets		30,000		10,000
		130,000		190,000
Long-term creditors		(20,000)		(20,000)
Deferred taxation		(10,000)		(10,000)
Total net assets		100,000		160,000
Share capital and reserves				
Ordinary shares capital		50,000		50,000
Other reserves		20,000		20,000
Profit and loss account		30,000		50,000
		100,000		120,000

2.12 The company is expecting to increase its net assets in the next year by £60,000 (£160,000 – £100,000) but expects retained profits for the year to be only £20,000 (£50,000 – £30,000). There is an excess of net assets over share capital and reserves amounting to £40,000 (£160,000 – £120,000), which is a **funding deficit**. The company must consider ways of obtaining extra cash (eg by borrowing) to cover the deficit. If it cannot, it will need to keep its assets below the forecast amount, or to have higher short-term creditors.

2.13 A revised projected balance sheet can then be prepared by introducing these new sources of funds. This should be checked for realism (eg by **ratio analysis**) to ensure that the proportion of the balance sheet made up by fixed assets and working capital, etc is sensible.

2.14 **Balance sheet-based forecasts** have **two main uses**:

(a) As longer-term (strategic) estimates, to assess the scale of funding requirements or cash surpluses the company expects over time

(b) To act as a check on the realism of cash flow-based forecasts (The estimated balance sheet should be **roughly** consistent with the net cash change in the cash budget, after allowing for approximations in the balance sheet forecast assumptions.)

Deriving cash flow from profit and loss account and balance sheet information

2.15 The previous paragraphs concentrated on preparing a forecast balance sheet, with estimated figures for debtors, creditors and stock. Cash requirements might therefore be presented as the 'balancing figure'. However, it is possible to derive a forecast figure for cash flows using both the balance sheet and **profit and loss account**. The profit before interest and tax is adjusted first of all for items not involving cash, such as depreciation. This is further adjusted for changes in the levels of working capital (eg debtors and creditors) to arrive at operational cash flows.

2.16 This is examined in the example below. For the time being, assume that there is no depreciation. The task is to get from profit to operational cash flow, by taking into account movements in working capital.

	Profit	Operational cash flow
	£	£
Sales	200,000	200,000
Opening debtors (∴ received in year)		15,000
Closing debtors (outstanding at year end)		(24,000)
Cash in		191,000
Cost of sales	170,000	170,000
Closing stock (purchased, but not used, in year)		21,000
Opening stock (used, but not purchased, in year)		(12,000)
Purchases in year		179,000
Opening creditors (∴ paid in year)		11,000
Closing creditors (outstanding at year end)		(14,000)
Cash out		176,000
Profit/operational cash flow	30,000	15,000

This may be summarised as:

		£	£
Profit			30,000
(Increase)/Decrease in stocks	Opening	12,000	
	Closing	(21,000)	
			(9,000)
(Increase)/Decrease in debtors	Opening	15,000	
	Closing	(24,000)	
			(9,000)
Increase/(Decrease) in creditors	Closing	14,000	
	Opening	(11,000)	
			3,000
Operational cash flow			15,000

2.17 In practice, of course, a business will make many other adjustments. The profit figure includes **items which do not involve the movement of cash,** such as the annual depreciation charge, which will have to be added back to arrive at a figure for cash.

2.18 Both 'receipts and payments' forecasts and forecasts based on financial statements could be used alongside each other. The cash management section and the financial controller's section should reconcile differences between forecasts on a continuing basis, so that the forecast can be made more accurate as time goes on.

Quality control of forecasts

2.19 When actual results differ from budget, it can be tempting to conclude that plans never work out in practice. However, as planning is a vital management activity, and if actual results differ from the plan, it is important to find out whether the **planning processes** can be improved.

2.20 **Accuracy of cash flow forecasts** can be enhanced by:

(a) Reviewing actual cash flows against the forecasts, learning from past mistakes, and

(b) Preparing updated rolling forecasts or revised forecasts, where useful, to replace earlier, less reliable forecasts

2.21 **A constant monthly amount** for receipts and payments will often indicate either sloppy cash forecasting practice, or a high degree of uncertainty in the forecast, since it is rare for a specific receivables and payables to remain unchanged except when there is a formal arrangement.

2.22 As a financial year progresses, the actual cash flows for the past months could show large variances from budget, but a rolling forecast indicates that the original budget for the end-of-year cash balance will still be achieved. This could occur if the rolling forecast has been prepared by adjusting the forecast for the unexpired months of the year, in order to keep the annual budget (on paper at least) for the end-of-year cash position. Where this occurs, suspicion must arise that the **rolling forecast has been prepared with little thought.**

2.23 **Unchanged figures over a number of months** of revised forecast submissions are also an indication of a weak forecasting system. It could be that business expectations have not changed; however there are few businesses that do not fluctuate with market conditions. A more likely explanation is that the rolling cash forecast has been prepared by copying the figures from the previous forecast or that a new revised forecast has not been prepared at all.

3 MODELLING CASH FLOW FORECASTS

Pilot paper

Cash flow forecasts (budgets)

3.1 When **budgets** are prepared, it may be the case that some of the factors to consider (for example levels of customer demand, interest rates, the inflation rate and so on) may vary, and each will have its own effect on the overall profit predicted for the period. For example customer demand for a product may not only be affected by selling price but also by interest rates. Both of these variables have an effect on sales revenue.

3.2 In a manual system, several **proforma** budgets would need to be prepared taking into account the effect of these different variables. It would take an enormous amount of time to prepare these budgets manually. The use of a **spreadsheet package**, whereby a model is devised and the values of each variable altered at will, **speeds up** this process as the results are known immediately.

Cash forecasting model

3.3 A cash forecasting model would be intended to provide a **cash flow plan or target.** The model should include all the factors (variables) which have a significant influence on cash flow.

3.4 Once the planning model has been constructed, the same model can be used again and again, simply by **changing the values of the variables** to produce new outputs for cash inflows, cash outflows, net cash flows and cash/bank balance.

3.5 **Computerised models** can incorporate actual results, period by period, and carry out the necessary calculations to produce budgetary control reports.

3.6 The use of a model also allows the budget for the remainder of the year to be **adjusted** once it is clear that the circumstances on which the budget was originally based have changed.

Sensitivity analysis

3.7 In a well-designed spreadsheet model a great number of '**what-if**' questions can be asked and answered quickly by simply changing the relevant data or variables.

3.8   **For example**, in a cash flow forecast model, managers may wish to know the cash flow impact if sales growth per month is nil, $\frac{1}{2}$%, 1%, 1$\frac{1}{2}$%, 2$\frac{1}{2}$% or minus 1% and so on. The information obtained should provide management with a better understanding of what the cash flow position in the future might be, and what factors are critical to ensuring that the cash position remains reasonable. It might be found, for example, that the cost of sales must remain less than 67% of sales value, or that sales growth of at least 1$\frac{1}{2}$% per month is essential to achieve a satisfactory cash position.

Three-dimensional spreadsheets

3.9   A spreadsheet file produced using a popular package such as Microsoft Excel or Lotus 1-2-3 may consist of **many individual sheets**. A cell in one sheet may **refer to data or formulae held in a different sheet**. The other sheet may be contained within the same spreadsheet file, or could be held in an entirely separate file.

3.10 Spreadsheets can therefore be described as **three dimensional.** This feature is often used to consolidate information from **two or more similar business units**. For example, a spreadsheet file may consist of three sheets (structured identically) named 'Branch A', 'Branch B' and 'Total'. Data would be input to the sheets 'Branch A' and 'Branch B', and the 'Total' sheet would contain **three-dimensional formulae combining the data held in the two feeder sheets.**

3.11 EXAMPLE: A MODEL BUDGET

The management accountant of Edgar Ltd wants to set up a spreadsheet for forecasting purposes. He has already prepared the input section of the spreadsheet which is as shown below.

3.12 This input was derived from the following information which is available for use in the budgeting process for the year to 31 December 2001.

(a) **Sales at selling price per product unit £24**

	2001				2002
	Quarter 1	Quarter 2	Quarter 3	Quarter 4	Quarter 1
Product units	126,000	84,000	75,600	117,600	100,800

(b) **Stock levels**

At 31 December 2000:	Finished product A	31,500 units
	Raw material X	73,500 kg

Closing stocks of finished product A at the end of each quarter are budgeted as a percentage of the sales units of the following quarter as follows.

(i)   At the end of quarters 1 and 2: 25%
(ii) At the end of quarters 3 and 4: 35%

Closing stock of raw material X is budgeted to fall by 6,300 kg at the end of each quarter in order to reduce holdings by 25,200 kg during 2001.

(c) **Product A unit data**

Material X	4 kg at £1.60 per kg
Direct labour	0.6 hours at £3.50 per hour

	A	B	C	D	E	F	G
1							
2	Selling price (£)	24					
3							
4	*Sales forecasts*		*Q1 01*	*Q2 01*	*Q3 01*	*Q4 01*	*Q1 02*
5	Units		126,000	84,000	75,600	117,600	100,800
6							
7	*Stock levels*						
8	Product A - units	31,500					
9	Material X - kg	73,500					
10	Closing stocks percentage		0.25	0.25	0.35	0.35	
11	Fall in material per quarter (kg)	6,300					
12							
13	*Product A unit data*						
14	Material X (kg)	4					
15	Material X (£/kg)	1.6					
16	Direct labour - hours	0.6					
17	Direct labour (£/hour)	3.5					
18							
19	Unit cost (£)	8.5					
20							
21	*Other expenditure*		945,000	1,008,000	987,000	1,050,000	
22	Fixed overhead			1,050,000			
23	Capital expenditure						
24							
25							
26	*Balances b/f*						
27	Debtors	840,000					
28	Bad debts	42,000					
29	Bank balance	462,000					
30	Creditors	201,600					
31	Fixed assets	10,500,000					
32							
33	*Cash flow timing*						
34	Sales revenues						
35	Quarter of sale	0.6					
36	Next quarter	0.38					
37	Bad debts	0.02					
38	Material X						
39	Quarter of purchase	0.7					
40	Next quarter	0.3					
41	Other expenditure						
42	Quarter incurred	1					
43	Next quarter	0					
44							
45	Depreciation rate	0.05					

(d) **Other quarterly expenditure**

	Quarter 1 £	Quarter 2 £	Quarter 3 £	Quarter 4 £
Fixed overhead	945,000	1,008,000	987,000	1,050,000
Capital expenditure		1,050,000		

(e) **Forecast balances at 31 December 2000**

Debtors	840,000
Bad debts provision	42,000
Bank balance	462,000
Creditors: materials	201,600
Fixed assets (at cost)	10,500,000

(f) **Cash flow timing information**

(i) Sales revenue: 60% receivable during the quarter of sale, 38% during the next quarter, the balance of 2% being expected bad debts.

(ii) Material X purchases: 70% payable during the quarter of purchase, the balance of 30% during the next quarter.

(iii) Direct wages, fixed overhead and capital expenditure: 100% payable during the quarter in which they are earned or incurred.

(g) Fixed assets are depreciated on a straight-line basis of 5% per annum, based on the total cost of fixed assets held at any point during a year and assuming nil residual value.

(h) All forecast balances at 31 December 2000 will be received or paid as relevant during the first quarter of 2001.

(i) Stocks of product A are valued on a marginal cost basis for internal budgeting purposes.

3.13 The budgets are given on the next two pages together with the formulae showing how each line is calculated.

Left section (columns A–G)

	A	B	C (Q1 01)	D (Q2 01)	E (Q3 01)	F (Q4 01)	G (Q1 02)
2	Selling price (£)	24					
4	Sales forecasts		Q1 01	Q2 01	Q3 01	Q4 01	Q1 02
5	Units		126,000	84,000	75,600	117,600	100,800
7	Stock levels						
8	Product A - units	31,500					
9	Material X - kg	73,500					
10	Closing stocks percentage		0.25	0.25	0.35	0.35	
11	Fall in material per quarter (kg)	6,300					
13	Product A unit costs						
14	Material X (kg)	4					
15	Material X (£/kg)	1.6					
16	Direct labour - hours	0.6					
17	Direct labour (£/hour)	3.5					
19	Unit cost (£)	8.5					
21	Other expenditure		945,000	1,008,000	987,000	1,050,000	
22	Fixed overhead		1,050,000				
23	Capital expenditure						
26	Balances b/f						
27	Debtors	840,000					
28	Bad debts	42,000					
29	Bank balance	462,000					
30	Creditors	201,600					
31	Fixed assets	10,500,000					
33	Cash flow timing						
34	Sales revenues						
35	Quarter of sale	0.6					
36	Next quarter	0.38					
37	Bad debts	0.02					
38	Material X						
39	Quarter of purchase	0.7					
40	Next quarter	0.3					
41	Other expenditure						
42	Quarter incurred	1					
43	Next quarter	0					
45	Depreciation rate	0.05					

Right section (columns H–M)

	H	I (Q1 01)	J (Q2 01)	K (Q3 01)	L (Q4 01)	M (Q1 02)
1	MATERIALS PURCHASES BUDGET					
2	Product A	Q1 01	Q2 01	Q3 01	Q4 01	Q1 02
3	Opening stock	-31,500	-18,900	-21,000	-41,160	
4	Sales units	126,000	84,000	75,600	117,600	100,800
5	Closing stock	21,000	18,900	41,160	35,280	
6	Production	115,500	81,900	97,860	111,720	
7	Raw materials					
8	Production	462,000	327,600	391,440	446,880	
9	Opening stock	-73,500	-67,200	-60,900	-54,600	
10	Closing stock	67,200	60,900	54,600	48,300	
11	Purchases (kg)	455,700	321,300	385,140	440,580	
13	Cost of purchases (£)	729,120	514,080	616,224	704,928	
26	CASHFLOW					
27	Receipts					
28	Q4 2000	798,000				
29	Q1 2001	1,814,400	1,49,120			
30	Q2 2001		1,209,600	766,080		
31	Q3 2001			1,088,640	689,472	
32	Q4 2001				1,693,440	
33	Total income	2,612,400	2,358,720	1,854,720	2,382,912	
	Payments					
	Creditors					
	Q4 2000	201,600				
	Q1 2001	510,384	218,736			
	Q2 2001		359,856	154,224		
	Q3 2001			431,357	184,867	
	Q4 2001				493,450	
	Total creditors	711,984	578,592	585,581	678,317	
	Wages	242,550	171,990	205,506	234,612	
	Overhead	945,000	1,008,000	987,000	1,050,000	
	Capital expenditure	0	1,050,000	0	0	
	Total expenditure	1,899,534	2,808,582	1,778,087	1,962,929	
	Net cash flow	712,866	-449,862	76,633	419,983	
	Opening cash balance	462,000	1,174,866	725,004	801,637	
	Closing cash balance	1,174,866	725,004	801,637	1,221,620	
	PROFIT AND LOSS ACCOUNT					
	Sales		£	£	9,676,800	
	Opening stock		267,750			
	Production		3,459,330			
	Closing stock		-299,880			
	Cost of sales			-3,427,200		
	Gross profit			6,249,600		
	Bad debts		193,536			
	Depreciation		577,500			
	Fixed overheads		3,990,000			
	Net loss			-4,761,036		
				1,488,564		

	H	I	J	K	L	M
1	MATERIALS PURCHASES BUDGET					
2	*Product A*	Q101	Q201	Q301	Q401	Q102
3	Opening stock	=-B8	=-I5	=-J5	=-K5	
4	Sales units	=C5	=D5	=E5	=F5	=G5
5	Closing stock	=D5*C10	=E5*D10	=F5*E10	=G5*F10	
6	Production	=SUM(I3:I5)	=SUM(J3:J5)	=SUM(K3:K5)	=SUM(L3:L5)	
7	*Raw materials*					
8	Production	=I6*B14	=J6*B14	=K6*B14	=L6*B14	
9	Opening stock	=-B9	=-I10	=-J10	=-K10	
10	Closing stock	=B9-B11	=I10-B11	=J10-B11	=K10-B11	
11	Purchases (kg)	=SUM(I8:I10)	=SUM(J8:J10)	=SUM(K8:K10)	=SUM(L8:L10)	
12						
13	Cost of purchases (£)	=I11*B15	=J11*B15	=K11*B15	=L11*B15	
14						
15	CASHFLOW					
16	*Receipts*					
17	Q4 1997	=B27-B28				
18	Q1 1999	=B2*C5*B35	=B2*C5*B36			
19	Q2 1999		=B2*D5*B35	=B2*D5*B36		
20	Q3 1999			=B2*E5*B35	=B2*E5*B36	
21	Q4 1999				=B2*F5*B35	
22	Total income	=SUM(I17:I21)	=SUM(J17:J21)	=SUM(K17:K21)	=SUM(L17:L21)	
23						
24	*Payments*					
25	Creditors					
26	Q4 1997	=B30				
27	Q1 1999	=I13*B39	=I13*B40			
28	Q2 1999		=J13*B39	=J13*B40		
29	Q3 1999			=K13*B39	=K13*B40	
30	Q4 1999				=L13*B39	
31	Total creditors	=SUM(I26:I30)	=SUM(J26:J30)	=SUM(K26:K30)	=SUM(L26:L30)	
32	Wages	=I6*B16*B17	=J6*B16*B17	=K6*B16*B17	=L6*B16*B17	
33	Overhead	=C21	=D21	=E21	=F21	
34	Capital expenditure	=C22	=D22	=E22	=F22	
35	Total expenditure	=SUM(I31:I34)	=SUM(J31:J34)	=SUM(K31:K34)	=SUM(L31:L34)	
36						
37	Net cash flow	=I22-I35	=J22-J35	=K22-K35	=L22-L35	
38	Opening cash balance	=B29	=I39	=J39	=K39	
39	Closing cash balance	=SUM(I37:I38)	=SUM(J37:J38)	=SUM(K37:K38)	=SUM(L37:L38)	
40						
41	PROFIT AND LOSS ACCOUNT		£	£		
42	Sales			=SUM(C5:F5)*B2		
43	Opening stock		=B8*B19			
44	Production		=SUM(I6:L6)*B19			
45	Closing stock		=-(L5*B19)			
46	Cost of sales			=-SUM(J43:J45)		
47	Gross profit			=K42+K46		
48	Bad debts		=K42*B37			
49	Depreciation		=(B31+D22)*B45			
50	Fixed overheads		=SUM(C21:F21)			
51				=-SUM(J48:J50)		
52	Net loss			=K47+K51		
53						

4   FORECAST FINANCIAL STATEMENTS: EXAMPLE

4.1   In the *Financial Strategy* paper, you could be presented with a requirement to construct forecast financial statements, which need not be presented in published accounts format, based upon first or base year data. Below, we work though such a question in detail.

4.2   EXAMPLE: FINANCIAL STATEMENT FORECASTING

You are a consultant working for a company called CC Drains plc, which started trading four years ago in 20X3 and which manufactures plastic rainwater drainage goods. You have the following information.

(a)   Sales and cost of sales are expected to increase by 10% in each of the financial years ending 31 December 20X7, 20X8 and 20X9. Operating expenses are expected to increase by 5% each year.

(b)   The company expects to continue to be liable for tax at the marginal rate of 30%. You can assume that tax is paid or refunded 12 months after the year end.

(c)   The ratios of **debtors to sales** and **creditors to cost of sales** will remain the same for the next three years.

(d) Fixed assets comprise land and buildings, for which no depreciation is provided. Other assets used by the company, such as machinery and vehicles, are hired on operating leases.

(e) The company plans for dividends to grow at 25% in each of the financial years 20X7, 20X8 and 20X9.

(f) The company plans to purchase new machinery to the value of £500,000 during 20X7, to be depreciated straight line over ten years. The company charges a full year's depreciation in the first year of purchase of its assets. Capital allowances at 25% reducing balance are available on this expenditure.

(g) Stock was purchased for £35,000 at the beginning of 20X7. The value of stock after this purchase is expected to remain at £361,000 for the foreseeable future.

(h) No decision has been made on the type of finance to be used for the expansion programme. The company's directors believe that they can raise new medium-term secured debt if necessary.

(i) The average P/E ratio of listed companies in the same industry as CC Drains plc is 15.

The company's objectives include the following.

(a) To earn a pre-tax return on the closing book value of shareholders' funds of 35% pa
(b) To increase dividends per share by 25% per year
(c) To obtain a quotation on a recognised stock exchange within the next three years

A summary of the financial statements for the year to 31 December 20X6 is set out below.

CC DRAINS PLC
SUMMARISED PROFIT AND LOSS ACCOUNT
FOR THE YEAR TO 31 DECEMBER 20X6

	£'000
Turnover	1,560
Cost of sales	950
Gross profit	610
Operating expenses	325
Interest	30
Tax liability	77
Net profit	178
Dividends declared	68

SUMMARISED BALANCE SHEET AT 31 DECEMBER 20X6

	£'000
Fixed assets (net book value)	750
Current assets	
Stock	326
Debtors	192
Cash and bank	50
Current liabilities	
Trade creditors	(135)
Other creditors (including tax and dividends)	(145)
Total assets less current liabilities	1,038

Financing	£'000
Ordinary share capital (ordinary shares of £1)	500
Retained profits to 31 December 20X5	128
Retentions for the year to 31 December 20X6	110
10% debenture redeemable 20Z0	300
Total financing	1,038

Required

Using the information given:

(a) Prepare forecast profit and loss accounts for the years 20X7, 20X8 and 20X9, and calculate whether the company is likely to meet its stated financial objective (return on shareholders' funds) for these three years.

(b) Prepare cash flow forecasts for the years 20X7, 20X8 and 20X9, and estimate the amount of funds which will need to be raised by the company to finance its expansion.

Notes

(1) You should ignore interest or returns on surplus funds invested during the three-year period of review.

(2) You may ignore the timing of cash flows within each year and you should not discount the cash flows.

4.3 ANSWER

(a) CC DRAINS PLC PROFIT AND LOSS ACCOUNTS

	Actual		*Forecast*	
	20X6	*20X7*	*20X8*	*20X9*
	£'000	£'000	£'000	£'000
Turnover (increase 10% pa)	1,560	1,716	1,888	2,076
Cost of sales (increase 10% pa)	(950)	(1,045)	(1,150)	(1,264)
Gross profit	610	671	738	812
Operating expenses (increase 5% pa)	(325)	(341)	(358)	(376)
Depreciation (10% pa × £500,000)		(50)	(50)	(50)
Operating profit	285	280	330	386
Interest (assumed constant)	(30)	(30)	(30)	(30)
Profit before tax	255	250	300	356
Taxation (see working)	(77)	(53)	(77)	(101)
Net profit	178	197	223	255
Dividend (25% growth pa)	(68)	(85)	(106)	(133)
Retained profit	110	112	117	122
Reserves b/f	128	238	350	467
Reserves c/f	238	350	467	589
Share capital	500	500	500	500
Year end reserves	238	350	467	589
Year end shareholders' funds	738	850	967	1,089
Pre-tax return on shareholders funds	34.6%	29.4%	31.0%	32.7%

On the basis of these figures, the financial objective of a pre-tax return of 35% of year-end shareholders' funds is not achieved in any of the years.

Working: Tax payable

It is assumed that the company does not account for deferred taxation.

	Actual		*Forecast*	
	20X6	*20X7*	*20X8*	*20X9*
	£'000	£'000	£'000	£'000
Profit before tax	255	250	300	356
Add back depreciation		50	50	50
Less capital allowance (25% red./bal)		(125)	(94)	(70)
Taxable profit	255	175	256	336
Tax at 30%	77	53	77	101

(b) *Cash flow forecasts*

The 20X6 balance sheet figure for 'other creditors (including tax and dividends)' is simply the sum of tax and dividends in the profit and loss account. It is assumed that this will continue to be the case in the following three years. The annual change in net current assets can be computed as follows.

Changes in net current assets

	Actual	Forecast		
	20X6	20X7	20X8	20X9
	£'000	£'000	£'000	£'000
Stock (scenario note (7))	326	361	361	361
Debtors (12.31% of sales) *	192	211	232	256
Trade creditors (14.21% of cost of sales) *	(135)	(148)	(163)	(180)
Tax and dividends payable (sum of P&L figures)	(145)	(138)	(183)	(234)
Net current assets	238	286	247	203
Increase/(decrease) net current assets		48	(39)	(44)

* Alternatively debtors and creditors can be computed as a 10% increase each year.

The cash flow forecasts can then be constructed.

Cash flow forecasts

	20X7	20X8	20X9
	£'000	£'000	£'000
Retained profit for the year	112	117	122
Add back depreciation	50	50	50
(Investment in working capital)/release of working capital (see working)	(48)	39	44
Expenditure on fixed assets	(500)		
Surplus/(deficit) for the year	(386)	206	216
Cash/(deficit) b/f	50	(336)	(130)
Cash/(deficit) c/f	(336)	(130)	86

The company will need to find finance of £338,000 in 20X7 but this can be completely repaid in the following two years. However, interest costs have been ignored in this computation.

Appendices

1 *Cash receipts and payments*

	20X7	20X8	20X9
Receipts	£'000	£'000	£'000
Cash from sales			
(sales + opening debtors – closing debtors)	1,697	1,867	2,053
Payments			
For purchases (cost of sales + opening			
creditors – closing creditors)	1,032	1,135	1,248
Operating expenses	341	358	376
Additional stock purchase	35		
Machinery	500		
Interest (current year)	30	30	30
Tax (previous year)	77	53	77
Dividends (previous year)	68	85	106
	2,083	1,661	1,837
Net cash flow	(386)	206	216
Cash/(deficit) b/f	50	(336)	(130)
Cash/(deficit) c/f	(336)	(130)	86

2 *FRS 1 format*

	20X7	20X8	20X9
	£'000	£'000	£'000
Net cash inflow from operating activities			
(see working)	290	373	429
Interest paid	(30)	(30)	(30)
Dividends paid	(68)	(85)	(106)
Net cash inflow	192	258	293
Tax paid	(77)	(53)	(77)
Investing activities:			
Fixed assets	(500)		
Net cash outflow	(577)	(53)	(77)
Net cash flow before financing	(385)	205	216

Working: net cash inflow from operating activities

	20X6	20X7	20X8	20X9
	£'000	£'000	£'000	£'000
Stock	326	361	361	361
Debtors	192	211	232	256
Trade creditors	(135)	(149)	(163)	(180)
	383	423	430	437
Incremental working capital		(40)	(7)	(7)
Gross profit before depreciation		671	738	812
Less: operating expenses		(341)	(358)	(376)
Net cash inflow from operating activities		290	373	429

Chapter roundup

- **Cash forecasting** should ensure that sufficient funds will be available when needed, to sustain the activities of an enterprise at an acceptable cost.

- **Balance sheet based forecasts** can be used to assess the scale of funding requirements or cash surpluses expected over time, and to act as a check on the realism of cash flow based forecasts.

- **Forecast financial statements** can be constructed for a period of several years, from first year data, given certain assumptions. You will not need to present cash flow statements in FRS 1 format.

Quick quiz

1   Give three methods of funding a deficiency of cash.

2   What variables should typically be included in a cash budgeting model?

3   What three categories of business asset does strategic financial management distinguish for the purposes of working capital management?

4   How would you described each of the working capital policies A, B and C in the diagram below respectively?

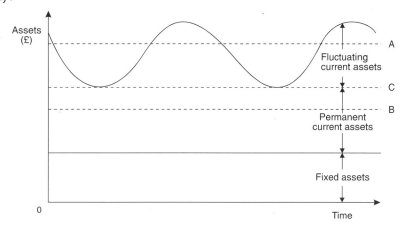

Answers to quick quiz

1   Borrowing; selling short-term financial investments; leading and lagging creditors and debtors.

2   (a)   Total sales

    (b)   Cash sales, perhaps as a percentage of total sales

    (c)   Credit sales, perhaps as a percentage of total sales

    (d)   Rate of growth in sales, or seasonal variations in sales

    (e)   Time taken by debtors to pay what they owe

        (i)   Percentage paying one month after invoice
        (ii)   Percentage paying two months after invoice
        (iii)   Percentage paying three months after invoice
        (iv)   Percentage of bad debts

    (f)   Purchases on credit

        (i)   Percentage paid within one month of receipt of invoice
        (ii)   Percentage paid within two months of receipt of invoice

    (g)   Wages and salaries

    (h)   Other cash expenses

    (i)   Dividends

    (j)   Taxation payments

    (k)   Capital expenditure

3   (a)   Assets needed for core activities
    (b)   Assets not needed for core activities which could be easily sold
    (c)   Less liquid assets not needed for core activities

4   A   Conservative
    B   Aggressive
    C   Balanced

Now try the question below from the Exam Question Bank

Number	Level	Marks	Time
4	Examination	50	90 mins

Chapter 5

DISTRIBUTION OF EARNINGS

Topic list	Syllabus reference	Ability required
1 Dividends and retentions	(i)	Evaluation
2 Dividend policy theory	(i)	Evaluation
3 Scrip dividends, scrip issue and stock splits	(i)	Evaluation
4 Share repurchase	(i)	Evaluation

Introduction

In this chapter, we deal with the question of how much should be paid out by a company to its shareholders, for example in the form of **dividends**. What is the effect of dividend policy on share prices? What are the practical influences on dividend policy, including the effects of taxation?

We shall be discussing the views on dividend policy of **Modigliani and Miller**. Part of the chapter is based on the **fundamental theory of share values**, which was covered in the *Finance* paper.

Learning outcomes covered in this chapter

- Evaluate the attainment of financial objectives

Syllabus content covered in this chapter

- Policies for distribution of earnings, eg dividends, share repurchase. (Note: theory of dividend relevance will not be tested.)

1   DIVIDENDS AND RETENTIONS

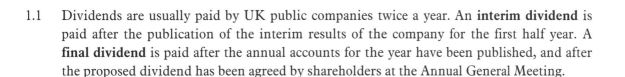

KEY TERM

A **dividend** is an amount payable to shareholders from profits or other distributable reserves.　　　　　　　　　　　　　　　　　　　　　　　　　　　*(OT 2000)*

1.1   Dividends are usually paid by UK public companies twice a year. An **interim dividend** is paid after the publication of the interim results of the company for the first half year. A **final dividend** is paid after the annual accounts for the year have been published, and after the proposed dividend has been agreed by shareholders at the Annual General Meeting.

1.2   It is usual for shareholders to have the power to vote to **reduce** the size of the final (proposed) dividend at the AGM, but not the power to **increase** the dividend. The directors of the company are therefore in a strong position, with regard to shareholders, when it comes to determining dividend policy. For practical purposes, shareholders will usually be

PUBLISHING

obliged to accept the dividend policy that has been decided on by the directors, or otherwise to sell their shares.

1.3 When deciding upon the dividends to pay out to shareholders, one of the main considerations of the directors will be the amount of earnings they wish to retain to meet **financing needs**. Funds generated internally are the single most important source of finance for UK companies – during the years 1992-1996 an average of 60.2% of funds were raised through **retained earnings.**

1.4 The major reasons for using retained earnings to finance new investments, rather than to pay higher dividends and then raise new equity funds for the new investments, are as follows.

(a) The dividend policy of a company is in practice determined by the directors. From their standpoint, funds from retained earnings are an attractive source of finance because **investment projects can be undertaken without involving either the shareholders or any outsiders.**

(b) The use of retained earnings as opposed to new shares or debentures **avoids issue costs.**

(c) The use of funds from retained earnings **avoids the possibility of a change in control** resulting from an issue of new shares.

1.5 As well as future financing requirements, the decision as to how much of a company's profits should be retained, and how much paid out to shareholders, will be influenced by:

(a) The **need to remain profitable** (Dividends are paid out of profits, and an unprofitable company cannot for ever go on paying dividends out of retained profits made in the past.)

(b) The **law on distributable profits**

(c) Any **dividend restraints** which might be imposed by loan agreements

(d) The **effect of inflation,** and the need to retain some profit within the business just to maintain its operating capability unchanged

(e) The company's **gearing level** (If the company wants extra finance, the sources of funds used should strike a balance between equity and debt finance. Retained earnings are the most readily available source of growth in equity finance.)

(f) The company's **liquidity position** (Dividends are a cash payment, and a company must have enough cash to pay the dividends it declares.)

(g) The ease with which the company could raise **extra finance** from sources other than retained earnings (Small companies which find it hard to raise finance might have to rely more heavily on retained earnings than large companies.)

(h) The **signalling effect** of dividends to shareholders and the financial markets in general – see below.

Dividends as a signal to investors

KEY TERM

Signalling is the use of dividend policy to indicate the future prospects of an enterprise.

1.6 The ultimate objective in any financial management decisions is to maximise shareholders' wealth. This wealth is basically represented by the current market value of the company, which should largely be determined by the **cash flows arising from the investment decisions** taken by management.

1.7 Although the market would **like** to value shares on the basis of underlying cash flows on the company's projects, such information is **not readily available to investors**. But the directors do have this information. The dividend declared can be interpreted as a **signal** from directors to shareholders about the strength of underlying project cash flows.

1.8 Investors usually expect a **consistent dividend policy** from the company, with stable dividends each year or, even better, **steady dividend growth**. A large rise or fall in dividends in any year can have a marked effect on the company's share price. Stable dividends or steady dividend growth are usually needed for share price stability. A cut in dividends may be treated by investors as signalling that the future prospects of the company are weak. Thus, **the dividend which is paid acts**, possibly without justification, **as a signal of the future prospects of the company.**

1.9 The signalling effect of a company's dividend policy may also be used by management of a company which faces a possible **takeover**. The dividend level might be increased as a defence against the takeover: investors may take the increased dividend as a signal of improved future prospects, thus driving the share price higher and making the company more expensive for a potential bidder to take over.

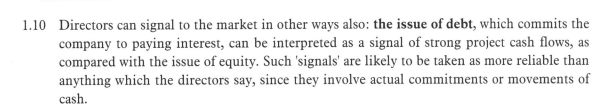

Exam focus point

You should make a point of showing in exam answers, where it is relevant, that you appreciate the signalling effect of dividends.

1.10 Directors can signal to the market in other ways also: **the issue of debt**, which commits the company to paying interest, can be interpreted as a signal of strong project cash flows, as compared with the issue of equity. Such 'signals' are likely to be taken as more reliable than anything which the directors say, since they involve actual commitments or movements of cash.

2 DIVIDEND POLICY THEORY

2.1 Having looked at the practical influence son dividend policy, we now look briefly at the main theory developed by **Modigliani and Miller (M&M)** in this area. It looks at the dividend decision from the viewpoint of the principal objective of financial management – maximisation of shareholders' wealth.

2.2 The question being asked here is: If a company chooses to fund a new investment by a cut in dividend rather than by raising new equity finance, how will this affect the wealth of the shareholders?

(a) M&M's **dividend irrelevancy theory** argues that existing shareholders will be **indifferent** between the two finance methods.

(b) However, **practical influences**, including market imperfections, mean that changes in dividend policy, particularly reduction in dividends paid, **can have an adverse effect** on shareholder wealth.

Dividend irrelevance

2.3 The basic thrust of M&M's argument was that the value of a company is determined solely by its **investment policy** – the selection of projects with positive net present values – and that the pattern of dividends paid out from the resultant net cash inflows would make no difference to the overall market value of the company.

2.4 MM argued that if a company with investment opportunities decides to pay a dividend, so that retained earnings are insufficient to finance all its investments, the shortfall in funds will be made up by obtaining additional funds from outside sources. **The consequent loss of value in the existing shares**, as a result of obtaining outside finance instead of using retained earnings, **is exactly equal to the amount of the dividend paid.** A company should therefore be indifferent between paying a dividend (and obtaining new outside funds) and retaining earnings.

Note. This argument can be 'proved' by use of the dividend valuation model, but you will not be required to do so.

2.5 The conditions under which M&M theory was held to be true included:

- No taxation
- No transaction costs on buying, selling or issuing shares
- All investors have free access to all relevant information

2.6 In answer to the practical point that, should a company choose not to pay any dividend at all, shareholders requiring a regular income would suffer, M&M argued that this could be overcome by the shareholders '**manufacturing**' their own dividends. This would be done by selling off some of their shares, which will have increased in value from the reinvestment of earnings; with no transaction costs or taxes, this would leave them in the same position as if they had received a dividend from the company.

2.7 In answer to criticisms that certain shareholders will show a preference either for **high dividends** or for **capital gains**, MM argued that if a company pursues a consistent dividend policy, 'each corporation would tend to attract to itself a clientele consisting of those preferring its particular payout ratio, but one clientele would be entirely as good as another in terms of the valuation it would imply for the firm'.

The case in favour of the relevance of dividend policy (and against MM's views)

2.8 There are strong arguments against MM's view that dividend policy is irrelevant as a means of affecting shareholder's wealth.

(a) **Differing rates of taxation** on dividends and capital gains can create a preference for a high dividend or one for high earnings retention – the **clientele effect**.

KEY TERM

The term **clientele effect** describes the tendency of companies to attract particular types of shareholders because of their management organisation and policies, particularly dividend policies.

(b) Dividend retention should be preferred by companies in a period of **capital rationing**.

(c) **Markets are not perfect.** Because of transaction costs on the sale of shares, investors who want some cash from their investments should prefer to receive dividends rather than to sell some of their shares to get the cash they want.

(d) **Information available to shareholders is imperfect,** and they are not aware of the future investment plans and expected profits of their company. Even if management were to provide them with profit forecasts, these forecasts would not necessarily be accurate or believable.

    (i)   As a consequence of imperfect information companies are normally expected at least to maintain the same level of dividends from one year to the next. They are expected to pay a constant dividend or an increased dividend, but not a lower dividend than the year before. **Failure to maintain the dividend level would undermine investors' confidence in the future –** the **signalling effect** discussed earlier.

    (ii)   In practice, undertaking a new investment project with a positive NPV **will not immediately increase the market value of shares** by the amount of the NPV because markets do not show strong-form efficiency. It is only gradually, as the profits from the investment begin to show up in the profits and dividends in historical financial statements, that the market value of the shares will rise.

(e) Perhaps the strongest argument against the MM view is that shareholders will tend to prefer a current dividend to future capital gains (or deferred dividends) because the future is **more uncertain.**

Question

Ochre plc is a company that is still managed by the two individuals who set it up 12 years ago. In the current year, the company acquired plc status and was launched on the second tier Alternative Investment Market (AIM). Previously, all of the shares had been owned by its two founders and certain employees. Now, 40% of the shares are in the hands of the investing public. The company's profit growth and dividend policy are set out below. Will a continuation of the same dividend policy as in the past be suitable now that the company is quoted on the AIM?

Year	Profits £'000	Dividend £'000	Shares in issue
4 years ago	176	88	800,000
3 years ago	200	104	800,000
2 years ago	240	120	1,000,000
1 year ago	290	150	1,000,000
Current year	444	222 (proposed)	1,500,000

Answer

Year	Dividend per share	Dividend as % of profit
4 years ago	11.0	50%
3 years ago	13.0	52%
2 years ago	12.0	50%
1 year ago	15.0	52%
Current year	14.8	50%

The company appears to have pursued a dividend policy of paying out half of after-tax profits in dividend. This policy is only suitable when a company achieves a stable EPS or steady EPS growth. Investors do not like a fall in dividend from one year to the next, and the fall in dividend per share in the current year is likely to be unpopular, and to result in a fall in the share price.

The company would probably serve its shareholders better by paying a dividend of at least 15p per share, possibly more, in the current year, even though the dividend as a percentage of profit would then be higher.

3 SCRIP DIVIDENDS, SCRIP ISSUES AND STOCK SPLITS

Scrip dividend

> ### KEY TERM
>
> A **scrip dividend** is a dividend paid by the issue of additional company shares, rather than by cash. *(OT 2000)*

3.1 Effectively, a scrip dividend converts profit reserves into issued share capital. When the directors of a company would prefer to retain funds within the business but consider that they must pay at least a certain amount of dividend, they might offer equity shareholders the choice of a cash dividend or a scrip dividend of more shares in the company. Recently (particularly since 1993) **enhanced scrip dividends** have been offered by a number of companies. With enhanced scrip dividends, the value of the shares offered is much greater than the cash alternative, giving investors an incentive to choose the shares. Scrip dividend schemes have become less popular as a result of the abolition of Advance Corporation Tax (ACT) in 1999.

3.2 A **scrip** or **bonus issue** (also known as a **capitalisation issue**) involves the issue of new shares, at no cost to existing shareholders, in proportion to their existing holdings. Such an issue has the effect of reducing the retained earnings (profit and loss) account and increasing the called up share capital account. Obviously there is **no net raising of cash, nor any increase in the value of shareholders' equity.**

3.3 Whether there is any point to the process (other than reducing the price per share and hence possibly increasing share trading liquidity) is open to debate. If there is, then it is either because shareholders are not as clever as we think they are, or because there are associated '**signals**' that commonly accompany the scrip issue, eg perhaps that the dividend per share is to be maintained on the increased number of shares and hence the directors believe future company cashflows will be favourable.

Stock split

3.4 This possible advantage of a scrip issue is also the reason for a **stock split**. A stock split occurs where, for example, each ordinary share of £1 each is split into two shares of 50p each, thus creating cheaper shares with **greater marketability**. There is possibly an added psychological advantage, in that investors may expect a company which splits its shares in this way to be planning for substantial earnings growth and dividend growth in the future.

3.5 As a consequence, the market price of shares may benefit. For example, if one existing share of £1 has a market value of £6, and is then split into two shares of 50p each, the market value of the new shares might settle at, say, £3.10 instead of the expected £3, in anticipation of strong future growth in earnings and dividends.

3.6 **The difference between a stock split and a scrip issue** is that a scrip issue converts equity reserves into share capital, whereas a stock split leaves reserves unaffected. Both are popular with investors as they are seen as likely to lead to increased dividends. Scrip dividends can, however, lead to tax complications for individual investors.

4 SHARE REPURCHASE

Why buy back the company's shares?

4.1 Until relatively recently, it was illegal for a UK company to repurchase its issued shares. The Companies Act 1981, and now the Companies Act 1985, have given companies rights to **buy back shares from shareholders** who are willing to sell them, subject to certain conditions.

4.2 For a **smaller private company** with few shareholders, the reason for buying back the company's own shares may be that there is no immediate willing purchaser at a time when a shareholder wishes to sell shares. For a public company, share repurchase could provide a way of withdrawing from the share market and 'going private'. **Larger public companies** also sometimes repurchase their own shares. Recently, for instance, a number of the privatised UK electricity companies have made significant share repurchases having gained shareholder approval to do so at the companies' annual meetings.

4.3 Repurchase of own shares is common among US companies and is gaining popularity in the UK. However, the practice remains rare in the rest of Europe. Share buybacks are indeed illegal in a number of European countries including Germany and in Scandinavia, although in some countries, including Sweden, Switzerland, and Ireland, there have been recent moves towards legalisation.

4.4 Among the possible **benefits of a share repurchase scheme** are the following.

(a) Finding a use for surplus cash, which may be a 'dead asset'.

(b) Increase in earnings per share through a reduction in the number of shares in issue - this should lead to a higher share price than would otherwise be the case, and the company should be able to increase dividend payments on the remaining shares in issue.

(c) Increase in gearing. Repurchase of a company's own shares allows debt to be substituted for equity, so raising gearing. This will be of interest to a company wanting to increase its gearing without increasing its total long-term funding.

(d) Readjustment of the company's equity base to more appropriate levels, for a company whose business is in decline.

(e) Possibly preventing a takeover or enabling a quoted company to withdraw from the stock market.

4.5 There are also possible **disadvantages**.

(a) It can be hard to arrive at a price which will be fair both to the vendors and to any shareholders who are not selling shares to the company.

(b) A repurchase of shares could be seen as an admission that the company cannot make better use of the funds than the shareholders.

(c) Some shareholders may suffer from being taxed on a capital gain following the purchase of their shares rather than receiving dividend income.

Case examples

In October 1994 it was reported that **Midlands Electricity plc** had purchased 21.16 million of its own shares. In making such a large repurchase, it had to pay a price of 725 pence, compared with a general market price on the day of 713 pence, up 25 pence on the previous day.

The objectives of the buy-back were to **boost earnings per share** and to help create a **'progressive'** **dividend policy** at a time when the company had cash available for the repurchase. An investment analyst was quoted in the press as approving of the move. Given what he saw as the utilities companies' poor record on diversification, he said that he would prefer seeing the company do this with its money than investing it abroad.

In October 2000, Redrow, the housebuilder, unveiled plans to buy back 30% of its shares via a tender offer at 170p (market price was 169.5p). This was to achieve a 'better match between debt and equity' on its balance sheet – the gearing level at the time being 4.5%.

Chapter roundup

- **Retained earnings** remain the most important single course of finance for UK companies, and financial managers should take account of the proportion of earnings which are retained as opposed to being paid as dividends.

- Companies generally **smooth out** dividend payments by adjusting only gradually to changes in earnings: large fluctuations might undermine **investors'** confidence.

- The dividends a company pays may be treated as a **signal** to investors. A company needs to take account of different **clienteles** of shareholders in deciding what dividends to pay.

- **Modigliani and Miller's theories** suggest that dividend policy is irrelevant to shareholder wealth in perfect capital markets. Given the imperfections in real-world markets and in taxation policies, the position is not so clear.

Quick quiz

1   What reasons are there in favour of using funds from retained earnings to finance new investments?

2   Give a definition of 'signalling' in the context of dividends policy.

3   Particular companies may attract particular types of shareholders. This is called the .... effect. (**Fill in the blank**.)

Answers to quick quiz

1   • No need for recourse to shareholders or others
    • No issue costs
    • No possibility of change in control from issue of new shares
    • Financial and taxation position of shareholders

2   The use of dividend policy to indicate the future prospects of an enterprise.

3   Clientele.

Now try the question below from the Exam Question Bank

Number	Level	Marks	Time
5	Introductory	n/a	15 mins

Part B
Business valuations

Chapter 6

VALUATION OF COMPANIES

Topic list	Syllabus reference	Ability required
1 Reasons for share valuations	(ii)	Application
2 Asset valuation bases	(ii)	Application
3 Earnings valuation bases	(ii)	Application
4 Cash flow valuation methods	(ii)	Application
5 Other valuation bases	(ii)	Application
6 Intangible assets and intellectual capital	(ii)	Application

Introduction

Our main interest in this section is with methods of valuing the entire equity in a company, perhaps for the purpose of making a takeover bid, rather than with the value of small blocks of shares which an investor might choose to buy or sell on the stock market.

Learning outcomes covered in this chapter

- Calculate values of organisations of different types, eg service, capital intensive.
- Identify and calculate the value of intangible assets in an organisation (including intellectual capital)

Syllabus content covered in this chapter

- Asset valuation bases (eg historic, replacement, realisable)
- Earnings valuation bases (eg price/earnings (P/E) multiples, earnings yield)
- Cash flow valuation bases (ie DCF, dividend yield, dividend growth model using the formula $P_0 = D_1/r - g$)
- Other valuation bases (eg earn out arrangements, super profits method)
- The strengths and weaknesses of each valuation method and when each method is most suitable
- Application of valuation bases to new issues
- The different forms of intellectual capital
- The methods of valuing intellectual capital

1   REASONS FOR SHARE VALUATIONS   5/01

1.1   Given quoted share prices on the Stock Exchange, why devise techniques for estimating the value of a share? A share valuation will be necessary:

    (a)   For **quoted companies,** when there is a takeover bid and the offer price is an estimated 'fair value' in excess of the current market price of the shares

KEY TERM

A **takeover** is the acquisition by a company of a controlling interest in the voting share capital of another company, usually achieved by the purchase of a majority of the voting shares.

(OT 2000)

    (b) For **unquoted companies**, when:

        (i)   The company wishes to 'go public' and must fix an issue price for its shares

        (ii)   There is a scheme of merger

        (iii) Shares are sold

        (iv) Shares need to be valued for the purposes of taxation

        (v)   Shares are pledged as collateral for a loan

    (c) For **subsidiary companies**, when the group's holding company is negotiating the sale of the subsidiary to a management buyout team or to an external buyer

1.2   Valuing **unquoted companies** presents some special considerations, for example:

    (a) **It may not be sensible to use P/E ratios** of a quoted company for comparative purposes because the market value of a quoted company is likely to include a premium to reflect the marketability of its shares.

    (b) A small unquoted company may be highly sensitive to the **loss of key employees** which may follow a merger or buyout. An arrangement to tie key employees in to the enterprise could be costly.

1.3   **Common bases for valuing shares**, each giving a different share valuation:

    • Asset based

    • Earnings based – P/E multiples, earnings yield, ARR

    • Cash flow based – dividends DCF

    • Other – super profits, earn out arrangements

Exam focus point

In an exam question as well as in practice, it is unlikely that one method would be used in isolation. Several valuations might be made, each using a different technique or different assumptions. The valuations could then be compared, and a final price reached as a compromise between the different values.

2   ASSET VALUATION BASES

The net assets method of share valuation

2.1   Using this method of valuation, the value of a share in a particular class is equal to the **net tangible assets attributable to that class,** divided by the **number of shares in the class.** **Intangible assets** (including goodwill) should be excluded, unless they have a market value (for example patents and copyrights, which could be sold).

    (a) **Goodwill**, if shown in the accounts, is unlikely to be shown at a true figure for purposes of valuation, and the value of goodwill should be reflected in another method of valuation (for example the earnings basis, the dividend yield basis or the super-profits method).

(b) **Development expenditure**, if shown in the accounts, would also have a value which is related to future profits rather than to the worth of the company's physical assets.

The valuation of intangible assets in general, and intellectual capital in particular, is discussed at the end of this chapter.

2.2 EXAMPLE: NET ASSETS METHOD OF SHARE VALUATION

The summary balance sheet of Cactus Ltd is as follows.

Fixed assets	£	£	£
Land and buildings			160,000
Plant and machinery			80,000
Motor vehicles			20,000
			260,000
Goodwill			20,000
Current assets			
Stocks		80,000	
Debtors		60,000	
Short-term investments		15,000	
Cash		5,000	
		160,000	
Current liabilities			
Creditors	60,000		
Taxation	20,000		
Proposed ordinary dividend	20,000		
		(100,000)	
			60,000
			340,000
12% debentures			(60,000)
Deferred taxation			(10,000)
			270,000
			£
Ordinary shares of £1			80,000
Reserves			140,000
			220,000
4.9% preference shares of £1			50,000
			270,000

What is the value of an ordinary share using the net assets basis of valuation?

2.3 SOLUTION

If the figures given for asset values are not questioned, the valuation would be as follows.

	£	£
Total value of net assets		340,000
Less intangible asset (goodwill)		20,000
Total value of tangible assets (net)		320,000
Less: preference shares	50,000	
debentures	60,000	
deferred taxation	10,000	
		120,000
Net asset value of equity		200,000
Number of ordinary shares		80,000
Value per share		£2.50

Which valuation bases should be used?

2.4   The difficulty in an asset valuation method is establishing the **asset values** to use. Values ought to be realistic. The figure attached to an individual asset may vary considerably depending on whether it is valued on a **going concern** or a **break-up** basis.

Possibilities include:

- Historic basis – unlikely to give a realistic value
- Replacement basis – if the asset is to be used on an on-going basis
- Realisable basis – if the asset is to be sold, or the business as a whole broken up

2.5   The following list should give you some idea of the factors that must be considered.

(a)   Do the assets need **professional valuation?** If so, how much will this cost?

(b)   Have the **liabilities** been accurately quantified, for example deferred taxation? Are there any contingent liabilities? Will any balancing tax charges arise on disposal?

(c)   How have the **current assets** been valued? Are all debtors collectable? Is all stock realisable? Can all the assets be physically located and brought into a saleable condition? This may be difficult in certain circumstances where the assets are situated abroad.

(d)   Can any **hidden liabilities** be accurately assessed? Would there be redundancy payments and closure costs?

(e)   Is there an **available market** in which the assets can be realised (on a break-up basis)? If so, do the balance sheet values truly reflect these break-up values?

(f)   Are there any **prior charges** on the assets?

When is the net assets basis of valuation used?

2.6   The net assets basis of valuation might be used in the following two circumstances.

(a)   **As a measure of the 'security' in a share value**. A share might be valued using an earnings basis (discussed next), and this valuation might be:

(i)   Higher than the net asset value per share (if the company went into liquidation, the investor could not expect to receive the full value of his shares when the underlying assets were realised.)

(ii)   Lower than the net asset value per share (if the company went into liquidation, the investor might expect to receive the full value of his shares and perhaps much more, when the underlying assets were realised.)

The **asset backing** for shares thus provides a measure of the possible loss if the company fails to make the expected earnings or dividend payments. It is often thought to be a good thing to acquire a company with valuable tangible assets, especially freehold property which might be expected to increase in value over time.

(b)   **As a measure of comparison in a scheme of merger**

KEY TERM

A **merger** is essentially a business combination of two or more companies, of which none obtains control over any other.

For example, if company A, which has a low asset backing, is planning a merger with company B, which has a high asset backing, the shareholders of B might consider that their shares' value ought to reflect this. It might therefore be agreed that a something should be added to the value of the company B shares to allow for this difference in asset backing.

(c) As a 'floor value' for a business that is up for sale – shareholders will be reluctant to sell for less than the NAV. However, if the sale is essential for cash flow purposes or to realign with corporate strategy, even the asset value may not be realised.

Case example

In November 2000, **Scottish & Newcastle**, the UK brewing and leisure group, sold off the holiday village business **Center Parcs** for £670 million, which fell significantly short of its £800 million net operating assets book valuation. Scottish & Newcastle shares fell by 2% following the announcement of the sale. The disposal was part of a strategy of Scottish & Newcastle to focus on beer and growth areas of its retail business, such as pubs/restaurants; the cash from the sale of Center Parcs was to help pay for the purchase of Kronenburg, the French brewer.

For these reasons, it is always advisable to calculate the net assets per share.

3 EARNINGS VALUATION BASES

The P/E ratio (earnings) method of valuation

3.1 This is a common method of valuing a controlling interest in a company, where the owner can decide on dividend and retentions policy. The P/E ratio relates earnings per share to a share's value.

$$\text{Since P/E ratio} = \frac{\text{Market value}}{\text{EPS}},$$

then market value per share $= \text{EPS} \times \text{P/E ratio}$

Case example

You will find frequent references to the P/E ratio in the financial press. For example, the *Financial Times* on 8 July 1997 reported the first day's trading in shares of the newly demutualised bank Woolwich plc as follows.

'"This is now the most expensive bank in Europe" said one analyst when Woolwich shares ended their first day of trading at 334p. By the close of trading, Woolwich stood at between 18 and 21 times prospective earnings. That compares with 16 times for Lloyds TSB and is considered unsustainable by many brokers unless a bid or merger offer appears.'

3.2 The P/E ratio produce an **earnings-based** valuation of shares. This is done by deciding a suitable P/E ratio and multiplying this by the EPS for the shares which are being valued. The EPS could be a historical EPS or a prospective future EPS. For a given EPS figure, a higher P/E ratio will result in a higher price. **A high P/E ratio may indicate:**

(a) **Expectations** that the EPS will grow rapidly in the years to come, so that a **high price is being paid for future profit prospects.** Many small but successful and fast-growing companies are valued on the stock market on a high P/E ratio. Some stocks (for example those of some internet companies in the late 1990s) have reached high valuations before making any profits at all, on the strength of expected future earnings.

Case examples

By April 1999, the internet 'portal' company 'Yahoo!', with only very limited assets, commanded a higher stock market value than Boeing the aircraft manufacturer. Amazon.com, the online bookseller, was valued at $20 billion but had yet to make a profit. eBay, the internet auctioneer was valued at 2,000 times prospective earnings.

Press comment at the time suggested that private investors, many of them trading through the internet, were mainly responsible for the volatility in internet stocks. These were 'momentum investors' who seemed to care little about the economic fundamentals underlying a business. If enough people pile in to buy stocks whose prices seem to rise inexorably, the prices are driven even higher perhaps until the 'bubble' bursts, and investors panic and sell *en masse*, when the price drops again sharply.

This was indeed seen to happen in the latter half of 2000 when high tech stocks dropped on average by 25% in the space of 6 weeks and many weaker dot.com companies died a death.

(b) **Security of earnings.** A well-established low-risk company would be valued on a higher P/E ratio than a similar company whose earnings are subject to greater uncertainty;

(c) **Status.** If a quoted company (the predator) made a share-for-share takeover bid for an unquoted company (the target), it would normally expect its own shares to be valued on a higher P/E ratio than the target company's shares. This is because a quoted company ought to be a lower-risk company; but in addition, there is an advantage in having shares which are quoted on a stock market: the shares can be readily sold. **The P/E ratio of an unquoted company's shares might be around 50% to 60% of the P/E ratio of a similar public company with a full Stock Exchange listing** (and perhaps 70% of that of a company whose shares are traded on the AIM).

Case examples

Some sample P/E ratios taken from the Financial Times on 14 November 2000:

Market indices

FTSE 100	23.6
FTSE all-share	23.1
FTSE all-small	23.1
FTSE fledgling	54.9
FTSE AIM	negative

Industry sector averages (main market)

Chemicals	13.4
Construction	9.8
Food retailers	23.0 (Tesco 25, Somerfield 6.5)
General retailers	17.0 (M&S 16.5, Matalan 59.3)
Health	30.9
Telecommunications	77.3 (BT 24, Vodafone, 52)
IT - hardware	26.7
- software	80.0+

3.3 EXAMPLE: EARNINGS METHOD OF VALUATION

Spider plc is considering the takeover of an unquoted company, Fly Ltd. Spider's shares are quoted on the Stock Exchange at a price of £3.20 and since the most recent published EPS of the company is 20p, the company's P/E ratio is 16. Fly Ltd is a company with 100,000 shares and current earnings of £50,000, 50p per share. How might Spider plc decide on an offer price?

3.4 SOLUTION

The decision about the offer price is likely to be preceded by the estimation of a 'reasonable' P/E ratio in the light of the particular circumstances.

(a) If Fly Ltd is in the **same industry** as Spider plc, its P/E ratio ought to be lower, because of its lower status as an unquoted company.

(b) If Fly Ltd is in a **different industry**, a suitable P/E ratio might be based on the P/E ratio that is typical for quoted companies in that industry.

(c) If Fly Ltd is thought to be **growing fast**, so that its EPS will rise rapidly in the years to come, the P/E ratio that should be used for the share valuation will be higher than if only small EPS growth is expected.

(d) If the acquisition of Fly Ltd would **contribute substantially to Spider's own profitability and growth**, or to any other strategic objective that Spider has, then Spider should be willing to offer a higher P/E ratio valuation, in order to secure acceptance of the offer by Fly's shareholders.

Of course, the P/E ratio on which Spider bases its offer will probably be lower than the P/E ratio that Fly's shareholders think their shares ought to be valued on. Some haggling over the price might be necessary.

Spider might decide that Fly's shares ought to be valued on a P/E ratio of $60\% \times 16 = 9.6$, that is, at $9.6 \times 50p = £4.80$ each.

Fly's shareholders might reject this offer, and suggest a valuation based on a P/E ratio of, say, 12.5, that is, $12.5 \times 50p = £6.25$.

Spider's management might then come back with a revised offer, say valuation on a P/E ratio of 10.5, that is, $10.5 \times 50p = £5.25$.

The haggling will go on until the negotiations either break down or succeed in arriving at an agreed price.

General guidelines for a P/E ratio-based valuation

3.5 When a company is thinking of acquiring an **unquoted** company in a takeover, the final offer price will be agreed by **negotiation**, but a list of some of the factors affecting the valuer's choice of P/E ratio is given below.

(a) General **economic** and **financial** conditions.

(b) The type of **industry** and the prospects of that industry.

(c) The **size** of the undertaking and its **status** within its industry. If an unquoted company's earnings are growing annually and are currently around £300,000 or so, then it could probably get a quote in its own right on the Alternative Investment Market, and a higher P/E ratio should therefore be used when valuing its shares.

(d) **Marketability**. The market in shares which do not have a Stock Exchange quotation is always a restricted one and a higher yield is therefore required. Because of restrictions on transfer given in their Articles, any 'private' market in the shares of private companies is likely to be particularly small. It is not uncommon for a quoted company to have a P/E ratio twice the size of that attributed to a private company in the same industry.

(e) The **diversity** of shareholdings and the **financial status** of any principal shareholders.

(f) The **reliability** of profit estimates and the past profit record.

(g) **Asset backing** and **liquidity**.

(h) The **nature of the assets**, for example whether some of the fixed assets are of a highly specialised nature, and so have only a small break-up value.

(i) **Gearing**. A relatively high gearing ratio will generally mean greater financial risk for ordinary shareholders and call for a higher rate of return on equity.

(j) The extent to which the business is dependent on the **technical skills** of one or more individuals.

3.6 A predator company may sometimes use their higher P/E ratio to value a target company. This assumes that the predator **can improve the target's business**, which is a dangerous assumption to make. It would be better to use an adjusted industry P/E ratio, or some other method.

Forecast growth in earnings

3.7 When one company is thinking about taking over another, it should look at the target company's **forecast earnings,** not just its historical results. Forecasts of the future earnings of a target company might be attempted by managers in the predator company, or, quite commonly they will make an initial approach to the board of directors of the target company, to sound them out about a possible takeover bid. If the target company's directors are amenable to a bid, they **might agree to produce forecasts** of their company's future earnings and growth. These forecasts (for the next year and possibly even further ahead) might then be used by the predator company in choosing an offer price.

3.8 Forecasts of **earnings growth** should only be used if:

(a) There are good reasons to believe that earnings growth will be achieved
(b) A reasonable estimate of growth can be made
(c) Forecasts supplied by the target company's directors are made in good faith

Question 1

Flycatcher Ltd wishes to make a takeover bid for the shares of an unquoted company, Mayfly Ltd. The earnings of Mayfly Ltd over the past five years have been as follows.

20X0	£50,000	20X3	£71,000
20X1	£72,000	20X4	£75,000
20X2	£68,000		

The average P/E ratio of quoted companies in the industry in which Mayfly Ltd operates is 10. Quoted companies which are similar in many respects to Mayfly Ltd are:

(a) Bumblebee plc, which has a P/E ratio of 15, but is a company with very good growth prospects
(b) Wasp plc, which has had a poor profit record for several years, and has a P/E ratio of 7

What would be a suitable range of valuations for the shares of Mayfly Ltd?

Answer

(a) **Earnings**. Average earnings over the last five years have been £67,200, and over the last four years £71,500. There might appear to be some growth prospects, but estimates of future earnings are uncertain.

A low estimate of earnings in 20X5 would be, perhaps, £71,500.

A high estimate of earnings might be £75,000 or more. This solution will use the most recent earnings figure of £75,000 as the high estimate.

(b) **P/E ratio**. A P/E ratio of 15 (Bumblebee's) would be much too high for Mayfly Ltd, because the growth of Mayfly Ltd earnings is not as certain, and Mayfly Ltd is an unquoted company.

On the other hand, Mayfly Ltd's expectations of earnings are probably better than those of Wasp plc. A suitable P/E ratio might be based on the industry's average, 10; but since Mayfly is an unquoted company and therefore more risky, a lower P/E ratio might be more appropriate: perhaps 60% to 70% of 10 = 6 or 7, or conceivably even as low as 50% of 10 = 5.

The valuation of Mayfly Ltd's shares might therefore range between:

high P/E ratio and high earnings: 7 × £75,000 = £525,000; and

low P/E ratio and low earnings: 5 × £71,500 = £357,500.

The earnings yield valuation method

3.9 $$\text{Earnings yield (EY)} = \frac{\text{EPS}}{\text{Market price per share}} \times 100\%$$

This method is effectively a variation on the P/E method (the EY being the inverse of the P/E ratio), using an appropriate earnings yield effectively as a discount rate to value the earnings:

$$\text{Market value} = \frac{\text{Earnings}}{\text{EY}}$$

3.10 Exactly the same guidelines apply to this method as for the P/E method. Note that where **high growth** is envisaged, **the EY will be low,** as current earnings will be low relative to a market price that has built in future earnings growth.

The accounting rate of return (ARR) method of share valuation

3.11 This method considers the **accounting** rate of return which will be required from the company whose shares are to be valued. It is therefore distinct from the P/E ratio method, which is concerned with the **market** rate of return required.

The following formula should be used.
$$\text{Value} = \frac{\text{Estimated future profits}}{\text{Required return on capital employed}}$$

3.12 For a takeover bid valuation, it will often be necessary to adjust the profits figure to allow for **expected changes** after the takeover. Those arising in an examination question might include:

(a) New levels of directors' remuneration

(b) New levels of interest charges (perhaps because the predator company will be able to replace existing loans with new loans at a lower rate of interest, or because the previous owners had lent the company money at non-commercial rates)

(c) A charge for notional rent where it is intended to sell existing properties or where the rate of return used is based on the results of similar companies that do not own their own properties

(d) The effects of product rationalisation and improved management

Note that such adjustments can also apply to earnings used in a P/E valuation approach.

3.13 EXAMPLE: ARR METHOD OF SHARE VALUATION

Chambers Ltd is considering acquiring Hall Ltd. At present Hall Ltd is earning, on average, £480,000 after tax. The directors of Chambers Ltd feel that after reorganisation, this figure could be increased to £600,000. All the companies in the Chambers group are expected to yield a post-tax accounting return of 15% on capital employed. What should Hall Ltd be valued at?

3.14 SOLUTION

$$\text{Valuation} = \frac{£600,000}{15\%} = £4,000,000$$

This figure is the maximum that Chambers should be prepared to pay. The first offer would probably be much lower.

3.15 An ARR valuation might be used in a takeover when the acquiring company is trying to assess the **maximum amount it can afford to pay**.

4 CASH FLOW VALUATION METHODS

The dividend yield method of share valuation

4.1 The **dividend yield method** of share valuation is suitable for the valuation of **small shareholdings in unquoted companies**. It is based on the principle that small shareholders are mainly interested in **dividends**, since they cannot control decisions affecting the company's profits and earnings. A suitable offer price would therefore be one which compensates them for the future dividends they will be giving up if they sell their shares.

4.2 This approach is similar to that of the earnings yield methods – a 'suitable dividend yield is applied as a discount rate to the expected level of dividend:

$$\text{Dividend yield} = \frac{\text{Dividend per share}}{\text{Market price per share}} \times 100\% \text{ and thus}$$

$$\text{Market price} = \frac{\text{Dividend}}{\text{Dividend yield}}$$

4.3 This method has the same problems as those of the earning based methods – the determination of a **'suitable' dividend yield**, and the appropriate level of **sustainable dividend** to use. Again, note that the dividend yield will be lower the higher the level of growth envisaged in the market price.

Using the dividend valuation model

4.4 The dividend yield approach is in fact a crude approximation to the application of the **dividend valuation model** that you studied in Paper 4.

Knowledge brought forward from Paper 4 (IFIN)

- The **dividend valuation model assumes that** the value of a share will be the discounted present value of all **future expected dividends on the share, discounted at the shareholders' cost of capital.**

- When the company is expected to pay **constant dividends** every year into the future, 'in perpetuity' the following formula applies. k_e is the shareholders' cost of capital (the required rate of return).

EXAM FORMULA

Ordinary (equity) share, paying a constant annual dividend d in perpetuity, where P_0 is the ex-div value:

$$P_0 = \frac{d_1}{k_e}$$

- When the company is expected to pay a dividend which increases at a constant rate g, every year into the future, the following **dividend growth model** may be used.

EXAM FORMULA

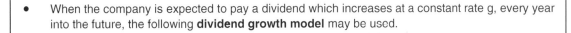

$$P_0 = \frac{d_1}{k_e - g} = \frac{d_0(1+g)}{k_e - g} \quad \left(\text{or } \frac{D_1}{r - g} \right)$$

where d_0 is the dividend in the current year (year 0) and so $d_0(1+g)$ is the expected future dividend in year 1 (d_1).

EXAM FORMULAE

Irredeemable preference share, paying a constant annual dividend, d, in perpetuity, where P_0 is the ex-div value:

$$P_0 = \frac{d}{\text{pref}}$$

and

Irredeemable (Undated) debt paying annual after tax interest, i(1–t), in perpetuity, where P_0 is the ex-interest value:

$$P_0 = \frac{i(1-t)}{k_{dnet}}$$

or without tax

$$P_0 = \frac{i}{k_d}$$

Exam focus point

These formulae are rearrangements of the cost of equity formula given to you in the exam.

4.5 Shares may be valued by the DVM using estimates of future growth rates and the required return by shareholders (possibly using the dividend yield of a similar company, with its expected growth adjusted out and taking account of differences in size, status etc).

Question 2

Target Ltd paid a dividend of £250,000 this year. The current return to shareholders of companies in the same industry as Target plc is 12%, although it is expected that an additional risk premium of 2% will be applicable to Target, being a smaller and unquoted company. Compute the expected valuation of Target Ltd, if:

(a) The current level of dividend is expected to continue into the foreseeable future, or
(b) The dividend is expected to grow at a rate of 4% pa into the foreseeable future

Answer

$k_e = 12\% + 2\% = 14\%\ (0.14)$ $\qquad d_0 = £250,000$ $\qquad\qquad$ g (in (b)) = 4% or 0.04

(a) $\quad P_0 = \dfrac{d_0}{k_e} = \dfrac{£250,000}{0.14} = £1,785,714$

(b) $\quad P_0 = \dfrac{d_0(1+g)}{k_e - g} = \dfrac{£250,000(1.04)}{0.14 - 0.04} = £2,600,000$

The discounted future cash flows method of share valuation

4.6 This method of share valuation may be appropriate when one company intends to buy the assets of another company and to make further investments in order to improve cash flows in the future.

4.7 We shall be looking at the discounted cash flow method (DCF) of investment appraisal later in the text; you should, however, be familiar with the basics from your earlier studies.

Knowledge brought forward from paper 4 (IFIN)

The net present value (NPV) method

- **Present value** (PV) can be defined as the cash equivalent now of a sum of money receivable or payable at a stated future date, discounted at a specified rate of return.

- **Net present value or NPV** is the value obtained by discounting all cash outflows and inflows of a capital investment project at a chosen target rate of return or cost of capital. The PV of cash inflows minus the PV of cash outflows is the NPV.

- **If the NPV is positive**, it means that the cash inflows from a capital investment will yield a return in excess of the cost of capital, and so the project should be undertaken if the cost of capital is the organisation's target rate of return.

- **If the NPV is negative**, it means that the cash inflows from a capital investment will yield a return below the cost of capital, and so the project should not be undertaken if the cost of capital is the organisation's target rate of return.

- The discount factor used in discounting is given by the following formula.

EXAM FORMULA

Present value of £1 payable or receivable in n years, discounted at r% per annum:

$$PV = \frac{1}{(1+r)^n}$$

- Discount tables for the present value of £1, for different values of r and t, are shown in the Appendix to this Study Text.

- Other relevant exam formulae:

EXAM FORMULAE

Future value of S, of a sum X, invested for n periods, compounded at r% interest:

$$S = X[1 + r]^n$$

Present value of an annuity of £1 per annum, receivable or payable for n years, commencing in one year, discounted at r% per annum:

$$PV = \frac{1}{r}\left[1 - \frac{1}{(1+r)^n}\right]$$

Present value of £1 per annum, payable or receivable in perpetuity, commencing in one year, discounted at r% per annum:

$$PV = \frac{1}{r}$$

Present value of £1 per annum, receivable or payable, commencing in one year, growing in perpetuity at a constant rate of g% per annum, discounted at r% per annum:

$$PV = \frac{1}{r - g}$$

4.8 EXAMPLE: DISCOUNTED FUTURE CASH FLOWS METHOD OF SHARE VALUATION

Diversification Ltd wishes to make a bid for Tadpole Ltd. Tadpole Ltd makes after-tax profits of £40,000 a year. Diversification Ltd believes that if further money is spent on additional investments, the after-tax cash flows (ignoring the purchase consideration) could be as follows.

Year	Cash flow (net of tax)
	£
0	(100,000)
1	(80,000)
2	60,000
3	100,000
4	150,000
5	150,000

The after-tax cost of capital of Diversification Ltd is 15% and the company expects all its investments to pay back, in discounted terms, within five years. What is the maximum price that the company should be willing to pay for the shares of Tadpole Ltd?

4.9 SOLUTION

The maximum price is one which would make the return from the total investment exactly 15% over five years, so that the NPV at 15% would be 0.

Year	Cash flows ignoring purchase consideration £	Discount factor (from tables) 15%	Present value £
0	(100,000)	1.000	(100,000)
1	(80,000)	0.870	(69,600)
2	60,000	0.756	45,360
3	100,000	0.658	65,800
4	150,000	0.572	85,800
5	150,000	0.497	74,550
Maximum purchase price			101,910

Selection of an appropriate cost of capital

4.10 In the above example, Diversification used its own cost of capital to discount the cash flows of Tadpole Ltd. There are a number of reasons why this may not be appropriate.

4.11 We shall be looking at the use of a current weighted average cost of capital (WACC) to appraise new investment in more detail later in the text; the main points to be made here are:

(a) The **business risk** of the new investment may not match that of the investing company. If Tadpole is in a completely different line of business from Diversification, its cash flows are likely to be subject to differing degrees of risk, and this should be taken into account when valuing them.

(b) The **method of finance** of the new investment may not match the current debt/equity mix of the investing company, which may have an effect on the cost of capital to be used.

Shareholder value analysis – free cash flows

4.12 In Chapter 1 we discussed Rappaport's concept of shareholder value analysis (SVA). This uses the basic concept of discounting company cash flows, under simplifying assumptions about the relationship between the various cash flow elements.

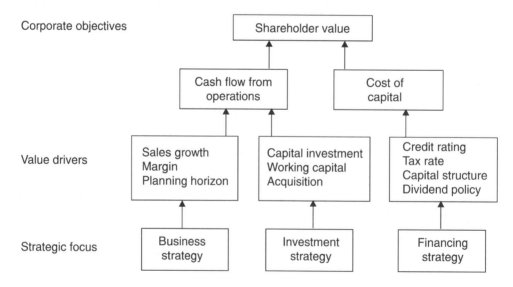

4.13 **Value drivers** are identified as being fundamental to the determination of value.

- Sales growth rate
- Operating profit margin
- Tax rate
- Fixed capital investment

- Working capital investment
- The planning horizon
- The required rate of return

4.14 **The model assumes** a constant percentage rate of sales growth and a constant operating profit margin. Tax is assumed to be a constant percentage of operating profit. Finally, fixed and working capital investments are assumed to be a constant percentage of changes in sales.

4.15 Using the free cash flows, **corporate value** is then computed using the company's WACC as a discount rate.

> **Corporate value = PV of free cash flows + current value of marketable securities and other non-operating investments**

Shareholder value can then be computed as **corporate value – debt.**

4.16 This approach is relatively simple to apply, is consistent with the concept of share valuation by DCF and creates management awareness of the key value variables (drivers). However, its drawbacks include:

(a) The constant percentage assumptions may be unrealistic

(b) The input data may not be easily available from current systems

(c) May be misused in target setting – giving managers a 12-month target cash flow may discourage longer term profitable investment

Economic value added

4.17 Economic value added (EVA) is closely associated with SVA and gives the economic value or profit added per year. It is not a means of valuing companies.

4.18 **EVA = NOPAT – (k × Net assets)**

where NOPAT = Net operating profit after tax
k = Cost of capital
Net assets = Book value of assets adjusted for depreciation distortions

Market value added

4.19 Market value added (MVA) is the difference between the **market value** and the **book value** of a **firm's capital.**

4.20 The MVA figure tends to correspond closely to the difference between the market value of equity and the book value of equity.

4.21 It is possible to have a positive MVA and a negative EVA, or a negative MVA and a positive EVA.

5 OTHER VALUATION BASES

The super-profits method of share valuation

5.1 This method, which is rather out of fashion at present, starts by applying a 'fair return' to the net tangible assets and comparing the result with the expected profits. Any excess of profits **(the super-profits)** is used to calculate goodwill. The goodwill is normally taken as a fixed number of years super-profits. The goodwill is then added to the value of the target company's tangible assets to arrive at a value for the business.

5.2 EXAMPLE: SUPER-PROFITS METHOD OF SHARE VALUATION

Light Ltd has net tangible assets of £120,000 and present earnings of £20,000. Doppler Ltd wants to take over Light Ltd and considers that a fair return for this type of industry is 12%, and decides to value Light Ltd taking goodwill at three years super-profits.

	£
Actual profits	20,000
Less fair return on net tangible assets: 12% × £120,000	14,400
Super-profits	5,600
Goodwill: 3 × £5,600	£16,800
Value of Light Ltd: £120,000 + £16,800	£136,800

5.3 The principal drawbacks to this valuation method are as follows.

(a) The rate of return required is chosen subjectively.

(b) The number of years purchase of super-profits is arbitrary. In the example above, goodwill was valued at three years of super-profits, but it could have been, for example, two years or four years of super-profits.

Earn-out arrangements

5.4 Earn-out arrangements were discussed in Chapter 3, whereby the buyer of a business agrees to pay the seller an additional amount of consideration if the acquired company achieves a certain level of performance.

5.5 For example, the consideration may be structured as follows.

(a) An initial amount payable at the time of acquisition

(b) A guaranteed minimum amount of deferred consideration, payable in, say, three years time

(c) An additional amount of deferred consideration, payable if a specified target performance is achieved over the next three years.

5.6 The total of the initial and guaranteed deferred consideration amounts may be based upon an assets based approach to valuation, or on an earnings basis, using, for example, the average level of expected profits over a given future period.

5.7 The additional amount of deferred consideration might be payable if the acquired company's average profits or revenues over the next three years exceeds a certain amount. Often, the amount payable would be specified as percentages of gross revenues or sales, because expenses can be more easily manipulated. For example, for a two year period, the seller might be paid 2% of gross sales over £2 million, and 3% of gross sales over £4 million.

5.8 This method would only be appropriate if the acquired company was to be run independently of the buyer's company, at least for the period upon which the contingent consideration is based. If the acquired business were to be immediately integrated within the buyer's, it would be difficult to identify separately the relevant sales or profits. In addition, the buying company's management would have influenced the performance, and they may end up paying for their own expertise.

5.9 Under these types of arrangement, then, the overall valuation of the business will have a variable element. The buyer will need to estimate the minimum, maximum and expected total amounts they may have to pay, with corresponding probabilities relating to the likelihood of the business reaching the specified targets. In particular, they will have to ensure that they could, if necessary, afford to pay the maximum amount, regardless of how unlikely that is to arise.

5.10 EXAMPLE: EARN-OUT ARRANGEMENT

Tripod plc is negotiating to buy Stratford Ltd, and has made a bid of £4 million, based upon an earnings-based valuation method. The directors of Tripod Ltd have rejected this offer, as they believe their business, which has only been established for five years, has greater earning potential than envisaged in this figure.

Tripod is therefore considering an earn-out arrangement, as follows.

If the average annual sales revenue of Stratford Ltd over the next three years exceeds £5 million, additional consideration will be payable at the end of that period, at the following rates:

10% of excess average profits of £5 million, up to £6 million
12% of excess average profits over £6 million, up to £8 million
15% of excess average profits over £8 million, up to a maximum of £12 million

It is estimated that the probabilities associated with these performance levels are 0.3, 0.15 and 0.05 respectively.

Compute the minimum, expected and maximum amounts of additional consideration Tripod will have to pay.

5.11 SOLUTION

Minimum amount = **0** (with probability $1 - (0.3 + 0.15 + 0.05) = $ **0.5**)
Maximum amount = $15\% \times £12$ million = **£1.8 million** (with probability **0.05**)

Expected amount, using mid values of ranges:

$0.3 \times 10\% \times £5.5$ million $+ 0.15 \times 12\% \times £7$ million $+ 0.05 \times 15\% \times £10$ million = **£366,000.**

Question 3

Profed Ltd provides a tuition service to professional students. This includes courses of lectures provided on their own premises and provision of study material for home study. Most of the lecturers are qualified professionals with many years' experience in both their profession and tuition. Study materials are written and word processed in-house, but sent out to an external printers.

The business was started fifteen years ago, and now employs around 40 full-time lecturers, 10 authors and 20 support staff. Freelance lecturers and authors are employed from time to time in times of peak demand.

The shareholders of Profed Ltd mainly comprise the original founders of the business who would now like to realise their investment. In order to arrive at an estimate of what they believe the business is worth, they have identified a long-established quoted company, City Tutors plc, who have a similar business, although they also publish texts for external sale to universities, colleges etc.

Summary financial statistics for the two companies for the most recent financial year are as follows.

	Profed Ltd	City Tutors Ltd
Issued shares (million)	4	10
Net asset values (£m)	7.2	15
Earnings per share (pence)	35	20
Dividend per share (pence)	20	18
Debt: equity ratio	1:7	1:65
Share price (pence)		362
Expected rate of growth in earnings/dividends	9% pa	7.5%

Notes

1   The net assets of Profed Ltd are the net book values of tangible fixed assets plus net working capital. However:

- A recent valuation of the buildings was £1.5m above book value.

- Stock includes past editions of text books which have a realisable value of £100,000 below their cost.

- Due to a dispute with one of their clients, an additional allowance for bad debts of £750,000 could prudently be made.

2   Growth rates should be assumed to be constant per annum; Profed's earnings growth rate estimate was provided by the marketing manager, based on expected growth in sales adjusted by normal profit margins. City Tutors' growth rates were gleaned from press reports.

3   Profed uses a discount rate of 15% to appraise its investments, and has done for many years.

You are required to:

(a)   Compute a range of valuations for the business of Profed Ltd, using the information available and stating any assumptions made.

(b)   Comment upon the strengths and weaknesses of the methods you used in (a) and their suitability for valuing Profed Ltd.

Answer

(a)   The information provided allows us to value Profed on three bases: net assets, P/E ratio and dividend valuation

All three will be computed, even though their validity may be questioned in part (b) of the answer.

Assets based

	£'000
Net assets at book value	7,200
Add: increased valuation of buildings	1,500
Less: decreased value of stocks and debtors	(850)
Net asset value of equity	7,850
Value per share	£1.96

P/E ratio

	Profed Ltd	City Tutors Ltd
Issued shares (million)	4	10
Share price (pence)		362
Market value (£m)		36.2
Earnings per shares (pence)	35	20
P/E ratio (share price ÷ EPS)		18.1

The P/E for a similar quoted company is 18.1. This will take account of factors such as marketability of shares, status of company, growth potential that will differ from those for Profed. Profed's growth rate has been estimated as higher than that of City Tutors, possibly because it is a younger, developing company, although the basis for the estimate may be questionable.

All other things being equal, the P/E ratio for an unquoted company should be taken as between one half to two thirds of that of an equivalent quoted company. Being generous, in view of the possible higher growth prospects of Profed, we might estimate an appropriate P/E ratio of around 12, assuming Profed is to remain a private company.

This will value Profed at 12 × £0.35 = £4.20 per share, a total valuation of £16.8m.

Dividend valuation model

The dividend valuation method gives the share price as

$$\frac{\text{Next year's dividend}}{\text{Cost of equity - growth rate}}$$

which assumes dividends being paid into perpetuity, and growth at a constant rate.

For Profed, next year's dividend = £0.20 × 1.09 = £0.218 per share

Whilst we are given a discount rate of 15% as being traditionally used by the directors of Profed for investment appraisal, there appears to be no rational basis for this. We can instead use the information for City Courses to estimate a cost of equity for Profed. This is assuming the business risks to be similar, and ignoring the small difference in their gearing ratio.

Again, from the DVM, cost of equity $= \dfrac{\text{next year's dividend}}{\text{market price}} + \text{growth rate}$

For City Tutors Ltd, cost of equity $= \dfrac{£0.18 \times 1.075}{£3.62} + 0.075 = 12.84\%$

Using, say, 13% as a cost of equity for Profed:

Share price $= \dfrac{£0.218}{0.13 - 0.09} = £5.45$

valuing the whole of the share capital at £21.8 million

Range for valuation

The three methods used have thus come up with a range of value of Profed Ltd as follows.

	Value per share £	Total valuation £m
Net assets	1.96	7.9
P/E ratio	4.20	16.8
Dividend valuation	5.45	21.8

(b) **Comment on relative merits of the methods used, and their suitability**

Asset based valuation

Valuing a company on the basis of its asset values alone is rarely appropriate if it is to be sold on a going concern basis. Exceptions would include property investment companies and investment trusts, the market values of the assets of which will bear a close relationship to their earning capacities.

Profed Ltd is typical of a lot of service companies, a large part of whose value lies in the skill, knowledge and reputation of its personnel. This is not reflected in the net asset values, and renders this method quite inappropriate. A potential purchaser of Profed Ltd will generally value its intangible assets such as knowledge, expertise, customer/supplier relationships, brands etc more highly than those that can be measured in accounting terms.

Knowledge of the net asset value (NAV) of a company will, however, be important as a floor value for a company in financial difficulties or subject to a takeover bid. Shareholders will be reluctant to sell for less than the net asset value even if future prospects are poor. (See Chapter 9 for further discussion of this point.)

P/E ratio valuation

The P/E ratio measures the multiple of the current year's earnings that is reflected in the market price of a share. It is thus a method that reflects the earnings potential of a company from a market point of view. Provided the marketing is efficient, it is likely to give the most meaningful basis for valuation.

One of the first things to say is that the market price of a share at any point in time is determined by supply and demand forces prevalent during small transactions, and will be dependent upon a lot of factors in addition to a realistic appraisal of future prospects. A downturn in the market, economies and political changes can all affect the day-to-day price of a share, and thus its prevailing P/E ratio. it is not known whether the share price given for City Tutors was taken on one particular day, or was some sort of average over a period. The latter would perhaps give a sounder basis from which to compute an applicable P/E ratio.

Even if the P/E ratio of City Tutors can be taken to be indicative of its true worth, using it as a basis to value a smaller, unquoted company in the same industry can be problematic.

The status and marketability of shares in a quoted company have tangible effects on value but these are difficult to measures.

The P/E ratio will also be affected by growth prospects – the higher the growth expected, the higher the ratio. The growth rate incorporated by the shareholders of City Tutors is probably based on a more rational approach than that used by Profed Ltd.

If the growth prospects of Profed, as would be perceived by the market, did not coincide with those of Profed management it is difficult to see how the P/E ratio should be adjusted for relative levels of growth.

In the valuation in (a) a crude adjustment has been made to City Tutors' P/E ratio to arrive at a ratio to use to value Profed's earnings. This can result in a very inaccurate result if account has not been taken of all the differences involved.

Dividend based valuation

The dividend valuation model (DVM) is a cash flow based approach, which valued the dividends that the shareholders expect to receive from the company by discounting them at their required rate of return. It is perhaps more appropriate for valuing a minority shareholding where the holder has no influence over the level of dividends to be paid than for valuing a whole company, where the total cash flows will be of greater relevance.

The practical problems with the dividend valuation model lie mainly in its assumptions. Even accepting that the required 'perfect capital market' assumptions may be satisfied to some extent, in reality, the formula used in (a) assumes constant growth rates and constant required rates of return in perpetuity.

Determination of an appropriate cost of equity is particularly difficult for a unquoted company, and the use of an 'equivalent' quoted company's data carries the same drawbacks as discussed above. Similar problems arise in estimating future growth rates, and the results from the model are highly sensitive to changes in both these inputs.

It is also highly dependent upon the current year's dividend being a representative base from which to start.

The dividend valuation model valuation provided in (a) results in a higher valuation than that under the P/E ratio approach. Reasons for this may be:

- The share price for City Courses may be currently depressed below its normal level, resulting in an inappropriately low P/E ratio.

- The adjustment to get to an appropriate P/E ratio for Profed may have been too harsh, particularly in light of its apparently better growth prospects.

- The cost of equity used in the dividend valuation model was that of City Courses. The validity of this will largely depend upon the relative levels of risk of the two companies. Although they both operate the same type of business, the fact that City Courses sells its material externally means it is perhaps less reliant on a fixed customer base.

- Even if business risks and gearing risk may be thought to be comparable a prospective buyer of Profed may consider investment in a younger, unquoted company to carry greater personal risk. His required return may thus be higher than that envisaged in the dividend valuation model, reducing the valuation.

---

6 INTANGIBLE ASSETS AND INTELLECTUAL CAPITAL

6.1 The asset based valuation method discussed earlier specifically excluded most intangible assets from the computation. This rendered this method unsuitable for the valuation of most established businesses, particularly those in the service industry. Here we consider the various types of intangible assets that a business may benefit from and how they might be valued.

> **KEY TERMS**
>
> **Intangible assets** are non-financial fixed assets that do not have physical substance but are identifiable and are controlled by the entity through custody or legal rights.
>
> *(FRS 10)*
>
> **Goodwill** (purchased) is the difference between the cost of an acquired entity and the aggregate of the fair value of that entity's identifiable assets and liabilities. *(FRS 10)*

6.2 The above definition of intangible assets, as given in FRS 10, *Goodwill and intangible assets,* distinguishes:

(a) Intangible assets from tangible assets, by the phrase 'do not have physical substance'.

(b) Intangible assets from goodwill, by the work 'identifiable', an identifiable asset is legally defined as one that can be disposed of separately without disposing of a business of the entity. Goodwill does not meet this separability criterion, although brands and publishing titles **are** included as intangible assets by FRS 10.

6.3 The strict accounting distinctions do not need to concern us here. We are interested in any element of business that may have some value. In fact we need to extend our scope of consideration beyond that of FRS 10 by including the additional elements coming under the heading of **intellectual capital.**

> **KEY TERM**
>
> **Intellectual capital** is knowledge which can be used to create value. Intellectual capital includes:
>
> (a) **Human resources**: the collective skills, experience and knowledge of employees
>
> (b) **Intellectual assets**: knowledge which is defined and codified such as a drawing computer program or collection of data
>
> (c) **Intellectual property**: intellectual assets which can be legally protected, such as patents and copyrights
> *(OT 2000)*

6.4 Whilst some of the examples included in the definition of intellectual capital are also included under FRS 10's definition of intangible assets, such as patents and copyrights, FRS 10 specifically **excludes** a company's workforce and clients as being beyond the company's control.

6.5 However, as the demand for knowledge-based products grows with the changing structure of the global economy, knowledge plays an expanding role in achieving competitive advantage. Employees may thus be extremely valuable to a business, and they should be included in a full assets based valuation.

6.6 The principles of valuation discussed below should be taken as applying to all assets, resources or property that are defined as intangible assets or intellectual capital, which will include:

- Patents, trademarks and copyrights
- Franchises and licensing agreements
- Research and development
- Brands
- Technology, management and consulting processes
- Know-how, education, vocational qualification
- Customer loyalty
- Distribution channels
- Management philosophy

Valuation of intangible assets

6.7 Two types of valuation may be distinguished:

- Valuation of the total intangible assets of an enterprise
- Valuation of individual intangible assets

Measurement of intangible assets of an enterprise

6.8 The expanding intellectual capital of firms accentuates the need for methods of valuation for comparative purposes, for example when an acquisition or buy-out is being considered.

6.9 Ramona Dzinkowski (*The measurement and management of intellectual capital*, Management Accounting) identifies the following three indicators, which are derived from audited financial statements and are independent of the definitions of intellectual capital adopted by the firm.

- **Market-to-book values**
- **Tobin's 'q'**
- **Calculated intangible value**

Market-to-book values

6.10 This method represents the value of a firm's intellectual capital as **the difference between the book value of tangible assets and the market value of the firm**. Thus, if a company's market value is £8 million and its book value is £5 million, the £3 million difference is taken to represent the value of the firm's intangible (or intellectual) assets.

6.11 Although obviously **simple**, this method's simplicity merely serves to indicate that it fails to take account of **real world complexities.** There may be imperfections in the market valuation, and book values are subject to accounting standards which reflect historic cost and amortisation policies rather than true market values of tangible fixed assets.

6.12 In addition, the accounting valuation does not attempt to value a company as a whole, but rather as a sum of separate asset values computed under particular accounting conventions. The market, in the other hand, values the entire company as a going concern, following its defined strategy.

Tobin's 'q'

6.13 The Nobel prize-winning economist James Tobin developed the 'q' method initially as a way of predicting investment behaviour.

6.14 'q' is the ratio of the **market capitalisation of the firm** (share price × number of shares) to the **replacement cost** of its assets.

6.15 If the replacement cost of assets is **lower** than the market capitalisation, **q is greater than unity** and the company is enjoying higher than average returns on its investment ('monopoly rents'). Technology and so called 'human-capital' assets are likely to lead to high q values.

6.16 Tobin's 'q' is affected by the same variables influencing market capitalisation as the market-to-book method. In common with that method, it is used most appropriately to make comparisons of the value of intangible assets of companies within an industry which serve the same markets and have similar tangible fixed assets. As such, these methods could serve as performance benchmarks by which to appraise management or corporate strategy.

Calculated intangible values

6.17 NCI Research has developed the method of **calculated intangible value (CIV)** for calculating the fair market value of a firm's intangible assets.

6.18 CIV calculates an 'excess return' on tangible assets. This figure is then used in determining the proportion of return attributable to intangible assets.

Case example: CIV

Stewart (Intellectual Capital: The New Wealth of Nations, 1997) uses Merck & Co to illustrate the CIV method.

- Merck's pre-tax earnings averaged $3.694 billion over 3 years.

- Average tangible assets per balance sheet over this period: $12.953 billion.

  $\Rightarrow$ Return on assets = 3.694 / 12.953 per cent = 29%

- Merck & Co is in the pharmaceutical industry. Suppose that this industry's average return on total assets is 10% (this must be less than the company's ROA for this method to work).

  $\Rightarrow$ $12.953bn $\times$ 10% = $1.2953bn, which represents the **average return** a pharmaceutical company would earn from Merck's amount of tangible assets.

  $\Rightarrow$ Subtracting this from Merck & Co's pretax earnings:

  $3.694 – $1.2953 = $2.4 billion, which represents, the **excess return** for Merck & Co.

- With tax at 31% for Merck & Co:

  $\Rightarrow$ After tax excess return = $2.4bn $\times$ 0.69 = $1.66bn

- If the industry's average cost of capital is 15%, the **net present value** of this premium in perpetuity is:

  $1.66 bn/0.15 = $11 billion - the calculated intangible value (CIV) for Merck & Co.

6.19 Whilst this seemingly straightforward approach, using readily available information, seems attractive, it does have two problems.

(a) It uses average industry ROA as a basis for computing excess returns, which may be distorted by extreme values.

(b) The choice of discount rate to apply to the excess returns to value the intangible asset needs to be made with care. To ensure comparability between companies and industries, some sort of average cost of capital should perhaps be applied. This again has the potential problems of distortion.

Valuation of individual intangible assets

6.20 Methods of valuing individual intangible assets include the following.

- **Relief from royalties method**
- **Premium profits method**
- **Capitalisation of earnings method**
- **Comparison with market transactions method**

Relief from royalties method

6.21 This method involves trying to determine:

(a) The value obtainable from licensing out the right to exploit the intangible asset to a third party, or

(b) The royalties that the owner of the intangible asset is relieved from paying through being the owner rather than the licensee

6.22 A **notional royalty rate** is estimated as a percentage of revenue expected to be generated by the intangible asset. The estimated royalty stream can then be **capitalised**, for example by discounting at a risk-free market rate, to find an estimated market value.

6.23 This relatively simple valuation method is easiest to apply if the intangible asset is already subject to licensing agreements. If they are not, the valuer might reach an appropriate figure from other comparable licensing arrangements.

Premium profits method

6.24 The premium profits method is often used for **brands**. It bases the valuation on capitalisation of the **extra profits generated** by the brand or other intangible asset in excess of profits made by businesses lacking the intangible asset or brand.

6.25 The premium profits specifically attributable to the brand or other intangible asset may be estimated (for example) by comparing the price of branded products and unbranded products. The estimated premium profits can then be capitalised by discounting at a risk-adjusted market rate.

6.26 Factors that may need to be taken into account in valuing brands will include:

(a) **The market sector**. Brand values will be higher for high sales/margins sectors, and in expanding markets.

(b) **Durability**. Brand names that have established customer loyalty over many years will support a higher valuation than those that may have shorter-term appeal.

(c) **Overseas markets**. the presence of a brand name in overseas markets will enhance its value.

(d) **Market position**. Market leader brand names will have greater value.

(e) **Advertising support**. Increased advertising expenditure could either indicate a weakening brand, or may significantly enhance sales, thus increasing its value.

(f) **Competition**. Increasing availability and/or awareness of substitutes for the branded products may detract from its value.

Capitalisation of earnings method

6.27 With the capitalised earnings method, the **maintainable earnings accruing to the intangible asset** are estimated. An **earnings multiple** is then applied to the earnings, taking account of expected risks and rewards, including the prospects for future earnings growth and the risks involved. This method of valuation is often used to value **publishing titles**.

Comparison with market transactions method

6.28 This method looks at **actual market transactions** in similar intangible assets. A multiple of turnover or earnings from the intangible asset might then be derived from a similar market transaction. A problem with this method is that many **intangible assets are unique** and it may therefore be difficult to identify 'similar' market transactions, although this might be done by examining acquisitions and disposals of businesses that include similar intangible assets.

6.29 The method might be used alongside other valuation methods, to provide a comparison.

Chapter roundup

- There are a number of different ways of **putting a value on a business**, or on shares in an unquoted company. It makes sense to use **several methods** of valuation, and to compare the values they produce. At the end of the day, however, what really matters is the final price that the buyer and the seller agree. The purchase price for a company will usually be discussed mainly in terms of:

  ° P/E ratios, when a large block of shares, or a whole business is being valued
  ° Alternatively, a cash flow DCF valuation
  ° To a lesser extent, the net assets per share

- **Dividend valuation methods** are more relevant to small shareholdings.

- The valuation of **intangible assets** and **intellectual capital** presents special problems.

Quick quiz

1 Give four circumstances in which the shares of an unquoted company might need to be valued.

2 How is the P/E ratio related to EPS?

3 What is meant by 'multiples' in the context of share valuation?

4 Value = Estimated future profits/Required return on capital employed. What is the name of this valuation model?

5 Suggest two circumstances in which net assets might be used as a basis for valuation of a company.

6 Give six examples of types of intangible assets.

7 Identify three methods of valuing the intellectual capital of a business.

Answers to quick quiz

1 • Setting an issue price if the company is floating its shares
  • When shares are sold
  • For tax purposes
  • When shares are pledged as collateral for a loan

2 P/E ratio = Share price/EPS.

3 The P/E ratio: the multiple of earnings at which a company's shares are traded.

4 Accounting rate of return method.

5 (a) As a measure of asset backing.
  (b) For comparison, in a scheme of merger.

6 Patents; trade marks; brands; copyrights; franchises; research and development.

7 Market-to-book values; Tobin's q; calculated intangible value.

Now try the question below from the Exam Question Bank

Number	Level	Marks	Time
6	Examination	25	45 mins

Chapter 7

SHARE VALUATION: MARKET EFFICIENCY

Topic list	Syllabus reference	Ability required
1 Share price behaviour	(ii)	Application
2 The efficient markets hypothesis	(ii)	Application

Introduction

In the last chapter we looked at methods of valuing businesses and individual shareholdings. Many of those techniques involved the use of market statistics, such as P/E ratios and dividend yields that were based upon **current market prices** of quoted shares. In this chapter we look at the **efficiency of the market** in incorporating various levels of information into those values, and how this can affect business valuations.

Learning outcomes covered in this chapter

- Calculate values of organisations of different types, eg service, capital intensive

Syllabus content covered in this chapter

- Application of the efficient market hypothesis (EMH) to business valuations
- Application of valuation bases to new issues

1   SHARE PRICE BEHAVIOUR

Investing in shares

1.1   Investors will buy shares to obtain an income from dividends and/or to make a capital gain from an increase in share prices. The market price of a security will depend on the return that investors expect to get from it.

1.2   The return from an **ordinary share** consists of dividends plus any capital gain.

    (a)   **Dividends.** In the UK these carry a tax credit equal to the lower rate of income tax 10% (in the tax year 2000/2001).

    (b)   The **capital gain (or loss)** is the difference between the price at which the investor bought the share, and the share's current market value. Capital gains are not taxable until the shareholder sells his or her shares, and realises the capital gain.

1.3   If the purpose of investing is **to earn dividend income,** an investor will try to buy shares which are expected to provide a **satisfactory dividend in relation to their market value.** The movement in share prices, which occurs from day to day on the stock market, means that an investor can improve his return by **buying at the right time.**

For example, if the share price is £1.50 on day 1, rising to £1.55 on day 2, falling to £1.48 on day 3 and rising to £1.50 on day 4, the investor will obtain the best return if he buys shares on day 3. However, if he predicts that the share price will fall even lower than £1.48 in one or two weeks time, he will prefer to wait until then before buying.

1.4 Similarly, the prediction of share price movements may help an investor to **maximise his capital gain** from buying and selling shares. Shares should be bought when prices are at their lowest and sold when they are at their highest. Since stockbrokers and investment advisers give advice to clients about when to buy and sell shares, they need a method of foretelling which way share prices will move, up or down, and when. It is therefore useful to consider the extent to which share prices and share price movements can be predicted.

The fundamental analysis theory of share values

KEY TERM

Fundamental analysis is the analysis of external and internal influences upon the operations of a company with a view to assisting in investment decisions. Information accessed might include fiscal/monetary policy, financial statements, industry trends, competitor analysis etc. *(OT 2000)*

1.5 The fundamental analysis theory of share values is based on the theory that the market price of a share can be predicted from **estimated future dividends** and knowledge of the **shareholders' required rate of return**.

1.6 These would then be used in the familiar dividend valuation model, which states that the market value of a share will be the present value of the future expected dividends, discounted at the shareholders' required rate of return.

1.7 If the fundamental analysis theory of share values is correct, the price of any share will be predictable, provided that all investors have the same information about a company's expected future profits and dividends, and a known cost of capital. So is it correct? Are share prices predictable? And if not, why not?

1.8 In general terms, fundamental analysis seems to be valid. This means that if an investment analyst can foresee before anyone else that:

(a) A company's future profits and dividends are going to be different from those currently expected, or

(b) Shareholders' cost of capital will rise or fall (for example in response to interest rate changes)

then the analyst will be able to predict a future share price movement, and so recommend clients to buy or sell the share before the price change occurs.

1.9 In practice however, share price movements are affected by day to day fluctuations, reflecting such factors as:

- Supply and demand in a particular period
- Investor confidence
- Market interest rate movements

1.10 Investment analysts want to be able to predict these fluctuations in prices, but fundamental analysis might be inadequate as a technique. Some analysts, known as **chartists**, therefore rely on technical analysis of share price movements.

Charting or technical analysis

1.11 **Chartists** or 'technical analysts' attempt to predict share price movements by assuming that **past price patterns will be repeated**. There is no real theoretical justification for this approach, but it can at times be spectacularly successful. Studies have suggested that the degree of success is greater than could be expected merely from chance. Nevertheless not even the most extreme chartist would claim that every major price movement can be predicted accurately and sufficiently early to make correct investment decisions.

> ### KEY TERM
>
> **Technical analysis** is the analysis of past movements in the prices of financial instruments, currencies, commodities etc, with a view to, by applying analytical techniques, predict future price movements. *(OT 2000)*

1.12 Chartists do not attempt to predict every price change. They are primarily interested in trend reversals, for example when the price of a share has been rising for several months but suddenly starts to fall.

1.13 A chartist will thus draw up charts of share price movements over time, and attempt to **identify particular features and patterns** in the charts, in advance of the market, that would be a **signal** to advise his clients to 'buy' or 'sell'. One of the main problems with this is that it is **often difficult to see a new trend until after it has happened**. By the time the chartist has detected a signal, other chartists will have as well, and the resulting masse movement to buy or sell will push the price so as to eliminate any advantage.

1.14 With the use of sophisticated computer programs to simulate the work of a chartist, academic studies have found that the **results obtained were no better or worse** than those obtained from a simple 'buy and hold' strategy of a **well diversified portfolio of shares.**

1.15 This may be explained by research that has found that there are no regular patterns or cycles in share price movements over time – they follow a **random walk.**

Random walk theory

1.16 Random walk theory is consistent with the fundamental theory of share values. It accepts that a share should have an **intrinsic (fundamental) price** dependent on the fortunes of the company and the expectations of investors. One of its underlying assumptions is that all relevant information about a company is available to all potential investors who will act upon the information in a rational manner. Thus the intrinsic **value will be altered as new information becomes available,** and that the behaviour of investors is such that the actual share price will fluctuate from day to day around the intrinsic value.

1.17 Random walk theory emerged in the late 1950s as an attempt to disprove chartist theory. H V Roberts challenged the idea that share price movements were systematic, and showed how sequences of random numbers can exhibit the same pattern as actual recorded changes of share prices on the Stock Exchange. Roberts was able to duplicate the chartists patterns of share price movements with random numbers, and he concluded that such 'patterns' are illusory and of no value for predicting share prices.

Random walks and an efficient stock market

1.18 Research was carried out in the late 1960s to explain why share prices in the stock market display a random walk phenomenon. This research led to the development of **the efficient market hypothesis**. It can be shown that random movements in share prices will occur if the stock market operates 'efficiently' and makes information about companies, earnings, dividends and so on, freely (or cheaply) available to all customers in the market. In displaying efficiency, the stock market also lends support to the fundamental analysis theory of share prices.

2 THE EFFICIENT MARKETS HYPOTHESIS

2.1 It has been argued that the UK and US stock markets are **efficient** capital markets, that is, markets in which:

(a) The prices of securities bought and sold reflect all the relevant information which is available to the buyers and sellers: in other words, share prices change quickly to reflect all new information about future prospects (specifically, this is **informational processing efficiency**)

(b) No individual dominates the market

(c) Transaction costs of buying and selling **are not so high as to discourage trading** significantly (**operational efficiency**)

2.2 If the stock market is efficient, share prices should vary in a rational way.

(a) If a company makes an investment with a positive net present value (NPV), shareholders will get to know about it and the market price of its shares will rise in anticipation of future dividend increases.

(b) If a company makes a bad investment shareholders will find out and so the price of its shares will fall.

(c) If interest rates rise, shareholders will want a higher return from their investments, so market prices will fall.

> **KEY TERM**
>
> **Efficient market hypothesis** is the hypothesis that the stock market responds immediately to all available information, with the effect that an individual investor cannot, in the long run, expect to obtain greater than average returns from a diversified portfolio of shares. *(OT 2000)*

2.3 The basic principles of the efficient market hypothesis (EMH) were studied earlier in Paper 4, and are revised below.

Knowledge brought forward from Paper 4 (IFIN)

The efficient market hypothesis

- The **information processing efficiency** of a stock market means the ability of a stock market to price stocks and shares fairly and quickly. An efficient market in this sense is one in which the **market prices of all the securities traded on it reflect all the available information.**

- There are three degrees or 'forms' of **'information processing'** efficiency: **weak form**, **semi-strong form** and **strong form**.

- Under the **weak form hypothesis** of market efficiency, current share prices **reflect all information available from past changes in the price**, undermining the value of chartist or technical analysis.

- The **semi-strong form** hypothesis of market efficiency states that current share prices reflect both:

  (a) All relevant information about past price movements and their implications, **and**
  (b) All knowledge which is **available publicly**

- For example, if a company is planning a rights issue of shares in order to invest in a new project, a semi-strong form efficient market hypothesis would predict that if there is **public knowledge before the issue is formally announced** of the issue itself and of the expected returns from the project, then the market price (cum rights) will change to reflect the anticipated profits before the issue is announced.

- The strong form hypothesis of efficiency states that share prices reflect all information available:

  (a) From past price changes
  (b) From public knowledge or anticipation **and**
  (c) From **specialists' or experts' insider knowledge** (eg investment managers)

- It would follow that in order to maximise the wealth of shareholders, management should concentrate simply on **maximising the net present value of its investments** and it need not worry, for example, about the effect on share prices of financial results in the published accounts because investors will make allowances for low profits or dividends in the current year if higher profits or dividends are expected in the future.

- Evidence suggests that **stock markets show efficiency that is at least weak form, but tending more towards a semi-strong form.** In other words, current prices of shares which are actively traded reflect all or most publicly available information about companies and their securities.

- The **implication for an investor** is that if the market shows strong form or semi-strong form efficiency, he can rarely spot shares at a bargain price that will soon rise sharply in value. This is because the market will already have anticipated future developments, and will have reflected these in the share price. All the investor can do, instead of looking for share bargains, is to concentrate on building up a good spread of shares (a portfolio) in order to achieve a satisfactory balance between risk and return.

2.4 Tests to prove semi-strong efficiency have concentrated on the ability of the market to anticipate share price changes before new information is formally announced. For example, if two companies plan a merger, share prices of the two companies will inevitably change once the merger plans are formally announced. The market would show semi-strong efficiency, however, if it were able to **anticipate** such an announcement, so that share prices of the companies concerned would change in advance of the merger plans being confirmed.

2.5 Research in both the UK and the USA has suggested that market prices anticipate mergers several months before they are formally announced, and the conclusion drawn is that the stock markets in these countries **do** exhibit semi-strong efficiency. It has also been argued that the market displays sufficient efficiency for investors to see through 'creative accounting' or 'window dressing' of accounts by companies which use loopholes in accounting standards to overstate profits.

2.6 EXAMPLE: EFFICIENT MARKET HYPOTHESIS

Company X has 3,000,000 shares in issue and company Y 8,000,000.

(a) On day 1, the market value per share is £3 for X and £6 for Y.

(b) On day 2, the management of Y decide, at a private meeting, to make a takeover bid for X at a price of £5 per share. The takeover will produce large operating savings with a present value of £8,000,000.

(c) On day 5, Y publicly announces an unconditional offer to purchase all shares of X at a price of £5 per share with settlement on day 20. Details of the large savings are not announced and are not public knowledge.

(d) On day 10, Y announces details of the savings which will be derived from the takeover.

Ignoring tax and the time value of money between day 1 and 20, and assuming the details given are the only factors having an impact on the share price of X and Y, determine the day 2, day 5 and day 10 share price of X and Y if the market is:

(a) Semi-strong form efficient
(b) Strong form efficient

in each of the following *separate* circumstances.

(a) The purchase consideration is cash as specified above.

(b) The purchase consideration, decided on day 2 and publicly announced on day 5, is five newly issued shares of Y for six shares of X.

2.7 SOLUTION

(a) **Semi-strong form efficient market (i) cash offer**

With a semi-strong form of market efficiency, shareholders know all the relevant historical data and publicly available current information.

(i) Day 1   Value of X shares: £3 each, £9,000,000 in total.

           Value of Y shares: £6 each, £48,000,000 in total.

(ii) Day 2   The decision at the **private** meeting does not reach the market, and so share prices are unchanged.

(iii) Day 5   The takeover bid is announced, but no information is available yet about the savings.

     (1) The value of X shares will rise to their takeover bid price of £5 each, £15,000,000 in total.

     (2) The value of Y shares will be as follows.

	£
Previous value (8,000,000 × £6)	48,000,000
Add value of X shares to be acquired, at previous market worth (3,000,000 × £3)	9,000,000
	57,000,000
Less purchase consideration for X shares	15,000,000
New value of Y shares	42,000,000
Price per share	£5.25

The share price of Y shares will fall on the announcement of the takeover.

(iv) Day 10 The market learns of the potential savings of £8,000,000 (present value) and the price of Y shares will rise accordingly to:

$$\frac{£42,000,000 + £8,000,000}{8,000,000\,\text{shares}} = £6.25 \text{ per share.}$$

The share price of X shares will remain the same as before, £5 per share.

Semi-strong form efficient market (ii) share exchange offer

(i) The share price will not change until the takeover is announced on day 5, when the value of the combined company will be perceived by the market to be (48 + 9) £57,000,000.

The number of shares in the enlarged company Y would be as follows.

Current	8,000,000
Shares issued to former X shareholders (3,000,000 × 5/6)	2,500,000
	10,500,000

The value per share in Y would change to reflect what the market expects the value of the enlarged company to be.

$$\frac{£57,000,000}{10,500,000} = £5.43 \text{ per share}$$

The value per share in X would reflect this same price, adjusted for the share exchange terms.

$$\frac{5}{6} \text{ of } £5.43 = £4.52$$

(ii) Day 10 The value of the enlarged company would now be seen by the market to have risen by £8,000,000 to £65,000,000 and the value of Y shares would rise to:

$$\frac{£65,000,000}{10,500,000} = £6.19 \text{ per share}$$

The value per X share would be:

$$\frac{5}{6} \text{ of } £6.19 = £5.16$$

(b) **Strong form efficient market (i) cash offer**

In a strong form efficient market, the market would become aware of **all** the relevant information when the private meeting takes place. The value per share would change as early as **day 2** to:

(i) X: £5
(ii) Y: £6.25

The share prices would then remain unchanged until day 20.

Strong form efficient market (ii) share exchange offer

In the same way, for the same reason, the value per share would change **on day 2** to:

(i) X: £5.16
(ii) Y: £6.19

and remain unchanged thereafter until day 20.

2.8   The different characteristics of a semi-strong form and a strong form efficient market thus affect the **timing** of share price movements, in cases where the relevant information becomes available to the market eventually. The difference between the two forms of market efficiency concerns **when** the share prices change, not **by how much** prices eventually change.

2.9   You should notice, however, that in neither case would the share prices remain unchanged until day 20. In a **weak form** efficient market, the price of Y's shares would not reflect the expected savings until after the savings had been achieved and reported, so that the takeover bid would result in a fall in the value of Y's shares for a considerable time to come.

Explaining share price movements

2.10   Events such as the 'crash' of October 1987, in which share prices fell suddenly by 20% to 40% on the world's stock markets, raise serious questions about the validity of random walk theory, the fundamental theory of share values and the efficient market hypothesis. If these theories are correct, how can shares that were valued at one level on one day suddenly be worth 40% less the next day, without any change in expectations of corporate profits and dividends? On the other hand, a widely feared crash late in 1989 failed to happen, suggesting that stock markets may not be altogether out of touch with the underlying values of companies.

2.11   Various types of anomaly appear to support the views that **irrationality** often drives the stock market, including the following.

(a)   Seasonal month-of-the-year effects, day-of-the-week effects and also hour-of-the-day effects seem to occur, so that share prices might tend to rise or fall at a particular time of the year, week or day.

(b)   There may be a short-run overreaction to recent events.

(c)   Individual shares or shares in small companies may be neglected.

2.12   According to **speculative bubble theory,** stock market behaviour is non-linear and based on inflating and bursting speculative bubbles, rather than economic forecasts. Security prices rise above their intrinsic prices reflecting expected cash returns because some investors believe that others will pay more for them in the future. This behaviour feeds upon itself and prices rise for a period, producing a bull market. However, at some point, investors will eventually react to all the information which they have previously ignored, losing confidence that prices can rise still further, and a market crash then occurs.

2.13   Zeeman (1974) divided all investors into two (non-mutually exclusive) classes: **'fundamentalists'**, who are guided in their investment strategies by economic analyses to construct forecasts based on rational expectations, and **'speculators'**, whose decisions reflect adaptive behaviour in response to technical analysis of recent stock market patterns. Instability in financial markets occurs if there is a substantial proportion of speculators, amplifying changes in market indices. If the index begins to rise/fall, there will be a rapid move into a bull/bear phase respectively.

The 'coherent market hypothesis'

2.14   A more recent approach, developed by Vaga in a 1991 publication and drawing upon catastrophe theory, is that known as the **coherent market hypothesis** (CMH). The CMH holds that financial markets may be in one of four states depending on the combination of economic fundamentals and group sentiment or crowd behaviour:

- Random walks (an efficient market with neutral fundamentals)
- Unstable transition (an inefficient market with neutral fundamentals)
- Coherence (crowd behaviour with bullish fundamentals)
- Chaos (crowd behaviour with mildly bearish fundamentals)

2.15 According to Vaga, the 1987 crash was pure crowd behaviour characteristic of a chaotic market and had little to do with information on economic fundamentals.

Chapter roundup

- In this chapter, we have looked at the theory behind the **movements in share prices** as explained by the three forms of the **efficient market hypothesis.**

- Knowledge of **what** and **when** information will be incorporated into a quoted share price is likely to influence how and when information regarding financial management decisions is made public.

- In particular, since current share prices can be crucial to the success or otherwise of **takeover bids** and **new share issues**, it will be important to be aware of how the market is likely to react to varying levels of information released.

Quick quiz

1 Identify three theories of share price behaviour.

2 The efficient market hypothesis (EMH) is concerned with the following form of efficiency (choose one):

A Allocative efficiency
B Operational efficiency
C Information processing efficiency

3 According to the semi-strong form of the EMH, current share prices reflect (choose all that apply):

A Information from past price changes
B Public knowledge
C Insider knowledge

Answers to quick quiz

1 • The fundamental analysis theory
   • Technical analysis (chartist theory)
   • Random walk theory

2 C.

3 A, B.

Now try the question below from the Exam Question Bank

Number	Level	Marks	Time
7	Introductory	n/a	25 mins

Chapter 8

CAPITAL STRUCTURE

Topic list	Syllabus reference	Ability required
1 Financial risk, WACC and market value	(ii)	Application
2 The traditional view of WACC	(ii)	Application
3 The net operating income (Modigliani-Miller (MM)) view of WACC	(ii)	Application
4 Modigliani-Miller theory adjusted for taxation	(ii)	Application

Introduction

The assets of a business must be financed somehow, and when a business is growing, the additional assets must be financed by additional capital. As you will by now be aware, **capital structure** refers to the way in which an organisation is financed, by a combination of equity capital (ordinary shares and reserves) and debt capital (preference shares, debentures, bank loans, convertible loan stock and so on).

Here we consider the impact of changing capital structure on the weighted average cost of capital (WACC) and, implicitly, the total market value of a company.

Learning outcomes covered in this chapter

- Calculate values of organisations of different types, eg service, capital intensive
- Calculate post merger values of companies

Syllabus content covered in this chapter

- The impact of changing capital structures on the market value of a company will be tested using the formula $V_g = V_u + DT_c$. An understanding of the principles of Modigliani and Miller's theory of gearing with and without tax will be expected, but no proof of their theory will be examined (ie arbitrage)

1   FINANCIAL RISK, WACC AND MARKET VALUE

KEY TERMS

Cost of capital in the minimum acceptable return on an investment, generally computed as a hurdle rate for use in investment appraisal exercises. The computation of the optimal cost of capital can be complex, and many ways of determining this opportunity cost have been suggested.

The **weighted average cost of capital** is the average cost of the country's finance (equity, debentures, bank loans) weighted according to the proportion each element bears to the total pool of capital. Weighting is usually based on market valuations, current yields and costs after tax.

(OT 2000)

BPP PUBLISHING

Market values, required returns and costs of capital

1.1 The **total market value** of a company is the sum of the market values of its long-term capital components, equity and debt. **The market value of each of these components** is determined by the relevant body of investors, who in theory will discount their **future expected returns** at their **required rate of return** (ie using the dividend valuation model, or its debt equivalent).

1.2 The individual required rates of return will determine the company's costs of capital; the **cost of equity** will equal the required return by shareholders, while the **cost of debt** will take account of the tax deductibility of interest payments, and will thus generally be lower than the actual rate of return paid to the debt holders. These individual costs are combined to give an overall **weighted average cost of capital (WACC)** to the company, with each individual cost weighted according to the proportion of total market value the related capital contributes.

1.3 The WACC for a company effectively measures the overall cost of dividends and post-tax interest relative to the total market value of the company. It therefore follows that WACC and total market value are interdependent – **if total market value rises** for a given level of earnings, **then WACC must fall, and vice versa.**

1.4 In this chapter, we are concerned with the effects of a company's **capital structure** on its total market value; this may be done directly, or indirectly, by looking at the effect on the WACC and thus deducing the effects on the total market value.

1.5 The computations of the costs of equity, debt and the WACC were covered in Paper 4.

Knowledge brought forward from Paper 4 (IFIN)

EXAM FORMULAE

Costs of capital

- The cost of irredeemable preference capital, paying an annual dividend d in perpetuity, and having a current ex-div price P_0:

$$k_{pref} = \frac{d}{P_0}$$

- The cost of ordinary (equity) share capital, paying an annual dividend d in perpetuity and having a current ex-div price P_0:

$$k_e = \frac{d}{P_0}$$

- The **cost of equity** (k_e) is derived from the dividend valuation model, and is given by

$$k_e = \frac{d_0(1+g)}{P_0} + g \qquad \text{or} \qquad k_e = \frac{d_1}{P_0} + g$$

where P_0 is the current ex-div market price
d_0 is the current year's dividend
g is the expected annual growth rate in dividends

- The **after-tax cost of irredeemable debt** ($k_{d\,net}$) is given by

$$k_{d\,net} = \frac{i(1-t)}{P_0}$$

where P_0 is the current ex-interest market price
   i is the annual interest
   t is the corporation tax rate

- The **after–tax cost of redeemable debt** is given by the IRR of the associated finance flows from the point of view of the company (current market value at t_0, net of tax interest payments times $1 - n$, redemption amount at time n).

- The **weighted average cost of capital (WACC, k_0)** is the average of the costs of equity and debt, weighted according to market values:

$$k_0 = k_{eg}\left[\frac{V_E}{V_E + V_D}\right] + k_d\left[\frac{V_D}{V_E + V_D}\right]$$

where k_{eg} is the cost of equity (the g denoting that it is a general company)

   k_d is the cost of debt
   V_E is the market value of equity in a firm
   V_D is the market value of debt in the firm

Question 1

The management of Custer Ackers plc are trying to decide on a cost of capital to apply to the evaluation of investment projects.

The company has an issued share capital of 500,000 ordinary £1 shares, with a current market value cum div of £1.17 per share. It has also issued £200,000 of 10% debentures, which are redeemable at par in two years time and have a current market value of £105.30 per cent, and £100,000 of 6% preference shares, currently priced at 40p per share. The preference dividend has just been paid, and the ordinary dividend and debenture interest are due to be paid in the near future.

The ordinary share dividend will be £60,000 this year, and the directors have publicised their view that earnings and dividends will increase by 5% a year into the indefinite future.

The fixed assets and working capital of the company are financed by the following.

	£
Ordinary shares of £1	500,000
6% £1 Preference shares	100,000
Debentures	200,000
Reserves	380,000
	1,180,000

Required

Advise the management. Ignore inflation, and assume corporation tax of 30%. Assume also that tax savings occur in the same year as the interest payments to which they relate.

Note. The cost of capital of a security is the IRR which equates the current market value of the security with its expected future cash flows. The balance sheet (accounting) values of the securities and reserves should be ignored.

Answer

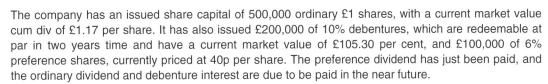

(a)   **Equity**. Given a 5% annual increase in dividend in perpetuity, the cost of equity capital may be estimated as

$$\frac{60,000(1 + 0.05)}{585,000 - 60,000 \text{ *}} + 0.05 = 0.17, \text{ ie } 17\%$$

   * Market value ex div

(b)   **Preference shares**. The cost of capital is $\dfrac{6p}{40p} \times 100\% = 15\%$

(c)   **Debentures**. The cost of capital is the IRR of the following cash flows.

Year	Cost	Interest	Tax relief	Net cash flows
	£	£	£	£
0	(95.30)			(95.30)
1		10	(3.00)	7.00
2	100.00	10	(3.00)	107.00

			Try 10%		Try 8%
Net cash flow			PV		PV
£		Discount factor	£	Discount factor	£
(95.30)		1.000	(95.30)	1.000	(95.30)
7.00		0.909	6.36	0.926	6.48
107.00		0.826	88.38	0.857	91.70
			(0.56)		2.88

The IRR is approx $\quad 8\% + \dfrac{2.88}{(2.88 - -0.56)} \times (10 - 8)\% = 9.67\%$

(d) **Weighted average cost of capital**

Item	Market value	Cost of capital	Product
	£		£
Ordinary shares*	525,000	17%	89,250
Preference shares	40,000	15%	6,000
Debentures*	190,600	9%	17,154
	755,600		112,404

* ex div and ex interest

$$\text{WACC} = \frac{112,404}{755,600} = 0.149 = 14.9\%, \text{ say } 15\%$$

(e) The management of Custer Ackers plc may choose to add a premium for risk on top of this 15% and apply a discount rate of, say, 18% to 20% in evaluating projects.

The cost of capital and risk

1.6 The cost of capital has three elements.

(a) The **risk-free rate of return** is the return which would be required from an investment if it were completely free from risk (such as the yield from government securities).

(b) The **premium for business risk** is an increase in the required rate of return due to the existence of uncertainty about the future and about a firm's business prospects. Business risk will be higher for some firms than for others, and some types of project undertaken by a firm may be more risky than other types of project that it undertakes.

(c) The **premium for financial risk** relates to the danger of high debt levels (high gearing). For ordinary shareholders, financial risk is evident in the variability of earnings after deducting payments to holders of debt capital. The higher the gearing of a company's capital structure, the greater will be the financial risk to ordinary shareholders, and this should be reflected in a higher risk premium and therefore a higher cost of capital.

1.7 Increasing gearing will have two effects:

(a) A higher proportion of (cheaper) debt finance in the pool of funds

(b) A greater risk to shareholders that is likely to lead to a higher cost of equity (and possibly, at very high gearing levels, a higher cost of debt)

These two will have opposing effects on the WACC. Therefore assuming a constant risk-free rate of return and level of business risk, **what overall effect will a change in gearing level have on the WACC and the total market value of a firm?**

1.8 There are two main theories about the effect of changes in gearing on the weighted average cost of capital (WACC) and share values. These are:

- The 'traditional' view
- The **net operating income approach (Modigliani and Miller)**

1.9 The assumptions on which these theories are based are as follows.

(a) The company pays out all its earnings after interest and tax as dividends.

(b) The gearing of the company can be changed immediately by issuing debt to repurchase shares, or by issuing shares to repurchase debt. There are no transaction costs for issues.

(c) The earnings of the company are expected to remain constant in perpetuity and all investors share the same expectations about these future earnings.

(d) Business risk is also constant, regardless of how the company invests its funds.

(e) Taxation, initially, is ignored.

2 THE TRADITIONAL VIEW OF WACC

2.1 The traditional view is as follows.

(a) As the level of gearing increases the cost of debt remains unchanged up to a certain level of gearing. Beyond this level, the cost of debt will increase.

(b) The cost of equity rises as the level of gearing increases.

(c) The weighted average cost of capital does not remain constant, but rather falls initially as the proportion of debt capital increases, and then begins to increase as the rising cost of equity (and possibly of debt) becomes more significant.

(d) The optimum level of gearing is where the company's weighted average cost of capital is minimised. At this point, **total market value is maximised.**

2.2 The traditional view about the cost of capital is illustrated in Figure 1. It shows that the weighted average cost of capital will be minimised at a particular level of gearing P. The traditional view is that the weighted average cost of capital, when plotted against the level of gearing, is saucer shaped. The optimum capital structure is where the weighted average cost of capital is lowest, at point P.

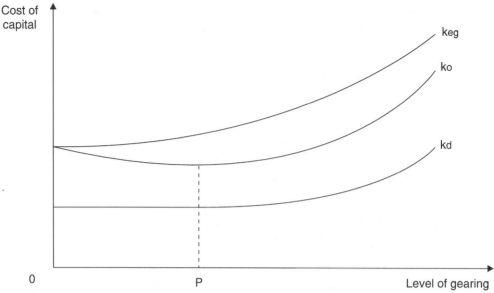

k_{eg} is the cost of equity in the geared company
k_d is the cost of debt
k_0 is the weighted average cost of capital

Figure 1

2.3 EXAMPLE: TRADITIONAL APPROACH

Gearing plc has the following capital structure (no tax):

		Constant annual payments to investors £m	Market value £m
Equity	dividends	27	150
Debt	interest	3	30
		30	180

The current cost of equity is thus $k_e = \dfrac{d_0}{P_0} = \dfrac{27}{150} = 18\%$

The current cost of debt is thus $k_d = \dfrac{i}{P_0} = \dfrac{3}{30} = 10\%$

Thus the WACC is $\dfrac{150}{180} \times 18\% + \dfrac{30}{180} \times 10\% = 16.67\%$

Note that in the case of constant dividends and interest, the WACC can be computed as

$$\text{WACC} = \frac{\text{Total payments to investors}}{\text{Total MV}} = \frac{£30m}{£180m} = 16.67\%$$

Conversely, discounting the total payments to investors by the WACC in perpetuity can derive the total MV:

$$\text{Total MV} = \frac{\text{Total payments to investors}}{\text{WACC}} = \frac{£30m}{0.1667} = £180m$$

Current gearing level, equity:debt, is 150:30 or 5:1

Now suppose the gearing is to be increased to (1) 3:1 or (2) 3:2 by the repurchase of shares, funded by new debt. It is estimated that the cost of equity will rise to compensate for the increase in gearing risk, by (1) 0.75% and (2) 3%, and that the cost of debt will rise, in the case of (2) only, by 0.5%.

What are the effects on WACC and total MV of each change?

New WACC under (1): $\frac{3}{4} \times 18.75\% + \frac{1}{4} \times 10\% = 16.56\%$

and, since total payments to investors will be unchanged,

Total MV under (1) $= \dfrac{£30m}{0.1656} = £181.16m$

New WACC under (2): $\frac{3}{5} \times 21\% + \frac{2}{5} \times 10.5\% = 16.8\%$

Total MV under (2) $= \dfrac{£30m}{0.168} = £178.57m$

Method (1), with the lower increase in gearing, had a small associated increase in the cost of equity, and the WACC went down – the impact of more cheaper debt outweighed the effect of the increased cost of equity. This led to a rise in the total MV.

Under Method (2), with the percentage of total capital represented by debt more than doubling, there was a much higher increase in the cost of equity, accompanied by an increase in the cost of debt. Despite the much higher proportion of cheap debt, the WACC went up, and the total MV fell.

Question 2

AB plc has a WACC of 16%. It is financed partly by equity (cost 18%) and partly by debt capital (cost 10%). The company is considering a new project which would cost £5,000,000 and would yield annual profits of £850,000 before interest charges. It would be financed by a loan at 10%. As a consequence of the higher gearing, the cost of equity would rise to 20%. The company pays out all profits as dividends, which are currently £2,250,000 a year.

(a) What would be the effect on the value of equity of undertaking the project?

(b) To what extent can you analyse the increase or decrease in equity value into two causes, the NPV of the project at the current WACC and the effect of the method of financing?

Ignore taxation. The traditional view of WACC and gearing is assumed in this exercise.

Answer

(a)

	£
Current profits and dividends	2,250,000
Increase in profits and dividends	
(£850,000 less extra interest 10% x £5,000,000)	350,000
New dividends, if project is undertaken	2,600,000
New cost of equity	20%

	£
New MV of equity	13,000,000
Current MV of equity	
(£2,250,000 ÷ 0.18)	12,500,000
Increase in shareholder wealth from project	500,000

(b) (i) NPV of project if financed at current WACC

$$= \frac{£850,000}{0.16} - £5,000,000 = + £312,500$$

(ii) The effect of financing on share values must be to increase the MV of equity by the remaining £187,500, which indicates that the effect of financing the project in the manner proposed will be to increase the company's gearing, but to reduce its WACC.

3 THE NET OPERATING INCOME (MODIGLIANI-MILLER (MM)) VIEW OF WACC

3.1 The net operating income approach takes a different view of the effect of gearing on WACC. In their 1958 theory, Modigliani and Miller (MM) proposed that the total market value of a company, in the absence of tax, will be determined only by two factors:

- The **total earnings** of the company
- The **level of operating (business) risk** attached to those earnings

The total market value would be computed by discounting the total earnings at a rate that is appropriate to the level of operating risk. This rate would represent the WACC of the company.

3.2 Thus Modigliani and Miller concluded that **the capital structure of a company would have no effect on its overall value of WACC.**

3.3 Modigliani and Miller made various assumptions in arriving at this conclusion, including:

(a) A **perfect capital market** exists, in which investors have the same information, upon which they act rationally, to arrive at the same expectations about future earnings and risks.

(b) There are no **tax or transaction costs.**

(c) **Debt is risk-free** and freely available at the same cost to investors and companies alike.

3.4 Modigliani and Miller justified their approach by the use of **arbitrage.**

> ### KEY TERM
>
> **Arbitrage** is the simultaneous purchase and sale of a security in different markets, with the aim of making a risk-free profit through the exploitation of any price difference between the markets.   *(OT 2000)*

3.5 Arbitrage can be used to show that once all opportunities for profit have been exploited, the market values of two companies with the same earnings in equivalent business risk classes will have moved to an equal value.

> ### Exam focus point
>
> The proof of Modigliani and Miller's theory by arbitrage is not examinable.

3.6 If Modigliani and Miller's theory holds, it implies:

(a) The cost of debt remains unchanged as the level of gearing increases.

(b) The cost of equity rises in such a way as to keep the weighted average cost of capital constant.

3.7 This would be represented on a graph as shown in Figure 2.

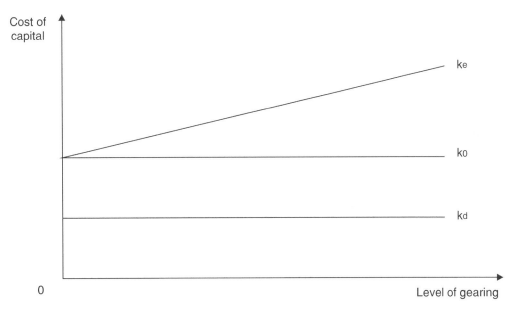

Figure 2

3.8 EXAMPLE: NET OPERATING INCOME APPROACH

A company has £5,000 of debt at 10% interest, and earns £5,000 a year before interest is paid. There are 2,250 issued shares, and the weighted average cost of capital of the company is 20%.

The market value of the company should be as follows.

Earnings	£5,000
Weighted average cost of capital	0.2
	£
Market value of the company (£5,000 ÷ 0.2)	25,000
Less market value of debt	5,000
Market value of equity	20,000

The cost of equity is therefore $\dfrac{5,000-500}{20,000} = \dfrac{4,500}{20,000} = 22.5\%$

and the market value per share is $\dfrac{4,500}{2,250} \times \dfrac{1}{0.225} = £8.89$

3.9 Suppose that the level of gearing is increased by issuing £5,000 more of debt at 10% interest to repurchase 562 shares (at a market value of £8.89 per share) leaving 1,688 shares in issue.

The weighted average cost of capital will, according to the net operating income approach, remain unchanged at 20%. The market value of the company should still therefore be £25,000.

Earnings	£5,000
Weighted average cost of capital	0.2
	£
Market value of the company	25,000
Less market value of debt	10,000
Market value of equity	15,000

Annual dividends will now be £5,000 – £1,000 interest = £4,000.

BPP
PUBLISHING

The cost of equity has risen to $\dfrac{4,000}{15,000} = 26.667\%$ and the market value per share is still:

$$\frac{4,000}{1,688} \times \frac{1}{0.2667} = £8.89$$

3.10 The conclusion of the net operating income approach is that the level of gearing is a matter of indifference to an investor, because it does not affect the market value of the company, nor of an individual share. This is because as the level of gearing rises, so does the cost of equity in such a way as to keep both the weighted average cost of capital and the market value of the shares constant. Although, in our example, the dividend per share rises from £2 to £2.37, the increase in the cost of equity is such that the market value per share remains at £8.89.

The Modigliani-Miller propositions, ignoring taxes

3.11 We can now set out the propositions of Modigliani and Miller, ignoring tax relief on the interest charged on debt capital.

3.12 The following symbols will be used.

V_u	=	the market value of an ungeared (all equity) company
V_D	=	the market value of the debt capital in a geared company which is similar in every respect to the ungeared company (same profits before interest and same business risk) except for its capital structure. The debt capital is assumed, for simplicity, to be irredeemable.
V_E	=	the market value of the equity in the geared company
k_{eu}	=	the cost of equity in an ungeared company
k_{eg}	=	the cost of equity in the geared company
k_d	=	the cost of debt capital

The total market value of the geared company V_g is then equal to (E + D).

The total market value of a company and the WACC (ignoring taxation)

3.13 MM suggested that the total market value of any company is independent of its capital structure, and is given by discounting its expected return at the appropriate rate. The value of a geared company is therefore as follows.

$$V_g = V_u$$

$$V_g = \frac{\text{Profit before interest}}{\text{WACC}\,(k_0 = k_{eu})}$$

$$V_u = V_g = \frac{\text{Earnings in an ungeared company}}{k_{eu}}$$

Note that since WACC (k_0) is unaltered by gearing, $k_0 = k_{eu}$ under this theory.

The cost of equity in a geared company (ignoring taxation)

3.14 MM went on to argue that **the expected return on a share in a geared company** equals the expected cost of equity in a similar but ungeared company, plus a premium related to financial risk.

3.15 The **premium for financial risk** can be calculated as the debt/equity ratio multiplied by the difference between the cost of equity for an ungeared company and the risk-free cost of debt capital.

> **EXAM FORMULA**
>
> $$k_{eg} = k_0 + [(k_0 - k_d) \times \frac{V_D}{V_E}]$$

3.16 Note the following points.

   (a) The part of the formula to the right of the plus sign is the value of the premium for financial risk.

   (b) The formula requires the debt ratio (debt: equity) to be used rather than the more common debt: (debt + equity).

   (c) Market values are used, not book values.

3.17 EXAMPLE: MM, IGNORING TAXATION (1)

The cost of equity in Minehead plc, an all equity company, is 15%. The WACC is therefore also 15%.

Another company, Dunster plc, is identical in every respect to the first, except that it is geared, with a debt: equity ratio of 1:4. The cost of debt capital is 5% and this is a risk-free cost of debt. What is Dunster plc's WACC?

3.18 SOLUTION

$k_{eg} = 15\% + ((15 - 5)\% \times \frac{1}{4}) = 17.5\%$.

	Weighting	*Cost*	*Product*
Equity	80%	17.5%	14%
Debt	20%	5.0%	1%
		WACC =	15%

The WACC in the geared company is the same as in the ungeared company.

3.19 EXAMPLE: MM, IGNORING TAXATION (2)

Loesch plc is an all equity company and its cost of equity is 12%.

Berelco plc is similar in all respects to Loesch plc, except that it is a geared company, financed by £1,000,000 of 3% debentures (current market price £50 per cent) and 1,000,000 ordinary shares (current market price £1.50 ex div).

What is Berelco's cost of equity and weighted average cost of capital?

3.20 SOLUTION

$$k_d = 3\% \times \frac{100}{50} = 6\%$$

$$k_{eg} = 12\% + [(12\% - 6\%) \times \frac{500}{1,500}] = 14\%$$

	Market value		*Cost*		
	£'000				£'000
Equity	1,500	×	0.14	=	210
Debt	500	×	0.06	=	30
	2,000				240

$$\text{WACC} = \frac{240}{2,000} = 0.12 = 12\%$$

This is the same as Loesch plc's WACC. As gearing is introduced, the cost of equity rises, but in such a way that the WACC does not change.

Weaknesses in MM theory

3.21 MM theory has been criticised on three main grounds.

(a) The **risks** for the investor may differ between personal gearing and corporate gearing, and the **cost** of borrowing for an individual is likely to be higher than the cost of borrowing for a company. MM's arbitrage 'proof' depends upon the assumptions that assume that the risk and cost is the same for personal and corporate borrowers.

(b) **Transaction costs** will restrict the arbitrage process.

(c) MM theory initially ignored *tax implications* (discussed below).

3.22 **Further weaknesses** in the MM theory are as follows.

(a) In practice, it may be impossible to identify firms with identical business risk and operating characteristics.

(b) Some earnings may be retained and so the simplifying assumption of paying out all earnings as dividends would not apply.

(c) Investors are assumed to act rationally which may not be the case in practice.

3.23 MM have acknowledged that **when the level of gearing gets high, the cost of debt will rise**. They argue, however, that this does not affect the weighted average cost of capital because the cost of equity falls at the same time as risk-seeking investors are attracted to buying shares in the company.

3.24 When a company's gearing reaches very high levels, it may be perceived as being in danger of insolvency, and its market value will be very low (instead of being very high, as MM would predict). MM ignored the possibility of **bankruptcy**, and so their theory may not be valid at very high levels of gearing.

4 MODIGLIANI-MILLER THEORY ADJUSTED FOR TAXATION

Exam focus point

Remember, follow any assumptions about taxation given in questions carefully. Tax rates assumed will not necessarily be those that currently apply in the real world.

4.1 Allowing for taxation reduces the cost of debt capital by multiplying it by a factor $(1 - T_c)$ where T_c is the rate of corporation tax (assuming the debt to be irredeemable). So far, our analysis of MM theory has ignored the tax relief on debt interest, which makes debt capital cheaper to a company, and therefore reduces the weighted average cost of capital where a company has debt in its capital structure.

4.2 MM modified their theory to admit that **tax relief on interest payments does lower the weighted average cost of capital.** They claimed that the weighted average cost of capital will continue to fall, up to gearing of 100%.

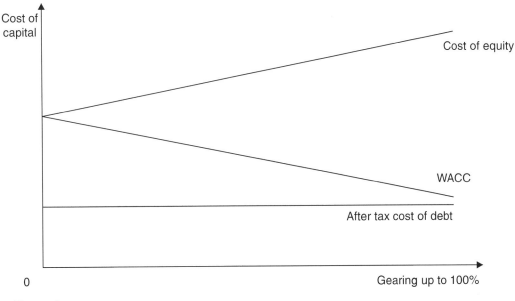

Figure 3

Adjustment to the MM cost of equity formula to allow for taxes

4.3 The formula for the cost of equity in a geared company becomes:

EXAM FORMULA

$$k_{eg} = k_{eu} + [k_{eu} - k_d] \frac{V_D \, (1-t)}{V_E}$$

where t is the corporation tax rate and k_d is the **pre-tax (gross)** cost of debt capital.

The financial risk premium is adjusted by a factor of $(1 - t)$.

4.4 From this formula we can derive the following formula:

EXAM FORMULA

$$r^* = r(1 - T^*L)$$

where r^* is the weighted average cost of capital of a geared company

r is the cost of equity and the WACC of a similar ungeared company

T^* is the tax saving due to interest payments expressed as a decimal, usually equal to the corporation tax rate (t)

L is equivalent to $\dfrac{V_D}{V_D + V_E}$

BPP PUBLISHING

(You are not expected to know the derivation, and so this is not given here. We shall return to this formula later, in Chapter 17.)

4.5 EXAMPLE (CONTINUED)

Thus, assuming a corporation tax rate of 30%, Dunster plc's cost of equity, using the information above, would be:

$$15\% + (1 - 0.30) [(15\% - 5\%) \times \tfrac{1}{4}] = 16.75\%$$

and its WACC would be:

$$15\% \left[1 - \frac{0.30 \times 1}{(1 + 4)} \right] = 15\% \times 0.94 = 14.1\%$$

4.6 This is below the ungeared company's WACC which is 15%. So higher gearing reduces the WACC.

Question 3

Apply the formulae given in Paragraphs 4.3 and 4.4 to find the cost of equity and WACC for Berelco plc, using the information given in Paragraph 3.16. The corporation tax rate is 30%.

Answer

Berelco plc's cost of equity would be

$$12\% + [(12 - 6)\% \times \frac{500(1 - 0.30)}{1,500}]$$

$$= 13.4\%$$

and its WACC would be

$$12\% \left[1 - \frac{0.30 \times 500}{1,500 + 500} \right] = 12\% \times 0.925 = 11.1\%$$

This is below Loesch plc's WACC of 12%.

Is there an optimum level of gearing?

4.7 We have now seen that MM modified their theory to say that when taxation is taken into account, the WACC will continue to fall as the level of gearing increases. The arbitrage process still operates, although the actions of investors will be influenced by their personal rates of taxation.

4.8 MM argued that since WACC falls as gearing rises, and the value of a company should rise as its WACC falls, **the value of a geared company will always be greater than its ungeared counterpart**, but only by the amount of the debt-associated tax saving of the geared company, assuming a permanent change in gearing.

where V_u is the value of the ungeared company, V_g is the value of the similar (equivalent) geared company, D is the value of debt, and a T_c is the rate of corporate tax.

4.9 The additional amount of value in the geared company, DT_c, is known as the value of the **'tax shield'** on debt.

4.10 However, the positive tax effects of debt finance will be exhausted where there is insufficient tax liability to use the tax relief which is available. This is known as **tax shield exhaustion**.

4.11 EXAMPLE: MM, WITH TAXES

Notnil plc and Newbegin plc are companies in the same industry. They have the same business risk and operating characteristics, but Notnil is a geared company whereas Newbegin is all equity financed. Notnil plc earns three times as much profit before interest as Newbegin plc. Both companies pursue a policy of paying out all their earnings each year as dividends.

The market value of each company is currently as follows.

		Notnil plc £m		*Newbegin plc* £m
Equity	(10m shares)	36	(20m shares)	15
Debt	(£12m of 12% loan stock)	14		
		50		15

The annual profit before interest of Notnil is £3,000,000 and that of Newbegin is £1,000,000. The rate of corporation tax is 30%. It is thought that the current market value per ordinary share in Newbegin plc is at the equilibrium level, and that the market value of Notnil's debt capital is also at its equilibrium level. There is some doubt, however, about whether the value of Notnil's shares is at its equilibrium level.

Apply the MM formula to establish the equilibrium price of Notnil's shares.

4.12 SOLUTION

$V_g = V_u + DT_c$

V_u = the market value of an equivalent ungeared company. Equivalence is in both **size** and **risk** of earnings. Since Notnil earnings (before interest) are three times the size of Newbegin's, V_u is three times the value of Newbegin's equity:

$3 \times £15,000,000 = £45,000,000.$

$DT_c = £14,000,000 \times 30\% = £4,200,000$

$V_g = £45,000,000 + £4,200,000 = £49,200,000.$

Since the market value of debt in Notnil plc is £14,000,000, it follows that the market value of Notnil's equity should be £49,200,000 − £14,000,000 = £35,200,000.

$$\text{Value per share} = \frac{£35,200,000}{10,000,000} = £3.52 \text{ per share}$$

Since the current share price is £3.60 per share, MM would argue that the shares in Notnil are currently over-valued by the market, by £800,000 in total or 8p per share. MM argue that this discrepancy would be rapidly removed by the process of arbitrage until the equity value of Notnil was as predicted by their model.

Empirical testing and conclusion

4.13 It might be imagined that empirical testing should have been carried out by now either to prove or to disprove MM theory. Given, however, that MM accept that the weighted average cost of capital declines after allowing for tax, and that traditional theorists argue in favour of a flattish bottom to the weighted average cost of capital curve, it is very difficult to prove that one theory is preferable to the other.

Question 4

The cost of equity in an ungeared company is 18%. The cost of risk free debt capital is 8%.

(a) What is the cost of equity in a similar geared company, according to MM, which is 75% equity financed and 25% debt financed, assuming corporation tax at a rate of 30%?

(b) What is the WACC of the geared company, allowing for taxation?

Answer

(a) $k_{eg} = 18\% + [(18-8)\% \times \dfrac{25(1-0.30)}{75}] = 20.333\%$

(b) $r^* = r \left[1 - \dfrac{T^* \times V_D}{(V_E + V_D)} \right] = 18\%[1 - \dfrac{25 \times 0.30}{(75 + 25)}]$

$= 18\% \times 0.925 = 16.7\%$

Question 5

CD plc and YZ are identical in every respect except for their gearing. The market value of each company is as follows.

CD plc		*YZ plc*	
	£m		£m
Equity (5m shares)	?	(8m shares)	24
Debt (£20m of 5% loan stock)	10		
	?		24

According to MM theory, what is the value of CD plc shares, given a corporation tax rate of 30%?

Answer

Value of CD plc in total $V_g = (V_u + DT_c)$ where V_u is the value of YZ plc.

$V_g = £24,000,000 + £10,000,000 \times 30\% = £27,000,000$.

CD plc's equity is valued at £27,600,000 – debt of £10,000,000 = £17,000,000, or £3.40 per share.

CASE STUDY LINK

In the case study, you may be told the business's capital structure is to be maintained or have to consider the potential impact on capital structure of various proposals.

Chapter roundup

- Some of the theories discussed in this chapter may seem to be far removed from the realities of day-to-day decision making. However, the directors of a company have a duty to act in the company's interests, and if there is an **optimum level of gearing** they should do their best to estimate and achieve it.

Quick quiz

1 Explain k_e, k_0, k_d and P in the diagram below illustrating the traditional view of the WACC.

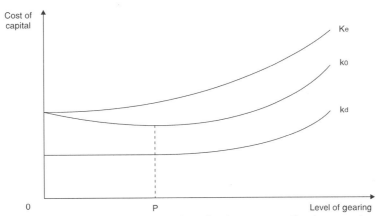

2 Sketch how the diagram in question 1 would look under the net operating income view of WACC.

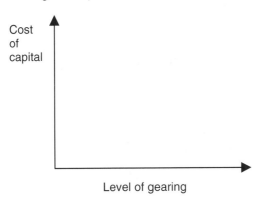

3 Now sketch the Modigliani-Miller view, allowing for taxation.

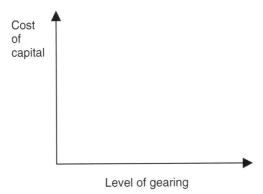

4 Define 'arbitrage'.

BPP PUBLISHING

Answers to quick quiz

1   k_e is the cost of equity in the geared company
    k_0 is the weighted average cost of capital
    k_d is the cost of debt
    P is the optimal level of gearing

2

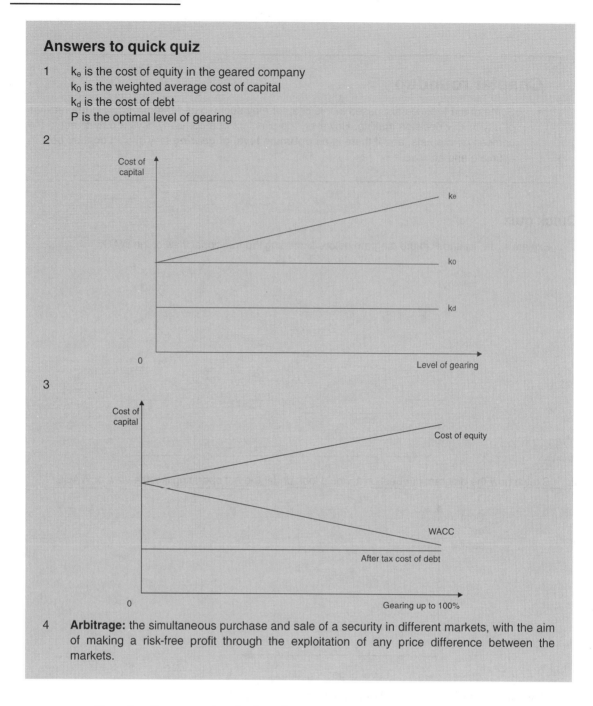

3

4   **Arbitrage:** the simultaneous purchase and sale of a security in different markets, with the aim of making a risk-free profit through the exploitation of any price difference between the markets.

Now try the question below from the Exam Question Bank

Number	Level	Marks	Time
8	Examination	25	45 mins

Chapter 9

AMALGAMATIONS AND RESTRUCTURING

Topic list	Syllabus reference	Ability required
1 Mergers and takeovers (acquisitions)	(ii)	Evaluation
2 Trends in takeover activity	(ii)	Evaluation
3 The conduct of a takeover	(ii)	Evaluation
4 Payment methods	(ii)	Evaluation
5 The position of shareholders in a merger/takeover	(ii)	Evaluation
6 Regulation of takeovers	(ii)	Evaluation
7 Post-acquisition integration	(ii)	Evaluation
8 Demergers and other forms of divestment	(ii)	Evaluation
9 Management buyouts (MBOs)	(ii)	Evaluation

Introduction

In this chapter, we are concerned with the issues of **business combinations** and **restructuring** from the point of view of financial management and financial strategy. It is often in such circumstances that the **valuations** discussed earlier are needed.

Learning outcomes covered in this chapter

- Identify and evaluate the financial and strategic implications of proposals for mergers, acquisitions, demergers and divestments

- Compare, contrast and recommend settlement methods and terms

- Calculate post merger values of companies

- Identify post acquisition value enhancement strategies

- Illustrate and explain the impact of regulation on take-overs

- Evaluate exit strategies

Syllabus content covered in this chapter

- The reasons for acquisitions (eg synergistic benefits, removing competition)

- Different payment methods (eg cash, shares, convertibles, earn out arrangements)

- The integration process following a take-over, eg transferring management, merging systems

- The implications of regulation in take-over situations (detailed knowledge of the City Code will not be tested)

- The priorities of different stakeholders in terms of business valuations

- The function/role of management buyouts, venture capitalists, including appropriate exit strategies

1   MERGERS AND TAKEOVERS (ACQUISITIONS)

KEY TERMS

Takeover: the **acquisition** by a company of a controlling interest in the voting share capital of another company, usually achieved by the purchase of a majority of the voting shares.   *(OT 2000)*

Merger: a business combination that results in the creation of a new reporting entity formed from the combining parties, in which the shareholders of the combining entities come together in a partnership for the mutual sharing of the risks and benefits of the combined entity, and in which no party to the combination in substance obtains control over any other, or is otherwise seen to be dominant, whether by virtue of the proportion of its shareholders' rights in the combined entity, the influence of its directors or otherwise.   *(FRS 6) (OT 2000)*

1.1   The distinction between mergers and takeovers (acquisitions) is not always clear, for example when a large company 'merges' with another smaller company. The methods used for mergers are often the same as the methods used to make takeovers. In practice, the number of genuine mergers is small relative to the number of takeovers.

Exam focus point

Business amalgamations (mergers and takeovers) are likely to be a key topic for exam questions.

The reasons for mergers and takeovers

1.2   When two or more companies join together, there should be a '**synergistic**' effect. Synergy can be described as the **2 + 2 = 5** effect, whereby a group after a takeover achieves combined results that reflect a better rate of return than was being achieved by the same resources used in two separate operations before the takeover. If company A, which makes annual profits of £200,000 merges with company B, which also makes annual profits of £200,000, the combined annual profits of the merged companies should be more than £400,000.

1.3   The main reasons why one company may wish to acquire the shares or the business of another may be categorised as follows.

(a)   **Operating economies**. There are many ways in which operating economies can be realised through a combination of companies. Duplicate (and competing) facilities can be eliminated.

(b)   **Management acquisition**. It is sometimes recognised that a company neither has, nor is likely to obtain in the immediate future, a management team of sufficient quality to ensure continued growth. In these circumstances it may be best to seek an amalgamation with another company which has aggressive and competent management.

(c)   **Diversification**. The management of many companies may feel that the long term interest of the shareholders will be best served by spreading risk through diversification.

(d) **Asset backing**. A company in a risky industry with a high level of earnings relative to the net assets may attempt to reduce its overall risk by acquiring a company with substantial assets.

(e) **The quality of earnings**. A company may reduce its risk by acquiring another with less risky earnings.

(f) **Finance and liquidity**. A company may be able to improve its liquidity and its ability to raise new finance through the acquisition of another more financially stable company.

(g) **Growth**. A company may achieve growth through acquisition more cheaply than through internal expansion.

(h) **Tax factors.** In exceptional cases, a cash-financed takeover may be a tax-efficient method of transferring cash out of the corporate sector. In the USA until recently, amalgamation provided a way of utilising tax losses by setting them against profits of another company: UK tax law precludes this possibility.

(i) **Defensive merger.** Companies may merge in order to prevent competitors from obtaining an advantage in some way.

1.4 The aim of a merger or acquisition should be to make profits **in the long term** as well as in the short term.

(a) **Acquisitions** may provide a means of entering a market at a lower cost than would be incurred if the company tried to develop its own resources, or a means of acquiring the business of a competitor. Acquisitions or mergers which might reduce or eliminate competition in a market may be prohibited in the UK by the Competition Commission.

(b) **Mergers**, especially in the UK, have tended to be more common in industries with a history of little growth and low returns. Highly profitable companies tend to seek acquisitions rather than mergers.

A strategic approach to takeovers

1.5 A strategic approach to takeovers would imply that acquisitions are only made after a full analysis of the underlying strengths of the acquirer company, and identification of candidates' **'strategic fit' with its existing activities**. Possible strategic reasons for a takeover are matched with suggested ways of achieving the aim in the following list from a publication of 3i (Investors in Industry), which specialises in offering advice on takeovers.

Strategic opportunities

Where you are	How to get to where you want to be
Growing steadily but in a mature market with limited growth prospects	Acquire a company in a younger market with a higher growth rate
Marketing an incomplete product range, or having the potential to sell other products or services to your existing customers	Acquire a company with a complementary product range
Operating at maximum productive capacity	Acquire a company making similar products operating substantially below capacity
Under-utilising management resources	Acquire a company into which your talents can extend

Strategic opportunities	
Where you are	**How to get to where you want to be**
Needing more control of suppliers or customers	Acquire a company which is, or gives access to, a significant customer or supplier
Lacking key clients in a targeted sector	Acquire a company with the right customer profile
Preparing for flotation but needing to improve your balance sheet	Acquire a suitable company which will enhance earnings per share
Needing to increase market share	Acquire an important competitor
Needing to widen your capability	Acquire a company with the key talents and/or technology

Factors in a takeover decision

1.6 Several factors will need to be considered before deciding to try to take over a target business. These include the following.

Price factors

(a) What would the **cost** of acquisition be?

(b) Would the acquisition be **worth** the price?

(c) Alternatively, factors (a) and (b) above could be expressed in terms of:
What is the **highest price** that it would be worth paying to acquire the business?

The value of a business could be assessed in terms of:

(i) Its earnings
(ii) Its assets
(iii) Its prospects for sales and earnings growth
(iv) How it would contribute to the strategy of the 'predator' company

The valuation of companies was covered in the previous chapter of this Study Text.

Other factors

(d) Would the takeover be regarded as **desirable** by the predator company's shareholders and (in the case of quoted companies) the stock market in general?

(e) Are the owners of the target company **amenable** to a takeover bid? Or would they be likely to adopt defensive tactics to resist a bid?

(f) What form would the **purchase consideration take?** An acquisition is accomplished by buying the shares of a target company. The purchase consideration might be cash, but the purchasing company might issue new shares (or loan stock) and exchange them for shares in the company taken over. If purchase is by means of a share exchange, the former shareholders in the company taken over will acquire an interest in the new, enlarged company.

(g) How would the takeover be **reflected in the published accounts** of the predator company?

(h) Would there be any **other potential problems** arising from the proposed takeover, such as future dividend policy and service contracts for key personnel?

2   TRENDS IN TAKEOVER ACTIVITY

UK takeover activity

2.1   There was a boom in takeover activity in the UK in the second half of the 1980s. As the increased level of expenditure on acquisitions took place at the same time as a surge in capital expenditure by industrial and commercial companies (ICCs), it appears that the increase in takeover activity must partly reflect a desire of companies to expand.

2.2   A more recent surge in takeover activity in the mid 1990s has included, for example, the £8.9 billion takeover of Wellcome by Glaxo, Europe's largest ever takeover by that time.

Largest ten acquisitions and mergers in the UK by UK companies 1st Quarter 2001

	Values in £m
Persimmon plc acquiring Beazer Group plc	560
Taylor Woodrow plc acquiring Bryant Group plc	556
Management buy-out of Burford Holdings plc	498
Fifthgrange Ltd acquiring Homebase Ltd	416
Pillar City plc acquiring Wates City of London Properties plc	373
Management buy-out of Fairview Holdings plc	307
Management buy-out of Frogmore Estates plc	293
Waste Recycling Group plc acquiring the Waste Management division of Hanson plc	185
Management buy-out of Perkins Foods plc	180
Liverpool Victoria Friendly Society acquiring Permanent Insurance Co Ltd	150

The values are taken from press or other media sources.   **Office for National Statistics**

International aspects of UK takeovers

2.3   Acquisition is one of the chief ways of carrying out **foreign direct investment** (FDI). Over the past fifteen years or so, approximately half of the UK's FDI was in the form of acquisition of share and loan capital overseas, of which a substantial proportion was related to takeovers.

2.4   A number of reasons for the expansion of UK companies into the **USA**, which occurred particularly during the late 1980s, can be identified.

   (a)   The same factors which led to the expansion in takeovers at home can be cited, especially the **strong financial position** of companies in this period.

   (b)   **US capital markets are open** and large bids, often hostile, can be made relatively easily.

   (c)   The **US product markets are large and diverse**.

   (d)   There is no **language barrier**.

   (e)   The **depreciation of the dollar** during the mid to late 1980s made acquisition targets more attractive.

2.5 Takeover transactions conducted by UK companies in the **European Union** (EU) have on average been much smaller (at around £10 million on average) than for takeovers in the USA in past years. However, the Single European Act and financial deregulation are factors contributing to a growth in importance in UK takeovers in the rest of the EU.

International comparisons of takeover activity

2.6 Official statistics for acquisitions are not available on a fully comparable basis internationally. It is clear that takeover activity was buoyant in the major OECD economies generally in the latter half of the 1980s, especially in the USA, Germany, France and Canada. However, distinctive features of the UK takeover boom have been the frequency of **hostile bids** (relative to other EU countries) and the greater emphasis **on equity finance** than in the USA. Hostile bids involve payment of a substantial premium over the pre-bid share price of the target firm and are therefore only feasible if the profitability of the joint assets can be improved to compensate for this premium.

Takeovers in the UK compared with other European countries

2.7 It has been suggested that UK companies are more vulnerable to takeover than their counterparts in other European countries. There are a number of reasons why this should be so.

2.8 Firstly, the equity markets in Britain are more highly developed than in other European countries and a greater proportion of companies are either quoted or are subsidiaries of quoted firms with publicly traded shares. In the rest of Europe by contrast there is a much greater proportion of firms in private ownership; this is especially true in Germany. Thus **access to ownership in Britain is easier.**

2.9 In addition, the capital structure of British firms is generally different to their European counterparts. In European firms there is frequently a large class of shares that do not have voting rights, unlike the ordinary shares that make up the major part of the equity for most UK companies. Thus in **Europe there is a greater division between ownership and control,** and access to the controlling shares is harder to obtain.

2.10 It has been argued that it is **easier to build a stake in a UK** firm due to the '3% rule' whereby a shareholder does not have to declare an interest until he holds 3% of the shares or 10% of any particular class of share. This is enhanced by the rule that a full bid need not be triggered until he owns 30%. It is difficult for a firm to mount a defence until a bid is declared, by which time the bidder already has a strong hand.

2.11 Government attitudes to the issues of ownership and control are also different to those in many other European countries. The prevalent **non-interventionist policies** mean that the government holds much fewer stakes and controlling interests in companies than say in France, and the 'national interest' lobby in the UK is also weaker.

2.12 Reporting requirements in the UK have been generally more rigorous than in Continental Europe. Annual reports contain more information and are more transparent than those of comparable European firms, and thus it is **easier for a predator to obtain a meaningful preliminary valuation of a potential target.** Although reporting rules in Europe have become stricter, enforcement is relatively weak, and annual accounts do not provide as full a picture of the company's position as in the UK.

Friendly and hostile takeovers: the UK, USA, Japan, Europe

2.13 In contrast to the UK and the USA, takeovers in Continental Europe and Japan are nearly always friendly. It has been argued that this difference results from different approaches to corporate governance in the Anglo-US markets compared with others.

2.14 In Continental Europe and Japan, the prevailing philosophy is that the objective of the organisation should be the maximisation of corporate wealth. In contrast to the Anglo-American emphasis on **maximisation of shareholder wealth,** this objective gives much more emphasis to the interests of other interest groups such as management, trade unions and suppliers. There are more often dual classes of voting shares, and strategic alliances (eg exchanges of shares between firms) and networks of close personal relationships play an important role. These factors mean that there are many more defences against unfriendly takeovers.

3 THE CONDUCT OF A TAKEOVER

Will the bidding company's shareholders approve of a takeover?

3.1 When a company is planning a takeover bid for another company, its board of directors should give some thought to **how its own shareholders might react** to the bid. A company does not have to ask its shareholders for their approval of every takeover.

   (a) When a large takeover is planned by a listed company involving **the issue of a substantial number of new shares by the predator company** (to pay for the takeover), Stock Exchange rules may require the company to obtain the formal approval of its shareholders to the takeover bid at a general meeting (probably an extraordinary general meeting, called specifically to approve the takeover bid).

   (b) If shareholders, and the stock market in general, think the takeover is not a good one the **market value of the company's shares is likely to fall.** The company's directors have a responsibility to protect their shareholders' interests, and are accountable to them at the annual general meeting of the company.

3.2 A takeover bid might seem **unattractive** to shareholders of the bidding company because:

   (a) It might reduce the EPS of their company

   (b) The target company is in a risky industry, or is in danger of going into liquidation

   (c) It might reduce the net asset backing per share of the company, because the target company will probably be bought at a price which is well in excess of its net asset value

Will a takeover bid be resisted by the target company?

3.3 Quite often, a takeover bid will be resisted. Resistance comes from the target company's board of directors, who adopt defensive tactics, and ultimately the target company's shareholders, who can refuse to sell their shares to the bidding company.

3.4 Resistance can be overcome by offering a higher price. In cases where an **unquoted** company is the target company, if resistance to a takeover cannot be overcome, the takeover will not take place, and negotiations would simply break down. Where the target company is a **quoted company**, the situation is different. The target company will have many shareholders, some of whom will want to accept the offer for their shares, and some of whom will not. In addition, the target company's board of directors might resist a takeover, even though their shareholders might want to accept the offer.

3.5 Because there are likely to be major **differences of opinion** about whether to accept a takeover bid or not, the Stock Exchange has issued formal rules for the conduct of takeover bids, in the City Code on Takeovers and Mergers. This and other regulatory issues are covered later in the chapter.

Exam focus point

Detailed knowledge of the City Code will not be tested in your examination, but you should be aware of its **implications**.

Contesting an offer: defensive tactics

3.6 The directors of a target company must **act in the interests of their shareholders, employees and creditors**. They may decide to contest an offer on several grounds.

   (a) The offer may be unacceptable because the terms are poor. Rejection of the offer may lead to an improved bid.

   (b) The merger or takeover may have no obvious advantage.

   (c) Employees may be strongly opposed to the bid.

   (d) The founder members of the business may oppose the bid, and appeal to the loyalty of other shareholders.

3.7 When a company receives a takeover bid which the board of directors considers unwelcome, the directors must act quickly to fight off the bid.

3.8 The steps that might be taken to **thwart a bid** or **make it seem less attractive** include:

   (a) Revaluing assets or issuing a forecast of attractive future profits and dividends to persuade shareholders that to sell their shares would be unwise, that the offer price is too low, and that it would be better for them to retain their shares to benefit from future profits, dividends and capital growth (Such profit and dividend forecasts can be included in 'defence documents' circulated to shareholders, and in press releases)

   (b) Lobbying the Office of Fair Trading and/or the Department of Trade and Industry to have the offer referred to the Competition Commission (see later in the chapter)

   (c) Launching an advertising campaign against the takeover bid (one technique is to attack the accounts of the predator company)

   (d) Finding a 'white knight', a company which will make a welcome takeover bid (see below)

   (e) Making a counter-bid for the predator company (this can only be done if the companies are of reasonably similar size)

   (f) Arranging a management buyout

   (g) Introducing a 'poison-pill' anti-takeover device (see below)

Case examples

In October 2000, Iberdrola, Spain second-largest electricity company, found a **white knight** in the largest, Endesa, fending off an unwelcome bid from Gas Natural, Spain's privatised gas monopoly. The Endesa offer was thought to be substantially lower than that of Gas Natural, the mix of shares and cash valuing at €16.82 per share, as against Gas Natural's €18 per share. A spokesman for Gas

Natural said 'We hope shareholders inside and outside Spain will press Iberdrola's board to explain why it accepted a less attractive offer'. Ironically, since the merger would now give the combined enterprise around 80% of Spain's electricity market, substantial divestment would be needed to reduce its market share to 50%, to comply with Spain's competition rules.

An example of a **poison pill** anti-takeover device was that used by Time Warner, the US media group in which Canada's Seagram drinks company had built up an 11 per cent stake in 1994. Seagram had announced plans to buy up to 15 per cent of Time Warner shares for investment purposes.

The Time Warner device was formally known as a 'shareholder rights plan' and is triggered if one investor buys more than 15 per cent of the company's stock. If that occurs, all other shareholders are given the right to buy stock at a large discount, thus diluting the 15 per cent shareholding. Time Warner pointed out that the device would not preclude a *bona fide* all-cash offer for the company which treated all shareholders equally; the 'poison pill' was designed to protect against 'abusive takeover tactics'. Seagram, on the other hand, questioned whether poison pills were in the best interests of shareholders, since they could interfere with choice and adversely affect share values.

Costs of contested takeover bids

3.9 Takeover bids, when contested, can be very expensive, involving:

- Costs of professional services, eg merchant bank and public relations agency
- Advertising costs
- Underwriting costs
- Interest costs
- Possible capital loss on buying/selling the target company's shares

Gaining the consent of the target company shareholders

3.10 A takeover bid will only succeed if the predator company can persuade enough shareholders in the target company to sell their shares. Shareholders will only do this if they are dissatisfied with the performance of their company and its shares, or they are attracted by a high offer and the chance to make a good capital gain.

3.11 The general functions of the various players in the stock market were covered in your earlier studies. Of particular relevance here are merchant banks and stockbrokers, and a brief revision of their roles is included here.

Knowledge brought forward from Paper 4 (IFIN)

Merchant banks

- Also known as **investment banks**, they provide various financial services to mainly corporate clients
- Some **clearing banks** also carry out merchant banking activities
- Activities include
  - Advice on, and organisation of, issue of new share and loan capital
  - Taking 'wholesale' deposits of funds in various currencies
  - Large scale lending to corporate borrowers
  - Providing venture capital
  - Foreign exchange dealing
  - Management of investments, eg for pension funds, insurance companies
  - Business advice on mergers and takeovers

Stockbrokers

- Deal in buying and selling shares on behalf of investors

Services of a merchant bank and stockbroker

3.12 During the acquisition process, a company may be assisted in the following ways by its merchant bank and stockbroker, or by one financial institution fulfilling both roles.

The merchant bank

(a) May provide the initial lead in identifying suitable acquisition targets; provides information on such target companies

(b) Can provide advice on and checks compliance with the City Code on Mergers and Takeovers, which is important from the very start of negotiations

(c) Will engage other advisors (for example, lawyers and reporting accountants)

(d) Will provide some advice on the valuation of target companies - however, the valuation can only be properly decided by the acquiring company's board and the advice given by the banker will tend to avoid legal liability

(e) Will advise on the best method of financing the issue - whether cash, or a share issue or loan stock issue, or a combination of these methods

(f) Will arrange the issue of finance

(g) Will handle much of the publicity surrounding the acquisition

The stockbroker

(a) Can sound out the opinions of major institutional investors on possible bids

(b) Can provide background stock market information, such as share prices, P/E ratios, equity beta factors

(c) Will deal with the detailed documentation for share issues, share exchanges and so on

4 PAYMENT METHODS

The purchase consideration

4.1 The terms of a takeover will involve a purchase of the shares of the target company for **cash** or for '**paper**' (shares, or possibly loan stock). A purchase of a target company's shares with shares of the predator company is referred to as a **share exchange**.

Cash purchases

4.2 If the purchase consideration is in **cash**, the shareholders of the target company will simply be bought out. For example, suppose that there are two companies.

	Big Ltd	*Small Ltd*
Net assets (book value)	£1,500,000	£200,000
Number of shares	100,000	10,000
Earnings	£2,000,000	£40,000

Big Ltd negotiates a takeover of Small Ltd for £400,000 in cash.

4.3 As a result, Big Ltd will end up with:

(a) Net assets (book value) of
£1,500,000 + £200,000 − £400,000 cash = £1,300,000

(b) 100,000 shares (no change)

(c) Expected earnings of £2,040,000, minus the loss of interest (net of tax) which would have been obtained from the investment of the £400,000 in cash which was given up to acquire Small Ltd

Purchases by share exchange

4.4 One company can acquire another company by **issuing shares** to pay for the acquisition. The new shares might be issued:

(a) **In exchange** for shares in the target company. Thus, if A plc acquires B Ltd, A plc might issue shares which it gives to B Ltd's shareholders in exchange for their shares. The B Ltd shareholders therefore become new shareholders of A plc. This is a takeover for a 'paper' consideration. Paper offers will often be accompanied by a **cash alternative.**

(b) **To raise cash** on the stock market, which will then be used to buy the target company's shares. To the target company shareholders, this is a cash bid.

4.5 Sometimes, a company might acquire another in a share exchange, but the shares are then **sold immediately** on a stock market to raise cash for the seller. For example, A plc might acquire B Ltd by issuing shares which it gives to B's shareholders; however A plc's stockbrokers arrange to 'place' these shares with other buyers, and so sell the newly issued shares for cash on behalf of the ex-shareholders of B Ltd. This sort of arrangement, which is a mixture of (a) and (b), is called a '**vendor placing**'.

4.6 Whatever the detailed arrangements of a takeover with paper, the end result will be an **increase in the issued share capital of the predator company**.

Use of convertible loan stock

4.7 Alternative forms of paper consideration, including debentures, loan stock and preference shares, are not so commonly used, due to:

- Difficulties in establishing a rate of return that will be attractive to target shareholders
- The effects on the gearing levels of the acquiring company
- The change in the structure of the target shareholders' portfolios
- The securities being potentially less marketable, and lacking voting rights

4.8 Issuing **convertible loan stock** will overcome some of these drawbacks, by offering the target shareholders the option of partaking in the future profits of the company if they wish.

> **KEY TERM**
>
> **Convertible loan stock** is a loan which gives the holder the right to convert to other securities, normally ordinary shares, at a predetermined price/rate and time. *(OT 2000)*

The choice between a cash offer and a paper offer

4.9 The choice between cash and paper offers (or a combination of both) will depend on how the different methods are viewed by the company and its existing shareholders, and on the attitudes of the shareholders of the target company. The factors that the directors of the bidding company must consider include the following.

(a) **The company and its existing shareholders**

    (i)   **Dilution of earnings per share.** A fall in the EPS attributable to the existing shareholders is undesirable but it might occur when the purchase consideration is in equity shares.

    (ii)   **The cost to the company.** The use of loan stock (or of cash borrowed elsewhere) will be cheaper to the acquiring company than equity as the interest will be allowable for tax purposes. A direct consequence of this is that dilution of earnings may be avoided. If convertible loan stock is used, the coupon rate could probably be slightly lower than with ordinary loan stock.

    (iii)   **Gearing.** A highly geared company may find that the issue of additional loan stock either as consideration or to raise cash for the consideration may be unacceptable to some or all of the parties involved.

    (iv)   **Control.** In takeovers involving a relatively large new issue of ordinary shares the effective control of the company can change considerably. This could be unpopular with the existing shareholders.

    (v)   **An increase in authorised share capital.** If the consideration is in the form of shares, it may be necessary to increase the company's authorised capital. This would involve calling a general meeting to pass the necessary resolution.

    (vi)   **Increases in borrowing limits.** A similar problem arises if a proposed issue of loan stock will require a change in the company's borrowing limit as specified in the Articles.

(b) **The shareholders in the target company**

    (i)   **Taxation.** If the consideration is in cash many investors may find that they face an immediate liability to tax on a realised capital gain, whereas the liability would be postponed if the consideration consisted of shares.

    (ii)   **Income.** Where the consideration is other than cash, it is normally necessary to ensure that existing income is at least maintained. A drop may, however, be accepted if it is compensated for by a suitable capital gain or by reasonable expectations of future growth.

    (iii)   **Future investments.** Shareholders in the target company might want to retain a stake in the business after the takeover, and so would prefer the offer of shares in the bidding company, rather than a cash offer.

    (iv)   **Share price.** If shareholders in the target company are to receive shares, they will want to consider whether the shares are likely to retain their value.

Mezzanine finance and takeover bids

4.10   When the purchase consideration in a takeover bid is cash, the cash must be obtained somehow by the bidding company, in order to pay for the shares that it buys. Occasionally, the company will have sufficient cash in hand to pay for the target company's shares. More frequently, the cash will have to be raised, possibly from existing shareholders, by means of **a rights issue** or, more probably, by **borrowing from** banks or other financial institutions.

4.11   When cash for a takeover is raised by borrowing, the loans would normally be **medium-term** and **secured**.

4.12   However, there have been many takeover bids, with a cash purchase option for the target company's shareholders, where the bidding company has arranged loans that:

(a)   Are short-to-medium term

(b)   Are unsecured (that is, 'junior' debt, low in the priority list for repayment in the event of liquidation of the borrower)

(c)   Because they are unsecured, attract a much higher rate of interest than secured debt (typically 4% or 5% above LIBOR)

(d)   Often, give the lender the option to exchange the loan for shares after the takeover

This type of borrowing is called **mezzanine finance** (because it lies between equity and debt financing) - a form of finance which is also often used in **management buyouts** (which are discussed later in this chapter).

Earn-out arrangements

4.13   The purchase consideration may not all be paid at the time of acquisition. Part of it may be deferred, payable upon the target company reaching certain performance targets. You should refer back to Chapter 3 for a definition of such arrangements, and to Chapter 6 for an illustration of their application.

5   THE POSITION OF SHAREHOLDERS IN A MERGER/TAKEOVER

The market values of the companies' shares during a takeover bid

5.1   **Market share prices** can be very important during a takeover bid. Suppose that Velvet plc decides to make a takeover bid for the shares of Noggin plc. Noggin plc shares are currently quoted on the market at £2 each. Velvet shares are quoted at £4.50 and Velvet offers one of its shares for every two shares in Noggin, thus making an offer at current market values worth £2.25 per share in Noggin. This is only the value of the bid so long as Velvet's shares remain valued at £4.50. If their value falls, the bid will become less attractive.

5.2   This is why companies that make takeover bids with a share exchange offer are always concerned that the market value of their shares should not fall during the takeover negotiations, before the target company's shareholders have decided whether to accept the bid.

Case example

In November 2000, **PricewaterhouseCoopers (PwC)**, the accountancy group, were about three days away from signing a $18bn deal with computer group Hewlett-Packard (HP) to sell HP PwC's consultancy division. Then HP announced that it had missed Wall Street earnings estimate by a wide margin, its share price dropped by nearly 13%, to $34.13, taking the share price down to a level 45% below that at which the talks had started. The bid, unsurprisingly, failed. With HP trading at well below its year-high price of $78, the acquisition would have been a pricey one.

5.3   If the market price of the target company's shares rises above the offer price during the course of a takeover bid, the bid price will seem too low, and the takeover is then likely to fail, with shareholders in the target company refusing to sell their shares to the bidder.

EPS before and after a takeover

5.4   If one company acquires another by issuing shares, its EPS will go up or down according to the P/E ratio at which the target company has been bought.

(a) If the target company's shares are bought at a higher P/E ratio than the predator company's shares, the predator company's shareholders will suffer a fall in EPS.

(b) If the target company's shares are valued at a lower P/E ratio, the predator company's shareholders will benefit from a rise in EPS.

5.5 EXAMPLE: MERGERS AND TAKEOVERS (1)

Giant plc takes over Tiddler Ltd by offering two shares in Giant for one share in Tiddler. Details about each company are as follows.

	Giant plc	*Tiddler Ltd*
Number of shares	2,800,000	100,000
Market value per share	£4	-
Annual earnings	£560,000	£50,000
EPS	20p	50p
P/E ratio	20	

By offering two shares in Giant worth £4 each for one share in Tiddler, the valuation placed on each Tiddler share is £8, and with Tiddler's EPS of 50p, this implies that Tiddler would be acquired on a P/E ratio of 16. This is lower than the P/E ratio of Giant, which is 20.

5.6 If the acquisition produces no synergy, and there is no growth in the earnings of either Giant or its new subsidiary Tiddler, then the EPS of Giant would still be higher than before, because Tiddler was bought on a lower P/E ratio. The combined group's results would be as follows.

	Giant group
Number of shares (2,800,000 + 200,000)	3,000,000
Annual earnings (560,000 + 50,000)	610,000
EPS	20.33p

If the P/E ratio is still 20, the market value per share would be £4.07, which is 7p more than the pre-takeover price.

5.7 EXAMPLE: MERGERS AND TAKEOVERS (2)

Redwood plc agrees to acquire the shares of Hawthorn Ltd in a share exchange arrangement. The agreed P/E ratio for Hawthorn's shares is 15.

	Redwood plc	*Hawthorn Ltd*
Number of shares	3,000,000	100,000
Market price per share	£2	-
Earnings	£600,000	£120,000
P/E ratio	10	

5.8 The EPS of Hawthorn Ltd is £1.20, and so the agreed price per share will be £1.20 × 15 = £18. In a share exchange agreement, Redwood would have to issue nine new shares (valued at £2 each) to acquire each share in Hawthorn, and so a total of 900,000 new shares must be issued to complete the takeover.

5.9 After the takeover, the enlarged company would have 3,900,000 shares in issue and, assuming no earnings growth, total earnings of £720,000. This would give an EPS of:

$$\frac{£720,000}{3,900,000} = 18.5p$$

The pre-takeover EPS of Redwood was 20p, and so the EPS would fall. This is because Hawthorne has been bought on a higher P/E ratio (15 compared with Redwood's 10).

Buying companies on a higher P/E ratio, but with profit growth

5.10 Buying companies on a higher P/E ratio will result in a fall in EPS unless there is profit growth to offset this fall. For example, suppose that Starving plc acquires Bigmeal plc, by offering two shares in Starving for three shares in Bigmeal. Details of each company are as follows.

	Starving plc	*Bigmeal plc*
Number of shares	5,000,000	3,000,000
Value per share	£6	£4
Annual earnings		
Current	£2,000,000	£600,000
Next year	£2,200,000	£950,000
EPS	40p	20p
P/E ratio	15	20

5.11 Starving plc is acquiring Bigmeal plc on a higher P/E ratio, and it is only the profit growth in the acquired subsidiary that gives the enlarged Starving group its growth in EPS.

	Starving group
Number of shares (5,000,000 + 2,000,000)	7,000,000

Earnings
    If no profit growth (2,000,000 + 600,000) £2,600,000   EPS would have been 37.24p
    With profit growth (2,200,000 + 950,000) £3,150,000   EPS will be 45p

If an acquisition strategy involves buying companies on a higher P/E ratio, it is therefore essential for continuing EPS growth that the acquired companies offer prospects of strong profit growth.

Reverse takeovers

5.12 A reverse takeover occurs when the smaller company takes over the larger one, so that the 'predator' company has to increase its voting equity by over 100% to complete the takeover.

Further points to consider: net assets per share and the quality of earnings

5.13 It might be concluded from what has been said above that dilution of earnings must be avoided at all cost. However, there are three cases where a dilution of earnings might be accepted on an acquisition if there were other advantages to be gained.

(a) **Earnings growth** may hide the dilution in EPS as above.

(b) A company might be willing to accept earnings dilution if the **quality of the acquired company's earnings** is superior to that of the acquiring company.

(c) A trading company with high earnings, but with few assets, may want to increase its assets base by acquiring a company which is strong in assets but weak in earnings so that assets and earnings get more into line with each other. In this case, **dilution in earnings is compensated for by an increase in net asset backing.**

5.14 EXAMPLE: MERGERS AND TAKEOVERS (3)

Intangible plc has an issued capital of 2,000,000 £1 ordinary shares. Net assets (excluding goodwill) are £2,500,000 and annual earnings average £1,500,000. The company is valued by the stock market on a P/E ratio of 8. Tangible Ltd has an issued capital of 1,000,000 ordinary shares. Net assets (excluding goodwill) are £3,500,000 and annual earnings average

BPP
PUBLISHING

£400,000. The shareholders of Tangible Ltd accept an all-equity offer from Intangible plc valuing each share in Tangible Ltd at £4. Calculate Intangible plc's earnings and assets per share before and after the acquisition of Tangible Ltd.

5.15 SOLUTION

(a) Before the acquisition of Tangible Ltd, the position is as follows.

$$\text{Earnings per share (EPS)} = \frac{£1,500,000}{2,000,000} = 75\text{p}$$

$$\text{Assets per share (APS)} = \frac{£2,500,000}{2,000,000} = £1.25$$

(b) Tangible Ltd's EPS figure is 40p (£400,000 ÷ 1,000,000), and the company is being bought on a multiple of 10 at £4 per share. As the takeover consideration is being satisfied by shares, Intangible plc's earnings will be diluted because Intangible plc is valuing Tangible Ltd on a higher multiple of earnings than itself. Intangible plc will have to issue 666,667 shares valued at £6 each (earnings of 75p per share at a multiple of 8) to satisfy the £4,000,000 consideration. The results for Intangible plc will be as follows.

$$\text{EPS} = \frac{£1,900,000}{2,666,667} = 71.25\text{p (3.75p lower than the previous 75p)}$$

$$\text{APS} = \frac{£6,000,000}{2,666,667} = £2.25 \text{ (£1 higher than the previous £1.25)}$$

If Intangible plc is still valued on the stock market on a P/E ratio of 8, the share price should fall by approximately 30p (8 × 3.75p, the fall in EPS) but because the asset backing has been increased substantially the company will probably now be valued on a higher P/E ratio than 8.

5.16 The shareholders in Tangible Ltd would receive 666,667 shares in Intangible plc in exchange for their current 1,000,000 shares, that is, two shares in Intangible for every three shares currently held.

		£
(a)	Earnings	
	Three shares in Tangible earn (3 × 40p)	1.200
	Two shares in Intangible will earn (2 × 71.25p)	1.425
	Increase in earnings, per three shares held in Tangible	0.225
(b)	Assets	£
	Three shares in Tangible have an asset backing of (3 × £3.5)	10.50
	Two shares in Intangible will have an asset backing of (2 × £2.25)	4.50
	Loss in asset backing, per three shares held in Tangible	6.00

The shareholders in Tangible Ltd would be trading asset backing for an increase in earnings.

Dividends and dividend cover

5.17 A further issue which may create some difficulties before a merger or takeover can be agreed is the level of dividends and dividend cover expected by shareholders in each of the companies concerned. Once the companies merge, a **single dividend policy** will need to be applied.

6 REGULATION OF TAKEOVERS

The Takeover Panel and the City Code on Takeovers and Mergers

6.1 The **City Code on Takeovers and Mergers** is a code of behaviour which companies are expected to follow during a takeover or merger, as a measure of self-discipline. The code has no statutory backing, although it is administered and enforced by the Takeover Panel. Once adopted, the 13th Company Law Directive of the EU will have statutory power in EU member states, bringing an end to the non-statutory approach to the regulation of bids and takeover deals currently used in the UK.

6.2 The nature and purpose of the City Code is described within the code itself as follows.

> 'The Code represents the collective opinion of those professionally involved in the field of takeovers on a range of business standards. It is not concerned with the financial or commercial advantages or disadvantages of a takeover, which are matters for the company and its shareholders, or with those wider questions which are the responsibility of the government, advised by the Competition Commission.

> The Code has not, and does not seek to have, the force of law, but those who wish to take advantage of the facilities of the securities markets in the United Kingdom should conduct themselves in matters relating to takeovers according to the code. Those who do not so conduct themselves cannot expect to enjoy those facilities and may find that they are withheld.'

6.3 Companies subject to the code include all public companies (listed or unlisted) and also some classes of private company.

The City Code: general principles

6.4 The City Code is divided into general principles and detailed rules which must be observed by persons involved in a merger or takeover transaction. The general principles include the following.

(a) 'All shareholders of the same class of an offeree company must be treated similarly by an offeror.' In other words, a company making a takeover bid cannot offer one set of purchase terms to some shareholders in the target company, and a different set of terms to other shareholders holding shares of the same class in that company.

(b) 'During the course of a takeover, or when such is in contemplation, neither the offeror nor the offeree company ...may furnish information to some shareholders which is not made available to all shareholders.'

(c) 'Shareholders must be given sufficient information and advice to enable them to reach a properly informed decision and must have sufficient time to do so. No relevant information should be withheld from them.'

(d) 'At no time after a *bona fide* offer has been communicated to the board of an offeree company ... may any action be taken by the board of the offeree company in relation to the affairs of the company, without the approval of the shareholders in general meeting, which could effectively result in any *bona fide* offer being frustrated or in the shareholders being denied an opportunity to decide on its merits.' In other words, directors of a target company are not permitted to frustrate a takeover bid, nor to prevent the shareholders from having a chance to decide for themselves.

(e) 'Rights of control must be exercised in good faith and the oppression of a minority is wholly unacceptable.' For example, a holding company cannot take decisions about a takeover bid for one of its subsidiaries in such a way that minority shareholders would be unfairly treated.

(f) 'Where control of a company is acquired ... a general offer to all other shareholders is normally required.' Control is defined as a 'holding, or aggregate holdings, of shares carrying 30% of the voting rights of a company, irrespective of whether that holding or holdings gives *de facto* control'.

The City Code: rules

6.5 In addition to its general principles, the City Code also contains a number of detailed rules, which are intended to govern the conduct of the parties in a takeover bid. These rules relate to matters such as:

(a) How the approach to the target company should be made by the predator company

(b) The announcement of a takeover bid

(c) The obligation of the target company board to seek independent advice (eg from a merchant bank)

(d) Conduct during the offer

(e) A time barrier to re-bidding if an offer fails

The Competition Commission

6.6 A UK company might have to consider whether its proposed takeover would be drawn to the attention of the Competition Commission (formerly called the Monopolies and Mergers Commission). Under the terms of the Monopolies and Mergers Act, the Office of Fair Trading (the OFT) is entitled to scrutinise all major mergers and takeovers. If the OFT thinks that a merger or takeover might be against the public interest, it can refer it to the Competition Commission. Proposed mergers can be notified to the OFT in advance. If no referral is made to the Competition Commission within (normally) 20 days, the merger can proceed without fear of a referral.

6.7 The function of the Competition Commission is to advise the government. The Commission can make recommendations to the Department of Trade and Industry (or to any other body, including the companies involved in the bid).

6.8 The result of an investigation by the Commission might be:

(a) Withdrawal of the proposal for the merger or takeover, in anticipation of its rejection by the Commission

(b) Acceptance or rejection of the proposal by the Commission

(c) Acceptance of the proposal by the Commission subject to the new company agreeing to certain conditions laid down by the Commission, for example on prices, employment or arrangements for the sale of the group's products

European Union regulations on mergers

6.9 In the past, EU competition policy was criticised for its limited scope. However, under a regulation introduced during 1990, the European Commission gained, for the first time, the power to intervene and to either block or authorise larger mergers. If the Commission finds that the merger raises serious doubts as to its compatibility with the European common market, it will initiate proceedings to block the merger.

7 POST-ACQUISITION INTEGRATION

7.1 Failures of takeovers often result from **inadequate integration** of the companies after the takeover has taken place. There is a tendency for senior management to devote their energies to the next acquisition rather than to the newly-acquired firm. The particular approach adopted will depend upon the **culture** of the organisation as well as the **nature** of the company acquired and **how it fits** into the amalgamated organisation (eg horizontally, vertically, or as part of a diversified conglomerate).

7.2 P F Drucker has suggested Five Golden Rules for the process of post-acquisition integration.

Rule 1. There should be a 'common core of unity' shared by the acquiror and acquiree. The ties should involve overlapping characteristics such as shared technology and markets, and not just financial links.

Rule 2. The acquiror should ask 'What can we offer them?' as well as 'What's in it for us?'

Rule 3. The acquiror should treat the products, markets and customers of the acquired company with respect, and not disparagingly.

Rule 4. The acquiring company should provide top management with relevant skills for the acquired company within a year.

Rule 5. Cross-company promotions of staff should occur within one year.

7.3 C S Jones has proposed a five-step 'integration sequence'.

Step 1 is to decide on and to communicate **initial reporting relationships.** This will reduce uncertainty. The issue of whether to impose relationships at the beginning, although these may be subject to change, or to wait for the organisation structure to become more established (see Step 5 below) needs to be addressed.

Step 2 is to achieve **rapid control of key factors,** which will require access to the right accurate information. Control of information channels needs to be gained without dampening motivation. Note that it may have been poor financial controls which led to the demise of the acquiree company.

Step 3 is the **resource audit**. Both physical and human assets are examined in order to get a clear picture.

Step 4 is to **re-define corporate objectives** and to **develop strategic plans,** to harmonise with those of the acquiror company as appropriate, depending on the degree of autonomy managers are to have to develop their own systems of management control.

Step 5 is to **revise the organisational structure**.

7.4 Successful post-acquisition integration requires careful management of the 'human factor' to avoid loss of motivation. Employees in the acquired company will want to know how they and their company are to fit into the structure and strategy of the amalgamated enterprise. Morale can, hopefully, be preserved by reducing uncertainty and by providing appropriate performance incentives, staff benefits and career prospects.

Service contracts for key personnel 5/01

7.5 When the target company employs certain key personnel, on whom the success of the company has been based, the predator company might want to ensure that these key people do not leave as soon as the takeover occurs. To do this, it might be necessary to insist as a condition of the offer that the key people should agree to sign **service contracts**, tying them to the company for a certain time (perhaps three years). Service contracts would have to be attractive to the employees concerned, perhaps through offering a high salary or other benefits such as share options in the predator company. Where key personnel are shareholders, they might be bound not to sell shares for a period.

Merging systems

7.6 The degree to which the information, control and reporting systems of the two companies involved in a takeover are merged will depend to some extent upon the **degree of integration** envisaged. There are two extremes of integration:

(a) **Complete absorption of the target firm**, where the cultures, operational procedures and organisational structures of the two firms are to be fused together. This approach is most suitable where significant cost reductions are expected to be achieved through economies of scale, and/or combining marketing and distribution effort can enhance revenues.

(b) **The preservation approach**, where the target company is to become an independent subsidiary of the holding company. This would be most beneficial for the merger of companies with very different products, markets and cultures.

7.7 In the circumstances of a complete absorption, the two companies will become one, and thus a **common operational system** must be developed. Care must be taken by the acquiring company's management not to impose immediately their own systems upon the target company's operations, assuming them to be superior. This is likely to **alienate** acquired employees.

7.8 It is probably best to **use the system already in place,** in the acquired company, initially supplemented by requests for additional reports felt to be immediately necessary for adequate information and control flows between the two management bodies. As the integration process proceeds, the best aspects of each of the companies' systems will be identified and a **common system developed.**

7.9 Where the two companies are to operate independently, it is likely that some changes will be needed to financial control procedures to get the two group companies in line. Essentially, however, the target company's management may **continue with their own cultures, operations and systems.**

Failure of mergers and takeovers

7.10 The aim of any takeover will be to **generate value for the acquiring shareholders.** Where this does not happen, there may be a number of reasons, including **a strategic plan that fails to produce the benefits expected,** or **over-optimism** about future market conditions, operating synergies and the amount of time and money required to make the merger work.

7.11 A third recurring reasons for failure is **poor integration management,** in particular:

(a) **Inflexibility** in the application of integration plans drawn up prior to the event. Once the takeover has happened, management must be prepared to adapt plans in the light of changed circumstances or inaccurate prior information.

(b) **Poor man management**, with lack of communication of goals and future prospects of employees, and failure to recognise and deal with the uncertainty and anxiety invariably felt by them.

7.12 A survey carried out in 1992, through the interviewing of senior executives of the UK's top 100 companies covering 50 deals, revealed some common factors contributing to the failure of mergers. In order of decreasing rate of incidence:

- Cultural differences and poor attitude of target management
- Little or no post-acquisition planning
- Lack of knowledge of industry or target company
- Poor management and poor practices in target company
- Little or no experience of acquisitions

The impact of mergers and takeovers on stakeholders

7.13 To what extent do the stakeholders in a merger or takeover benefit from it?

The following comments are based upon extensive empirical research.

(a) **Acquiring company shareholders**

At least half of mergers studied have shown a decline in profitability compared with industry averages. Returns to equity can often be poor relative to the market in the early years, particularly for equity-financed bids and first time players. Costs of mergers frequently outweigh the gains.

(b) **Target company shareholders**

In the majority of cases, it is the target shareholders who benefit most from a takeover. Bidding companies invariable have to offer a significant premium over the market price prevailing prior to the bid in order to achieve the purchase.

(c) **Acquiring company management**

The management of the newly enlarged organisation will often enjoy increased status and influence, as well as increased salary and benefits.

(d) **Target company management**

Whilst some key personnel may be kept on for some time after the takeover, a significant number of managers will find themselves out of a job. However, a 'golden handshake' and the prospect of equally remunerative employment elsewhere may lessen the blow of this somewhat.

(e) **Other employees**

Commonly the economy of scale cost savings anticipated in a merger will be largely achieved by the loss of jobs, as duplicated service operations are eliminated and loss-making divisions closed down. However, in some instances, the increased competitive strength of the newly enlarged enterprise can led to expansion of operations and the need for an increased workforce.

(f) **Financial institutions**

These are perhaps the outright winners. The more complex the deal, the longer the battle, and the more legal and financial problems encountered, the greater their fee income, regardless of the end result.

8 DEMERGERS AND OTHER FORMS OF DIVESTMENT

8.1 Mergers and takeovers are not inevitably good strategy for a business. In some circumstances, strategies of internal growth, no growth or even some form of **divestment** might be preferable.

> ## KEY TERM
>
> A **divestment** is a proportional or complete reduction in ownership stake in an organisation.
>
> *(OT 2000)*

Demergers

8.2 A **demerger** is the opposite of a merger. It is the **splitting up of a corporate body into two or more separate and independent bodies.** For example, the ABC Group plc might demerge by splitting into two independently operating companies AB plc and C plc. Existing shareholders are given a stake in each of the new separate companies.

8.3 Demerging, in its strictest sense, stops short of selling out, but is an attempt to ensure that share prices reflect the true value of the underlying operations. In large diversified conglomerates, such as those built up by Lord Hanson in the 1980s and early 1990s, so many different businesses are combined into one organisation that it becomes difficult for analysts to understand them fully. In addition, a management running ten businesses instead of two could be seen to lose some focus.

Case example

British Gas demerged into BG plc and Centrica plc in 1996, allowing Centrica to develop fully its retail business and BG to build up a strong investment portfolio. In March 2000, it was announced that BG itself was to demerge, separating its international business (BG International) from the UK part (Lattice). These two businesses are unrelated, the international part being focussed on oil and gas exploration and Lattice owning and operating the gas pipeline system in the UK, and this was an attempt to realise a fuller value for them.

The market looked upon the news of the demerger favourably, and BG's share price hit a five-year high shortly afterwards. BG International was widely seen as a takeover target, having important strategic assets in its field, but lacking in the critical mass thought necessary.

Just prior to the demerger date, BG's share price was 443p, as compared to analysts' estimates of break-up share values of 211p for BG International and 216p for Lattice. Takeover potential, however meat that shareholders were advised to hold on.

8.4 The potential disadvantages with demergers are as follows.

(a) Economies of scale may be lost, where the demerged parts of the business had operations in common to which economies of scale applied.

(b) The smaller companies which result from the demerger will have lower turnover, profits and status than the group before the demerger.

    (c)   There may be higher overhead costs as a percentage of turnover, resulting from (b).

    (d)   The ability to raise extra finance, especially debt finance, to support new investments and expansion may be reduced.

    (e)   Vulnerability to takeover may be increased.

Sell-offs

8.5   A **sell-off** is a form of **divestment** involving the sale of part of a company to a third party, usually another company. Generally, cash will be received in exchange.

8.6   A company may carry out a sell-off for one of the following reasons.

    (a)   As part of its strategic planning, it has decided to restructure, concentrating management effort on particular parts of the business. Control problems may be reduced if peripheral activities are sold off.

    (b)   It wishes to sell off a part of its business which makes losses, and so to improve the company's future reported consolidated profit performance. This may be in the form of a management buy-out (MBO) – see below.

    (c)   In order to protect the rest of the business from takeover, it may choose to sell a part of the business which is particularly attractive to a buyer.

    (d)   The company may be short of cash.

    (e)   A subsidiary with high risk in its operating cash flows could be sold, so as to reduce the business risk of the group as a whole.

    (f)   A subsidiary could be sold at a profit. Some companies have specialised in taking over large groups of companies, and then selling off parts of the newly-acquired groups, so that the proceeds of sales more than pay for the original takeovers.

Liquidations

8.7   The extreme form of a sell-off is where the entire business is sold off in a **liquidation**. In a voluntary dissolution, the shareholders might decide to close the whole business, sell off all the assets and distribute net funds raised to shareholders.

Spin-offs

8.8   In a **spin-off**, a new company is created whose shares are owned by the shareholders of the original company which is making the distribution of assets. There is no change in the ownership of assets, as the shareholders own the same proportion of shares in the new company as they did in the old company. Assets of the part of the business to be separated off are transferred into the new company, which will usually have different management from the old company. In more complex cases, a spin-off may involve the original company being split into a number of separate companies.

8.9   For a number of possible reasons such as those set out below, a spin-off appears generally to meet with favour from stock market investors.

    (a)   The change may make a merger or takeover of some part of the business easier in the future, or may protect parts of the business from predators.

    (b)   There may be improved efficiency and more streamlined management within the new structure.

(c) It may be easier to see the value of the separated parts of the business now that they are no longer hidden within a conglomerate.

(d) The requirements of regulatory agencies might be met more easily within the new structure, for example if the agency is able to exercise price control over a particular part of the business which was previously hidden within the conglomerate structure.

(e) After the spin-off, shareholders have the opportunity to adjust the proportions of their holdings between the different companies created.

Case example

In November 2000, **Invensys**, the UK automations and controls group, announced it was to spin off its power systems business in an attempt to improve the group's prospects by clearer recognition of the value of the division. The new company was to be listed on the London Stock Exchange, and up to 25% of Invensys's interest in the spun-off unit would be offered to investors. The market reacted positively to the news, with a rapid increase in Invensys's share price, though some reservations were expressed about the 'partial' nature of the flotation, with suggestions that it was a means of raising cash quickly or to fend off a takeover bid.

Going private

8.10 A public company **'goes private'** when a **small group of individuals**, possibly including existing shareholders and/or managers and with or without support from a financial institution, **buys all of the company's shares.** This form of restructuring is relatively common in the USA and may involve the shares in the company ceasing to be listed on a stock exchange.

8.11 Advantages in going private could include the following.

(a) The costs of meeting listing requirements can be saved.

(b) The company is protected from volatility in share prices which financial problems may create.

(c) The company will be less vulnerable to hostile takeover bids.

(d) Management can concentrate on the long-term needs of the business rather than the short-term expectations of shareholders.

(e) Shareholders are likely to be closer to management in a private company, reducing costs arising from the separation of ownership and control (the 'agency problem').

Case examples

One example of going private was Richard Branson's repurchase of shares in the **Virgin Company** from the public and from financial institutions. Another example was **SAGA** the tour operator which changed status from public to private in 1990. While public, 63% of the company was owned by one family. The family raised finance to buy all of the shares, to avoid the possibility of hostile takeover bids and to avoid conflicts between the long-term needs of the business and the short-term expectations which institutional shareholders in particular are often claimed to have.

More recently, the Matthews family have been considering an MBO (see below) to buy back the publicly held shares in their family turkey business, Bernard Matthews. It was held that the company was being undervalued by the stock market and, after 29 years as a listed company, the Matthews wanted it back. At the time of writing, there was a possibility of a counter bid being made by Sara Lee, another food producer.

9 MANAGEMENT BUYOUTS (MBOs)

> **KEY TERM**
>
> A **management buy-out** is a transaction in which the executive managers of a business join with financing institutions to buy the business from the entity which currently owns it.
>
> *(OT 2000)*

9.1 A **management buyout** is the purchase of all or part of a business from its owners by its managers. For example, the directors of a subsidiary company in a group might buy the company from the holding company, with the intention of running it as proprietors of a separate business entity.

    (a) **To the managers,** the buyout would be a method of setting up in business for themselves.

    (b) **To the group,** the buyout would be a method of **divestment**, selling off the subsidiary as a going concern.

9.2 In the later 1990s into 2000, MOB activity in the UK was dominated by a large, £250 million plus, deals, accounting for around two thirds of the total value of MBOs. In 1999, the total value was £14.4 billion, a figure already exceeded in the first three quarters of 2000. Examples of MBO transactions in 2000 included the **General Healthcare** and **Rank Hovis McDougall** £1 billion plus deals, and the largest **public-to-private** transaction to date, by property company **MEPC,** worth $3.5 billion.

The parties to a buyout

9.3 There are usually three parties to a management buyout.

    (a) A **management team** wanting to make a buyout. This team ought to have the skills and ability to convince financial backers that it is worth supporting.

    (b) **Directors** of a group of companies, who make the divestment decision.

    (c) **Financial backers** of the buyout team, who will usually want an equity stake in the bought-out business, because of the **venture capital risk** they are taking. Often, several financial backers provide the venture capital for a single buyout.

9.4 **The management team making the buyout** would probably have the aims of setting up in business themselves, being owners rather than mere employees; or avoiding redundancy, when the subsidiary is threatened with closure.

9.5 **A large organisation's board of directors** may agree to a management buyout of a subsidiary for any of a number of different reasons.

    (a) The subsidiary may be peripheral to the group's mainstream activities, and no longer fit in with the group's overall strategy.

    (b) The group may wish to sell off a loss-making subsidiary, and a management team may think that it can restore the subsidiary's fortunes.

    (c) The parent company may need to raise cash quickly.

    (d) The subsidiary may be part of a group that has just been taken over and the new parent company may wish to sell off parts of the group it has just acquired.

(e) The best offer price might come from a small management group wanting to arrange a buyout.

(f) When a group has taken the decision to sell a subsidiary, it will probably get better co-operation from the management and employees of the subsidiary if the sale is a management buyout.

9.6 **A private company's shareholders** might agree to sell out to a management team because they need cash, they want to retire, or the business is not profitable enough for them.

9.7 To help convince a bank or other institution that it can run the business successfully, the management team should prepare a **business plan** and estimates of sales, costs, profits and cash flows, in reasonable detail.

The role of the venture capitalist   5/01

9.8 The nature of venture capital was covered earlier in your studies. A brief reminder follows.

Knowledge brought forward from Paper 4 (IFIN)

Venture capital

- **Venture capital** is risk capital, normally provided in return for an equity stake.

- Examples of **venture capital organisations** in the UK are 3i, Equity Capital for industry and the various venture capital subsidiaries of the clearing banks.

- Venture capital **may be provided to fund** business start-ups, business development, MBOs and the purchase of shares from one of the owners of the business.

- Venture capital can also be provided through **venture capital funds**, which is a pool of finance provided by a variety of investors, which will then be applied to MBOs or expansion projects.

- Venture capitalists will normally require an **equity stake** in the company and may wish to have a **representative on the board** to look after its interests.

- A number of clearly defined **exit routes** will be sought by the venture capitalists in order to ensure the easy realisation of their investment when required.

9.9 Venture capitalists are far more inclined to fund MBOs, management buy-ins (MBI) and corporate expansion projects than the more risky and relatively costly early stage investments such as start-ups. The minimum investment considered will normally be around £100,000, with average investment of £1m-£2m.

9.10 Whilst the return required on venture capital for the high-risk, early stage investments may be as high as 80%, where the funding is for a well established business with sound management, it is more commonly around the 25-30% mark. Whilst this may be achieved by the successful investments, of course there will be many more that fail, and the overall returns on venture capital funds averages out at around 10-15%.

9.11 For MBOs and MBIs the venture capitalist will not necessarily provide the majority of the finance. A £50m buy-out may be funded by, say, £15m venture capital, £20m debt finance and £15m mezzanine debt, discussed earlier.

9.12 Venture capital funds may require:

- A 20-30% shareholding
- Special rights to appoint a number of directors
- The company to seek their prior approval for new issues or acquisitions

Exit strategies

9.13 Venture capitalists generally like to have a predetermined **target exit date,** the point at which they can recoup some or all of their investment in an MBO. At the outset, they will wish to establish various **exit routes**, the possibilities including:

- The sale of shares following a **flotation** on a recognised stock exchange
- The **sale** of the company to another firm
- The **repurchase** of the venture capitalist's shares by the company or its owners
- The sales of the venture capitalist's shares to an **institution** such as an investment trust

The appraisal of proposed buyouts

How likely is a management buyout to succeed?

9.14 Management-owned companies seem to achieve better performance probably because of:

- A favourable buyout price having been achieved
- Personal motivation and determination
- Quicker decision making and so more flexibility
- Keener decisions and action on pricing and debt collection
- Savings in overheads, eg in contributions to a large head office

However, many management buyouts, once they occur, begin with some redundancies to cut running costs.

How should an institutional investor evaluate a buyout?

9.15 An institutional investor (such as a venture capitalist) should evaluate a buyout before deciding whether or not to finance. Aspects of any buyout that ought to be checked are as follows.

(a) Does the management team have the full range of management skills that are needed (for example a technical expert and a finance director)? Does it have the right blend of experience? Does it have the commitment?

(b) Why is the company for sale? The possible reasons for buyouts have already been listed. If the reason is that the parent company wants to get rid of a loss-making subsidiary, what evidence is there to suggest that the company can be made profitable after a buyout?

(c) What are the projected profits and cash flows of the business? The prospective returns must justify the risks involved.

(d) What is being bought? The buyout team might be buying the shares of the company, or only selected assets of the company. Are the assets that are being acquired sufficient for the task? Will more assets have to be bought? When will the existing assets need replacing? How much extra finance would be needed for these asset purchases? Can the company be operated profitably?

(e) What is the price? Is the price right or is it too high?

(f) What financial contribution can be made by members of the management team themselves?

(g) What are the exit routes and when might they be taken?

The financial arrangements in a typical buyout

9.16 Typically, the **buyout team** will have a **minority** of the equity in the bought-out company, with the **various financial backers** holding a **majority** of the shares between them. A buyout might have several financial backers, each providing finance in exchange for some equity.

9.17 Investors of venture capital usually want the **managers to be financially committed**. Individual managers could borrow personally from a bank, say £20,000 to £50,000.

9.18 The suppliers of equity finance might insist on investing part of their capital in the form of **redeemable convertible preference shares**. These often have voting rights should the preference dividend fall in arrears, giving increased influence over the company's affairs. They are issued in a redeemable form to give some hope of taking out part of the investment if it does not develop satisfactorily, and in convertible form for the opposite reason: to allow an increased stake in the equity of a successful company.

Possible problems with buyouts

9.19 A common problem with management buyouts is that the managers have little or no experience in **financial management** or **financial accounting**.

9.20 Other problems are:

(a) Tax and legal complications

(b) Difficulties in deciding on a fair price to be paid

(c) Convincing employees of the need to change working practices

(d) Inadequate cash flow to finance the maintenance and replacement of tangible fixed assets

(e) The maintenance of previous employees' pension rights

(f) Accepting the board representation requirement that many sources of funds will insist upon

(g) The loss of key employees if the company moves geographically, or wage rates are decreased too far, or employment conditions are unacceptable in other ways

(h) Maintaining continuity of relationships with suppliers and customers

Buy-ins

9.21 'Buy-in' is a term used when a team of **outside managers**, as opposed to managers who are already running the business, mount a takeover bid and then run the business themselves. A management buy-in might occur when a business venture is running into trouble, and a group of outside managers see an opportunity to take over the business and restore its profitability.

CASE STUDY LINK

The issues discussed in this chapter may be very important when you come to take the case study. The May 2001 case study asked for various options including mergers, strategic alliances (and doing nothing) to be considered.

Chapter roundup

- Buying another company is a substantial undertaking for a company. The target company's shareholders must be persuaded of the benefits of the takeover. **Takeover bids** are not infrequent, and it is worth following one or two in the financial press, to see how the considerations set out in this chapter translate into practice.

- **Management buyouts** are a special sort of transaction, involving several parties. A buyout cannot go ahead unless all the parties are satisfied with the arrangements.

Quick quiz

1   What is the name for 'the acquisition by a company of a controlling interest in the voting share capital of another company, usually achieved by the purchase of a majority of the voting shares' (CIMA Official Terminology)?

2   What is meant by a 'white knight'?

3   What is a 'poison pill' in the context of takeovers and mergers?

4   A smaller company takes over a larger one, so that the smaller company must increase its voting equity by over 100% to complete the takeover. What is this process called?

5   Why might management owned companies achieve improved performance?

Answers to quick quiz

1   A takeover

2   A company which will make a welcome takeover bid

3   An anti-takeover device

4   A reverse takeover

5   • Personal motivation and determination
    • Quicker and more flexible decision making
    • Keener decisions, eg on pricing
    • Overhead savings

Now try the question below from the Exam Question Bank

Number	Level	Marks	Time
9	Examination	25	45 mins

Part C
Risk management

Chapter 10

RISKS AND THEIR MANAGEMENT

Topic list	Syllabus reference	Ability required
1 The types of risk faced by a business	(iii)	Analysis
2 Risk management	(iii)	Analysis
3 Diversification of risk	(iii)	Analysis
4 ·Reducing credit risk	(iii)	Analysis
5 Fraud	(iii)	Analysis
6 Risk analysis techniques	(iii)	Application

Introduction

Risk is something that all businesses must recognise, assess and manage. In this chapter we consider the various types of risk that arise in business and the ways in which they may be managed. Two of the main risks, **currency risk** and **interest rate risk** are covered in the following chapters. In this chapter we focus on **credit risk** and **fraud risk,** and also discuss the role of **diversification** in risk management. **Political** risk is covered in a later chapter. Finally, we revise the risk analysis techniques covered earlier in Paper 9.

Learning outcomes covered in this chapter

- Interpret the risks facing an organisation
- Evaluate risk management strategies

Syllabus content covered in this chapter

- Management of risk: cultural, economic, political, technological and fraud

- Minimising the risk of fraud (eg fraud policy statements, effective recruitment policies and good internal controls especially over procurement and cash)

- The principle of diversifying risk (no numerical calculations required)

- The risk of loss while goods are in transit and the risk of litigation in different countries (no specific country will be tested).

1   THE TYPES OF RISK FACED BY A BUSINESS   5/01

KEY TERM

Risk is a condition in which there exists a quantifiable dispersion in the possible outcomes from any activity.   *(OT 2000)*

The role of risk in business

1.1   All business will face risk. Only by the taking of some degree of risk can potentially profitable opportunities be exploited – it is what running a business is all about. However, all risks must be recognised, most managed to some extent, and some should be sought to be eliminated as being outside the scope of the remit of the management of a business run for, in general, risk-averse shareholders.

1.2   For example, a business in a high-tech industry, such as computing, which evolves rapidly within ever-changing markets and technologies, has to accept high risks in their research and development activities; but should they also be speculating on interest and exchange rates within their treasury activities?

1.3   Insurance premiums and transaction costs incurred in the reduction or elimination of risk can be expensive, and, as always, the costs must be balanced against the expected benefits.

1.4   Some of the benefits to be derived from the management of risk, possibly at the expense of profits are:

- Predictability of cash flows
- Limitation of the impact of potentially bankrupting events
- Increased confidence of its shareholders and other investors

1.5   There are many different types of risks faced by commercial organisations, particularly those with international activities. They may be categorised under the following headings.

- General business risk
- Trading risk
- Cultural risk
- Country and political risk
- Currency (foreign exchange) risk
- Interest rate risk
- Technological risk
- Fraud risk

1.6   The nature of these risks, and general methods that may be used to manage them are discussed briefly below. In this and the next few chapters we shall go on to look at the most significant areas and management techniques in greater depth.

General business risk

1.7   Business risk may be defined is **the potential volatility of profits caused by the nature and type of the business operations involved.**

1.8   Factors contributing to business risk will include:

- The types of industries/markets within which the business operated
- The state of the economy
- The actions of competitors
- The actions of unions or impact of government legislation
- The stage in a product's life cycle, higher risks in the introductory and declining stages
- The dependence upon inputs with fluctuating prices, eg wheat, oil etc
- The level of operating gearing – the proportion of fixed costs in total costs
- The flexibility of production processes to adapt to different specifications or products

1.9 There may be little management can do about some of these risks, they are inherent in business activity. However, strategies discussed later in the text such as **diversification**, the use of **commodity futures**, the **restructuring** of manufacturing processes and **real options** can contribute substantially to the reduction of many business risks.

Trading risks

1.10 Both domestic and international traders will face trading risks, although those faced by the latter will generally be greater due to the increased distances and times involved. The types of trading risk include:

(a) **Physical risk** – the risk of goods being lost or stolen in transit, or the documents accompanying the goods going astray

(b) **Credit risk** – the possibility of payment default by the customer. This is discussed further below

(c) **Trade risk** – the risk of the customer refusing to accept the goods on delivery (due to sub-standard/inappropriate goods), or the cancellation of the order in transit

(d) **Liquidity risk** – the inability to finance the credit

1.11 Such risks may be reduced with the help of banks, insurance companies, credit reference agencies and government agencies, including the UK's Export Credit Guarantee Department (ECGD). The company should also develop policies for debtor management and methods of payment that minimise these risks without jeopardising the business's commercial standing, particularly with regards to export trade.

Cultural risk

1.12 Where a business trades with, or invests in, a foreign country additional uncertainty is introduced by the existence of different customs, laws and language. Communication between parties can be hindered, and potential deals put into jeopardy by ignorance of the expected manner in which such transactions should be conducted.

1.13 Such risks can be minimised by adherence to international trading rules, such as those developed by the International Chamber of Commerce, although not all countries have accepted these. Above all, an organisation that wants to succeed in international dealings must ensure its management are fully aware of cultural differences that exist and how these should be dealt with.

Country and political risk

> **KEY TERMS**
>
> **Country risk** is the risk associated with undertaking transactions with, or holding assets in, a particular country. Sources of risk might be political, economic or regulatory instability affecting overseas taxation, repatriation of profits, nationalisation, currency instability etc. *(OT 2000)*
>
> **Political** risk is the risk that political action will affect the position and value of a company.

1.14 Country risk, of which political risk will be a significant element, will be particularly relevant to businesses that invest overseas, eg setting up a foreign subsidiary. Whilst some governments will take positive action to encourage foreign investment, the main concern will be actions that have an adverse affect of the value of a firm.

1.15 Examples of such actions will include:

(a) **Exchange controls** – where the extent to which a country's currency may be used to transfer funds is restricted, or there are limitations on the amount of foreign currency that may be converted to another currency

(b) **Tax regulations** – increases in tax rates or new taxes introduced

(c) **Expropriation of assets** – where the foreign government confiscates privately owned property, for example by nationalisation

(d) **Regulations on the use of local resources** – the government may require that products must contain a certain amount of local labour and locally produced materials

(e) **Pricing regulations** – where a firm may be restricted in its price setting

(f) **Restriction on local finance** – a firm's access to local loans may be limited

1.16 Even if political risk is considered to be high, the investment may well be justified by expectations of high returns. The impact of such risk may be minimised by the way the investment is set up. This is discussed further in Chapter 16, on international investment appraisal.

Currency risk

> **KEY TERM**
>
> **Currency risk** is the possibility of loss or gain due to future changes in exchange rates.
>
> *(OT 2000)*

1.17 When a firm trades with an overseas supplier or customer, and the invoice is in the overseas currency, it will expose itself to exchange rate or currency risk. Movement in the foreign exchange rates will create risk in the settlement of the debt – ie the final amount payable/receivable in the home currency will be uncertain at the time of entering into the transaction. Investment in a foreign country or borrowing in a foreign currency will also carry this risk.

1.18 There are three types of currency risk.

(a) **Transaction risk** – arising from exchange rate movements between the time of entering into an international trading transaction and the time of cash settlement.

(b) **Translation risk** - the changes in balance sheet values of foreign assets and liabilities arising from retranslation at different prevailing exchange rates at the end of each year.

(c) **Economic risk** – the effect of exchange rate movements on the international competitiveness of the organisation, eg in terms of relative prices of imports/exports, the cost of foreign labour etc.

1.19 Of these three, transaction risk has the greatest immediate impact on day to day cash flows of a firm, and there are many ways of reducing or eliminating this risk, for example by the use of **hedging** techniques. These and other currency risk management strategies are discussed in detail in Chapters 12 and 13.

Interest rate risk

1.20 As with foreign exchange rates, future interest rates cannot be easily predicted. If a firm has a significant amount of variable (floating) rate debt, interest rate movements will give rise to uncertainty about the cost of servicing this debt. Conversely, if a company uses a lot of fixed rate debt, it will lose out if interest rates begin to fall.

1.21 There are many arrangements and financial products that a firm's treasury department can use to reduce its exposure to interest rate risk for example, involving **hedging** techniques similar to those used for the management of currency risk. The topic of interest rate risk is covered in greater depth in Chapter 11.

Technological risk

1.22 All businesses depend to some extent on technology either in the support of its business activities (eg the computers used by the accounts, stores and treasury departments), or more directly in its production or marketing activities.

1.23 The development of the world class manufacturer, who will strive to achieve flexibility in its production processes to produce high-quality goods to the customers' specifications at a minimum cost, has lead to an increased use of **computer integrated manufacturing**. Computers are used throughout the designing, testing and production stages of a product, both to reduce the times within which such activities are carried out and to assist in their co-ordination monitoring and control.

1.24 The increasing use of the **Internet** for both marketing and trading (e-commerce) brings technology to the forefront of any business's strategic considerations.

1.25 In addition, the **product** itself may well be highly dependent upon technology such as those produced in the IT, telecommunications, and video industries.

1.26 As technology evolves and develops, firms can find themselves using out of date equipment and marketing methods, which may leave them at a **competitive disadvantage**. Products in a high-tech industry have a very short life-cycle, and a firm must recognise and plan for continual replacement and upgrading of products if it is not to lose market share.

1.27 Management of this risk can include the **leasing** of equipment rather than purchasing outright, so that updating is easily achieved at less cost. **Research and development** departments must be given sufficient resources to ensure the high-tech firm keeps up with, or indeed itself brings about, changes in technology. A careful eye must be kept on the development of e-commerce, with strategic decisions made as to when, and to what extent, the firm should participate in internet based activities.

Fraud risk

1.28 All businesses run the risk of loss through the fraudulent activities of employees including management. This is perhaps one of the risk areas over which the company can exert the greatest control, through a coherent corporate strategy set out in a **fraud policy statement** and the setting up of strict **internal controls**. This is covered later in this chapter.

BPP
PUBLISHING

2 RISK MANAGEMENT

> **KEY TERM**
>
> **Risk management** is the process of understanding and managing the risks that the organisation is inevitably subject to in attempting to achieve its corporate objectives.
>
> *(OT 2000)*

2.1 In discussing the particular types of risk above, various methods and techniques were mentioned in the context of their management. Some of these will be developed in this and later chapters of the text. Here we shall look at the general principles a business will need to follow in developing its risk management strategy.

2.2 In the UK, the **Turnbull report** on internal control has provided organisations with guidelines on the setting up of systems of risk management. In doing so, management should **identify** and **evaluate** the risks to which they will be exposed in the achievement of their corporate objectives. These will include both the traditional areas of risk discussed above, but also those increasingly arising for intangible assets, such as reputation and branding.

2.3 The effective evaluation and control of risks will ensure:

- The enhancement of competitive advantages
- The recognition of potential opportunities
- The reduction of management time wasted on fire-fighting
- The increased confidence of shareholders

2.4 As previously discussed, risk management is not necessarily the **elimination of risk**, as a certain amount of risk needs to be faced if opportunities are to be exploited and higher returns achieved. It is up to the mangers of a particular business to select the risks the business might take and those it wishes to avoid.

Identifying risks

2.5 In order to control risks, they need to be identified. This identification exercise must cover risks specific to the organisation and market circumstances, and should cover strategic, operational and financial areas.

2.6 The specific operational risks covered above are only part of the story. In a recent study, some of the principal strategic and operational risks faced by companies were identified by financial managers as:

- The failure to manage major projects successfully, especially technological ones
- The failure to be sufficiently innovative
- Problems arising from poor reputation or weak brand management
- Lack of employee motivation

2.7 Relevant risks will be identified from information provided both by senior management and more detailed operational knowledge lower down the hierarchy. The risk management system must provide a route by which such information is effectively collected, classified and assessed in order to determine a company's risk profile.

Assessment and prioritisation of risks

2.8 **Financial risk** analysis will very much depend upon commercial judgement, but the following questions may be used as a framework for the assessment of their impact on company value:

- What is the effect on present and future cash flow?
- What is the effect on the underlying present and future profitability of the business?
- What is the effect on the present and future liquidity and value of assets employed?
- What is the effect on the present and future debt structure of the business?

2.9 Whilst these questions concentrate on the impact in financial terms, consideration should also be made of the potential effect on the achievement of **corporate objectives.**

2.10 The **relative likelihood** of the events giving rise to the risks also need to be addressed. This can then be combined with the level of impact to prioritise the risks, eg

- **High impact, high likelihood** – immediate action required
- **High impact low likelihood** – contingency plan needed
- **Low impact, high likelihood** – consider taking action
- **Low impact, low likelihood** – no action now, but review periodically

Control strategy

2.11 Once risks have been prioritised, management needs to decide what to do about them, and how they can be managed and monitored in the future.

2.12 Strategies for management of a given risk include:

- Acceptance
- Transfer   - eg by insurance of joint venture
- Elimination - by hedging, or ceasing the activity/operation
- Control   - by building in operational controls

2.13 The Turnbull report stresses that risk control should be **embedded in the culture and processes of the business**, rather than being the subject of a completely separate management system. Each person in the organisation should be aware of, and manage, the significant risks related to the tasks they perform.

2.14 Directors will need to review and monitor risk control issues continually. The board should regularly review **reports on internal control** from line managers and, where appropriate, from internal auditors and other specialists. **Regular discussion** of risk and control issues at board meetings should be encouraged. **Risk analysis and assessment** should form part of the evaluation of every major capital investment or proposed acquisition.

Case examples

In the 1999 annual report of **Hilton Group plc**, a review of the group's treasury management activities included the following extracts.

Financial risk management. The group's treasury function provides a centralised service for the provision of finance and the management and control of liquidity, foreign exchange and interest rates. The function operates as a cost centre and manages the group's treasury exposure to reduce risk in accordance with policies approved by the board.

Derivative financial instruments such as spot and forward foreign exchange contracts, currency swaps and interest rate swaps are used to assist in the management of the group's financial risk ... it is not the policy of the group to trade in or enter into speculative transactions.

Kingfisher's 2000 report included the statement that 'the main financial risks faced by the group and managed by its treasury function are funding risk, interest rate risk and currency risk. The board regularly reviews these risks and proves written treasury policies covering the use of financial instruments to manage these risks.

Funding risk. Treasury ensures that the group has sufficient secure resources to meet its business objectives and manages the group's exposure to liquidity risk by promoting a diversity of funding sources and debt maturities.

Interest rate and currency risk management – Interest rate and foreign currency policies provide a degree of flexibility, whilst ensuring that the overall level of risk is maintained with agreed limits.'

---

3 DIVERSIFICATION OF RISK

3.1 One of the main strategies available to organisations in managing risk arising from a particular type of activity, business or market is that of **diversification** whereby it spreads it investments across a range of businesses and markets, with the aim of offsetting gains and losses.

3.2 The technique of diversification within an individual investor's portfolio was covered earlier in your studies, and no numerical calculations are required in this paper. However, you should be aware of the basic principles as revised below, as these will apply similarly to companies' investments.

Knowledge brought forward from Paper 4 (IFIN)

Portfolio theory – diversification of risk

- When investments are combined within a portfolio, **expected returns** will combine on a weighted average basis, but the ways that risks combine will depend upon the nature and extent of **correlation** between the investments.

- There will be **positive correlation** when the returns from the separate investment tend to move in the same direction under the same change of market/economic conditions.

- There will be **negative correlation** when the returns tend to move in opposite directions – the returns on one will increase as a response to the change, whilst the returns on the other will decrease.

- The **correlation coefficient (R) is** used to measure the strength and nature of the correlation between investments – the nearer it is to +1, the greater the positive correlation; the nearer it is to –1, the stronger the negative correlation.

- Combining investments with perfect positive correlation (R = +1) will result in a portfolio risk equal to the weighted average of the individual risks, and there has been **no diversification**.

- Combining investments with anything other than perfect positive correlation will result in **some of the individual risks being diversified away** (cancelled out) and the resulting portfolio risk will be less than a weighted average.

- The nearer R is to – 1, the greater the extent of diversification.

- The element of an investment's risk that can be diversified away by including it in a well-diversified portfolio is known as the **unsystematic (or specific) risk.** This is the variability of returns that is attributable to factors particular to that company or its market sector.

- The element of risk that is left to contribute to overall portfolio risk is the **systematic (or market) risk.** This is the variation in returns caused by factors affecting the market as a whole, eg economic, political, fiscal.

3.3 Just as an investor can reduce the risk of variable returns by diversifying into a portfolio of different securities, a company can reduce its own risk and so stabilise its profitability if it invests in a portfolio of different projects or operations, assuming that any positive correlation between returns is weak.

(a) If a company which manufactures garden tables diversifies into manufacturing umbrellas for garden tables, it is unlikely that the diversification will reduce risk, because the returns from trading in garden tables and garden table umbrellas will be positively correlated, both depending on the strength of demand for garden furniture.

(b) On the other hand, if a company which manufactures and sells computer equipment were to diversify into trading in video recorders, children's clothing, industrial paints, domestic plumbing and electrical services, it is probable that its risk of variable profits would be reduced.

Should companies try to diversify?

3.4 The answer to this question is not clear-cut, and you can probably think of examples of large companies today which concentrate mainly on a single industry or product range and **conglomerates** which are **widely diversified** (for example, the 'guns-to-buns' Tomkins group, which, however, demerged its Rank Hovis McDougall subsidiary in late 1999 to reduce its degree of diversification).

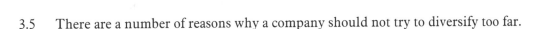

KEY TERM

Conglomerate is an entity comprising a number of dissimilar businesses.   *(OT 2000)*

3.5 There are a number of reasons why a company should not try to diversify too far.

(a) A company may employ people with particular skills, and it will get the best out of its employees by allowing them to stick to **doing what they are good at**. A manager with expert knowledge of the electronics business, for example, might not be any good at managing a retailing business. Some managers can adapt successfully to running a diversified business, and a company can acquire employees with the necessary skills by taking over other companies. Even so, diversification will not necessarily succeed, because a company may lack the skills and expertise to be a successful diversified business.

(b) When companies try to grow, they will often find the best opportunities to make **extra profits in industries or markets** with which they are familiar. If a market opens up for say, a new electronic consumer product, the companies which are likely to exploit the market most profitably are those which already have experience in producing electronic consumer products.

(c) **Conglomerates** are **vulnerable** to **takeover bids** where the buyer plans to 'unbundle' the companies in the group and sell them off individually at a profit. A reason why conglomerates are vulnerable to takeover bids is that their returns will often be mediocre rather than high, and so the stock market will value the shares on a fairly low P/E ratio. Separate companies within the group would be valued according to their individual performance and prospects, often at P/E ratios that are much higher than for the conglomerate as a whole.

(d) A company can reduce its business risk by **diversifying** and lower business risk would protect the company's shareholders; however, a shareholder does not need the company to reduce investment risk on his behalf. The shareholder can reduce risk himself by diversifying into shares in a range of different companies. Why should a company try to reduce risk when investors can do this themselves?

(e) Investors can probably **reduce investment risk more efficiently** than companies. They have a wider range of investment opportunities. Investments with uncorrelated or negatively correlated returns will be easier to identify. Estimates of beta factors will be more reliable for quoted companies' shares than for companies' capital expenditure projects.

3.6 These arguments suggest that a company should not necessarily diversify widely into completely different products and markets. On the other hand, it would be against the interests of shareholders if a company were to be so unprofitable that it went into liquidation. Companies should try to obtain some protection against short-term profit changes, and some diversification will help to provide this protection.

Limitations of portfolio analysis for the financial manager

3.7 **Portfolio analysis** offers a way in which the financial manager can deal with risk by diversifying through the investment decisions which are made by the firm. However, portfolio theory applied to the selection of investment proposals has a number of limitations.

(a) In practice, it may require guesswork to **estimate probabilities** of different outcomes, for example when a new product is to be developed. In other cases, such as machine replacement, sufficient information may however be available to make relatively good probability estimates.

(b) It will be difficult in practical cases to know what are **shareholders' preferences** between risk and return and therefore to reflect these preferences in decision-making.

(c) The **agency problem** in management's relationship to the company is relevant. Portfolio theory is based on the notion of managers assessing the relevant probabilities and deciding the combination of activities that a business will be involved in. Managers have the security of their jobs to consider, while the shareholder can easily buy and sell securities. It is arguable that managers are as a result more risk-averse than shareholders, and this may distort managers' investment decisions.

(d) Projects may be of such a size that they are **not easy to divide** in accordance with recommended diversification principles.

(e) The theory assumes that there are **constant returns to scale**, in other words that the percentage returns provided by a project are the same however much is invested in it. In practice, there may be economies of scale to be gained from making a larger investment in a single project.

(f) Other aspects of risk not covered by the theory may need to be considered, eg **bankruptcy costs**.

International portfolio diversification

3.8 Given the increased liberalisation of domestic capital markets and the increasing internationalisation of the financial system, the investor or company seeking a diversified portfolio does not need to restrict its choice to domestic investments.

3.9 Approximately 7% of total world equities has been estimated to comprise cross-border holdings. Even so, it is arguable that there remains a domestic bias among many types of investor, which can be attributed to a number of **barriers** to international investment, including the following.

(a) Legal restrictions exist in some markets, limiting ownership of securities by foreign investors.

(b) Foreign exchange regulations may prohibit international investment or make it more expensive.

(c) Double taxation of income from foreign investment may deter investors.

(d) There are likely to be higher information and transaction costs associated with investing in foreign securities.

(e) Some types of investor may have a parochial 'home bias' for domestic investment.

Diversification of risk

3.10 There are a number of arguments in favour of international portfolio diversification. A portfolio which is diversified internationally should in theory be less risky than a purely domestic portfolio. This is of advantage to any risk-averse investor. As with a purely domestic portfolio, the extent to which risk is reduced by international diversification will depend upon the degree of correlation between individual investments in the portfolio. The lower the degree of correlation between returns on the investments, the more risk can be avoided by diversification.

3.11 On the international dimension, a number of factors help to ensure that there is often low correlation between returns on investments in different countries and therefore enhance the potential for risk reduction, including the following.

(a) Different countries are often at **different stages** of the **trade cycle** at any one time.

(b) Monetary, fiscal and exchange rate policies differ internationally.

(c) Different countries have different endowments of natural resources and different industrial bases.

(d) Potentially risky political events are likely to be localised within particular national or regional boundaries.

On the other hand, for countries within the same region having closely linked economies, such as the USA and Canada, correlations are relatively high.

3.12 A study published in *Financial Analysts Journal* (1974) found that a fully diversified international portfolio had less than half the risk (measured as the variance of portfolio return ÷ variance of return on a typical security) of a fully diversified US domestic portfolio.

Risks and returns

3.13 Securities markets in different countries differ considerably in the combination of risk and return which they offer. For example, a study of fifteen major stock markets over the period 1973 to 1982 found that the Hong Kong, Singapore and UK stock markets were characterised by high risk but high returns while the US market displayed low risk and low returns.

Exchange rates

3.14 Exchange rate fluctuations will generally have implications for international portfolio diversification where the investment is in a country whose **currency floats** against that of the investor's own country's currency. Indeed, the volatility in exchange rates between major currencies in recent years is sometimes cited as a barrier to international investment.

3.15 Foreign exchange markets can often be almost as volatile as stock markets. Overall, fluctuations in exchange rates make international investment more risky, but this does not negate the fact that international portfolio diversification is worthwhile for investors wishing to reduce the risk of a portfolio.

Are multinational firms less risky than domestic firms?

3.16 The evidence on this issue suggests that, unlike a portfolio of stocks drawn from different international markets, the **share price behaviour** of multinational companies closely **reflects** that of **non-multinational domestic firms**. It follows that the reduction of risk (ie the reduction in the variance of portfolio return) which international portfolio diversification can achieve is not likely to be gained through the strategy of investing in a domestically based multinational.

4 REDUCING CREDIT RISK

KEY TERM

Credit risk is the possibility that a loss may occur from the failure of another party to perform according to the terms of a contract. *(OT 2000)*

4.1 The elements of a basic credit or debtor management strategy were covered in some detail in your earlier studies. Revising these briefly:

Knowledge brought forward from Paper 4 (IFIN)

Debtor management policies and procedures

- Assess the **creditworthiness** of new customers before extending credit, by obtaining trade, bank and credit agency references and making use of information from financial statements and salesmen's reports.

- Set **credit limits** and **credit periods** in line with those offered by competitors, but taking account of the status of individual customers.

- Set up a system of **credit control** that will ensure that credit checks and terms are being adhered to.

- Set out clear **debt collection procedures** to be followed.

- **Monitor** the efficiency of the system by the regular production and review of **reports** such as age analysis, credit and bad debt ratios and statistical analyses of incidences and causes of default and bad debts amongst different types of customer and trade.

- Consider the use of a **debt factor** to assist in the management, collection and financing of debts where this is cost effective.

4.2 Where a company trades overseas, the risk of bad debts is potentially increased by the lack of direct contact with, and knowledge of, the overseas customers and the business environment within which they operate. Whilst the basic methods of minimising foreign credit risk will be as set out above, we shall here consider the additional options available to the exporter.

4.3 Methods of reducing the risks of bad debts in foreign trade include:

- **Export factoring**
- **Forfaiting**
- **Documentary credits**
- **International credit unions**
- **Export credit insurance**

Export factoring

4.4 **Export factoring** is essentially the same as factoring domestic trade debts. Factoring, as compared with forfaiting which we discuss below, is widely regarded as an appropriate mechanism for trade finance and collection of receivables for small to medium-sized exporters, especially where there is a flow of small-scale contracts.

4.5 A factoring service typically offers prepayment of up to 80% against approved invoices. Service charges vary between around 0.75% and 3% of total invoice value, plus finance charges at levels comparable to bank overdraft rates for those taking advantage of prepayment arrangements.

Forfaiting

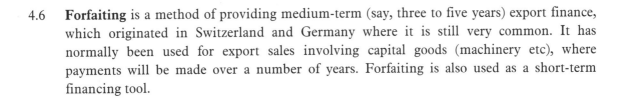

KEY TERM

Forfaiting is the purchase of financial instruments such as bills of exchange or letters of credit on a non-recourse basis by a forfaiter, who deducts interest (in the form of a discount) at an agreed rate for the period covered by the notes. The forfaiter assumes the responsibility for claiming the debt from the importer (buyer) who initially accepted the financial instrument drawn by the seller of the goods. Traditionally forfaiting is fixed-rate medium-term (one to five year) finance. *(OT 2000)*

4.6 **Forfaiting** is a method of providing medium-term (say, three to five years) export finance, which originated in Switzerland and Germany where it is still very common. It has normally been used for export sales involving capital goods (machinery etc), where payments will be made over a number of years. Forfaiting is also used as a short-term financing tool.

4.7 Forfaiting works as follows.

(a) An exporter of capital goods finds an overseas buyer who wants medium-term credit to finance the purchase. The buyer must be willing:

(i) To pay some of the cost (perhaps 15%) at once

(ii) To pay the balance in **regular instalments** (perhaps every six months) normally for the next five years

(b) The buyer will either:

(i) Issue a series of promissory notes, or

(ii) Accept a series of drafts

with a final maturity date, say, five years ahead but providing for regular payments over this time, in other words, a series of promissory notes maturing every six months, usually each for the same amount.

(c) If the buyer has a very good credit standing, the exporter might not ask for the promissory notes (or drafts) to be guaranteed. In most cases, however, the buyer will be required to find a bank which is willing to guarantee (**avalise**) the notes or drafts.

(d) At the same time, the exporter must find a bank that is willing to be a 'forfaiter'. Some banks specialise in this type of finance.

(e) Forfaiting is the business of **discounting (negotiating)** medium-term promissory drafts or bills. Discounting is normally at a fixed rate, notified by the bank (forfaiter) to the exporter when the financing arrangement is made. If the exporter arranges forfaiting with a bank before the export contract is signed with the buyer, the exporter will be able to incorporate the cost of discounting into the contract price.

(f) The exporter will deliver the goods and receive the avalised promissory notes or accepted bills. He will then sell them to the forfaiter, who will purchase them **without recourse to the exporter**. The forfaiter must now bear the following risks:

   (i) Risks of non-payment

   (ii) Political risks in the buyer's country

   (iii) The transfer risk that the buyer's country might be unable to meet its foreign exchange obligations

   (iv) Foreign exchange risk (The forfaiter holds the promissory notes and has paid cash to the exporter, and therefore it is the forfaiter who accepts the exchange risk.)

   (v) Collection of payment from the avalising bank

4.8 The following diagram should help to clarify the procedures.

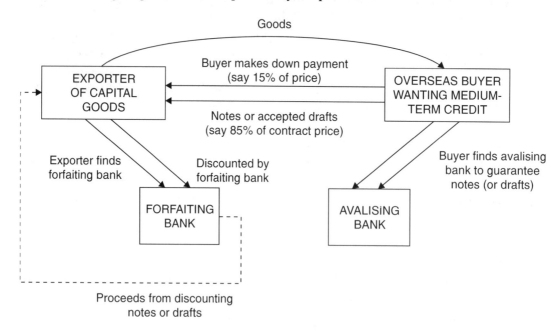

4.9 Forfaiting can be an expensive choice and arranging it takes time. However, it can be a useful way of enabling trade to occur in cases where other methods of ensuring payment and smooth cash flow are not certain, and in cases where trade may not be possible by other means.

Documentary credits

4.10 **Documentary credits ('letters of credit')** provide a method of payment in international trade which gives the exporter a risk-free method of obtaining payment.

4.11 At the same time, documentary credits are a method of obtaining short-term finance from a bank, for working capital. This is because a bank might agree to discount or negotiate a bill of exchange.

(a) The exporter receives immediate payment of the amount due to him, less the discount, instead of having to wait for payment until the end of the credit period allowed to the buyer.

(b) The buyer is able to get a period of credit before having to pay for the imports.

Banks may advance pre-shipment finance to help with manufacture.

4.12 The buyer (a foreign buyer, or a UK importer) and the seller (a UK exporter or a foreign supplier) first of all agree a contract for the sale of the goods, which provides for payment through a documentary credit. The **buyer** then requests a bank in his country to issue a **letter of credit** in favour of the exporter. This bank which issues the letter of credit is known as the **issuing bank.** The buyer is known as the **applicant** for the credit and the exporter is known as the **beneficiary** (because he receives the benefits).

4.13 The issuing bank, by issuing its letter of credit, guarantees payment to the beneficiary. Banks are involved in the credits, not in the underlying contracts. The cost of issuing a letter of credit is usually borne by the buyer.

4.14 A documentary credit arrangement must be made between the exporter, the buyer and participating banks **before the export sale takes place**. Documentary credits are slow to arrange, and administratively cumbersome; however, they might be considered essential where the risk of non-payment is high, or when dealing for the first time with an unknown buyer.

International credit unions

4.15 **International credit unions** are organisations or associations of finance houses or banks in different countries (in Europe). The finance houses or banks have reciprocal arrangements for providing instalment credit finance. When a buyer in one country wants to pay for imported goods by instalments the exporter can approach a member of the credit union in his own country which will then arrange for the finance to be provided through a credit union member in the importer's country. The exporter receives immediate payment without recourse to himself. The buyer obtains instalment credit finance. Without the existence of international co-operation between members of a credit union, importers would have more difficulty in obtaining instalment credit finance.

4.16 Suppose, for example, that an exporter in the UK wishes to sell some capital goods to a customer in Germany and the customer wants to pay for the goods by instalment.

(a) The exporter can approach a member of an international credit union in the UK, and ask for the necessary instalment finance to be arranged through a German member of the credit union.

(b) Details of the proposed sale will be given to the German finance house or bank, which will then decide on the terms of instalment credit it will offer to the German buyer (in accordance with the German laws and practice).

(c) The UK finance house will receive full payment for the goods from the German finance house and pay the exporter. The German finance house is then left with a normal hire purchase agreement with the German buyer.

4.17 This type of scheme has advantages for small exporters who cannot afford to allow lengthy credit periods to its overseas customers. Examples of international credit unions are the European Credit Union and Eurocredit.

Export credit insurance

4.18 Export credit insurance is insurance against the risk of non-payment by foreign customers for export debts. Not all exporters take out export credit insurance because premiums are very high and the benefits are sometimes not fully appreciated; but, if they do, they will obtain an insurance policy from a private insurance company that deals in export credit insurance.

4.19 Although a number of private sector companies in the UK (such as Trade Indemnity) offer export credit insurance, the largest provider is NCM UK, which insures more than 6,000 British companies in trade with 200 countries. The UK government's **Export Credit Guarantee Department (ECGD)** also exists to providing long-term guarantees to banks on behalf of exporters.

4.20 Export credit insurance is not essential, eg when exporters are reasonably confident that all their customers are trustworthy. You might be wondering why export credit insurance should ever be necessary, when exporters can pursue non-paying customers through the courts in order to obtain payment. The answer is as follows.

(a) If a credit customer defaults on payment, the task of pursuing the case through the courts will be lengthy, and it might be a long time before payment is eventually obtained.

(b) There are various reasons why non-payment might happen. Export credit insurance provides insurance against non-payment for a variety of risks in addition to the buyer's failure to pay on time. The types of risk covered are described later.

The short-term guarantee

4.21 As already mentioned, NCM UK provides of credit insurance for short-term export credit business. A credit insurance policy for export trade on short-term credit (up to 180 days) or on cash terms is known as a short-term guarantee.

4.22 Exporters can choose to obtain credit insurance:

- For all their export business on a regular basis
- For selected parts of their export business
- For occasional, high-value export sales

However, NCM UK prefers to provide comprehensive insurance for an exporter's entire export business.

5   FRAUD

Fraud

5.1   Give an employee responsibility, and he may manage the resources under his control dishonestly. The incidence of **financial fraud**, including fraud in a computer environment, appears to be increasing fast. This trend, together with the increasing sophistication of fraudsters, creates difficult problems for management.

> **KEY TERM**
>
> In a famous court case, **fraud** was defined as:
>
> 'a false representation of fact made with the knowledge of its falsity, or without belief in its truth, or recklessly careless, whether it be true or false.'

Types of fraud

5.2   Some of the most common methods of fraud are described briefly in the following paragraphs.

Ghost employees

5.3   These are imaginary employees for whom the wages department prepare wage packets which are distributed amongst the fraudsters. This type of fraud arises when there is extensive reliance on casual workers, and minimal record keeping for such workers. Inflated overtime claims can also result from poor time recording systems.

Miscasting of the payroll

5.4   This fraud often succeeds due to its simplicity. If there are twenty employees, each to be paid £100, then the computer program for the payroll could be adjusted so that an extra £50 is added to the total added up for the amounts to be paid. Thus management approve a payment of £2,050 for the period's wages, each employee gets his £100 and the fraudster collects his extra £50. Manual payroll systems can be manipulated in a similar way. When employees are paid in cash, this type of fraud can be hard to trace.

Stealing unclaimed wages

5.5   This is effectively confined to wages paid in cash and can occur when an employee leaves without notice or is away sick. In the case of a subsequent claim for unpaid wages, it could be claimed that the cash in the original pay packet was paid back into the bank.

Collusion with external parties

5.6   This could involve suppliers, customers or their staff. Possible frauds are overcharging on purchase invoices, undercharging on sales invoices or the sale of confidential information (eg customer lists, expansion plans) to a competitor. Management should watch out for unusual discounts or commissions being given or taken, or for an excessive zeal on the part of an employee to handle all business with a particular company.

Teeming and lading

5.7   This is a 'rolling' fraud rather than a 'one-off' fraud. It occurs when a clerk has the chance to misappropriate payments from debtors or to creditors. Cash received by the company is 'borrowed' by the cashier rather than being kept as petty cash or banked. (It is also possible, although riskier and more difficult to organise, to misappropriate cheques made payable to the company.) When the cashier knows that a reconciliation is to be performed, or audit visit planned, he pays the money back so that everything appears satisfactory at that point, but after the audit the teeming and lading starts again. Surprise visits by auditors and independent checking of cash balances should discourage this fraud.

5.8   A common fraud, arising when one employee has sole control of the sales ledger and recording debtors' cheques, is to pay cheques into a separate bank account, either by forged endorsement or by opening an account in a name similar to the employer's.

5.9   The clerk has to allocate cheques or cash received from other debtors against the account of the debtor whose payment was misappropriated. This prevents other staff from asking why the account is still overdue or from sending statements etc to the debtors. However, the misallocation has to continue as long as the money is missing. This fraud, therefore, never really stops.

5.10   It can be detected by independent verification of debtors balances (eg by circulation) and by looking at unallocated payments, if the sales ledger is organised to show this. In addition, sending out itemised monthly statements to debtors should act as a deterrent, although in a really elaborate fraud the clerk may be keeping two sets of books, so that the statements show the debtor's own analysis of amounts due and paid off in the month, but do not agree with the books.

Altering cheques and inflating expense claims

5.11   These are self-explanatory.

Stealing assets

5.12   Using the company's assets for personal gain and stealing fully depreciated assets are both encountered in practice. Whether or not the private use of company telephones and photocopiers is a serious matter is up to the company to judge, but it may still be fraudulent. More serious examples include the sale by employees of unused time on the computer, which is a growing fraud.

Issuing false credit notes

5.13   Another way of avoiding detection when cash and cheques received from debtors have been misappropriated is to issue a credit note which is not sent to the customer (who has paid his account) but is recorded in the books. Again, the issue of itemised statements monthly should show this up, as the customer would query the credit note. A similar tactic is to write a debt off as bad to cover up the disappearance of the payment.

Failing to record all sales

5.14   A very elaborate fraud may be perpetrated in a business with extremely poor controls over sales recording and minimal segregation of duties. In such circumstances, a dishonest bookkeeper may invoice customers but fail to record the invoices so that the customer's payments never have to be recorded and the misappropriation is not missed.

Managing fraud risk

5.15 Fraud risk may be minimised by management taking the following steps.

- Identify fraud risks in the industry
- Identify the fraud risks in the company
- Examine how particular circumstances within the organisation create fraud risk
- Review how the company manages risk
- Review how internal controls reduce the risk.

Identifying fraud risks in the industry

5.16 External factors, such as increased competition, technological development, new regulations or changing customer needs might change the risk of fraud.

- Technology changes might change the cost structure significantly.
- Increased competition may provide the motivation for manipulating results.

Identifying fraud risks in the company

5.17 There may be:

- Factors increasing the risk of fraud (personnel, culture or company structure)
- Specific risks to which a company may be exposed (handling large volumes of cash)

Circumstances creating fraud risk

5.18 Examples include:

- New staff
- New information system
- Rapid growth
- New technology
- New activities
- Corporate restructuring
- New foreign trading operations

How the company manages fraud risk

5.19 To fight fraud effectively demands a coherent corporate strategy. **Fraud policy statements** communicate this through the organisation.

Reviewing how controls manage fraud risk

5.20 The cost of controls must be balanced against the risk of fraud, whose cost is of course more difficult to quantify. (Risk management is supposed to protect profit, not to create costs.)

Prevention of fraud

5.21 Fraud will only be prevented successfully if potential fraudsters perceive the risk of detection as being high, and if personnel are adequately screened before employment and given no incentive to turn against the company once employed. The following safeguards should therefore be implemented:

- A good internal control system, in particular segregation of duties
- Continuous supervision of all employees
- Surprise audit visits
- Thorough personnel procedures

5.22 **The work of employees must be monitored** as this will increase the perceived risk of being discovered. Actual results must regularly be compared against budgeted results, and employees should be asked to explain significant variances.

5.23 **Surprise audit visits** are a valuable contribution to preventing fraud.

(a) If a cashier is carrying out a teeming and lading fraud and is told that an audit visit is due the following week, he may be able to square up the books before the visit so that the auditors will find nothing wrong.

(b) However, if the threat of a surprise visit is constantly present, the cashier will not be able to carry out a teeming and lading fraud without the risk of being discovered, and this risk is usually sufficient to prevent the fraud. The auditors do not need to carry out any sophisticated audit tests during their surprise visit. The fraud deterrent effect on the employee is highly significant, because the employee thinks that every figure is being checked.

5.24 Finally, **personnel procedures** must be adequate to prevent the occurrence of frauds.

(a) Whenever a fraud is discovered, the fraudster should be dismissed and the police should be informed. Too often an employee is 'asked to resign' and then moves on to a similar job where the fraud is repeated, often because management fear loss of face or investor confidence. This is a self-defeating policy.

(b) On recruitment, all new employees should be required to produce adequate references from their previous employers.

(c) If an employee's lifestyle changes dramatically, explanations should be sought.

(d) Every employee must be made to take his annual holiday entitlement. Often in practice the employee who is 'so dedicated that he never takes a holiday' is in fact not taking his leave for fear of his fraud being discovered by his replacement worker while he is away.

(e) Pay levels should be adequate and working conditions of a reasonable standard. If employees feel that they are being paid an unfairly low amount or 'exploited', they may look for ways to supplement their pay dishonestly.

Management fraud

5.25 So far, we have concentrated on employee fraud. However, arguably more serious (and very much more difficult to prevent and detect) is the growing problem of **management fraud**. While employee fraud is usually undertaken purely for the employee's financial gain, management fraud is often undertaken to improve the company's apparent performance, to reduce tax liabilities or to improve manager's promotion prospects.

5.26 Managers are often in a position to override internal controls and to intimidate their subordinates into collusion or turning a blind eye. This makes it difficult to detect such frauds. In addition, where the company is benefiting financially rather than the manager, it can be difficult to persuade staff that any dishonesty is involved.

5.27 This clash of interest between loyalty to an employer and professional integrity can be difficult to resolve and can compromise an internal auditor's independence. Management fraud often comes to light after a takeover or on a change of audit staff or practices. Its consequences can be far reaching for the employing company in damaging its reputation or because it results in legal action. Because management usually have access to much larger sums of money than more lowly employees, the financial loss to the company can be immense.

Advance fee fraud

5.28 This type of fraud involves the fraudster taking a fee or deposit up-front, promising to deliver in the future goods and services which never materialise.

5.29 Many companies have been exposed to such frauds from international sources. In recent years, for example, the highest incidence of such fraud led to the Central Bank of Nigeria publishing warnings around the world. Hopefully, wide publicity about the details of such fraud schemes will mean that fewer such frauds will be perpetrated successfully.

Case example

Advance fee fraud in Nigeria

The advance fee fraud is normally perpetrated by the sending of a letter that promises to transfer millions of US dollars to the addressee's bank account. In order to gain access to the funds, the addressee is requested to assist in paying various 'taxes' and 'fees' that will allow the funds to be processed. The fraudsters often make use of fake Government, Central Bank and Nigerian National Petroleum Corporation documents and go to considerable lengths to give the scam the appearance of a legitimate offer. They request confidentiality about the transaction.

The gathering of advance fees, made up of supposed legal fees, registration fees, VAT and so on is the actual objective of the scam.

Two recent variants of the scam have been reported. The first, normally directed at religious and charitable organisations, is the request for fees to process bogus inheritances from a will. The second is an offer to use chemicals to transform paper into US dollar bills with the proceeds being shared by both parties.

Responsibility for reporting fraud to management

5.30 A company's **external auditors** are required to report all instances of fraud that they find to the company's management, unless they suspect management of being involved in the fraud. If they uncover fraud by management, they should report the matter to the appropriate **public authorities** or seek **legal advice**. The external auditors should also report to management any material (ie significant) **weakness in the company's systems of accounting and internal control.**

5.31 If **internal auditors** uncover instances of fraud, they should also report this to executive management. If they discover management fraud, they should make use of lines of communication to the company's **audit committee**, which should be in place as a matter of good corporate governance practice. The audit committee should have the authority to take appropriate action, which is likely to include discussion of the matter with the external auditors.

6 RISK ANALYSIS TECHNIQUES

> **KEY TERMS**
>
> **Uncertainty** is the inability to predict the outcomes from an activity due to a lack of information about the required input/output relationships or about the environment within which the activity takes place. *(OT 2000)*

6.1 We conclude this chapter by reviewing the techniques you may be required to use in decision-making questions where conditions of uncertainty and/or risk exist. Most of this was covered in your earlier studies of Paper 9, and is only briefly revised here.

6.2 There are basically two ways of analysing risk and uncertainty.

(a) One approach takes the view that estimates of future costs, sales demand and revenues will at best be based on **rational opinions** and assumptions, and actual results might easily be better or worse than estimated. Just how much better or worse than what is estimated is unquantifiable.

(b) Another approach takes the view that we can provide **quantified estimates** of how the future outcomes might vary. These quantified estimates will often be expressed as probabilities that a particular outcome will occur. For example, estimates of future sales demand might be made as follows.

Sales demand	Probability
Units	
10,000	0.2
12,000	0.5
15,000	0.2
20,000	0.1

6.3 Analysing possible future outcomes can be done using either approach (a) or approach (b). Approach (a) might be described as **uncertainty analysis**, whereas the more quantifiable approach (b) might be described in contrast as **risk analysis**. The distinction between **uncertainty** and **risk**, if you are called on to make one, is basically a matter of whether or not the variability of future outcomes can be quantified or not.

6.4 The methods or techniques of analysing uncertainty and risk, and of taking uncertainty and risk into consideration when reaching a decision, include the following.

(a) **Conservative estimates** can be made. Here outcomes are estimated in a conservative manner in order to provide a built-in safety factor. However, the method fails to consider explicitly a range of outcomes and, by concentrating only on conservative figures, may also fail to consider the expected or most likely outcomes.

(b) We can look at the **worst possible and best possible outcomes,** as well as the **most likely** outcome, and reach a decision which takes these into account.

(c) **Sensitivity analysis** can be used.

(d) We can assess probabilities and calculate for each decision alternative:

    (i) The **expected value** of costs or benefits and also, possibly, the **standard deviation** of the possible outcomes

    (ii) A **probability distribution** of the possible outcomes

Decision trees might be used to show the alternatives facing the decision maker. Computerised decision models might also be used.

(e) We can assess the **value of having more information** to help the decision maker to reach a decision.

Knowledge brought forward from Paper 9 (IDEC)

Sensitivity analysis

- Sensitivity analysis is a modelling procedure in which changes are made to significant variables in order to determine the effect of these changes on the planned outcome. Those variables that are identified as being of particular significance to the decision are thereafter given particular attention.

- Margin or error sensitivity analysis assesses, for one variable input of a decision computation, the amount by which that variable could change from its current value before the decision changes

- One of the most common applications that you may come across is in the context of NPV investment appraisal. Sensitivity analysis can be applied to individual sales volumes, activity levels, discount rates and project duration to determine the value at which each in turn will cause the NPV to change from positive to negative.

- The general rule for a NPV cash flow margin of error is as follows:

$$\% \text{ change required in variable to take NPV to 0} = \frac{\text{NPV project}}{\text{PV of cash flows relating to variable}}$$

- Sensitivity analysis in its simplest form can be unrealistic as it assumes only one variable changing at a time. It also ignores the likelihood of variability.

Probability estimates of cash flows

- Where a probability distribution for possible cash flows can be derived, the **expected value** of the cash flow can be used $= \Sigma(\text{cash flow} \times \text{probability})$

- To take account of **risk** we can calculate:

  ° The best and worst outcomes, with their probabilities
  ° The probability that a loss, or a negative NPV, will be made

Decision trees

- Decision trees are used where a decision involves a number of chance outcomes and sub-decisions. it is a pictorial representation of the logic of the decision, incorporating cash flows and probabilities.

- The decision is evaluated by 'rolling back' through the tree from right to left, computing expected values at chance forks and making decisions based on these values at decisions point.

Question 1

A project has a net present value at 12% of £4,270. There is, however, uncertainty about a cost at year 2 which is estimated to be £50,000. What percentage increase in this cost would make the project non-viable?

Answer

The present value of the cost is £50,000 × 0.797 = £39,850.

The required increase is £4,270/£39,850 = 0.10715 = 10.715%, or about 11%.

Question 2

Elsewhere Ltd is considering the production of a new consumer item with a five year product lifetime. In order to manufacture this time it would be necessary to build a new plant. After having considered several alternative strategies, management are left with the following three possibilities.

Strategy A: build a large plant at an estimated cost of £600,000

This strategy faces two types of market conditions: high demand with a probability of 0.7 or low demand with a probability of 0.3. If the demand is high the company can expect to receive a net annual cash inflow of £250,000 for each of the next five years. If the demand is low there would be a net annual cash outflow of £50,000.

Strategy B: build a small plant at an estimated cost of £350,000

This strategy also faces two types of market conditions: high demand with a probability of 0.7 or low demand with a probability of 0.3. The net annual cash inflow of the five-year period for the small plant is £25,000 if the demand is low and is £150,000 if the demand is high.

Strategy C: do not build a plant initially

This strategy consists of leaving the decision for one year whilst more information is collected. The resulting information can be positive or negative with estimated probabilities of 0.8 and 0.2 respectively. At the end of this time management may decide to build either a large plant or a small plant at the same costs as at present providing the information is positive. If the resulting information is negative, management would decide to build no plant at all. Given positive information the probabilities of high and low demand change to 0.9 and 0.1 respectively, regardless of which plant is built. The net annual cash inflows for the remaining four-year period for each type of plant are the same as those given in strategies A and B.

All costs and revenues are given in present value terms and should not be discounted.

Required

(a) Draw a decision tree to represent the alternative courses of action open to the company.

(b) Determine the expected return for each possible course of action and hence decide the best course of action for the management of Elsewhere Ltd.

Answer

(a) Decision tree for a possible new plant

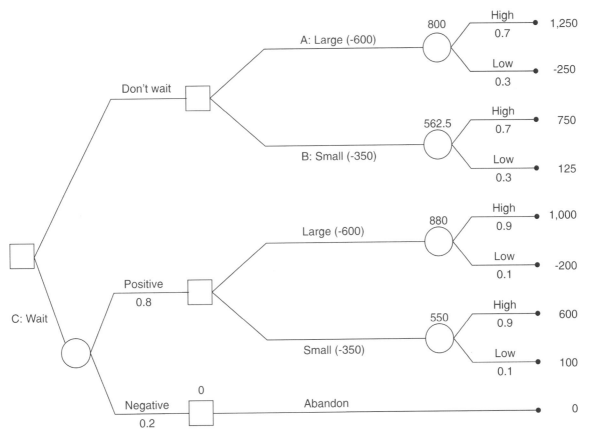

Key
☐ Decision point
○ Outcome point

(b) Evaluation of the decision tree (see above) shows that the best course of action is to wait a year, and then build a large plant if positive information is received, but abandon the project if negative information is received.

Expected values (in thousands of pounds) are calculated as follows.

Large plant now (A)	$(0.7 \times 5 \times 250) - (0.3 \times 5 \times 50) - 600$	= 200
Small plant now (B)	$(0.7 \times 5 \times 150) + (0.3 \times 5 \times 25) - 350$	= 212.5

Large plant following positive information

$$(0.9 \times 4 \times 250) - (0.1 \times 4 \times 50) - 600 \qquad = 280$$

Small plant following positive information

$$(0.9 \times 4 \times 150) + (0.1 \times 4 \times 25) - 350 \qquad = 200$$

Positive information: higher of 280 and 180, ie 280

Waiting (C)	$(0.8 \times 280) + (0.2 \times 0)$	= 224

224 is higher than either 200 or 212.5, hence the recommendation to wait.

6.5 Other techniques for dealing with risk and uncertainty include:

(a) Adjusting the discount rate in NPV appraisal

(b) Applying a time limit to the payback period (normal/discounted)

(c) The certainty equivalent approach – reducing future cash flows by a certain margin to arrive at a revised present value. This margin may increase over time, so for example, you might include in the NPV appraisal 80% of what you estimate year 1 cash flows are most likely to be, 70% of what you estimate year 2 cash flows are most likely to be and so on. This is covered in more detail in Chapter 17.

Adjusting the discount rate

6.6   With this method of allowing for risk, a premium is added to the discount rate used in appraising investments as a safety margin. Marginally profitable projects are then less likely to have a positive NPV. For example, if a company's cost of capital is say 10%, a very risky project might be discounted at, say, 15% and a less risky project might be evaluated at a discount rate of, say, 12%.

6.7   This method recognises that risky investments ought to earn a higher return as reward for the risks that are taken. The problem with the method is that the size of the risk premium to be added is chosen arbitrarily unless a model such as the CAPM is used (see later).

Applying a time limit to the payback period

6.8   Estimates of future cash flows are difficult to make at the best of times, and estimates of cash flows several years ahead are quite likely to be inaccurate. It is also difficult to control capital projects over a long period of time, to ensure that the expected benefits are fully realised.

6.9   A method of limiting the risk on a capital project is to apply a **payback time limit**, so that a project should not be undertaken unless it pays back within, say, four years. There are two ways of applying a payback time limit.

(a)   A project might be expected to pay back within a certain time limit, and in addition show a positive NPV from its net cash flows.

(b)   Alternatively, a project might be expected to pay back **in discounted cash flow terms** within a certain time period. For example, a project might be required to have a positive NPV on its cumulative cash flows by year 4.

Chapter roundup

- All businesses face **risk.** Some risks are necessary if profitable opportunities are to be exploited. Other risks need to be reduced and/or eliminated where possible.

- The risks faced by businesses include those arising from **general business, trading, cultural, political, currency, interest rate, technology and fraud.**

- **Risk management** needs to be recognised as an integral part of a business's operating and reporting systems.

- **Diversification** may be used to reduce risk by investing across industries, markets and **countries.**

- Management of **credit risk** is of particular importance to exporters and various instruments and other arrangements are available to assist in this.

- Potential losses arising from **fraud** can be significant and a company must seek to minimise the risk by clear fraud policy statements, effective requirement policies and good internal controls, especially over procurement and cash.

Quick quiz

1 Reducing or eliminating risk can often reduce potential profits. Give three reasons why this can be beneficial.

2 What is physical trading risk?

3 Give three examples of restrictions that may be defined as political risk

4 How has the Turnbull report contributed to risk management?

5 What is a conglomerate?

6 List ways of minimising fraud risk.

7 A fraudster takes an up-front deposit, promising to deliver at a future date, goods which never appear. What is the name for this kind of fraud?

8 'A condition in which there exists a quantifiable dispersion in the possible outcomes from any activity'. What does this define?

Answers to quick quiz

1 (a) Predictability of cash flows
   (b) Limitation of the impact of potentially bankrupting events
   (c) Increased confidence of its shareholders and other investors

2 The risk of goods being lost or stolen in transit, or the documents accompanying the goods going astray

3 Exchange controls, tax regulations, regulations on the use of local resources

4 By providing guidelines on setting up a system of risk management

5 An entity comprising a number of dissimilar businesses

6 Fraud policy statements, good internal controls, supervision of employees, surprise audit visits, effective personnel procedures

7 Advance fee fraud

8 Risk

Now try the question below from the Exam Question Bank

Number	Level	Marks	Time
10	Examination	25	45 mins

Chapter 11

INTEREST RATE RISK

Topic list		Syllabus reference	Ability required
1	Interest rate risk	(iii)	Application
2	Interest rate futures	(iii)	Application
3	Interest rate swaps	(iii)	Application
4	Interest rate options	(iii)	Application
5	Hedging strategy alternatives: example	(iii)	Application

Introduction

Here we consider **interest rate risk** and some of the financial instruments which are now available for managing financial risks, including '**derivatives**' such as **options** and **swaps**. The risk of interest rate changes is however less significant in most cases than the risk of currency fluctuations which, in some circumstances, can fairly easily wipe out profits entirely if it is not hedged. **Currency risk** or **foreign exchange risk** is considered in later chapters of this Study Text.

Learning outcomes covered in this chapter

* Identify appropriate methods for managing interest rate risk
* Demonstrate how and when to convert fixed to floating rate interest

Syllabus content covered in this chapter

* Management of interest rate risk including the use of interest rate swaps (simple calculations to illustrate an interest rate swap may be required)

* Forward rate agreements and interest rate guarantees (numerical questions will not be set on these topics)

* Illustration and interpretation of interest options using simple graphs to show caps, floors and collars (numerical questions will not be set)

1 INTEREST RATE RISK

Managing a debt portfolio

1.1 The corporate treasurers will be responsible for managing the company's **debt portfolio**, that is, in deciding how a company should obtain its short-term funds so as to:

(a) Be able to repay debts as they mature

(b) Minimise any inherent risks, notably invested foreign exchange risk, in the debts the company owes and is owed

Three important considerations in this respect are:

(a) **Maturity mix**

The treasurer must avoid having **too much debt becoming repayable** within a short period.

(b) **Currency mix**

Foreign currency debts create a risk of losses through adverse movements in foreign exchange rates before the debt falls due for payment. Foreign currency management involves **hedging** against foreign currency risks, for example by means of forward exchange contracts, or having debts in several currencies, some of which will strengthen and some of which will weaken over time.

(c) **The mix of fixed interest and floating rate debts**

    (i) Too much fixed interest rate debt creates an unnecessary cost when market interest rates fall. A company might find itself committed to high interest costs that it could have avoided.

    (ii) Too much borrowing at a floating, or variable, rate of interest (such as bank overdrafts and medium-term bank lending) leads to high costs when interest rates go up.

1.2 There are a number of situations in which a company might be exposed to risk from interest rate movements.

(a) **Fixed rate versus floating rate debt.** A company can get caught paying higher interest rates by having fixed rather than floating rate debt, or floating rather than fixed rate debt, as market interest rates change.

(b) **Currency of debt.** This is also a foreign currency exposure. A company can face higher costs if it borrows in a currency for which exchange rates move adversely against the company's domestic currency. The treasurer should seek to match the currency of the loan with the currency of the underlying operations/assets that generate revenue to pay interest/repay the loans.

(c) **Term of loan.** A company can be exposed by having to repay a loan earlier than it can afford to, resulting in a need to re-borrow, perhaps at a higher rate of interest.

(d) **Term loan or overdraft facility?** A company might prefer to pay for borrowings only when it needs the money as with an overdraft facility: the bank will charge a commitment fee for such a facility. Alternatively, a term loan might be preferred, but this will cost interest even if it is not needed in full for the whole term.

1.3 Where the magnitude of the risk is **immaterial** in comparison with the company's overall cash flows, one option is to **do nothing** and to accept the effects of any movement in interest rates which occur.

Exam focus point

Bear in mind this possibility - the decision *not* to take action to reduce interest rate risk - when answering questions in the exam.

Case examples

In their 2000 annual report, **Kingfisher** discussed its management of interest rate risk: 'The interest rate exposure of the group arising from its borrowing and deposits is managed by the use of fixed and floating rate debt and investment, interest rate swaps, cross currency interest rate swaps and interest futures. Against the backdrop of market conditions which prevailed during the year, the majority of the Group's borrowings and investments have remained at floating rates of interest.'

Tate and Lyle noted in its 2000 annual report that: 'The Groups policy is that no interest rate fixings are undertaken for more than 12 years and between 30% and 75% of Group net debt is fixed for more than one year ... If the interest rates applicable to the Group's floating rate debt rise from the levels at the end of March 2000 by an average of 1%, or 5% over the year to March 2001, this would reduce Group profit by £1 million and £5 million respectively.

Hedge efficiency

KEY TERM

Hedge is a transaction to reduce or eliminate an exposure to risk.   *(OT 2000)*

1.4   **Hedging** is the process of financial risk management. Hedging has a cost, either a fee to a financial institution or a reduction in profit, but companies might well consider the costs to be justified by the reduction in financial risks that the hedging achieves. The degree to which the exposure is covered is termed the **hedge efficiency**: a perfect hedge has 100% efficiency.

Question 1

Explain what is meant by hedging in the context of interest rate risk.

Answer

Hedging is a means of reducing risk. Hedging involves coming to an agreement with another party who is prepared to take on the risk that you would otherwise bear. The other party may be willing to take on that risk because he would otherwise bear an opposing risk which may be 'matched' with your risk; alternatively, the other party may be a speculator who is willing to bear the risk in return for the prospect of making a profit. In the case of interest rates, a company with a variable rate loan clearly faces the risk that the rate of interest will increase in the future as the result of changing market conditions which cannot now be predicted.

Many financial instruments have been introduced in recent years to help corporate treasurers to hedge the risks of interest rate movements. These instruments include forward rate agreements, financial futures, interest rate swaps and options.

Interest rate risk management

1.5   Methods of reducing interest rate risk include:

- Forward rate agreements (FRAs)
- Interest rate futures
- Interest rate options (or interest rate guarantees)
- Interest rate swaps

In the remainder of this section, we look at FRAs, before considering interest rate futures, swaps and options.

Forward rate agreements (FRAs)

> **KEY TERM**
>
> **Forward rate agreements (FRAs)** are agreements, typically between a company and a bank, about the interest rate on future borrowing or bank deposits.

1.6 A company can enter into a FRA with a bank that fixes the rate of interest for borrowing at a certain time in the future. If the actual interest rate proves to be higher than the rate agreed, the bank pays the company the difference. If the actual interest rate is lower than the rate agreed, the company pays the bank the difference.

1.7 One **limitation** on FRAs is that they are usually only available on loans of at least £500,000. They are also likely to be **difficult to obtain for periods of over one year**.

1.8 An **advantage** of FRAs is that, for the period of the FRA at least, they **protect the borrower** from adverse market interest rate movements to levels above the rate negotiated for the FRA. With a normal variable rate loan (for example linked to a bank's base rate or to LIBOR) the borrower is exposed to the risk of such adverse market movements. On the other hand, the borrower will similarly not benefit from the effects of favourable market interest rate movements.

1.9 The **interest rates** which banks will be willing to set for FRAs will reflect their current expectations of interest rate movements. If it is expected that interest rates are going to rise during the term for which the FRA is being negotiated, the bank is likely to seek a higher fixed rate of interest than the variable rate of interest which is current at the time of negotiating the FRA.

Gap analysis of interest rate risk

1.10 The degree to which a firm is exposed to interest rate risk can be identified by using the method of **gap analysis**.

1.11 Some of the interest rate risks to which a firm is exposed may **cancel each other out**, where there are both assets and liabilities with which there is exposure to interest rate changes. If interest rates rise, more interest will be payable on loans and other liabilities, but this will be compensated for by higher interest received on assets such as money market deposits.

1.12 The effect of interest rate changes depends upon whether interest rates for the assets and liabilities are floating or fixed.

(a) **Floating** interest rates, of course, move up and down according to general market conditions.

(b) With **fixed** interest rates, the interest on the asset or liability will only be repriced at the date of maturity in the light of prevailing market conditions. If a fixed interest rate liability matures at the same time as a fixed rate asset, then the interest rate risks arising from the repricing of the two instruments will cancel each other out.

1.13 Gap analysis is based on the principle of **grouping together** assets and liabilities which are sensitive to interest rate changes according to their maturity dates. Two different types of 'gap' may occur.

(a) **A negative gap**. A negative gap occurs when a firm has a larger amount of interest-sensitive liabilities maturing at a certain time or in a certain period than it has interest-sensitive assets maturing at the same time. The difference between the two amounts indicates the net exposure.

(b) **A positive gap**. There is a positive gap if the amount of interest-sensitive assets maturing in a particular time exceeds the amount of interest-sensitive liabilities maturing at the same time.

1.14 With a **negative** gap, the company faces exposure if interest rates **rise** by the time of maturity. With a **positive** gap, the company will lose out if interest rates **fall** by maturity. The company's interest rate hedge should be based on the size of the gap.

2 INTEREST RATE FUTURES

KEY TERM

Futures contract is a contract relating to currencies, commodities or shares that obliges the buyer (issuer) to purchase (sell) the specified quantity of the item represented in the contract at a pre-determined price at the expiration of the contract.

Unlike forward contracts, which are entered into privately, futures contracts are traded on organised exchanges, carry standard terms and conditions, have specific maturities, and are subject to rules concerning margin requirements. *(OT 2000)*

2.1 Most LIFFE (London International Financial Futures and Options Exchange) futures contracts involve interest rates (**interest rate futures**), and these offer a means of hedging against the risk of interest rate movements. Such contracts are effectively a gamble on whether interest rates will rise or fall. Like other futures contracts, interest rate futures offer a way in which **speculators can 'bet'** on market movements just as they offer others who are more risk-averse a way of **hedging risks.**

KEY TERM

Futures market is an exchange-traded market for the purchase or sale of a standard quantity of an underlying item such as currencies, commodities or shares, for settlement at a future date at an agreed price. *(OT 2000)*

2.2 Interest rate futures are similar in effect to FRAs, except that the terms, amounts and periods are **standardised**. For example, a company can contract to buy (or sell) £100,000 of a notional 30-year Treasury bond bearing an 8% coupon, in, say, 6 months time, at an agreed price. The basic principles behind such a decision are:

(a) The futures price is likely to vary with changes in interest rates, and this acts as a **hedge** against adverse interest rate movements. We shall see how this works in a later example.

(b) The outlay to buy futures is much less than for buying the financial instrument itself, and so a company can hedge large exposures of cash with a relatively **small initial employment of cash.**

2.3 LIFFE provides a market for futures contracts in long-dated, medium-dated and short-dated gilt-edged stocks, American, German and Japanese government bonds, short-term sterling and eurocurrency interest rates. The **Chicago Mercantile Exchange (CME)** and the **Chicago Board of Trade (CBOT)** are other important exchanges for the trading of interest rate futures.

Pricing futures contracts

2.4 The **pricing** of an interest rate futures contract is determined by prevailing interest rates. For example, if three month eurodollar time deposit interest rates are 8%, a three month eurodollar futures contract will be priced at 92 (100 − 8). If interest rates are 11%, the contract price will be 89 (100 − 11). This decrease in price, or value, of the contract, reflects the reduced attractiveness of a fixed role deposit in time of rising interest rates.

> **KEY TERM**
>
> The minimum amount by which the price of a interest rate futures contract can move is called a **tick**.

2.5 A **tick** or **basis point of price** has a known, measurable value. Here are some examples.

(a) In the case of 3-month eurodollar futures, the amount of the underlying instrument is a 3-month deposit of $1,000,000. As a tick is 0.01% (or one-hundredth of one per cent), the value of a tick is $25 (0.01% × $1,000,000 × 3/12).

(b) In the case of long gilt futures, the underlying instrument is £50,000 of notional gilts. Given that a tick is 1/32 of one per cent, the value of one tick is £15.625 (1/32 × 1% × £50,000).

2.6 Interest rate futures are not all priced in the same way.

(a) Prices of **short-term interest rate futures**, which, as already indicated, reflect the interest rates on the underlying financial instrument, are quoted at a **discount to a par value of 100**. For example, a price of 93.40 indicates that the underlying money market deposit is being traded at a rate of 6.6% (100 − 93.40).

(b) Pricing for **long-term bond futures** is as a **percentage of par value**, similarly to the pricing of bonds themselves.

   (i) In the case of US Treasury bond futures, prices are quoted in 32nds of each full percentage point of price. The number of 32nds is shown as a number following a hyphen. For example, 91-23 denotes a price of $91^{23/32}$ per 100 nominal value and 91-16 denotes a price of $91^{1/2}$ per 100 nominal value.

   (ii) For other types of bond future, decimal pricing is used, so that if Italian government bond futures are quoted at 92.75, this indicates a price of $92^{3/4}$ per 100 nominal value.

2.7 EXAMPLE: FUTURES PRICE MOVEMENTS (1)

June 3-month ecu futures fell in price on a particular day from 96.84 to 96.76. Privet plc has purchased June futures, having a 'long' position on five contracts ie they have bought now to sell later. Calculate the change in value of the contracts on the day concerned, given the value of one tick is 25 ecus (size 0.01%).

2.8 SOLUTION

The fall in price represents 8 ticks (96.84 − 96.76 = 0.08 and the tick size is 0.01%). The value of one tick is 25 ecus. Each contract has fallen in value by $25 \times 8 = 200$ ecus. Privet plc has bought five contracts and so the day's price movement represents for the company a loss on the contracts of $200 \times 5 = 1,000$ ecus.

2.9 EXAMPLE: FUTURES PRICE MOVEMENTS (2)

September long gilts sterling futures fell in price on a particular day from 99-9 to 98-27. Privet plc has sold September futures, having a 'short' position of 10 contracts, ie they have sold now to match with a later purchase. Calculate the change in value of the contract on the day concerned, given that the tick size is 1/32 of 1%.

2.10 SOLUTION

The fall in price represents 14 ticks ($99^{9/32} - 98^{27/32} = {}^{14/32}$ and the tick size is $^{1/32}$ of 1%). The value of one tick for long gilts sterling futures is £15.625. Each contract has fallen in value by $£15.625 \times 14 = £218.75$. For Privet plc, which has sold 10 contracts, the day's price movement represents a profit of $£218.75 \times 10 = £2,187.50$, (ie it will cost them less to purchase the contracts to sell).

Question 2

The following futures price movements were observed during a week in October.

Contract	Price at start of week	Price at end of week
December short sterling	90.40	91.02
December US Treasury bonds	92-16	92-06
December Japanese government bond	93.80	94.25

Hawthorn plc has the following positions in these contracts:

(a) A short position (seller) of ten December short sterling contracts (tick value = £12.50, size 0.01%)

(b) A long position (buyer) of six December US Treasury bonds contracts (Tick value = $31.25, size 1/32 of 1%)

(c) A long position of eight December Japanese government bonds contracts (tick value = Y10,000, size 0.01%)

Required

Calculate the profit or loss to the company on the futures contracts.

Answer

Short sterling

Increase in price (91.02 − 90.40 = 0.62)	62 ticks
Value per tick	£12.50
Increase in value of one contract (62 × £12.50)	£775

The company is a seller of ten contracts and would lose £7,750 (£775 × 10)

US Treasury bond futures

Fall in price ($92^{16/32} - 92^{6/32} = 10/32$)	10 ticks
Value per tick	$31.25
Fall in value of one contract (10 × $31.25)	$312.50

The company is a buyer of six contracts and would lose $1,875 ($312.50 × 6)

Japanese government bonds

Increase in price (94.25 – 93.80 = 0.45)	45 ticks
Value per tick	Y10,000
Increase in value of one contract (45 × Y10,000)	Y450,000

The company is a buyer of eight contracts and would gain Y3,600,000 (Y450,000 × 8)

2.11 EXAMPLE: INTEREST RATE HEDGE USING FUTURES

Yew plc has taken a 3 month $1,000,000 eurodollar loan with interest payable of 8%, the loan being due for rollover on 31 March. At 1 January, the company treasurer considers that interest rates are likely to rise in the near future. The futures price is 91 representing a yield of 9%. Given a standard contract size of $1,000,000 the company **sells** a eurodollar three month contract to hedge against interest on the three month loan required at 31 March (to **sell** a contract is to commit the seller to take a deposit). At 31 March the spot interest rate is 11%.

(a) What is the cost saving to Yew plc?

(b) Calculate the hedge efficiency.

2.12 SOLUTION

(a) The company can **buy back** the future at 89 (100 – 11). The cost saving is the **profit on the futures contract**.

$$\$1,000,000 \times (91 - 89) \times {}^3/_{12} = \$5,000$$

(b) The **additional interest cost** resulting from the increase in interest rates is $1,000,000 $\times (11 - 8) = 3\% \times {}^3/_{12} = \$7,500$. Hedge efficiency = $\$5,000 \div 7,500 = 66.7\%$.

The hedge has effectively reduced the new annual interest cost by 2%. Instead of a cost of 11% at 31 March ($27,500) for a three month loan, the net cost is $22,500 ($27,500 – $5,000), a 9% annual cost.

Use of interest rate futures

2.13 The standardised nature of interest rate futures is a limitation on their use by the corporate treasurer as a means of hedging, because they **cannot always be matched** with specific interest rate exposures. However, their use is growing. Futures contracts are frequently used by banks and other financial institutions as a means of hedging their portfolios: such institutions are often not concerned with achieving an exact match with their underlying exposure.

2.14 The seller of a futures contract does not have to own the underlying instrument, but may need to deliver it on the contract's delivery date if the buyer requires it. Many, but not all, interest rate contracts are **settled for cash** rather than by delivery of the underlying instrument.

2.15 Interest rate futures offer an attractive means of **speculation** for some investors, because there is no requirement that buyers and sellers should actually be lenders and borrowers (respectively) of the nominal amounts of the contracts. A relatively small investment can lead to substantial gains, or alternatively to substantial losses. The speculator is in effect 'betting' on future interest rate movements.

BPP
PUBLISHING

Basis risk

2.16 The concept of hedge efficiency was introduced earlier. There are two reasons why it is often not possible to achieve a perfect (100%) hedge with futures, as follows.

(a) The fact that futures are available only in certain standard sizes means that the contracts may not fit exactly the company's needs.

(b) There is also **basis risk,** arising from the fact that the price of the futures contract may not move as expected in relation to the value of the instrument which is being hedged. There are two main reasons for basis risk.

   (i) **Cashflow requirements** may differ, altering the relative values of the underlying financial instrument and the derivative futures contract. This is because usually no payment is required when a forward contract is entered into, while an initial margin must be deposited for a futures contract.

   (ii) The **financial instrument** which the firm is seeking to hedge may be different from the financial instrument which underlies the futures contract. For example, a firm may wish to hedge interest rates which are linked to bank base interest rates using a futures contract which is based on the London Inter-Bank Offered Rate (LIBOR). This type of hedge is called **cross hedging**, and there will be basis risk because LIBOR will not always move exactly in line with bank base interest rates.

Hedge ratio

2.17 The **hedge ratio** is the ratio of the amount of the futures contracts bought or sold to the amount of the underlying financial instrument being hedged. For example, if a company is exposed to interest rate risk on a loan of £210,000 and it takes a position in futures contracts for £200,000, the hedge ratio is:

$$\frac{200,000}{210,000} = 95.2\%$$

3 INTEREST RATE SWAPS

> **KEY TERM**
>
> **Swap** is an arrangement whereby two organisations contractually agree to exchange payments on different terms, eg in different currencies, or one at a fixed rate and the other at a floating rate. *(OT 2000)*

3.1 **Interest rate swaps** are transactions that exploit different interest rates in different markets for borrowing, to reduce interest costs for either fixed or floating rate loans.

3.2 An **interest rate swap** is an arrangement whereby two companies, or a company and a bank, swap interest rate commitments with each other. In a sense, each simulates the other's borrowings, with the following effects.

(a) A company which has debt at a fixed rate of interest can make a swap so that it ends up paying interest at a variable rate.

(b) A company which has debt at a variable rate of interest (floating rate debt) ends up paying a fixed rate of interest.

3.3   Note that the parties to a swap retain their obligations to the original lenders. This means that the parties must accept **counterparty risk**. An example is illustrated in Figure 1.

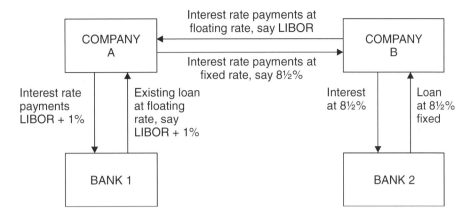

Figure 1 Interest rate swap

3.4   In this example, company A can use a swap to change from paying interest at a floating rate of LIBOR + 1% to one of paying fixed interest of (8½% + 1%) = 9½%.

3.5   A swap may be arranged with a bank, or a counterparty may be found through a bank or other financial intermediary.

3.6   Interest rate swaps could be arranged in different currencies, for example between a fixed rate in US dollars and a floating rate in sterling. Where this happens, the swaps are normally reversed with the principal eventually swapped back at the original exchange rate. For example, a UK company and a US company can arrange a back-to-back loan and currency swap (Figure 2).

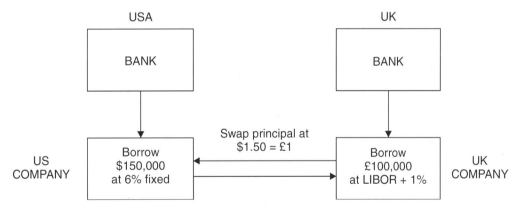

Figure 2 Back-to-back loan and currency swap

3.7   The companies can service each other's debt (interest rate swap) and also exchange the principal, with the UK company taking $150,000 and the US company taking £100,000 (currency swap). Each company will eventually repay the principal on each other's loans at a rate of $1.50 = £1.

3.8   EXAMPLE: INTEREST RATE SWAPS

Goodcredit plc has been given a high credit rating. It can borrow at a fixed rate of 11%, or at a variable interest rate equal to LIBOR, which also happens to be 11% at the moment. It would like to borrow at a variable rate.

BPP PUBLISHING

Secondtier plc is a company with a lower credit rating, which can borrow at a fixed rate of 12½% or at a variable rate of LIBOR plus ½%. It would like to borrow at a fixed rate.

(a) Without a swap, Goodcredit would borrow at LIBOR which is currently 11%, and Secondtier would borrow at 12½% fixed.

(b) With a swap:

   (i)   Goodcredit would borrow at a fixed rate (11%)

   (ii)   Secondtier would borrow at a variable rate (LIBOR plus ½%), currently 11½%

   (iii) They would then agree a rate for swapping interest, perhaps with:

          (1) Goodcredit paying Secondtier variable rate interest, at LIBOR
          (2) Secondtier paying Goodcredit fixed rate interest, say at 11½%

3.9 The net result is as follows.

Goodcredit plc		*Secondtier plc*	
Pays		Pays	
to bank	(11%)	to bank	(LIBOR plus ½%)
in swap	(LIBOR)	in swap	(11½%)
Receives		Receives	
in swap	11½%	in swap	LIBOR
Net interest cost	LIBOR less ½%	Net interest cost	12%

The results of the swap are that Goodcredit ends up paying variable rate interest, but at a lower cost than it could get from a bank, and Secondtier ends up paying fixed rate interest, also at a lower cost than it could get from investors or a bank.

Other advantages of swaps

3.10 Interest rate swaps have several further attractions.

(a) They are easy to arrange.
(b) They are flexible. They can be arranged in any size and, if required, reversed.
(c) The transaction costs are low, limited to legal fees.

As with all hedging methods, interest rate swaps can alternatively be used as a means of financial speculation. In cases receiving much publicity, local authority treasurers in the UK have engaged in such speculation with disastrous results.

4 INTEREST RATE OPTIONS

KEY TERM

An **option** gives the holder the **right** to buy (**call**) or sell (**put**) a specific asset on predetermined terms on, or before, a future date.

Interest rate options (guarantees)

4.1 An **option** is an agreement giving the right to buy or sell a specific quantity something (eg shares) at a known or determinable price within a stated period. Pure options are financial instruments such as **share options** which are created by exchanges rather than by the company. As with other types of option, share options can be used by investors either as a means of speculation or as a means of risk reduction (hedging). The financial manager seeking to hedge exchange rate risk or interest rate risk is however more likely to come across **currency options** or **interest rate options**, and we now look at the latter in more detail.

4.2 An **interest rate option** grants the buyer of it the right, but **not the obligation,** to deal at an agreed interest rate (strike rate) at a future maturity date. On the date of expiry of the option, the buyer must decide whether or not to exercise the right. Clearly, a buyer of an option to borrow will not wish to exercise it if the market interest rate is now below that specified in the option agreement. Conversely, an option to lend will not be worth exercising if market rates have risen above the rate specified in the option by the time the option has expired.

4.3 The term **interest rate guarantee (IRG)** refers to an interest rate option which hedges the interest rate for a single period of up to one year.

4.4 Tailor-made **'over-the-counter' interest rate options** can be purchased from major banks, with specific values, periods of maturity, denominated currencies and rates of agreed interest. The cost of the option is the **'premium'.** Interest rate options offer more flexibility than and are more expensive than FRAs.

Caps, floors and collars

4.5 Various **cap** and **collar** agreements are possible. An interest rate **cap** is an option which sets an interest rate ceiling. A **floor** is an option which sets a lower limit to interest rates. Using a 'collar' arrangement, the borrower can buy an interest rate cap and at the same time sell an interest rate floor which fixes the cost for the company. The cost is lower than for a cap alone. However, the borrowing company forgoes the benefit of movements in interest rates below the floor limit in exchange for this cost reduction. A **zero cost collar** can even be negotiated sometimes, if the **premium** paid for buying the cap equals the premium received for selling the floor.

4.6 EXAMPLE: CAP AND COLLAR

Suppose the prevailing interest rate for a company's borrowing is 10%. The company treasurer considers that a rise in rates above 12% will cause serious financial difficulties for the company. How can the treasurer make use of a 'cap and collar' arrangement?

4.7 SOLUTION

The company can buy an interest rate cap from the bank. The bank will reimburse the company for the effects of a rise in rates above 12%. As part of the arrangements with the bank, the company can agree that it will pay at least 9%, say, as a 'floor' rate. The bank will pay the company for agreeing this. In other words, the company has sold the floor to the bank, which partly offsets the costs of the cap. The bank benefits if rates fall below the floor level.

A graphical approach to options

4.8 A graphical approach to options may help you to understand options more fully and may provide a means of illustrating options in answers to exam questions. The examples illustrated below generally refer to **share prices**. In the case of other types of option (eg interest rate options or currency options), then it will be the value or price of the particular underlying investment (eg the interest rate or the currency) which is relevant.

4.9   Figure 1 shows the position of a **call option holder**.

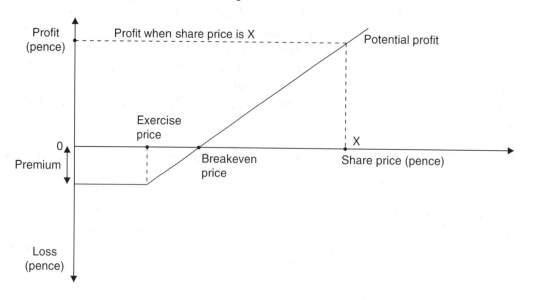

Figure 1 Call option holder ('long call position')

4.10   The holder of the call option will not exercise the option unless the share price is at least equal to the **exercise price** (or **strike price**) at the exercise date. If the share price is above that level, he can cut his losses (up to the break-even price) or make profits (if the share price is above the break-even price). Holding a call option is called having a **long position** in the option.

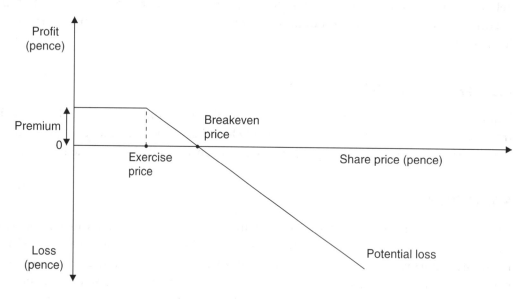

Figure 2 Call option writer ('short call position')

4.11   Any profit made by the holder of the option is reflected by the loss of the other party to the transaction - the writer of the option. Accordingly, Figure 2, illustrating the potential outcomes for the writer of the option, looks like a 'mirror image' of Figure 1. Selling or writing a call option is called taking a **short call position**. It can be seen from Figure 2 that the writer of the call option is exposed to potentially unlimited losses.

4.12 The position of the **buyer of a put option** is illustrated in Figure 3. The maximum potential profit is equal to the exercise price, which is the position if the share price falls to zero. Then, the put option holder has the option to sell worthless shares at the exercise price. You should be able to appreciate that the put option can be used to protect a holder of shares against a fall in their value. As Figure 3 shows, the loss on the option is limited to the size of the premium.

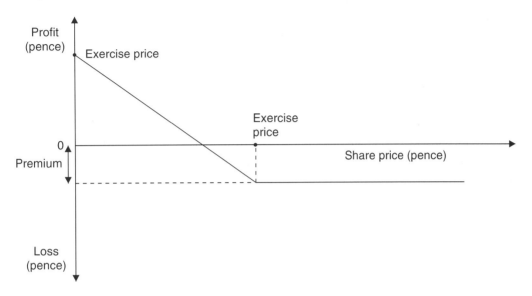

Figure 3 Put option holder ('long put position')

4.13 You will probably by now be able to guess what a graph illustrating the position of a put option writer will look like.

Question 3

See if you can sketch such a graph and then look at Figure 4.

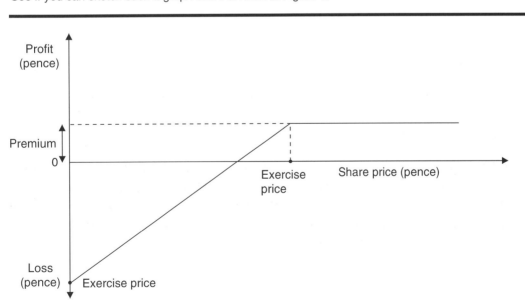

Figure 4 Put option writer ('short put position')

Question 4

Reasoning from what you have already learned about options, check that you can explain Figure 4. Note that the maximum loss for the writer or seller of the put option is the exercise price.

4.14 Figures 1 to 4 illustrate the basic positions which can be taken in options. It is also possible to combine different option positions in various ways, depending on the combination of risks and returns which are sought from different outcomes.

4.15 Interest rate caps, collars and floors can be illustrated graphically, and this approach may help in understanding the effect of such arrangements.

4.16 Figure 5 illustrates a collar arrangement for a bank loan. The bank subsidises its client to the extent represented by shaded area A when the market interest rate exceeds the capped level, while the bank gains to the extent of area B when interest rates dip below the floor level.

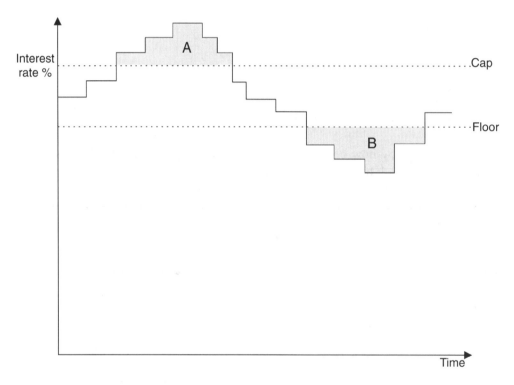

Figure 5 Interest rate collar through time

4.17 In the example shown in Figure 6, a company has a loan at LIBOR (London Inter-Bank Offered Rate). Suppose that for an annual cost of 1% of principal, it can buy a cap at 8%. When LIBOR is between 6% and 8%, the vertical distance between the two lines on the graph represents the cost of the cap. The cap begins to pay off when LIBOR rises above 8%, with a break-even point where LIBOR is 9%.

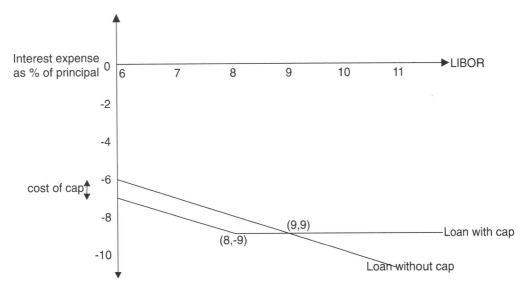

Figure 6 Loan with Interest rate cap

4.18 Part or all of the cost of the cap may be set off by agreeing to an interest rate floor, thus making a collar. In the case of a **zero cost collar**, the cost of the cap is fully offset by the proceeds of the floor.

4.19 Figure 7 illustrates the profit/loss profile for a zero cost collar. This might be achieved by combining a floor with the arrangement illustrated in Figure 6. The interest expense cannot exceed 8% and cannot be less than 5%. Between 5% and 8%, the interest expense matches LIBOR.

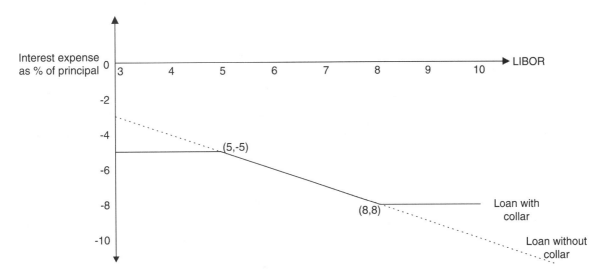

Figure 7 Loan with interest rate collar

4.20 Note that numerical questions will not be set on interest rate options in the CIMA Financial Strategy exam.

Traded interest rate options

4.21 Exchange-traded interest rate options are available as **options on interest rate futures,** which give the holder the right to buy (call option) or sell (put option) one futures contract on or before the expiry of the option at a specified price. The best way to understand the pricing of interest rate options is to look at a schedule of prices. The schedule below (from the *Financial Times*) is for 12 October in a particular year.

UK long gilt futures options (LIFFE) £100,000 100ths of 100%

Strike Price	Calls Nov	Dec	Jan	Puts Nov	Dec	Jan
11,350	0.87	1.27	1.34	0.29	0.69	1.06
11,400	0.58	0.99	1.10	0.50	0.91	1.32
11,450	0.36	0.76	0.88	0.77	1.18	1.60

4.22   This schedule shows that an investor could pay 1.34/100 × 100% × £100,000 = £1,340 to purchase the right to buy a sterling futures contract in January at a price of £113,50 per £100 stock.

4.23   If, say, in December, January sterling futures are priced **below** £113.50 (reflecting an interest rate **rise**), the option will be exercised. In calculating any gain from the option, the premium cost must also be taken into account.

The profit for each contract is:

(113.50 – current futures price – 1.34) × 100 ticks

To evaluate a hedge, this profit will be set against extra interest costs incurred due to the interest rate increase.

4.24   If the futures price moves **higher,** as it is likely to if interest rates **fall,** the option will not be exercised. To evaluate a hedge, there is only the option premium to set against the interest saving from the lower interest rates.

4.25   The profit/loss profile from the use of an option can be illustrated **graphically,** and this is covered, with other types of options, in Chapter 13.

Valuation of options

4.26   The widespread use of derivatives involving options has resulted in much attention being paid to the **valuation of options**. In this Study Text, we have looked at the use of interest rate and currency options in the hedging of interest rate risk and currency risk. Another common form of option identified was the share option, giving the right but not the obligation to buy or to sell a quantity of a company's shares at a specified price within a specified period.

4.27   Using share options as an example, the main variables which determine the value of a call option (the right to **buy** shares at a fixed price) can be identified as:

(a)   The current value of the share – option values **increases** with this

(b)   The exercise price of the option - option value **decreases** with this

(c)   The time to expiry of the option – affects the **risk** and the **time value** (see below) of an option

(d)   Variability of the price of the share – the higher the variability, the greater the chance of favourable gains and thus the higher the value

(e)   The risk-free rate of interest – option value **increases** with this due to greater potential earnings on cash saved by buying the option rather than the share

Time value and valuation of options

4.28 We need to consider further the **time value of an option**. Holding a call option can be seen effectively as the deferred purchase of the underlying asset (eg shares), since the exercise price does not have to be paid until a later date.

4.29 The time value of an option will be affected by the level of interest rates. The higher the level of interest rates, the higher will be the value of the option as the present value of the exercise price of the option will be correspondingly lower. The longer the time to expiration, the higher will the value of the option be, as its present value will be lower. Furthermore, the longer is the period to expiration, the more opportunity there is for volatility in the markets to lead to higher share values.

4.30 We can illustrate the limits of valuation of options graphically (Figure 8).

   (a) An upper limit to the value of an option is the value of the underlying share (or other asset). It will never be worthwhile to pay more for an option than the price of the asset which the option enables you to buy.

   (b) The lower limit to the value of an option shown on Figure 8 represents the **intrinsic** value of the option - ie the extent to which it is '**in the money**'. This lower limit is zero up to the exercise price and at higher share prices is the difference between the share price and the exercise price.

   (c) In practice, the value of most options will lie somewhere between these limits, as illustrated by lines A, B and C in Figure 8.

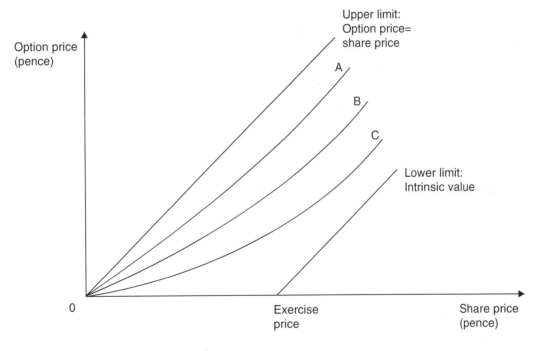

Figure 8 Limits to call option values

4.31 Options theory can be applied to business decisions beyond the areas of financial instruments such as traded share options, currency options and interest rate options. The following are examples from the range of possible applications.

   (a) **Convertible loan stock** provides a combination of a conventional loan with a call option. If the option is exercised, the loan is exchanged for a specified number of shares in the company.

(b) **Share warrants** provide the holder with an option to purchase shares from the company at a specified exercise price during a specified time period.

(c) **Government loan guarantees** effectively provide a put option to holders of risky loans, giving the holders an opportunity to exercise an option of obtaining reimbursement from the government if a borrower defaults.

(d) **Insurance** more generally is a form of put option which is exercised when an insurance claim is made.

(e) **Share purchase** at the prevailing market price can be seen as equivalent to the purchase of a call option combined with the sale of a put option, while putting the remaining amount on deposit at a risk-free rate of return over the option period.

(f) Option valuation theory which is used in valuing share options can be extended to various options which financial managers may meet in making **capital investment decisions.** We discuss these **real options** in a later chapter.

5 HEDGING STRATEGY ALTERNATIVES: EXAMPLE

5.1 Different hedging instruments often offer alternative ways of managing risk in a specific situation. In this section, after initial discussion of three possible hedging methods, we work through an example in which different ways in which a company can hedge interest rate risk are evaluated, covering both interest rate futures and interest rate options (interest rate guarantees).

5.2 EXAMPLE: HEDGING ALTERNATIVES

It is 31 December. Octavo plc needs to borrow £6 million in three months' time for a period of six months. For the type of loan finance which Octavo would use, the rate of interest is currently 13% per year and the Corporate Treasurer is unwilling to pay a higher rate.

The treasurer is concerned about possible future fluctuations in interest rates, and is considering the following possibilities:

(a) Forward rate agreements (FRAs)
(b) Interest rate futures
(c) Interest rate guarantees or short-term interest rate caps

Required

Explain briefly how each of these three alternatives might be useful to Octavo plc.

5.3 SOLUTION

Forward rate agreements (FRAs)

Entering into a FRA with a bank will allow the treasurer of Octavo plc to effectively lock in an interest rate for the six months of the loan. This agreement is independent of the loan itself, upon which the prevailing rate will be paid. If the FRA were negotiated to be at a rate of 13%, and the actual interest rate paid on the loan were higher than this, the bank will pay the difference between the rate paid and 13% to Octavo plc. Conversely, if the interest paid by Octavo turned out to be lower than 13%, they would have to pay the difference to the bank. Thus the cost of Octavo will be 13% regardless of movements in actual interest rates.

Interest rate futures

Interest rate futures have the same effect at FRAs, in effectively locking in an interest rate, but they are standardised in terms of size, duration and terms. They can be traded on an exchange (such as LIFFE in London), and they will generally be closed out before the maturity date, yielding a profit or loss that is offset against the loss or profit on the money transaction that is being hedged. So, for example, as Octavo is concerned about rises in interest rates, the treasurer can sell future contracts now; if that rate does rise, their value will fall, and they can then be bought at a lower price, yielding a profit which will compensate for the increase in Octavo's loan interest cost. If interest rates fall, the lower interest cost of the loan will be offset by a loss on their futures contracts.

There may not be an exact match between the loan and the future contract (100% hedge), due to the standardised nature of the contracts, and margin payments may be required whilst the futures are still held (see Chapter 13), where margins are discussed the context of currency futures).

Interest rate guarantees

Interest rate guarantees (or short term interest rate options) give Octavo the opportunity to benefit from favourable interest rate movements as well as protecting them from the effects of adverse movements. They give the holder the **right** but not the **obligation** to deal at an agreed interest rate at a future maturity date. This means that if interest rates rise, the treasurer would exercise the option, and 'lock in' to the predetermined borrowing rate. If, however, interest rates fall, then the option would simply lapse, and Octavo would feel the benefit of lower interest rates.

The main disadvantage of options is that a premium will be payable to the seller of the option, whether or not it is exercised. This will therefore add to the interest cost. The treasurer of Octavo will need to consider whether this cost, which can be quite expensive, is justified by the potential benefits to be gained form favourable interest rate movements.

Chapter roundup

- **Interest rates**, like **exchange rates**, can be very volatile.
- Factors involving **interest rate risk** include the following.
  - Fixed rates versus floating rate debt
  - The term of the loan
- A variety of financial instruments are available for reducing exposure to interest rate risk, including **FRAs**, **futures**, **swaps** and **options**.
- An **interest rate guarantee** is a form of interest rate option.

Quick quiz

1 Identify three aspects of a debt in which a company may be exposed to risk from interest rate movements. (Example: Fixed rate *versus* floating rate debt.)

2 What are 'FRAs'?

3 Apart from FRAs, identify three other types of financial instrument which might be used to reduce interest rate risk.

4 What name is given to the degree or percentage to which risk exposure is covered?

5 Complete the following definition of a futures contract (from *OT 2000*).

'A contract relating to currencies, commodities or shares that obliges the buyer/issuer to ....'

6   Complete the following (from *OT 2000*).

'Unlike (1) ...., which are entered into privately, futures contracts are traded on (2) ...., carry standard (3) ...., have specific (4) ...., and are subject to rules concerning (5) .... requirements.

7   Fill in the blanks in the following definition of a *swap*, from *OT 2000*.

'An arrangement whereby two (1) .... contractually agree to exchange (2) .... on different terms, eg in different (3) ...., or one at a (4) .... rate and the other at a (5) .... rate.

8   Fill in the blanks.

With a *collar*, the borrower buys (1) .... and at the same time sells (2) ....

Answers to quick quiz

1   Here are four aspects.

   (a)   Fixed rate *versus* floating rate debt
   (b)   Debt in different currencies
   (c)   Different terms of loan
   (d)   Term loan or overdraft facility

2   Forward interest rate agreements.

3   (a)   Interest rate futures
   (b)   Interest rate options
   (c)   Interest rate swaps

   Other answers may also be valid.

4   Hedge efficiency.

5   ' ... purchase/sell the specified quantity of the item represented in the contract at a predetermined price at the expiration of the contract.'

6   (1)   Forward contracts
   (2)   Organised exchanges
   (3)   Terms and conditions
   (4)   Maturities
   (5)   Margin

7   (1)   Organisations
   (2)   Payments
   (3)   Currencies
   (4)   Fixed
   (5)   Floating

8   (1)   An interest rate cap
   (2)   An interest rate floor

Now try the question below from the Exam Question Bank

Number	Level	Marks	Time
11	Examination	25	45 mins

Chapter 12

CURRENCY RISK I

Topic list		Syllabus reference	Ability required
1	Currency risk	(iii)	Analysis
2	Exchange rates	(iii)	Analysis
3	Factors influencing exchange rates	(iii)	Analysis
4	Management of currency risk	(iii)	Analysis
5	Forward exchange contracts	(iii)	Analysis

Introduction

The rôle of the treasurer is increasingly concerned with identifying and managing **risks** of various types. In this chapter and the next, we look at risks relating in particular to **exchange rate fluctuations**.

Learning outcomes covered in this chapter

- Interpret the impact of currency risk
- Calculate the impact of different national inflation rates on forecasting exchange rates
- Explain exchange rate theory
- Recommend foreign exchange risk management strategies

Syllabus content covered in this chapter

- Transaction, translation and economic risk

- Interest rate parity, purchasing power parity and the Fisher effect

- Forward contracts and money market hedges (numerical questions will be set including the need to be able to use cross rates)

- Internal hedging techniques, eg netting and matching

- Predict changing exchange rates using the purchasing power parity method or interest rate parity

1 CURRENCY RISK

Pilot paper

1.1 Currency risk arises from unexpected movements in exchange rates. A company may become exposed to **currency risk** (or '**exchange rate risk**') in a number of ways, including the following.

- As an exporter of goods or services
- As an importer of goods or services
- Through having an overseas subsidiary
- Through being the subsidiary of an overseas company
- Through transactions in overseas capital markets

1.2 The following different types of foreign exchange risk (or 'currency risk') may be distinguished.

(a) **Transaction risk** is the risk of adverse exchange rate movements occurring in the course of **normal international trading transactions**. This arises when export prices are fixed in foreign currency terms, or imports are invoiced in foreign currencies. Below, we discuss various methods for reducing this type of exposure to risk.

(b) **Translation risk** arises from differences in the currencies in which **assets and liabilities** are denominated. If a company has different proportions of its assets and liabilities denominated in particular currencies, then exchange rate movements are likely to have varying effects on the value of these assets and liabilities. This could influence investors' and lenders' attitudes to the financial worth and creditworthiness of the company. Such risk can be reduced if assets and liabilities denominated in particular currencies can be **held in balanced amounts**.

(c) **Economic risk** refers to the effect of exchange rate movements on the **international competitiveness** of a company. For example, a UK company might use raw materials which are priced in US dollars, but export its products mainly within the European Union. A depreciation of sterling against the dollar or an appreciation of sterling against other EU currencies will both erode the competitiveness of the company. **Diversification of the supplier and customer base** across different countries may reduce this kind of exposure to risk.

Case examples

In the 1999 Annual Report of the **Hilton Group plc,** the Group's management of its exposure to currency risk was reviewed as following.

'Due to the international nature of its core activities, the group's reported profits, net assets and gearing are all affected by movements in foreign exchange rates. The group seeks to mitigate the effect of any structural currency exposure that may arise from the translation of the foreign currency assets by borrowing in foreign currencies to match at least 75% of the foreign currency assets.... Although the group carries out operations through a number of foreign enterprises, group exposure to currency risk at a transactional level is minimal. The day-to-day transactions of overseas subsidiaries are carried out in local currency.'

The 1999 Annual Report of **John Laing plc,** the property development and construction groups, notes that 'The Group seeks to cover exposure to exchange rate movements on trade receivables and payables – provided that the cost of doing so would not, in the opinion of the directors, be prohibitive. Contingent or uncertain exposures are hedged when, in the opinion of the directors, the risk justifies doing so'.

2 EXCHANGE RATES

Spot rates

KEY TERM

The **spot rate** is the exchange or interest rate currently offered on a particular currency or security.

2.1 The **spot rate** is the rate of exchange in currency for **immediate delivery**.

2.2   If an importer has to pay a foreign supplier in a foreign currency, he might ask his bank to sell him the required amount of the currency. For example, suppose that a bank's customer, a trading company, has imported goods for which it must now pay US$10,000.

(a)   The company will ask the bank to sell it US$10,000. If the company is buying currency, the bank is selling it.

(b)   When the bank agrees to sell US$10,000 to the company, it will tell the company what the spot rate of exchange will be for the transaction. If the bank's selling rate (known as the **'offer'**, or **'ask'** price) is, say $1.7935 for the currency, the bank will charge the company:

$$\frac{\$10,000}{\$1.7935 \text{ per } £1} = £5,575.69$$

2.3   Similarly, if an exporter is paid, say, US$10,000 by a customer in the USA, he may wish to exchange the dollars to obtain sterling. He will therefore ask his bank to buy the dollars from him. Since the exporter is selling currency to the bank, the bank is buying the currency.

If the bank quotes a buying spot rate (known as the **'bid'** price) of, say $1.8075, for the currency the bank will pay the exporter:

$$\frac{\$10,000}{\$1.8075 \text{ per } £1} = £5,532.50$$

2.4   A bank expects to make a profit from selling and buying currency, and it does so by offering a rate for selling a currency which is different from the rate for buying the currency.

2.5   If a bank were to buy a quantity of foreign currency from a customer, and then were to re-sell it to another customer, it would charge the second customer more (in sterling) for the currency than it would pay the first customer. The difference would be profit. For example, the figures used for illustration in the previous paragraphs show a bank selling some US dollars for £5,575.69 and buying the same quantity of dollars for £5,532.50, at selling and buying rates that might be in use at the same time. The bank would make a profit of £43.19. The bank 'buys high' (at $1.8075) and 'sells low' (at $1.7935).

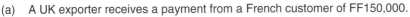

Question 1

Calculate how much sterling exporters would receive or how much sterling importers would pay, ignoring the bank's commission, in each of the following situations, if they were to exchange currency and sterling at the spot rate.

(a)   A UK exporter receives a payment from a French customer of FF150,000.
(b)   A UK importer buys goods from a Japanese supplier and pays 1 million yen.

Spot rates are as follows.

	Bank sells (offer)		Bank buys (bid)
France FF/£	9.4340	-	9.5380
Japan Y/£	203.65	-	205.78

Answer

(a)   The bank is being asked to buy the French francs and will give the exporter:

$$\frac{150,000}{9.5380} = £15,726.57 \text{ in exchange}$$

(b)   The bank is being asked to sell the yen to the importer and will charge for the currency:

$$\frac{1,000,000}{203.65} = £4,910.39$$

Direct and indirect currency quotes

2.6 A **direct quote** is the amount of **domestic** currency which is equal to **one foreign currency unit**. An **indirect quote** is the amount of **foreign** currency which is equal to **one domestic currency unit**.

2.7 Currencies may be quoted in either direction. In the UK indirect quotes are invariably used but, in most countries, direct quotes are more common. For example the US dollar and German mark may be quoted as DM/$ = 1.723 or $/DM = 0.580. In other words, DM1.723 = $1 and $0.580 = DM1. One rate is simply the reciprocal of the other.

2.8 A further complication to be aware of is that the offer rate in one country becomes the bid rate in the other. For example, Malaysian Ringgit (MR) are quoted in London like this:

	Bank sells (offer)		Bank buys (bid)
MR/£	4.0440	-	4.0910

However, in Kuala Lumpur you would see:

	Bank sells (offer)		Bank buys (bid)
MR/£	4.0910	-	4.0440

Exam focus point

The examination is not confined to the activities of UK companies. Exchange rates given in the examination could be as quoted in any countries. Because of these complications you should always double-check which rate you are using when choosing between the bid or offer rate. One sure method is to recognise that the bank makes money out of the transaction and will therefore offer you the worse of the two possible rates!

Forward rates

KEY TERM

Forward exchange rate is an exchange rate set for the exchange of currencies at some future date. *(OT 2000)*

2.9 For reasons discussed later, a forward exchange rate might be higher or lower than the spot rate. If it is higher, the quoted currency will be cheaper forward than spot. For example, if in the case of Italian lire against sterling (i) the spot rate is 2,156 - 2,166 and (ii) the three months forward rate is 2,207 - 2,222:

(a) A bank would sell 2,000,000 lire:

    (i)   At the spot rate, now, for   £927.64

$$\left(\frac{2,000,000}{2,156}\right)$$

(ii)   In three months time, under a forward contract, for   £906.21

$$\left(\frac{2,000,000}{2,207}\right)$$

(b)   A bank would buy 2,000,000 lire:

(i)   At the spot rate, now, for   £923.36

$$\left(\frac{2,000,000}{2,166}\right)$$

(ii)   In three months time, under a forward contract, for   £900.09

$$\left(\frac{2,000,000}{2,222}\right)$$

2.10   In both cases, the quoted currency (lire) would be worth less against sterling in a forward contract than at the current spot rate. This is because it is quoted forward cheaper, or 'at a discount', against sterling. If the forward rate is higher than the spot rate, then it is 'at a premium' to the spot rate.

3   FACTORS INFLUENCING EXCHANGE RATES

3.1   The exchange rate between two currencies - ie the buying and selling rates, both 'spot' and forward - is determined primarily by **supply and demand** in the foreign exchange markets. Demand comes from individuals, firms and governments who want to buy a currency and supply comes from those who want to sell it.

3.2   Supply and demand for currencies are in turn influenced by:

- The rate of inflation, compared with the rate of inflation in other countries
- Interest rates, compared with interest rates in other countries
- The balance of payments
- Sentiment of foreign exchange market participants regarding economic prospects
- Speculation
- Government policy on intervention to influence the exchange rate

3.3   Other factors influence the exchange rate through their relationship with the items identified above. For example:

(a)   Total income and expenditure (demand) in the domestic economy determines the demand for goods, including:

(i)   Imported goods

(ii)   Goods produced in the country which would otherwise be exported if demand for them did not exist in the home markets

(b)   Output capacity and the level of employment in the domestic economy might influence the balance of payments, because if the domestic economy has full employment already, it will be unable to increase its volume of production for exports.

(c)   The growth in the money supply influences interest rates and domestic inflation.

Interest rate parity (International Fisher Effect)

> **KEY TERM**
>
> **Interest rate parity** method is a method of predicting foreign exchange rates based on the hypothesis that the difference between the interest rates in the two countries should offset the difference between the spot rates and the forward foreign exchange rates over the same period. *(OT 2000)*

3.4 **The difference between spot and forward rates reflects differences in interest rates.** If this were not so, then investors holding the currency with the lower interest rates would switch to the other currency for (say) three months, ensuring that they would not lose on returning to the original currency by fixing the exchange rate in advance at the forward rate. If enough investors acted in this way (known as **arbitrage**), forces of supply and demand would lead to a change in the forward rate to prevent such risk-free profit making.

3.5 The principle of **interest rate parity** links the foreign exchange markets and the international money markets. The principle can be stated as follows.

> **EXAM FORMULA**
>
> $$\text{Forward rate US\$/£} = \text{Spot US\$/£} \times \frac{1 + \text{nominal US interest rate}}{1 + \text{nominal UK interest rate}}$$

This equation is based on US dollar/sterling exchange and interest rates as shown in the formulae provided in the exam, but of course can be generalised to other cases. It shows that:

Difference in interest rates determines the difference between forward and spot rates

3.6 EXAMPLE: INTEREST RATE PARITY

Exchange rates between two currencies, the Northland florin (NF) and the Southland dollar (S$) are listed in the financial press as follows.

Spot rates	4.7250	NF/$S
	0.21164	$S/NF
90 day rates	4.7506	NF/$S
	0.21050	$S/NF

The money market interest rate for 90 day deposits in Northland florins is 7.5% annualised. What is implied about interest rates in Southland?

Assume a 365-day year. (*Note.* In practice, foreign currency interest rates are often calculated on an alternative **360-day** basis, one month being treated as 30 days.)

3.7 SOLUTION

Today, $S1.000 buys NF4.7250.

NF4.7250 could be placed on deposit for 90 days to earn interest of NF(4.7250 × 0.075 × 90/365) = NF0.0874, thus growing to NF(4.7250 + 0.0874) = NF4.8124.

This is then worth $S 1.0130 at the 90 day exchange rate.

This tells us that the annualised expected interest rate on 90-day deposits in Southland is $0.013 \times 365/90 = 5.3\%$.

3.8 Alternatively, applying the formula given earlier, we have the following.

Northland interest rate on 90 day deposit $= r_n = 7.5\% \times 90/365 = 1.85\%$

Southland interest rate on 90 day deposit $= r_s$

90-day forward exchange rate $= f_{s/n} = 0.21050$

Spot exchange rate $= s_{s/n} = 0.21164$

$$\frac{1 + r_s}{1 + 0.0185} = \frac{0.21050}{0.21164}$$

$1 + r_s \quad = \quad 1.0185 \times 0.21050 \div 0.21164 = 1.013$

$r_s \qquad = \quad 0.013$, or 1.3%

Annualised, this is $0.013 \times 365/90 = 5.3\%$

Purchasing power parity

KEY TERM

Purchasing power parity theory states that the exchange rate between two currencies is the same in equilibrium when the purchasing power of currency is the same in each country. *(OT 2000)*

3.9 Interest rate parity should not be confused with **purchasing power parity**. Purchasing power parity theory predicts that the exchange value of foreign currency depends on the relative purchasing power of each currency in its own country and that **spot exchange rates will vary over time according to relative price changes**.

Formally, purchasing power parity can be expressed in the following formula.

EXAM FORMULA

Forward rate US$/£ = Spot US$/£ $\times \dfrac{1 + \text{US inflation rate}}{1 + \text{UK inflation rate}}$

Note that the term 'forward rate' is used here as meaning the expected future spot rate and will not necessarily coincide with the 'forward exchange rate' currently quoted.

3.10 EXAMPLE: PURCHASING POWER PARITY

The exchange rate between UK sterling and the French franc is £1 = 8.00 francs. Assuming that there is now purchasing parity, an amount of a commodity costing £110 in the UK will cost 880 French francs. Over the next year, price inflation in France is expected to be 5% while inflation in the UK is expected to be 8%. What is the 'expected spot exchange rate' at the end of the year?

Using the formula above:

Future (forward) rate, $S_t = 8 \times \dfrac{(1.05)}{1.08}$

$$= 7.78$$

3.11 This is the same figure as we get if we compare the inflated prices for the commodity. At the end of the year:

UK price	=	£110 × 1.08 = £118.80
France price	=	FF880 × 1.05 = FF924
S_t	=	924 ÷ 118.80 = 7.78

3.12 In the real world, exchange rates move towards purchasing power parity only over the **long term**. However, the theory is sometimes used to predict future exchange rates in **investment appraisal problems** where forecasts of relative inflation rates are available.

The Fisher effect

3.13 The term **Fisher effect** is sometimes used in looking at the relationship between **interest rates** and expected rates of **inflation**.

3.14 The rate of interest can be seen as made up of two parts: the real required rate of return plus a premium for inflation. Then:

EXAM FORMULA

[1 + nominal (money) rate] = [1 + real interest rate] [1 + inflation rate]

3.15 Countries with relatively high rates of inflation will generally have high nominal rates of interest, partly because high interest rates are a mechanism for reducing inflation and partly because of the Fisher effect: higher nominal interest rates serve to allow investors to obtain a high enough real rate of return where inflation is relatively high.

3.16 According to the **international Fisher effect**, interest rate differentials between countries provide an unbiased predictor of future changes in spot exchange rates. The currency of countries with relatively high interest rates is expected to depreciate against currency's with lower interest rates, because the higher interest rates are considered necessary to compensate for the anticipated currency depreciation. Given free movement of capital internationally, this idea suggests that the real rate of return in different countries will equalise as a result of adjustments to spot exchange rates.

3.17 The Fisher effect can be expressed as:

$$\frac{1 + r_f}{1 + r_{uk}} = \frac{1 + i_f}{1 + i_{uk}}$$

where

r_f is the nominal interest rate in the foreign country, with inflation rate i_f
r_{uk} is the nominal interest rate in the home country, with inflation rate i_{uk}

4   MANAGEMENT OF CURRENCY RISK

4.1   We shall now look at the various means by which a business can manage its exposure to currency, or exchange rate, risk. We are principally concerned here with the risk that has a direct effect on immediate cash flows – transaction risk. This risk is illustrated in the following question.

Question 2

Bulldog Ltd, a UK company, buys goods from Redland which cost 100,000 Reds (the local currency). The goods are re-sold in the UK for £32,000. At the time of the import purchase the exchange rate for Reds against sterling is 3.5650 - 3.5800.

Required

(a)   What is the expected profit on the re-sale?
(b)   What would the actual profit be if the spot rate at the time when the currency is received has moved to:

        (i)   3.0800 - 3.0950
        (ii)   4.0650 - 4.0800?

Ignore bank commission charges.

Answer

(a)   Bulldog must buy Reds to pay the supplier, and so the bank is selling Reds. The expected profit is as follows.

	£
Revenue from re-sale of goods	32,000.00
Less cost of 100,000 Reds in sterling (÷ 3.5650)	28,050.49
Expected profit	3,949.51

(b)   (i)   If the actual spot rate for Bulldog to buy and the bank to sell the Reds is 3.0800, the result is as follows.

	£
Revenue from re-sale	32,000.00
Less cost (100,000 ÷ 3.0800)	32,467.53
Loss	(467.53)

        (ii)   If the actual spot rate for Bulldog to buy and the bank to sell the Reds is 4.0650, the result is as follows.

	£
Revenue from re-sale	32,000.00
Less cost (100,000 ÷ 4.0650)	24,600.25
Profit	7,399.75

This variation in the final sterling cost of the goods (and thus the profit) illustrates the concept of transaction risk.

Direct risk reduction methods   **Pilot paper**

4.2   The **forward exchange contract** is perhaps the most important method of obtaining cover against risks, where a firm decides that it does not wish to speculate on foreign exchange. This is discussed later in the chapter. However, there are **other methods of reducing risk** which we shall consider first:

- Currency of invoice
- Matching receipts and payments
- Leads and lags
- Matching long term assets and liabilities
- Money market hedges

Currency of invoice

4.3 One way of avoiding exchange risk is for an exporter to **invoice his foreign customer in his own domestic currency**, or for an importer to arrange with his foreign supplier to be invoiced in his domestic currency.

   (a) If a UK exporter is able to quote and invoice an overseas buyer in sterling, then **the foreign exchange risk is in effect transferred to the overseas buyer.**

   (b) Similarly, a UK-based importer may be able to persuade the overseas supplier to invoice in sterling rather than in a foreign currency.

4.4 Although either the exporter or the importer avoids exchange risk in this way, only one of them can. The other must accept the exchange risk, since there will be a period of time elapsing between agreeing a contract and paying for the goods (unless payment is made with the order).

4.5 An alternative method of achieving the same result is to negotiate contracts expressed in the foreign currency but specifying **a fixed rate of exchange** as a condition of the contract.

4.6 There is a possible **marketing advantage** to be obtained by proposing to **invoice in the buyer's own currency**, when there is competition for the sales contract. The foreign buyer, invoiced in his own currency, will not have the problem of deciding whether to protect himself against exchange risks.

   (a) If the exporter believes that he is in danger of not winning the contract, owing to competition from other sellers overseas, and if the buyer's own currency is weak and likely to depreciate against sterling, the exporter might offer to invoice the buyer in his own (weak) currency in order to win the contract. The exporter would in effect be offering the buyer a price discount due to the probability of a movement in exchange rates favourable to the buyer and therefore unfavourable to the exporter.

   (b) In some export markets, foreign currency (often the US dollar) is the normal trading currency, and so UK exporters might have to quote prices in that currency for customers to consider buying from them. By arranging to sell goods to customers in a foreign currency, a UK exporter might be able to obtain a loan in that currency at a lower rate of interest than in the UK, and at the same time obtain cover against exchange risks by arranging to repay the loan out of the proceeds from the sales in that currency.

4.7 There are certain other aspects to the currency of invoicing that an exporter might wish to consider.

   (a) **Pricing and price lists**. If the exporter issues price lists in foreign currency, he should be aware of the need to revise price lists as the value of his domestic currency fluctuates against the value of the foreign currency. For example, if a UK exporter issues a price list in US dollars, and sterling strengthens against the US dollar, the exporter will earn less sterling when he sells his US dollar receipts, and so his profit margins will be cut. He might therefore need to raise his prices to maintain profit margins. On the other hand, if the US dollar strengthened against sterling, the UK exporter could cut his prices whilst still maintaining his sterling profit margins.

   (b) **Customer relations**. A switch from invoicing in a foreign currency to invoicing in sterling might not be easy to achieve, at least not without giving adequate warning to the customer. The ability of an exporter to make a change might be thwarted by the resistance of a customer with bargaining strength.

(c) **Accounting systems**. Accounting procedures for invoicing in foreign currency, or borrowing in a foreign currency, are a little more complex than for invoicing and borrowing in sterling.

Matching receipts and payments

4.8 A company can reduce or eliminate its foreign exchange transaction risk exposure by matching receipts and payments. Wherever possible, a company that expects to make payments and have receipts in the same foreign currency should plan to **offset its payments against its receipts in the currency.**

4.9 The process of matching is made simpler by having **foreign currency accounts** with a bank. UK residents are allowed to have bank accounts in any foreign currency. Receipts of foreign currency can be credited to the account pending subsequent payments in the currency. (Alternatively, a company might invest its foreign currency income in the country of the currency - for example it might have a bank deposit account abroad - and make payments with these overseas assets/deposits).

4.10 Offsetting (matching payments against receipts) will be **cheaper** than arranging a forward contract to buy currency and another forward contract to sell the currency, provided that receipts occur before payments, and the time difference between receipts and payments in the currency is not too long. Any **differences** between the amounts receivable and the amounts payable in a given currency may be covered by a forward exchange contract to buy/sell the amount of the difference.

Leads and lags

4.11 Companies might try to use:

(a) **Lead payments:** payments in advance, or
(b) **Lagged payments:** delaying payments beyond their due date

in order to take advantage of foreign exchange rate movements. With a lead payment, paying in advance of the due date, there is a finance cost to consider. This is the interest cost on the money used to make the payment.

4.12 EXAMPLE: LEADS AND LAGS

A company owes $30,000 to a US supplier, payable in 90 days. It might suspect that the US dollar will strengthen against sterling over the next three months, because the US dollar is quoted forward at a premium against sterling on the foreign exchange market. The spot exchange rate is $1.50 = £1.

(a) The company could pay the $30,000 now, instead of in 90 days time. This would cost £20,000 now, which is a payment that could have been delayed by 90 days.

(b) The cost of this lead payment would be interest on £20,000 for 90 days, at the company's borrowing rate or its opportunity cost of capital.

(c) This cost needs to be compared against the potential benefit derived from saving an increased sterling cost that would have arisen if the $ had strengthened against the £.

Netting

4.13 Unlike matching, netting is not technically a method of managing exchange risk. However, it is conveniently dealt with at this stage. The objective is simply to save transactions costs by netting off inter-company balances before arranging payment. Many **multinational groups** of companies engage in **intra-group trading**. Where related companies located in different countries trade with one another, there is likely to be inter-company indebtedness denominated in different currencies.

> ### KEY TERM
>
> **Netting** is a process in which credit balances are netted off against debit balances so that only the reduced net amounts remain due to be paid by actual currency flows.

4.14 In the case of **bilateral netting,** only two companies are involved. The lower balance is netted off against the higher balance and the difference is the amount remaining to be paid.

4.15 EXAMPLE: BILATERAL NETTING

A and B are respectively UK and US based subsidiaries of a German based holding company. At 31 March 19X5, A owed B DM300,000 and B owed A DM220,000. Bilateral netting can reduce the value of the intercompany debts: the two intercompany balances are set against each other, leaving a net debt owed by A and B of DM 80,000 (DM300,000 – 220,000).

Multilateral netting

4.16 As you will have guessed, **multilateral netting** is a more complex procedure in which the debts of more than two group companies are netted off against each other. There are different ways of arranging multilateral netting. The arrangement might be co-ordinated by the company's own central treasury or alternatively by the company's bankers.

4.17 The **common currency** in which netting is to be effected needs to be decided upon, as does the method of establishing the exchange rates to use for netting purposes. So that it is possible to agree the outstanding amounts in time but with minimum risk of exchange rate fluctuations in the meantime, this may involve using the exchange rates applying a few days before the date at which payment is to be made.

4.18 Netting has the following advantages.

    (a) **Foreign exchange purchase** costs, including commission and the spread between selling and buying rates, and money transmission costs are **reduced**.

    (b) There is **less loss in interest** from having money in transit.

4.19 **Local laws and regulations** need to be considered before netting is used, as netting is restricted by some countries. In some countries, bilateral netting is permitted but multinational netting is prohibited; in other cases, all payments can be combined into a single payment which is made on a 'gross settlements' basis.

4.20 EXAMPLE: MULTILATERAL NETTING

A group of companies controlled from the USA has subsidiaries in the UK, South Africa and France. Below, these subsidiaries are referred to as UK, SA and FR respectively. At 30 June 20X5, inter-company indebtedness is as follows.

Debtor	Creditor	Amount
UK	SA	1,200,000 South African rand (R)
UK	FR	480,000 French francs (FF)
FR	SA	800,000 South African rand
SA	UK	£74,000 sterling
SA	FR	375,000 French francs

It is the company's policy to net off inter-company balances to the greatest extent possible. The central treasury department is to use the following exchange rates for this purpose.

US$1 equals R 6.126 / £0.6800 / F 5.880.

You are required to calculate the net payments to be made between the subsidiaries after netting off of inter-company balances.

4.21 SOLUTION

The first step is to convert the balances into US dollars as a common currency.

Debtor	Creditor	Amount in US dollars
UK	SA	1,200,000 ÷ 6.126 = $195,886
UK	FR	480,000 ÷ 5.880 = $81,633
FR	SA	800,000 ÷ 6.126 = $130,591
SA	UK	£74,000 ÷ 0.6800 = $108,824
SA	FR	375,000 ÷ 5.880 = $63,776

	Paying subsidiaries			
Receiving subsidiaries	*UK*	*SA*	*FR*	*Total*
	$	$	$	$
UK	-	108,824	-	108,824
SA	195,886	-	130,591	326,477
FR	81,633	63,776	-	145,409
Total payments	(277,519)	(172,600)	(130,591)	580,710
Total receipts	108,824	326,477	145,409	
Net receipt/(payment)	(168,695)	153,877	14,818	

The UK subsidiary should pay $153,877 to the South African subsidiary and $14,818 to the French subsidiary.

Matching long-term assets and liabilities

4.22 When an international company has an operating subsidiary abroad, it may try to **finance the subsidiary's long-term assets with a matching long-term loan in the same currency.** For example, suppose that a UK company with a French subsidiary decides to purchase extra premises in France which must be paid for in francs. The company may try to finance the purchase by raising a loan in francs, which it would then repay out of the operating profits (in francs) from the use of the French premises.

Money market hedges

4.23 An exporter who invoices foreign customers in a foreign currency can hedge against the exchange risk by:

(a) Borrowing an amount in the foreign currency now

(b) Converting this foreign currency amount into domestic currency at the 'spot' rate

(c) Repaying the loan with interest out of the eventual foreign currency receipts from debtors

4.24 EXAMPLE: MONEY MARKET HEDGE

An exporter is expecting to receive DM70,000 from a German customer in one year's time. He wishes to cover this transaction by a money market hedge. The current spot rate is DM3.2 = £1, and the appropriate DM borrowing rate is 4% per annum.

The hedge can be illustrated diagrammatically as follows.

Now   *In one year*
Borrow DM67,308*—— add interest ($\times 1.04$)——►Repay DM70,000 from customer payment
      |
Convert at spot
      |
      ▼
Sterling receipt

$$\frac{DM67,308}{3.2} = £21,875$$

*The amount of DM loan required was computed as DM70,000/1.04

The uncertain sterling value of the future receipt of DM70,000 has been converted to a certain £21,875 now.

Note that in order to establish the 'effective' forward rate achieved here, we would need to add in the (fixed) interest receivable on a year sterling deposit of £21,875.

4.25 Similarly, if a company has to make a foreign currency **payment** in the future, it can buy the currency now at the spot rate and put it on **deposit**, using the principal and the interest earned to make the foreign currency payment when it falls due. These forms of **money market hedge** are an alternative method of covering foreign exchange risk to using **forward exchange contracts** (considered next).

Forward exchange contracts versus money market hedge

4.26 Is one of these methods of cover likely to be cheaper than the other? The answer is perhaps, but not by much. There will be very little difference between borrowing in foreign currency and repaying the loan with currency receivables and borrowing in sterling and selling forward the currency receivables. This is because the premium or discount on the forward exchange rate reflects the interest differential between the two countries, as explained in the next section.

5 FORWARD EXCHANGE CONTRACTS

Pilot paper

Forward exchange contracts

> **KEY TERM**
>
> A **forward exchange contract** is:
>
> (a) An immediately firm and binding contract between a bank and its customer
>
> (b) For the purchase or sale of a specified quantity of a stated foreign currency
>
> (c) At a rate of exchange fixed at the time the contract is made
>
> (d) For performance (delivery of the currency and payment for it) at a future time which is agreed upon when making the contract (This future time will be either a specified date, or any time between two specified dates.)

5.1 **Forward exchange contracts** hedge against transaction exposure by allowing a trader who knows that he will have to buy or sell foreign currency at a date in the future, to make the purchase or sale at a predetermined rate of exchange. The trader will therefore know in advance either how much local currency he will receive (if he is selling foreign currency to the bank) or how much local currency he must pay (if he is buying foreign currency from the bank).

Forward rates and future exchange rate movements

5.2 Interest rate parity predicts that the forward rate is the spot price ruling on the day a forward exchange contract is made plus or minus the interest differential for the period of the contract. **It is wrong to think of a forward rate as a forecast of what the spot rate will be on a given date in the future**, and it will be a coincidence if the forward rate turns out to be the same as the spot rate on that future date.

5.3 It is however likely that the spot rate will move in the direction indicated by the forward rate. Currencies with high interest rates are likely to depreciate in value against currencies with lower interest rates: the attraction of higher interest persuades investors to hold amounts of a currency that is expected to depreciate.

Expectations theory of forward exchange rates

5.4 On the assumption that risk is absent, the **expectations theory of forward exchange rates** predicts that **the percentage difference between forward and spot rates now equals the expected change in spot rates over the period.**

5.5 Thus, given expectations of interest rates and inflation rates, the spot rate three months from now is expected to equal the three-months forward rate quoted now, for example. Because on average the forward rate equals the future spot rate, and overestimates it about as often as it underestimates it, the forward market is said to be an **unbiased predictor** of exchange rates.

Fixed and option contracts

5.6 A forward exchange contract may be either **fixed** or **option**.

(a) 'Fixed' means that performance of the contract will take place on a specified date in the future. For example, a two months forward **fixed** contract taken out on 1 September will require performance on 1 November.

(b) 'Option' means that performance of the contract may take place, at the option of the customer, either

    (i) At any date from the contract being made up to and including a specified final date for performance, or

    (ii) At any date between two specified dates

Option forward exchange contracts are different from **currency options**, which are explained later.

5.7 EXAMPLE: FORWARD EXCHANGE CONTRACTS (1)

A UK importer knows on 1 April that he must pay a foreign seller 26,500 Swiss francs in one month's time, on 1 May. He can arrange a forward exchange contract with his bank on 1 April, whereby the bank undertakes to sell the importer 26,500 Swiss francs on 1 May, at a fixed rate of, say, 2.64.

The UK importer can be certain that whatever the spot rate is between Swiss francs and sterling on 1 May, he will have to pay on that date, at this forward rate,

$$\frac{26{,}500}{2.64} = £10{,}037.88.$$

(a) If the spot rate is lower than 2.64, the importer would have successfully protected himself against a weakening of sterling, and would have avoided paying more sterling to obtain the Swiss francs.

(b) If the spot rate is higher than 2.64, sterling's value against the Swiss franc would mean that the importer would pay more under the forward exchange contract than he would have had to pay if he had obtained the francs at the spot rate on 1 May. He cannot avoid this extra cost, because a forward contract is binding.

Option forward exchange contracts

5.8 As we saw above, **option contracts** are forward exchange contracts where the customer has the option to call for performance of the contract:

- At any date from the contract being made up to a specified date in the future, or
- At any date between two dates both in the future

The contract **must be performed at some time:** the customer cannot avoid performance altogether (this distinguishes it from a currency option).

5.9 Option contracts are normally used to cover whole months straddling the likely payment date, where the customer is not sure of the exact date on which he will want to buy or sell currency. (The purpose of an option contract is to avoid having to renew a forward exchange contract and extend it by a few days, because extending a forward contract can be expensive.)

5.10 Option contracts can also be used bit by bit. For example, if a customer makes an option forward contract to sell DM 100,000 at any time between 3 July and 3 August, he might sell DM 20,000 on 5 July, DM 50,000 on 15 July and DM 30,000 on 1 August.

5.11 When a customer makes an option forward exchange contract with his bank, the bank will quote the rate which is most favourable to itself out of the forward rates for all dates within the option period. This is because the customer has the option to call for performance of the contract on any date within the period, and the bank will try to ensure that the customer does not obtain a favourable rate at the bank's expense.

What happens if a customer cannot satisfy a forward contract?

5.12 A customer might be unable to satisfy a forward contract for any one of a number of reasons.

   (a) An **importer** might find that:

      (i) His supplier fails to deliver the goods as specified, so the importer will not accept the goods delivered and will not agree to pay for them

      (ii) The supplier sends fewer goods than expected, perhaps because of supply shortages, and so the importer has less to pay for

      (iii) The supplier is late with the delivery, and so the importer does not have to pay for the goods until later than expected

   (b) An **exporter** might find the same types of situation, but in reverse, so that he does not receive any payment at all, or he receives more or less than originally expected, or he receives the expected amount, but only after some delay.

Close-out of forward contracts

5.13 If a customer cannot satisfy a forward exchange contract, the bank will make the customer fulfil the contract.

   (a) If the customer has arranged for the bank to **buy** currency but then cannot deliver the currency for the bank to buy, the bank will:

      (i) Sell currency to the customer at the spot rate (when the contract falls due for performance)

      (ii) Buy the currency back, under the terms of the forward exchange contract

   (b) If the customer has contracted for the bank to **sell** him currency, the bank will:

      (i) Sell the customer the specified amount of currency at the forward exchange rate

      (ii) Buy back the unwanted currency at the spot rate

5.14 Thus, the bank arranges for the customer to perform his part of the forward exchange contract by either selling or buying the 'missing' currency at the spot rate. These arrangements are known as **closing out** a forward exchange contract.

5.15 EXAMPLE: FORWARD EXCHANGE CONTRACTS (2)

Shutter Ltd arranges on 1 January with a US supplier for the delivery of a consignment of goods costing US$96,000. Shutter Ltd will have to pay for the goods in six months time, on 1 July. The company therefore arranges a forward exchange contract for its bank to sell it US$96,000 six months hence.

In the event, the size of the consignment is reduced and, on 1 July, Shutter Ltd only needs US$50,000 to pay its supplier. The bank will therefore arrange to close out the forward exchange contract for the US$46,000 which Shutter Ltd does not need. This is called a **partial close-out**.

Exchange rates between the US dollar and sterling are as follows.

1 January
    Spot $1.5145 - 1.5155
    6 months forward $1.5050 - $1.5070
1 July
    Spot $1.5100 - 1.5110

Compute the cost to Shutter Ltd of the whole transaction, ignoring commission.

5.16 SOLUTION

On 1 July the bank will sell Shutter Ltd US$96,000, to fulfil the original forward contract. The bank will then buy back the unwanted US$46,000 at the prevailing spot rate, thus closing out the contract.

	£
Sale of US$96,000 at $1.5050	63,787.38
Purchase of US$46,000 at $1.5110	30,443.41
Cost to Shutter Ltd	33,343.97

Extensions of forward contracts

5.17 When a forward exchange contract reaches the end of its period, a customer might find that he has not yet received the expected currency from an overseas buyer, or does not yet have to pay an overseas seller. The customer still wants to buy or sell the agreed amount of currency in the forward exchange contract, but he wants to **defer the delivery date** for the currency under the contract. The customer can then ask the bank to close out the old contract at the appropriate spot rate, and ask for a new contract for the extra period, with the rate being calculated in the usual way.

5.18 An alternative would be for the bank to **extend the contract,** by changing the bank's selling or buying rate in the contract. The bank would then arrange a new forward exchange contract with the customer at a rate that is slightly more favourable to the customer than for an ordinary forward exchange contract. This type of arrangement is, however, frowned upon by the Bank of England as it might encourage companies to conceal losses, and banks will only permit it in the rarest of cases.

Chapter roundup

- There are a number of techniques for **exchange rate risk management**.

- **Hedging strategies** are possible involving various financial instruments including **options**, **swaps** and **futures**. We look at these alternatives in the next chapter.

- Examination questions may focus on the selection of the cheapest **appropriate** technique, so it is important to grasp not only the mathematics of these techniques but also what financial commitments are necessary to use each one.

Quick quiz

1   Identify the three types of currency risk.

2   Which factors influence the supply and demand for currencies?

3   The principle of purchasing power parity must always hold.

    True   ☐

    False   ☐

4   A company might make payments earlier or later in order to take advantage of exchange rate movements. What is this called?

5   Define a 'forward exchange rate'.

6   Fill in the boxes in the diagram with (A) to (E), to indicate which factors are linked by which theory.

  (A)   Purchasing powering parity theory
  (B)   Expectations theory
  (C)   Fisher effect
  (D)   International Fisher effect
  (E)   Interest rate parity

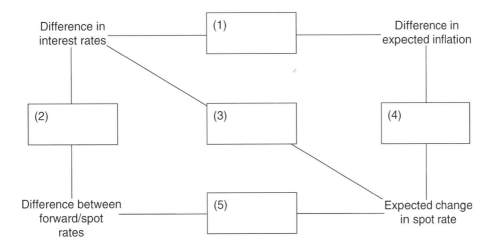

Now try the question below from the Exam Question Bank

Number	Level	Marks	Time
12	Examination	25	45 mins

BPP
PUBLISHING

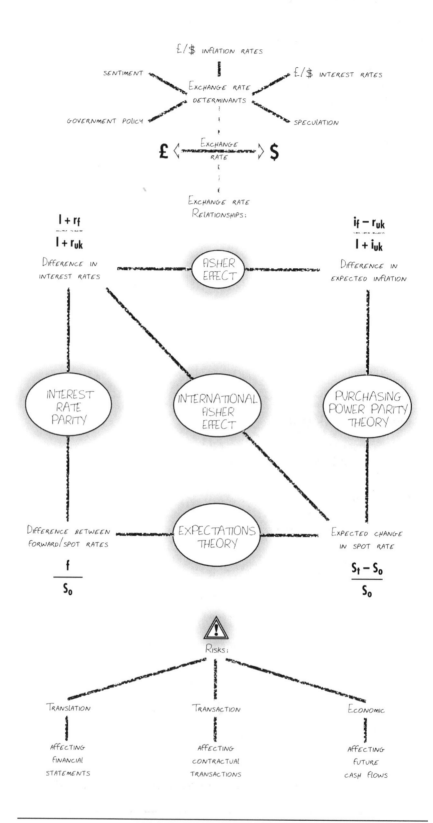

£/$ INFLATION RATES

SENTIMENT

£/$ INTEREST RATES

EXCHANGE RATE DETERMINANTS

GOVERNMENT POLICY

SPECULATION

£ ⟨ EXCHANGE RATE ⟩ $

EXCHANGE RATE RELATIONSHIPS:

$$\frac{1 + r_f}{1 + r_{uk}}$$

DIFFERENCE IN INTEREST RATES

FISHER EFFECT

$$\frac{i_f - r_{uk}}{1 + i_{uk}}$$

DIFFERENCE IN EXPECTED INFLATION

INTEREST RATE PARITY

INTERNATIONAL FISHER EFFECT

PURCHASING POWER PARITY THEORY

DIFFERENCE BETWEEN FORWARD/SPOT RATES

EXPECTATIONS THEORY

EXPECTED CHANGE IN SPOT RATE

$$\frac{f}{S_0}$$

$$\frac{S_t - S_0}{S_0}$$

RISKS:

TRANSLATION

TRANSACTION

ECONOMIC

AFFECTING FINANCIAL STATEMENTS

AFFECTING CONTRACTUAL TRANSACTIONS

AFFECTING FUTURE CASH FLOWS

FINANCIAL STRATEGY: EXCHANGE RATES

Chapter 13

CURRENCY RISK II

Topic list	Syllabus reference	Ability required
1 Choosing a hedging method	(iii)	Analysis
2 Currency futures	(iii)	Analysis
3 Currency options	(iii)	Analysis
4 Swaps	(iii)	Analysis

Introduction

In this chapter, we extend our discussion of **currency risk management** and consider the choice of appropriate hedging methods as well as some of the plethora of **financial instruments** which are now available for managing **financial risks** of various kinds.

Learning outcomes covered in this chapter

- Interpret the impact of currency risk
- Recommend foreign exchange risk management strategies
- Calculate and interrupt real options (abandonment, follow-on, deferment)

Syllabus content covered in this chapter

- Currency futures and options including tick values (numerical questions including tick values but ignoring basis risk will be set: the Black Scholes option pricing model will not be tested numerically, however, an understanding of the variables which will influence the value of an option should be appreciated)

- Currency swaps (calculations to illustrate a currency swap may be set)

1 CHOOSING A HEDGING METHOD

Pilot paper

1.1 When a company expects to receive or pay a sum of foreign currency in the next few months, it can choose between using the **forward exchange market** and the **money market** to hedge against the foreign exchange risk. Both of these methods were introduced in the previous chapter. The cheaper option available is the one that ought to be chosen. Other methods may also be possible, such as making **lead payments**.

1.2 EXAMPLE: CHOOSING THE CHEAPEST METHOD

Trumpton plc has bought goods from a US supplier, and must pay $4,000,000 for them in three months time. The company's finance director wishes to hedge against the foreign exchange risk, and the three methods which the company usually considers are:

(a) Using forward exchange contracts
(b) Using money market borrowing or lending

(c)   Making lead payments

The following annual interest rates and exchange rates are currently available.

	US dollar		Sterling	
	Deposit rate	*Borrowing rate*	*Deposit rate*	*Borrowing rate*
	%	%	%	%
1 month	7	10.25	10.75	14.00
3 months	7	10.75	11.00	14.25

	$/£ exchange rate ($ = £1)
Spot	1.8625 - 1.8635
1 month forward	1.8565 – 1.8577
3 months forward	1.8445 – 1.8460

Which is the cheapest method for Trumpton plc? Ignore commission costs. (The bank charges for arranging a forward contract or a loan.)

1.3   SOLUTION

The three choices must be compared on a similar basis, which means working out the cost of each to Trumpton either **now** or **in three months time**. Here the cost to Trumpton now will be determined.

Choice 1: the forward exchange market

1.4   Trumpton must buy dollars in order to pay the US supplier. The exchange rate in a forward exchange contract to buy $4,000,000 in three months time (bank sells) is $1.8445/£.

The cost of the $4,000,000 to Trumpton in three months time will be:

$$\frac{\$4,000.000}{1.8445} = £2,168,609.38$$

1.5   This is the cost **in three months**. To work out the cost **now**, we could say that by deferring payment for three months, the company is:

(a)   Saving having to borrow money now at 14.25% a year to make the payment now, or
(b)   Avoiding the loss of interest on cash on deposit, earning 11% a year

The choice between (a) and (b) depends on whether Trumpton plc needs to borrow to make any current payment (a) or is cash rich (b). Here, assumption (a) is selected, but (b) might in fact apply.

1.6   At an annual interest rate of 14.25% the rate for three months is approximately 14.25/4 = 3.5625%. The 'present cost' of £2,168,609.38 in three months time is:

$$\frac{£2,168,609.38}{1.035625} = £2,094,010.27$$

Choice 2: the money markets

1.7   Using the money markets involves:

(a)   Borrowing in the foreign currency, if the company will eventually receive the currency
(b)   Lending (depositing) in the foreign currency, if the company will eventually pay the currency

Here, Trumpton will pay $4,000,000 and so it would **lend** US dollars.

1.8 It would lend enough US dollars for three months, so that the principal repaid in three months time plus interest will amount to the payment due of $4,000,000.

(a) Since the US dollar deposit rate is 7%, the rate for three months is approximately 7/4 = 1.75%.

(b) To earn $4,000,000 in three months time at 1.75% interest, Trumpton would have to lend now:

$$\frac{\$4,000,000}{1.0175} = \$3,931,203.93$$

1.9 These dollars would have to be purchased now at the spot rate of (bank sells) $1.8625. The cost would be:

$$\frac{\$3,931,203.93}{1.8625} = £2,110,713.52$$

By lending US dollars for three months, Trumpton is matching eventual receipts and payments in US dollars, and so has hedged against foreign exchange risk.

Choice 3: lead payments

1.10 Lead payments should be considered when the currency of payment is expected to strengthen over time, and is quoted forward at a premium on the foreign exchange market.

Here, the cost of a lead payment (paying $4,000,000 now) would be $4,000,000 ÷ 1.8625 = £2,147,651.01.

1.11 In this example, the present value of the costs are as follows.

	£
Forward exchange contract	2,094,010.27 (cheapest)
Money markets	2,110,713.52
Lead payment	2,147,651.01

2 CURRENCY FUTURES

> **KEY TERMS**
>
> A **futures contract** can be defined as 'a standardised contract covering the sale or purchase at a set future date of a set quantity of a commodity, financial investment or cash'.
>
> A **financial future** is a futures contract which is based on a financial instrument, rather than a physical commodity. There are financial futures for interest rates, currencies and stock market indices.
>
> A **currency future** is a futures contract to buy or sell a currency.

2.1 **Currency futures** are not nearly as common as forward contracts, and their market is much smaller. On the currency futures markets, currencies such as the pound, deutschmark, yen, Swiss franc and French franc are all priced in US dollars. There is no contract for the US dollar itself.

2.2 On financial futures exchanges, most trading is in **interest rates** and **stock exchange indices**. **LIFFE** started trading in currency futures in 1982 but quickly abandoned them because of competition from the huge London-based forward foreign exchange market. LIFFE now trades futures and options concerned with short-term and long-term interest rates, the FTSE 100 and 250 indices and some commodities (eg wheat, coffee).

2.3 A London-based firm wishing to deal in currency futures could not therefore use LIFFE but would need to use a foreign exchange. The largest market for currency futures is the International Monetary Market (IMM), a division of the Chicago Mercantile Exchange. Another alternative is Singapore International Monetary Exchange (SIMEX).

KEY TERM

The **contract size** is the fixed minimum quantity of commodity which can be bought or sold using a futures contract.

2.4 Dealing in this amount is referred to as buying or selling one contract. In general, dealing on futures markets must be in a whole number of contracts.

KEY TERM

The **contract price** is the price at which the futures contract can be bought or sold.

2.5 For all currency futures the contract price is in US dollars (e.g. \$/DM 0.5800 as used in the last example). Most commodities are also priced in dollars, though other currencies (eg pounds) are also used. The contract price is the figure which is traded on the futures exchange. It changes continuously and is the basis for computing gains or losses.

KEY TERM

The **settlement date** (or delivery date, or expiry date) is the date when trading on a particular futures contract stops and all accounts are settled.

2.6 On IMM, the settlement dates for all currency futures are at the end of March, June, September and December. The period for which a currency contract is traded before the settlement date is normally a maximum of nine months. This means that for each currency there will be three contracts being traded at any time, each to a different settlement date. For example from April to June, the currency futures being traded will be the June contract, the September contract and the December contract.

POSITIONS	
Buyer of futures contract	Long position
Seller of futures contract	Short position

KEY TERM

One tick (or the **tick size**) is the smallest measured movement in the contract price. For currency futures this is a movement in the fourth decimal place.

2.7 The value of one tick = contract size × tick size. A movement in the price of the D-Mark contract from \$/DM 0.5800 to 0.5801 is a one-tick movement. The **value of a tick** is the gain or loss which is made if there is one tick price movement. This value depends on the contract size. Examples of tick values and contract sizes are shown in the following table.

Currency future	Contract size	Tick	Value of one tick
Deutschmark	DM 125,000	\$0.0001 per DM	\$12.50
Swiss franc	SFr 125,000	\$0.0001 per SFr	\$12.50
Japanese yen	Y 12.5 million	\$0.0001 per Y100	\$12.50
Sterling	£62,500	\$0.0001 per £	\$6.25
Euro	€125,000	\$0.0001 per €	\$12.50

2.8 Market traders will compute gains or losses on their futures positions by reference to the number of ticks by which the contract price has moved. For instance, the futures market gain in the previous example could have been computed as follows.

Bought at	0.5800
Sold at	0.6000
Gain	0.0200 = 200 ticks.

8 contracts × 200 ticks × \$12.50 = \$20,000.

KEY TERM

When futures contracts are bought or sold, a **deposit** known as the **initial margin** must be advanced.

2.9 The size of this margin depends on the actual contract but might typically amount to about 5% of the value of contracts dealt in. This deposit is refunded when the contract is closed out.

2.10 The objective of the initial margin is to cover any possible losses made from the first day's trading. Thereafter, any variations in the contract price are covered by a **variation** margin. Profits are advanced to the trader's account but losses must be covered by advancing further collateral. This process is known as **marking to market**.

2.11 The fact that futures trading can be carried out **on the margin** in this fashion makes it very attractive to speculators. For example, if you buy \$580,000 worth of futures contracts, you might only have to advance \$29,000 initial margin. Thereafter, if the value of the contract increases steadily over the next month to \$600,000, you need advance no more. When you close out you make a gain of \$20,000 and your \$29,000 is refunded. Your percentage return in one month is \$20,000/\$29,000 = 69% compared with the 3.45% you would have made if you had to advance the full \$580,000.

2.12 Under volatile trading conditions, percentage gains can be far higher than this. It goes without saying, however, that similar percentage *losses* can be made, sometimes amounting to several times the initial outlay.

KEY TERM

A future's price may be different from the spot price, and this difference is the **basis**.

Basis = spot price – futures price

2.13 (Some books show it the other way round, so that the basis is the amount by which the futures price exceeds the spot price.) The basis will move towards zero at the delivery date. If it did not, **arbitrage profits** would be possible. If, for example, the basis was negative at the delivery date, profits could be earned by selling futures contracts (at the higher price) and simultaneously buying in the cash market (at the lower price) goods - gold, pork bellies, dollars or whatever - for delivery to the futures buyers.

2.14 The futures markets have grown rapidly as more and more speculators have become involved and this has increased short-term volatility. However, hedgers who need to buy or sell the underlying currency or commodity do not use the margin to trade more than they otherwise would and can use the futures markets quite safely provided they understand how the system operates. The only risk to hedgers is that the futures market does not always provide a perfect hedge. This can result from two causes.

   (a) The first reason is that amounts must be **rounded to a whole number of contracts**, causing inaccuracies.

   (b) The second reason is **basis risk** - the risk that the futures contract price may move by a different amount from the price of the underlying currency or commodity. The actions of speculators may increase basis risk.

2.15 When deciding to use futures to hedge currency risk, you need to consider the following things when **setting up** the hedge.

   - **Which contract** out of a number of contracts with different settlement dates?
   - **What type** of futures contract - are you looking for a **buy** or **sell** contract?
   - **Which settlement date**?

Which contract settlement date?

2.16 Currency futures are traded for a period of about nine months before the settlement date is reached. This means that at any time there will be a choice of three settlement dates to choose from. To hedge currency receipts and payments a futures contract must have a settlement date **after** the date that the actual currency is needed. Usually the best hedge is achieved by selecting the contract which matures **next after** the actual cash is needed.

Which type of contract?

2.17 One of the limitations of currency futures is that currencies can only be bought or sold for US dollars. The basic rules are given below.

   (a) If you need to **buy** a currency on a future date with US dollars, take the following action.

      Step 1. **Buy** the **appropriate currency futures** contracts now

      Step 2. Close out by **selling** the **same number of futures** contracts on the date that you buy the actual currency

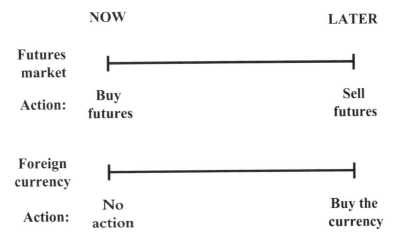

This was the procedure we used in the examples involving deutschmarks in the previous section.

(b) If you need to **sell** a currency on a future date for US$, take the following steps.

Step 1. **Sell** the **appropriate currency futures** contracts now

Step 2. Close out by **buying** the **same number** of **futures** contracts on the date that you sell the actual currency

How many contracts?

2.18 We have already made the point that futures can only be bought or sold as a whole number of contracts. When hedging, there is no necessary advantage in rounding **up** because futures trading can produce a loss as regularly as a profit. The problem which has not yet been covered is **how many contracts to use when the receipt or payment is in US dollars**. The method normally used is to convert to the other currency using the exchange rate implicit in the futures contract (i.e. today's contract price) and then divide by the futures contract size.

2.19 EXAMPLE: CURRENCY FUTURES

Great Eastern plc, a British company, has purchased steel worth Y100 million from Japan and needs to pay for this in 90 days' time. How can it hedge the cost of the purchase by using currency futures? On IMM the Japanese yen future is trading at $0.8106 per 100 yen and the Sterling future is trading at $1.6250 per pound.

2.20 SOLUTION

The company must buy yen futures and sell sterling futures. The size of the Japanese yen futures contract is Y12.5 million. The number of yen futures to buy is 100/12.5 = 8.

$$8 \text{ contracts represent } \frac{8 \times 12,500,000 \times \$0.8106}{100} = \$810,600.$$

$810,600, converted at the sterling futures price, gives £ 810,600/1.6250 = £498,831. The sterling contract size is £62,500. The company should sell £498,831/£62,500 = 7.98 contracts, rounded to 8 contracts.

Summary. Today, buy 8 yen contracts and sell 8 sterling contracts. In 90 days, close out by selling 8 yen contracts and buying 8 sterling contracts.

Dealing with a futures question

2.21 A number of possible stages are involved.

Step 1. **The setup process**

This may involve the following steps.

(a) **Choose which contract**

You must chose an expiry date after the underlying exposure.

(b) **Choose type of contract**

A €125,000 contract will be to buy or sell €. If the company owes €, it will wish to buy € so will **buy € futures**. However a UK company receiving $ will wish to sell $ or buy £. As the contract size noted in 2.20 is quoted in £, £62,500, the company will **buy £ futures**.

(c) **Choose number of contracts**

You need to divide the amount being hedged by the size of contract, rounding to the nearest whole contract.

You may also need to calculate how much of the currency of the future is needed. You do this by using today's price for the futures contract to convert the amount being hedged into the currency of the futures contract, and then divide by the size of the futures contract.

(d) **Calculate tick size**

Tick size = Minimum price movement × standard contract size

Remember that the minimum price has to be calculated to the **fourth** decimal place, for example $0.0001 per £.

Step 2. **Estimate the closing futures price**

You should be given this in the question.

Step 3. **Hedge outcome**

(a) **Calculate spot market outcome**

This will be the amount paid or received in the spot market at the closing spot rate.

(b) **Calculate futures market outcome**

This will be

Tick movement × tick value × number of contracts

(c) **Calculate net outcome**

Spot market payment or receipt
+ Futures market profit/(loss)

As with 3(a), the currency used for this calculation will be the opposite to the currency of the receipt/payment being hedged. If therefore, a dollar receipt or payment is being hedged, the value of the futures profit or loss will have to be converted using the **closing spot rate**.

The gain or loss on the future will accrue during the contract. In exam questions you will take this gain or loss at the end of the contract at the prevailing closing spot rate.

2.22 EXAMPLE: FUTURES CONTRACT

A US company buys goods worth €720,000 from a German company payable in 30 days. The US company wants to hedge against the € strengthening against the dollar.

Current spot is 0.9215 – 0.9221 $/€ and the € futures rate is 0.9245 $/€.

The standard size of a 3 month € futures contract is €125,000.

In 30 days time the spot is 0.9345 – 0.9351 $/€.

Closing futures price will be 0.9367.

Evaluate the hedge.

2.23 SOLUTION

Step 1. **Setup**

(a) **Which contract?**

We assume that the three month contract is the best available.

(b) **Type of contract**

We need to buy € or sell $.

As the futures contract is in €, we need to buy futures.

(c) **Number of contracts**

$$\frac{720,000}{125,000} = 5.76, \text{ say 6 contracts}$$

(d) **Tick size**

Minimum price movement × contract size = $0.0001 \times 125,000 = \$12.50$

Step 2. **Closing futures price**

We're told it will be 0.9367

Step 3. **Hedge outcome**

(a) **Outcome in spot market**

	$
At opening spot rate (720,000 × 0.9221 $/€)	663,912
At closing spot rate (720,000 × 0.9351 $/€)	673,272
Opportunity profit/(loss)	(9,360)

(b) **Outcome in futures market**

Opening futures price	0.9245	Buy at low price
Closing futures price	0.9367	Sell at high price
Movement in ticks	122 ticks	Profit

Futures profit/loss   122 × $12.50 × 6 contracts = $9,150

(c) **Net outcome**

	$
Spot market payment	673,272
Futures market profit	(9,150)
	664,122

Choosing between forward contracts and futures contracts

2.24 A futures market hedge attempts to achieve the same result as a forward contract, that is to fix the exchange rate in advance for a future foreign currency payment or receipt. As we have seen, hedge inefficiencies mean that a futures contract can only fix the exchange rate subject to a margin of error.

2.25 It is useful at this stage to consider the advantages and disadvantages of futures hedges over forward contracts and then to work some examples which compare the two.

2.26 Forward contracts are agreed 'over the counter' between a bank and its customer. Futures contracts are standardised and traded on futures exchanges. This results in the following advantages and disadvantages.

Advantages of futures over forward contracts

(a) **Transaction** costs should be **lower**.

(b) The **exact date** of **receipt** or **payment** of the currency does **not have to be known**, because the futures contract does not have to be closed out until the actual cash receipt or payment is made. In other words, the futures hedge gives the equivalent of an 'option forward' contract, limited only by the expiry date of the contract.

Disadvantages of futures compared with forward contracts

(a) The **contracts cannot be tailored** to the user's exact requirements.

(b) **Hedge inefficiencies** are **caused** by having to deal in a whole number of contracts and by basis risk.

(c) **Only a limited number of currencies** are the subject of futures contracts (although the number of currencies is growing, especially with the rapid development of Asian economies).

(d) The **procedure for converting** between two currencies neither of which is the US dollar is twice as complex for futures as for a forward contract.

In general, the disadvantages of futures mean that the market is much smaller than the currency forward market.

3   CURRENCY OPTIONS

Pilot paper

The nature of an option

> **KEY TERM**
>
> An **option** is a right of an option holder to buy or sell a specific asset on predetermined terms on, or before, a future date.   *(OT 2000)*

3.1 We looked at the use of interest rate options in Chapter 11. Now, we turn to currency options.

Currency options

3.2 There is a major drawback to forward exchange contracts as a means of managing foreign exchange risk. A forward exchange contract is an agreement to buy or sell a given quantity of foreign exchange, which **must be carried out** because it is a binding contract. Some exporters might be uncertain about the amount of currency they will earn in several months time, and so would be unable to enter forward exchange contracts without the risk of contracting to sell more or less currency to their bank than they will actually earn when the time comes. An alternative method of obtaining foreign exchange cover, which overcomes much of the problem, is the **currency option**.

> **KEY TERM**
>
> A **currency option** is an agreement involving an option, but not an obligation, to buy or to sell a certain amount of currency at a stated rate of exchange (the exercise price) at some time in the future.

3.3 The exercise price for the option may be the same as the current spot rate, or it may be more favourable or less favourable to the option holder than the current spot rate. Options are 'at-the-money', 'in-the-money' or 'out-of-the-money' accordingly.

3.4 Companies can choose whether to buy:

  (a) A tailor-made currency option from a bank, suited to the company's specific needs. These are **over-the-counter** (OTC) or **negotiated** options, or

  (b) A standard option, in certain currencies only, from an options exchange. Such options are **traded** or **exchange-traded** options.

3.5 As with other types of option, buying a currency option involves paying a premium, which is the most the buyer of the option can lose. Selling (or 'writing') options, unless covered by other transactions, is extremely risky because the seller ('writer') bears the whole of the cost of the variation and can face potentially unlimited losses. Such risks received much publicity with the Barings Bank failure in 1995.

3.6 **Currency options are not the same as forward exchange option contracts,** although the similarity in names might seem confusing. Unlike a forward exchange contract (option or otherwise), a currency option **does not have to be exercised**. Instead, when the date for exercising the option arrives, the importer or exporter can either exercise the option or let the option lapse.

> **KEY TERMS**
>
> There are two types of currency option, both of which can be bought and sold.
>
> (a) A **call option** is an option to buy a specified underlying asset at a specified exercise price on, or before, a specified exercise date.
>
> (b) A **put option** is an option to sell a specified underlying asset at a specified exercise price, on, or before, a specified exercise date.   *(OT 2000)*

The purpose of currency options

3.7 The purpose of currency options is to reduce or eliminate exposure to currency risks, and they are particularly useful for companies in the following situations:

BPP PUBLISHING

(a) Where there is uncertainty about foreign currency receipts or payments, either in timing or amount. Should the foreign exchange transaction not materialise, the option can be sold on the market (if it has any value) or exercised if this would make a profit.

(b) To support the tender for an overseas contract, priced in a foreign currency

(c) To allow the publication of price lists for its goods in a foreign currency

(d) To protect the import or export of price-sensitive goods. If there is a favourable movement in exchange rates, options allow the importer/exporter to profit from the favourable change (unlike forward exchange contracts, when the importer/exporter is tied to a fixed rate of exchange by the binding contract). This means that the gains can be passed on in the prices to the importer's or exporter's customers.

In both situations (b) and (c), the company would not know whether it had won any export sales or would have any foreign currency income at the time that it announces its selling prices. It cannot make a forward exchange contract to sell foreign currency without becoming exposed in the currency.

3.8 EXAMPLE: CURRENCY OPTIONS

Tartan plc has been invited to tender for a contract in Blueland with the bid priced in Blues (the local currency). Tartan thinks that the contract would cost £1,850,000. Because of the fierce competition for the bid, Tartan is prepared to price the contract at £2,000,000, and since the exchange rate is currently B2.80 = £1, it puts in a bid of B5,600,000. The contract will not be awarded until after six months.

3.9 What can happen to Tartan with the contract? Consider the following possible outcomes.

(a) Tartan plc decides to hedge against the currency risk, and on the assumption that it will be awarded the contract in six months time, it enters into a **forward exchange contract** to sell B5,600,000 in six months time at a rate of B2.8 = £1.

As it turns out, the company fails to win the contract and so it must buy B5,600,000 spot to meet its obligation under the forward contract. The exchange rate has changed, say, to B2.5 = £1.

	£
At the outset:	
Tartan sells B5,600,000 forward at B2.8 to £1	2,000,000
Six months later:	
Tartan buys B5,600,000 spot to cover the hedge, at B2.5 to £1	(2,240,000)
Loss	(240,000)

(b) Alternatively, Tartan plc might decide not to make a forward exchange contract at all, but to **wait and see** what happens. As it turns out, Tartan is awarded the contract six months later, but by this time, the value of the Blue has fallen, say, to B3.2 = £1.

Question

Have a go at calculating the outcome, before looking at the calculation below.

	£
Tartan wins the contract for B5,600,000, which has a sterling value of (B3.2 = £1)	1,750,000
Cost of the contract	(1,850,000)
Loss	(100,000)

(c) A **currency option** would, for a fixed cost, eliminate these risks for Tartan plc. When it makes its tender for the contract, Tartan might purchase a currency option to sell B5,600,000 in six months time at B2.8 to £1, at a cost of £40,000.

3.10 The worst possible outcome for Tartan plc is now a loss of £40,000.

(a) If the company **fails to win the contract,** Tartan will **abandon** the option (unless the exchange rate has moved in Tartan's favour and the Blue has weakened against sterling so that the company can make a profit by buying B5,600,000 at the spot rate and selling it at B2.8 = £1).

(b) If the company **wins the contract** and the exchange rate of the Blue has **weakened** against sterling, Tartan will **exercise** the option and sell the Blues at 2.80.

	£	£
Proceeds from selling B5,600,000		2,000,000
Cost of contract	1,850,000	
Cost of currency option	40,000	
		1,890,000
Net profit		110,000

(c) If the Blue has **strengthened** against sterling, Tartan will **abandon** the option. For example, if Tartan wins the contract and the exchange rate has moved to B2.5 = £1, Tartan will sell the B5,600,000 at this rate to earn £2,240,000, and will incur costs, including the abandoned currency option, of £1,890,000.

	£	£
Proceeds from selling B5,600,000		2,240,000
Cost of contract	1,850,000	
Cost of currency option	40,000	
		1,890,000
Net profit		350,000

Comparison of currency options with forward contracts and futures contracts

3.11 In the last chapter, we saw that a hedge using a currency future will produce approximately the same result as a currency forward contract, subject to hedge inefficiencies. When comparing currency options with forward or futures contracts we usually find the following.

(a) If the currency movement is adverse, the option will be exercised, but the hedge will not normally be quite as good as that of the forward or futures contract; this is because of the **premium cost of the option.**

(b) If the currency movement is favourable, the option will not be exercised, and the result will normally be better than that of the forward or futures contract; this is because the option allows the holder to **profit from the improved exchange rate.**

These points are illustrated by the next series of examples.

3.12 EXAMPLE: CURRENCY OPTIONS (2)

Crabtree plc is expecting to receive 20 million Austrian schillings (Sch) in one month's time. The current spot rate is Sch/£ 19.3383 - 19.3582. Compare the results of the following actions.

(a) The receipt is hedged using a forward contract at the rate 19.3048.

(b) The receipt is hedged by buying an over-the-counter (OTC) option from the bank, exercise price Sch/£ 19.30, premium cost 12 pence per 100 schillings.

(c) The receipt is not hedged.

In each case compute the results if, in one month, the exchange rate moves to:

(a) 21.00

(b) 17.60

3.13 SOLUTION

The target receipt at today's spot rate is 20,000,000/19.3582 = £1,033,154.

(a) The receipt using forward contract is fixed with certainty at 20,000,000/19.3048 = £1,036,012. This applies to both exchange rate scenarios.

(b) The cost of the option is 20,000,000/100 × 12/100 = £24,000. This must be paid at the start of the contract.

The results under the two scenarios are as follows.

Scenario	(a)	(b)
Exchange rate	21.00	17.60
Exercise price	19.30	19.30
Exercise option?	YES	NO
Exchange rate used	19.30	17.60
	£	£
Pounds received	1,036,269	1,136,364
Less option premium	24,000	24,000
Net receipt	1,012,269	1,112,364

(c) The results of not hedging under the two scenarios are as follows.

Scenario	(a)	(b)
Exchange rate	21.00	17.60
Pounds received	£952,381	£1,136,364

Summary. The option gives a result between that of the forward contract and no hedge. If the Austrian schilling weakens to 21.00, the best result would have been obtained using the forward market (£1,036,012). If it strengthens to 17.60, the best course of action would have been to take no hedge (£1,136,364). In both cases the option gives the second best result, being £24,000 below the best because of its premium cost.

3.14 EXAMPLE: CURRENCY OPTIONS (3)

In **Example: currency options** (2), by how much would the exchange rate have moved if the forward and option contracts gave the same result? Comment on your answer.

3.15 SOLUTION

The forward contract gives a receipt of £1,036,012 whatever the movement in exchange rate. If the option is to give a net receipt of £1,036,012, it must give a gross amount (before deducting the premium) of £1,036,012 + £24,000 = £1,060,012. This implies that the exchange rate has moved to 20,000,000/1,060,012 = 18.87 schillings to the pound.

The option will not be exercised at this exchange rate. It is allowed to lapse, giving an exchange gain which just covers the premium cost. The option becomes advantageous over a forward contract if the exchange rate strengthens beyond 18.87 schillings to the pound.

3.16 As with futures, a number of complications are encountered when using traded options. The most important of these complications are:

- Choosing the correct type of option (call or put)
- Choosing the strike price and the number of contracts to be used
- Surplus cash when the number of contracts is rounded
- Closing out when traded options still have time to run
- Use of collars to reduce the option premium cost

Choosing the correct type of option

3.17 In the previous example the American company needed to sell pounds sterling. It therefore purchased options to sell pounds, which are sterling put options. Note that the vast majority of options examples which we consider are concerned with **hedgers** who **purchase** options in order to reduce risk. We are seldom concerned with option writers. The only times that we normally consider selling options are either when we wish to close out options which have already been purchased or when we wish to create a 'collar'. Both of these situations are dealt with later.

3.18 So, given that we are normally going to *purchase* options, should we **purchase puts or calls?** With OTC options there is usually no problem in making this decision. If, for example, we may need to buy US dollars at some stage in the future, we can hedge by purchasing a US dollar call option. With traded options, however, we run into the same problem as with futures. Only a limited number of currencies are available and there is no US dollar option as such. We have to **rephrase the company's requirements,** as we did with futures.

3.19 For example, a UK company wishing to sell US dollars in the future can hedge by purchasing £ sterling call options (ie options to buy sterling with dollars). Similarly, a German company which needs to buy US dollars can hedge by purchasing D-Mark put options.

Choosing the strike price and the number of contracts to be used

3.20 When the American company wished to sell £3.75 million, the computation of the number of contracts was easy (£3,750,000/£31,250 = 120 option contracts). A problem arises when a non-US company wishes to buy or sell US dollars using traded options. The amount of US dollars must first be converted into the home currency. For this purpose the best exchange rate to use is the **exercise price**, which means that the number of contracts may vary according to which exercise price is chosen.

Surplus cash when the number of contracts is rounded

3.21 Assume that the company chooses to hedge the receipt of $10 million by purchasing 229 June £ call option contracts, exercise price 1.400 $/£. Demonstrate the result if the spot rate on June 30 is (i) 1.55; (ii) 1.35.

3.22 The premium cost is 229 × $0.0574 × 31,250 = $410,769. This must be purchased at today's spot $/£ rate, which is 1.4461, giving a cost of £284,053.

Scenario (i)

The option will be exercised and £31,250 × 229 = £7,156,250 will be purchased with 7,156,250 × 1.40 = $10,018,750. The customer provides $10,000,000, but $18,750 has to be purchased at the June 30 spot rate of 1.55 $/£, giving an additional cost of £12,097. (Note that this additional amount *could* have been covered on the forward market, but that this would have created an exchange loss under Scenario (ii) when the option is abandoned. We therefore assume that forward cover is not taken).

The total sterling amount received from the sale of $10 million is:

	£
Option premium paid	(284,053)
£ purchased by exercising option	7,156,250
Purchase of surplus $ on 30 June	(12,097)
Net £ received	6,860,100

Note. An approximate result can be obtained by converting $10,000,000 at 1.4574 (the sum of the exercise price and the option premium) giving £6,861,534. However, this method ignores the fact that the premium is paid in advance and that surplus $ must be purchased at the end.

Scenario (ii)

The option is abandoned. $10,000,000 is converted at the spot rate 1.35, giving £7,407,407. After subtracting the option premium of £284,053, the net receipt is £7,123,354.

By way of comparison, a forward contract would have yielded 10,000,000/1.4101 = £7,091,696.

Closing out when traded options still have time to run

3.23 The above example assumes that the traded option is at its expiry date when the decision needs to be made between exercising or abandoning. In practice, most traded options arc **closed out**, like futures contracts, because the date when the cash is required does not match the option expiry date.

3.24 Suppose that the company in the above example was due to receive $10 million on 10 June. Then June option contracts would still be used, but on 10 June the decision that needs to be made is whether to close out the option, to exercise it or to allow it to lapse. Closing out will be more beneficial than exercising or allowing to lapse if the option still has a positive time value.

3.25 Assume that the company purchased 229 June sterling call option contracts, exercise price 1.400, and that on 10 June two possible scenarios are as follows.

(a) Spot rate is 1.55 and the 1.400 call option premium has risen to 15.35 cents per pound
(b) Spot rate is 1.35 and the 1.400 call option premium has fallen to 0.43 cents per pound

In *Scenario (a)* the intrinsic value of the option is $(1.55 - 1.40) = 15 cents. If the option is exercised, a gain of 15 cents per £ will be made, as opposed to a gain of 15.35 cents per £ if the call option is sold. Consequently the contracts will be sold for a premium of $0.1535 × 31,250 × 229 = $1,098,484.

	$	£
Option premium paid at start		(284,053)
Option premium received at end	1,098,484	
Cash from customer	10,000,000	
Total dollars received	11,098,484	
Converted to sterling at 1.55:		7,160,312
Net sterling received		6,876,259

In *Scenario (b)* the intrinsic value of the option is zero, so it will be sold in order to realise the small time value: $0.0043 × 31,250 × 229 = $30,772.

	$	£
Option premium paid at start		(284,053)
Option premium received at end	30,772	
Cash from customer	10,000,000	
Total dollars received	10,030,772	
Converted to sterling at 1.35:		7,430,202
Net sterling received		7,146,149

3.26 Because of the complications, it is best to use a similar method to the method we used for futures to assess the impact of options.

Step 1. Set up the hedge

(a) Choose contract date
(b) Decide whether put or call option required
(c) Decide which strike price applies
(d) How many contracts
(e) Tick size
(f) The premium may need to be converted using the spot rate

Step 2. Ascertain closing price

You should be given this.

Step 3. Calculate outcome of hedge

You may have to calculate the outcome under more than one closing spot rate.

(a) Outcome in spot market

(b) Outcome in options market. This will include deciding whether to exercise the option

(c) Net outcome

3.27 EXAMPLE: CURRENCY OPTIONS (6)

A UK company owes a US supplier $2,000,000 payable in July. The spot rate is 1.5350-1.5370 $/£ and the UK company is concerned that the $ might strengthen.

The details on the Philadelphia Stock Exchange for $/£ £31,250 options (cents per £1) are as follows.

	Calls			Puts		
Strike price	*June*	*July*	*August*	*June*	*July*	*August*
1.4750	6.34	6.37	6.54	0.07	0.19	0.50
1.5000	3.86	4.22	4.59	0.08	0.53	1.03
1.5250	1.58	2.50	2.97	0.18	1.25	1.89

Show how traded $/£ currency options can be used to hedge the risk at 1.525. Calculate the sterling cost of the transaction if the spot rate in July is:

(a) $1.46-$1.4620
(b) $1.61-$1.6120

BPP
PUBLISHING

3.28 SOLUTION

Step 1. **Set up the hedge**

    (a)   Which date contract?   July

    (b)   Put or call?   Put, we need to put (sell) pounds in order to generate the dollars we need

    (b)   Which strike price?   1.5250

    (d)   How many contracts

$$\frac{2,000,000 \div 1.525}{31,250} \approx 42 \text{ contracts}$$

    (e)   Tick size $= 31,250 \times 0.0001 = \$3.125$

    (f)   Premium $= \dfrac{1.25}{100} \times 31,250 \times 42$

$$= \$16,406 \ @ \ 1.5350$$

$$= £10,688$$

We need to pay for the option in \$ now. Therefore the bank sells low at 1.5350.

Step 2. **Closing spot and futures prices**

Case (a) \$1.46
Case (b) \$1.61

Assume here the price to use for options calculation is the same as the closing spot rate.

Step 3. **Outcome**

    (a)   **Spot market**

	Case (a) £	*Case (b)* £
At opening spot rate \$2 million/1.5350	1,302,932	1,302,932
At closing spot rate \$2 million/closing spot	1,369,863	1,242,236
Opportunity profit/(loss)	(66,931)	60,696

    (b)   **Options market outcomes**

Strike price put (sell at)	1.5250	1.5250
Closing futures price (buy at)	1.46	1.61
Exercise?	Yes	No
If exercised, tick movement	650	–
Outcome of options position	650×42	–
	\$3.125	
	= \$85,313	

    (c)   **Net outcome**

	£	£
Spot market payment	(1,369,863)	(1,242,236)
Option market 85,313/1.46	58,434	–
Option premium	(10,688)	(10,688)
Net outcome	(1,322,117)	(1,252,924)

3.29 Drawbacks of currency options

- The cost depends on the expected volatility of the exchange rate.
- Options must be paid for as soon as they are bought.

- Tailor-made options lack negotiability.
- Traded options are not available in every currency.

Graphical illustration of currency options

3.30 Above, we have used options on shares as the main type of example. A similar graphical approach can be used to illustrate other kinds of options, for example currency options.

3.31 Suppose that a UK-based company expects to receive an amount of export income in dollars ($) in three months' time. Figure 6 illustrates the profit/loss profile of different strategies.

(a) Selling dollars and buying sterling in the **forward market** eliminates all uncertainty. The outcome is represented by a horizontal line.

(b) Relying on the **spot market** results in a net gain or loss compared with the forward market if the spot exchange rate in three months' time turns out to be below or above $X per pound respectively.

(c) If a **call option** is used, it will not be exercised if the exchange rate is less than $X per pound. A currency call option reduces the potential gain compared with the spot market strategy (b) by the amount of the premium on the option, but has the advantage that potential losses are contained as they will not exceed the value of the premium.

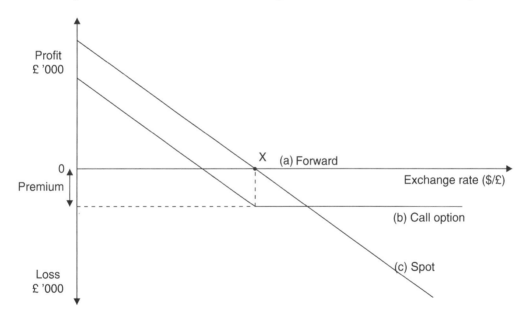

Figure 1 Currency call option, forward and spot markets: profit/loss profile

4   SWAPS   5/01

> **KEY TERM**
>
> A **swap** is 'an arrangement whereby two organisations contractually agree to exchange payments on different terms, eg in different currencies, or one at a fixed rate and the other at a floating rate'.   (*OT 2000*)

4.1 We discussed the use of interest rate swaps in Chapter 11. Now we consider currency swaps.

Currency swaps

4.2　In a **currency swap**, the parties agree to swap equivalent amounts of currency for a period. This effectively involves the exchange of debt from one currency to another. As with interest rate swaps (discussed earlier), liability on the principal is not transferred and the parties are liable to counterparty risk: if the other party defaults on the agreement to pay interest, the original borrower remains liable to the lender. This can present complicated legal problems, and some borrowers are unwilling to get involved in swap transactions for this reason.

Benefits of currency swaps

4.3　Swaps are **easy to arrange** and are **flexible** since they can be arranged in any size and are reversible. **Transaction costs are low**, only amounting to legal fees, since there is no commission or premium to be paid. The main benefits to be derived from currency swaps are as follows.

(a)　The parties can obtain the currency they require without subjecting themselves to the uncertainties of the foreign exchange markets.

(b)　The company can gain access to debt finance in another country and currency where it is little known, and consequently has a poorer credit rating, than in its home country. It can therefore take advantage of lower interest rates than it could obtain if it arranged the currency loan itself.

(c)　Currency swaps may be used to restructure the currency base of the company's liabilities. This may be important where the company is trading overseas and receiving revenues in foreign currencies, but its borrowings are denominated in the currency of its home country. Currency swaps therefore provide a means of reducing exchange rate exposure.

(d)　At the same time as exchanging currency, the company may also be able to convert fixed rate debt to floating rate or vice versa. Thus it may obtain some of the benefits of an interest rate swap in addition to achieving the other purposes of a currency swap.

(e)　A currency swap could be used to absorb excess liquidity in one currency which is not needed immediately, to create funds in another where there is a need.

4.4　A simple example would be one in which a UK company agrees with a US company to swap capital amounts at an agreed rate of exchange. Suppose a UK company is selling satellite equipment to NASA in the USA but will not be paid (in US dollars) for two years. The UK company could agree with another company to swap capital at an agreed rate of exchange in two years' time. The UK company will give the counterparty US dollars and receive sterling in return.

4.5　Consider a UK company X with a subsidiary Y in France which owns vineyards. Assume a spot rate of £1 = 10 French francs. Suppose the parent company X wishes to raise a loan of 10 million French francs for the purpose of buying another French wine company. At the same time, the French subsidiary Y wishes to raise £1 million to pay for new up-to-date capital equipment imported from the UK. The UK parent company X could borrow the £1 million sterling and the French subsidiary Y could borrow the 10 million francs, each effectively borrowing on the other's behalf. They would then swap currencies. This is known as a back-to-back loan.

KEY TERM

A **back-to-back loan** is a form of financing whereby money borrowed in one country or currency is covered by lending an equivalent amount in another.   *(OT 2000)*

4.6   A variation on currency swaps is **international interest arbitrage financing** or 'arbiloans'. This can be of value for an enterprise which operates in a country where interest rates are high and credit is hard to obtain. A subsidiary in a low-interest country borrows the amount required, converting it into the domestic currency of the parent company at the spot rate. The UK parent signs an agreement to repay the amount in the foreign currency at the end of the term, and purchases a forward contract for repayment at the same date.

4.7   In practice, most currency swaps are conducted between banks and their customers. An agreement may only be necessary if the swap were for longer than, say, one year.

4.8   EXAMPLE: HEDGING STRATEGY USING A SWAP

Adventurer Ltd, a UK company, is considering a contract to supply a telephone system to Blueland Telecom. All operating cash flows would be in the local currency, the Blue, as follows.

Time from start	Cash flow
	Blues
0	(700,000)
6 months	(400,000)
12 months	1,800,000

4.9   Because of high inflation in Blueland, the directors of Adventurer Ltd are very concerned about foreign exchange risk. However, the only available form of cover is a currency swap at a fixed rate of 9 Blues to the pound, for 1,100,000 Blues, to take effect in full at the start of the project and to last for a full year. The interest rate chargeable on the Blues would be 18% a year. This compares to a UK opportunity cost of capital for Adventurer Ltd of 22%.

4.10   The alternative to the swap is to convert between sterling and Blues at the spot rate, currently 10 Blues to the pound. The Blue floats freely on world currency markets. Inflation in Blueland and the UK over the year for which the project will last is forecast to be as follows.

UK	Blueland	Probability
%	%	
2	10	0.2
3	30	0.3
4	70	0.5

Required

Show whether or not Adventurer Ltd should use the available swap. Do not discount receipts and payments to a single time.

4.11   SOLUTION

The first step is to calculate the exchange rate in each of the different inflation scenarios. The rates can be found if we assume **purchasing power parity** between the two countries. Then, with inflation rates expressed as decimals:

$$\text{Exchange rate after a year} = \text{current spot rate} \times \frac{1 + \text{Blueland inflation rate}}{1 + \text{UK inflation rate}}$$

Now as our flows are six monthly, we need to convert this to an equivalent relationship over $^1/_2$ year, which is achieved taking the **square root** of the inflation factor:

$$\text{Exchange rate after six months} = \text{current spot rate} \times \sqrt{\frac{1 + \text{Blueland inflation rate}}{1 + \text{UK inflation rate}}}$$

Month	Inflation Blueland	UK	Exchange rate B/£
0			10.00
6	0.10	0.02	10.38
12	0.10	0.02	10.78
0			10.00
6	0.30	0.03	11.23
12	0.30	0.03	12.62
0			10.00
6	0.70	0.04	12.79
12	0.70	0.04	16.35

4.12 The **expected values** will not be calculated since these have little real meaning. Instead, the swap will be evaluated using the currency markets **for each of the three scenarios**. The effects of the exchange rate on the investments and returns can now be calculated. It is assumed that Adventurer Ltd will have to borrow funds in the UK to finance the deal, and therefore interest will be calculated at the opportunity cost of funds, 22%. The interest rate for six months will be $\sqrt{1.22} - 1 = 0.1045 = 10.45\%$.

(a) **Using the currency markets**

(i) Inflation rates 2% and 10%:

	Blues	£	Interest £
Investment - month 0	(700,000)	(70,000)	(15,400)
Investment - month 6	(400,000)	(38,536)	(4,027)
		(108,536)	(19,427)
Interest		(19,427)	
Total cost		(127,963)	
Price received	1,800,000	166,976	
Net profit/(loss)		39,013	

(ii) Inflation rates 3% and 30%:

	Blues	£	Interest £
Investment - month 0	(700,000)	(70,000)	(15,400)
Investment - month 6	(400,000)	(35,619)	(3,722)
		(105,619)	(19,122)
Interest		(19,122)	
Total cost		(124,741)	
Price received	1,800,000	142,631	
Net profit/(loss)		17,890	

(iii) Inflation rates 4% and 70%:

	Blues	£	Interest £
Investment - month 0	(700,000)	(70,000)	(15,400)
Investment - month 6	(400,000)	(31,274)	(3,268)
		(101,274)	(18,668)
Interest		(18,668)	
Total cost		(119,942)	
Price received	1,800,000	110,092	
Net profit/(loss)		(9,850)	

(b) **Using the currency swap**

Adventurer Ltd will have to borrow sterling funds in the UK to finance the swap. The cost of funds in the UK is 22%. However, swaps involve the transfer of interest rate liabilities as well as of principal, and therefore the interest cost will be calculated at the swap rate of 18%.

It is assumed that no interest will be earned on the 400,000 Blues which will be lying idle until month 6. The sterling investment required before interest is £1,100,000/9 = £122,222.

The price received will depend on the inflation rates. 1,100,000 Blues will be at the swap rate of 9 Blues to the pound, yielding £122,222, equal to the initial sterling outlay; the balance (700,000 Blues) will be at the prevailing year end rate. The sterling value of interest payments (198,000 Blues) will also depend on the exchange rate. It is assumed that no interest will be paid until the end of the year.

Inflation rates	Spot rate receipts £	Interest £	Profit £	Profit/(loss) without swap £
2% and 10%	64,935	18,367	46,568	39,013
3% and 30%	55,468	15,689	39,779	17,890
4% and 70%	42,813	12,110	30,703	(9,850)

4.13 Whatever the inflation rates, Adventurer Ltd will make a bigger profit with the swap than without it. It should therefore use the swap.

Chapter roundup

- A variety of financial instruments are available for reducing exposure to exchange rate risk. The markets for hedging instruments such as **futures**, **options** and **swaps** have undergone huge growth in recent years. Futures contracts have the practical disadvantage that they are for standardised amounts.

- Financial managers and strategists can use **options theory** in a variety of situations. However, where there is no market for the option concerned, such as there is with traded options, the exercise is likely to be a more subjective one involving a greater level of estimation to be made of the different factors affecting the value of the option.

Quick quiz

1   What does *CIMA Official Terminology* define as 'a right of an option holder to buy or sell a specific asset on predetermined terms on, or before, a future date'.

2   In the context of currency options, a put option gives the option buyer the right to buy the underlying currency at a fixed rate of exchange.

    True ☐

    False ☐

3   What are the main variables determining the value of a share (call) option?

4   In a currency swap, the parties agree to swap equivalent amounts of currency for a period.

    True ☐

    False ☐

5   What is the name given to 'a form of financing whereby money borrowed in one country or currency is covered by lending an equivalent amount in another' *(OT 2000)*?

Answers to quick quiz

1   An option.

2   False. This is true of a call option, not a put option.

3   (a)   The current value of the share
     (b)   The exercise price of the option
     (c)   The time to expiry of the option
     (d)   Variability of the price of the share
     (e)   The risk-free rate of interest

4   True.

5   A back-to-back loan.

Now try the question below from the Exam Question Bank

Number	Level	Marks	Time
13	Examination	25	45 mins

Part D
Advanced investment appraisal

Chapter 14

INVESTMENT APPRAISAL METHODS

Topic list	Syllabus reference	Ability required
1 Capital investment appraisal	(iv)	Analysis
2 The use of appraisal methods in practice	(iv)	Analysis
3 Allowing for inflation in DCF	(iv)	Analysis
4 Allowing for taxation in DCF	(iv)	Analysis
5 Project control	(iv)	Analysis

Introduction

The managers of all businesses will find themselves faced, from time to time, by capital investment decisions. Indeed, such decisions are fundamental to the long-term profitability of the business. In this chapter, we begin our coverage of investment and decision-making by revising some of the principles of appraising a project.

Learning outcomes covered in this chapter

- Evaluate investment proposals (domestic)
- Identify and describe procedures for the control of investments

Syllabus content covered in this chapter

- Calculate the net present value and internal rate of return
- Investment controls in practice (eg procedural controls, project management)
- The effect of taxation

KEY TERM

Capital investment appraisal: the application of a set of methodologies (generally based on the discounting of projected cash flows) whose purpose is to give guidance to managers with respect to decisions as to how best to commit long-term investment funds. *(OT 2000)*

1   CAPITAL INVESTMENT APPRAISAL

1.1 Most **capital investment decisions** will have a direct effect on future profitability, either because they will result in an **increase in revenue** or because they will bring about an increase in efficiency and a **reduction in costs**. Whatever level of management authorises a capital expenditure, the proposed investment should be properly **evaluated**, and found to be **worthwhile**, before the decision is taken to go ahead with the expenditure.

1.2   **Capital** expenditures differ from day to day **revenue** expenditures in that:

   (a)   They often involve a bigger outlay of money.

   (b)   The benefits will accrue over a long period of time, usually well over one year and often much longer, so that the benefits cannot all be set against costs in the current year's profit and loss account.

1.3   The planning steps in the process of developing a new programme of capital investment are as follows.

   •   Identification of an investment opportunity
   •   Consideration of the alternatives to the project being evaluated
   •   Acquiring relevant information
   •   Detailed planning
   •   Taking the investment decision

1.4   The **identification of an investment opportunity** is the most difficult part of the capital investment process. Indeed, for many businesses, and particularly small ones, it is the only stage; projects are undertaken without any form of sophisticated investment appraisal. There are often two or more ways of getting a job done, or achieving an objective. The different investment alternatives ought to be identified, and compared.

1.5   Acquiring the **relevant data** to form the basis for an informed decision is one of the most important aspects in practice. Large capital investments that turn out to be unprofitable can usually be abandoned only at a substantial loss, and therefore the time and effort spent in market research and acquiring data about relevant costs and benefits is rarely wasted. This activity helps to **focus managers' minds** on the reality of the projections as they are forecasting and so **weed out poor projects** at an early stage, before they are subjected to intensive financial scrutiny.

1.6   The principal methods of evaluating capital projects are as follows.

   (a)   The return on investment method, or accounting rate of return method

   (b)   The payback method

   (c)   Discounted cash flow (DCF):

         (i)   the net present value method (NPV)
         (ii)   the internal rate of return method (IRR)

   Of these, DCF should be by far the most important, although (a) and (b) are used more in practice by small and medium-sized firms.

1.7   The principles and mechanics of these methods were covered in your studies of Paper 9 *Decision making*. Before we go on to look at the more advanced aspects, and their application to international investment appraisal, we briefly revise the main points here, followed by some questions for you to brush up your knowledge.

Knowledge brought forward from Paper 9 (IDEC)

The accounting rate of return (ARR) method of investment appraisal

•   This method uses **financial accounting based figures** in arriving at a rate of return on a project, which is compared with a target rate of return to decide on its acceptability.

•   There are various **definitions** of the ARR, the most common of which is

---

$$\text{ARR} = \frac{\text{Estimated average annual profits, after depreciation, before interest and tax}}{\text{Average book value of capital employed}}$$

- The main disadvantages of the ARR are that it uses **subjective accounting profits** rather than cash flows; it does not take account of the **timing** of flows, and it can be computed under **various definitions**, which makes comparisons difficult.

The payback method of investment appraisal

- The **payback period** is the time required for the cash inflows from a capital investment project to equal the cash outflows.

- The payback should not be used as the sole appraisal method, as it ignores the cash flows after the payback period, but may be used as a **first screening method**, particularly when applied to risky projects.

- The payback period may be estimated by computing the **accumulated cash inflows** year by year until the initial capital investment is covered.

Discounted cash flow (DCF) methods of investment appraisal

- **DCF** is an appraisal technique which uses **cash flows,** takes account of both the **time value** of money and also the **total profitability** over a project's life, and is thus a method superior to both the ARR and payback methods.

- The time value of money (why £1 now is worth more than £1 in the future) arises from considerations of **investment opportunities, risk** and **inflation.**

- **Basic discounting** of cash flows using an appropriate opportunity cost of capital principally takes account of the first of these considerations, although the method can be adapted to take account of both risk and inflation, as we shall see later.

- The cash flows used in DCF methods are those that are **relevant** – the **changes** in **future cash flows** of the business that will arise as a result of undertaking the project.

- There are two methods of applying the DCF technique to project appraisal: net present value **(NPV)** and internal rate of return **(IRR).**

- The **NPV** approach applies a **specific discount rate** to the cash flows of the project to arrive at an **absolute** measure the NPV, which, if positive, implies the project is acceptable. The basic mechanics of this approach were revised in Chapter 6.

- The **IRR** approach is to calculate the **discount rate at which the NPV of the project would be zero**, indicating the maximum cost of capital at which the project would be viable. Provided the investing business's cost of capital is less than this, the project may be accepted.

- The IRR is found approximately by using interpolation, using the results from MPV computations at two different discount rates:

$$\text{IRR} \sim \text{A} + \frac{N_A}{N_A - N_B}(\text{B} - \text{A}) \quad \text{where} \quad \begin{array}{l} \text{A} = \text{lower discount rate used with NPV} = N_A \\ \\ \text{B} = \text{higher discount rate used with NPV} = N_B \end{array}$$

EXAM FORMULA

Present value of £1 payable or receivable in n years, discounted at r% per annum:

$$\text{PV} = \frac{1}{(1+r)^n}$$

Question 1

A company has a target accounting rate of return of 20% (using the definition given above), and is now considering the following project.

Capital cost of asset	£80,000
Estimated life	4 years
Estimated profit before depreciation	
Year 1	£20,000
Year 2	£25,000
Year 3	£35,000
Year 4	£25,000

The capital asset would be depreciated by 25% of its cost each year, and will have no residual value. Should the project be undertaken?

Answer

	£
Total profit before depreciation over four years	105,000
Total profit after depreciation over four years	25,000
Average annual profit after depreciation	6,250
Original cost of investment	80,000
Average net book value over the four year period $\dfrac{(80,000+0)}{2}$	40,000

The average ARR is 6,250 ÷ 40,000 = 15.625%.

The project would not be undertaken because it would fail to yield the target return of 20%.

Question 2

LCH Ltd manufactures product X which it sells for £5 a unit. Variable costs of production are currently £3 a unit, and fixed costs 50p a unit. A new machine is available which would cost £90,000 but which could be used to make product X for a variable cost of only £2.50 a unit. Fixed costs, however, would increase by £7,500 a year as a direct result of purchasing the machine. The machine would have an expected life of four years and a resale value after that time of £10,000. Sales of product X are estimated to be 75,000 units a year. If LCH Ltd expects to earn at least 12% a year from its investments, should the machine be purchased? (Ignore taxation.)

Answer

Savings are 75,000 × £(3.00 – 2.50) = £37,500 a year.
Additional costs are £7,500 a year.
Net cash savings are therefore £30,000 a year.

It is assumed that the machine will be sold for £10,000 at the end of year 4.

Year	Cash flow £	PV factor 12%	PV of cash flow £
0	(90,000)	1.000	(90,000)
1	30,000	0.893	26,790
2	30,000	0.797	23,910
3	30,000	0.712	21,360
4	40,000	0.636	25,440
		NPV	+7,500

The NPV is positive and so the project is expected to earn more than 12% a year and is therefore acceptable.

Note

The timing of cash flows: conventions used in DCF

The following guidelines may be applied unless a question indicates that they should not be.

(a) A cash outlay to be incurred at the beginning of an investment project, that is now, occurs in year 0. The present value of £1 in year 0 is £1.

(b) A cash outlay, saving or inflow which occurs during the course of a time period (say, one year) is assumed to occur all at once at the end of the time period. Therefore receipts of £10,000 during the first year are taken to occur at the end of that year. That point in time is called 'year 1'.

(c) A cash outlay, saving or inflow which occurs at the beginning of a time period (say at the beginning of the second year) is taken to occur at the end of the previous year. Therefore a cash outlay of £5,000 at the beginning of the second year is taken to occur at year 1.

Question 3

A company is trying to decide whether to buy a machine for £80,000 which will save £20,000 a year for five years and which will have a resale value of £10,000 at the end of year 5. What would the IRR of the investment project be?

Answer

The return on investment is $\dfrac{20{,}000 - \text{depreciation of } 14{,}000}{\dfrac{1}{2} \text{ of } (80{,}000 + 10{,}000)} = \dfrac{6{,}000}{45{,}000} = 13.3\%$

Two thirds of this is 8.9% and so we can start by trying 9%.

The IRR is the rate for the cost of capital at which the NPV = 0.

Year	Cash flow £	PV factor 9%	PV of cash flow £
0	(80,000)	1.000	(80,000)
1-5	20,000	3.890	77,800
5	10,000	0.650	6,500
		NPV	4,300

This is fairly close to zero. It is also positive, which means that the IRR is more than 9%. We will try 12% next.

Year	Cash flow £	PV factor 12%	PV of cash flow £
0	(80,000)	1.000	(80,000)
1-5	20,000	3.605	72,100
5	10,000	0.567	5,670
		NPV	(2,230)

This is fairly close to zero and negative. The IRR is therefore greater than 9% but less than 12%. We shall now use the two NPV values to estimate the IRR, using the formula given above.

Internal rate of return $= 9 + \left[\dfrac{4{,}300}{4{,}300 - -2{,}230} \times (12-9) \right] = 10.98\%$, say 11%

Further aspects of the DCF methods

Working capital

1.8 **Increases** in working capital **reduce** the net cash flow of the period to which they relate. So for example, if a project lasts for five years with a £20,000 working capital requirement at the end of year 1, rising to £30,000 at the end of year 2, the DCF calculation will show £20,000 as a year 1 cash outflow and £10,000 (30,000 – £20,000) as a year 2 cash outflow.

1.9 Working capital is assumed to be **recovered** at the end of the project. In our example, this will be shown by a £30,000 cash inflow at year 5.

Question 4

Elsie Ltd is considering the manufacture of a new product which would involve the use of both a new machine (costing £150,000) and an existing machine, which cost £80,000 two years ago and has a current net book value of £60,000. There is sufficient capacity on this machine, which has so far been under-used.

Annual sales of the product would be 5,000 units, selling at £32 a unit. Unit costs would be as follows.

	£
Direct labour (4 hours at £2)	8
Direct materials	7
Fixed costs including depreciation	9
	24

The project would have a five year life, after which the new machine would have a net residual value of £10,000. Because direct labour is continually in short supply, labour resources would have to be diverted from other work which currently earns a contribution of £1.50 per direct labour hour. The fixed overhead absorption rate would be £2.25 an hour (£9 a unit) but actual expenditure on fixed overhead would not alter.

Working capital requirements would be £10,000 in the first year, rising to £15,000 in the second year and remaining at this level until the end of the project, when it will all be recovered. The company's cost of capital is 20%. Ignore taxation.

Is the project worthwhile?

Answer

Working		£
Years 1-5	Contribution from new product	
	5,000 × £(32 – 15)	85,000
	Less contribution forgone	
	5,000 × (4 × £1.50)	30,000
		55,000

Year	Equipment £	Working capital £	Contribution £	Net cash flow £	Discount factor 20%	PV of net cash flow £
0	(150,000)	(10,000)		(160,000)	1.000	(160,000)
1		(5,000)		(5,000)	0.833	(4,165)
1-5			55,000	55,000	2.991	164,505
5	10,000	15,000		25,000	0.402	10,050
					NPV =	10,390

The NPV is positive and the project is worthwhile, although there is not much margin for error. Some risk analysis of the project is recommended.

Note. The discount factor 2.991 applied to the annual contribution is an example of an **annuity factor**, which can be used for a series of equal annual cash flows starting at time 0. Annuity factors may be found from the table or from the formula (viii), both given in the Appendix at the end of this text.

Other formula

1.10   You may also find the following formulae useful.

(a)   For **non-annual cash flows**, the period interest rate r is related to the annual interest rate R by the following formula.

$$r = \sqrt[n]{1 + R} - 1$$

where n is the number of periods per annum.

For example, if the annual interest rate is 18%, the monthly interest rate $r = \sqrt[12]{1.18} - 1$ = 0.0139, ie 1.39%.

(b) **Changes in interest rate** can be reflected as in the following example.

In years 1, 2 and 3, the interest rate is 10%, 12% and 14% respectively.

$$\text{Then, Year 3 discount factor} \quad = \frac{1}{(1 + r_1)(1 + r_2)(1 + r_3)}$$

$$= \frac{1}{1.10 \times 1.12 \times 1.14} = 0.712$$

NPV or IRR?

1.11 Given that there are two methods of using DCF, the NPV method and the IRR method, the relative merits of each method have to be considered. Which is better?

1.12 The main advantage of the IRR method is that the information it provides is more easily understood by managers, especially non-financial managers. For example, it is fairly easy to understand the meaning of the following statement.

> 'The project has an initial capital outlay of £100,000, and will earn a yield of 25%. This is in excess of the target yield of 15% for investments.'

It is not so easy to understand the meaning of this statement.

> 'The project will cost £100,000 and have an NPV of £30,000 when discounted at the minimum required rate of 15%.'

1.13 In other respects, the IRR method has serious disadvantages.

(a) It might be tempting to confuse the IRR and the accounting ROCE. The accounting ROCE and the IRR are two completely different measures. If managers were given information about both ROCE (or ROI) and IRR, it might be easy to get their meanings and significance mixed up.

(b) It ignores the relative size of investments. Both the following projects have an IRR of 18%.

	Project A	Project B
	£	£
Cost, year 0	350,000	35,000
Annual savings, years 1-6	100,000	10,000

Clearly, project A is bigger (ten times as big) and so more profitable but if the only information on which the projects were judged were to be their IRR of 18%, project B would seem just as beneficial as project A.

(c) If the cash flows from a project are not conventional (with an outflow at the beginning resulting in inflows over the life of a project) there may be more than one IRR. This could be very difficult for managers to interpret. For example, the following project has cash flows which are not conventional, and as a result has two IRRs of approximately 7% and 35%.

Year	Project X
	£'000
0	(1,900)
1	4,590
2	(2,735)

This deficiency can be overcome by using the modified internal rate of return. This method assumes that all cash flows after the initial investment can be reinvested at the cost of capital, and converts all the flows to a single cash inflow at the end of the project's life.

(d) The IRR method should not be used to select between mutually exclusive projects. This follows on from point (b) and it is the most significant and damaging criticism of the IRR method.

1.14 EXAMPLE: MUTUALLY EXCLUSIVE OPTIONS

A company is considering two mutually exclusive options, option A and option B. The cash flows for each would be as follows.

Year		Option A	Option B
		£	£
0	Capital outlay	(10,200)	(35,250)
1	Net cash inflow	6,000	18,000
2	Net cash inflow	5,000	15,000
3	Net cash inflow	3,000	15,000

The company's cost of capital is 16%. Which option should be chosen?

1.15 SOLUTION

The NPV of each project is calculated below.

		Option A		Option B	
Year	Discount factor	Cashflow	Present value	Cashflow	Present value
	16%	£	£	£	£
0	1.000	(10,200)	(10,200)	(35,250)	(35,250)
1	0.862	6,000	5,172	18,000	15,516
2	0.743	5,000	3,715	15,000	11,145
3	0.641	3,000	1,923	15,000	9,615
		NPV	+610		+1,026

However, the IRR of option A is 20% and the IRR of option B is only 18% (workings not shown). On a comparison of NPVs, option B would be preferred but, on a comparison of IRRs, option A would be preferred.

1.16 Option B should be chosen. This is because the differences in the cash flows between the two options, when discounted at the cost of capital of 16%, show that the present value of the incremental benefits from option B compared with option A exceed the PV of the incremental costs. This can be re-stated in the following ways.

(a) The NPV of the differential cash flows (option B cash flows minus option A cash flows) is positive, and so it is worth spending the extra capital to get the extra benefits.

(b) The IRR of the differential cash flows exceeds the cost of capital of 16%, and so it is worth spending the extra capital to get the extra benefits.

2 THE USE OF APPRAISAL METHODS IN PRACTICE

2.1 A survey of the use of capital investment evaluation methods in the UK carried out by RH Pike in 1992 produced the following results on the frequency of use of different methods by 100 large UK firms.

Capital investment evaluation methods in 100 large UK firms: frequency of use (1992)

	Total	Always	Mostly	Often	Rarely
Firms using	%	%	%	%	%
Payback	94	62	14	12	6
Accounting rate of return	56	21	5	13	17
Internal rate of return	81	54	7	13	7
Net present value	74	33	14	16	11

(Source: Pike & Neale, *Corporate Finance and Investment*)

2.2 Almost two-thirds of the firms surveyed by Pike used three or more appraisal techniques, indicating that DCF techniques complement rather than replace more traditional approaches.

2.3 The following points are worth noting.

(a) The **payback method** is used in the great majority (94%) of companies surveyed. Although it remains a traditional 'rule-of-thumb method' with limited theoretical justification because it ignores the profile of cash flows and cash flows beyond the payback period, it will provide in practice a fair approximation to the net present value method. Its widespread use is perhaps then not so reprehensible given the uncertainty of future cash flows and the tendency of cash flows following the payback period to be similar in form to earlier cash flows in most cases.

(b) In spite of its theoretical limitations (notably, its failure to take account of the time value of money), the **ARR method** was used in half of the companies surveyed. This is perhaps to be expected, given the importance in practice of the rate of return on capital as a financial goal.

(c) The data shows a preference for the **IRR method** over the **NPV method**. It would appear that, in spite of theoretical reasons for favour NPV, the IRR method is preferred by managers as a convenient way of ranking projects in percentage terms.

AMT and investment appraisal

2.4 There has been much criticism in recent management accounting literature of the short-term orientation of many organisations' investment appraisal systems and their effect of slowing down the adoption of **advanced manufacturing technology (AMT)** by British firms.

2.5 Some writers have criticised the short-term quantitative and financial orientation of many investment appraisal techniques. These techniques fail to consider the unquantifiable long-term benefits which are an implicit part of AMT projects.

2.6 **Strategic investment appraisal** has been defined as 'linking corporate strategy to costs and benefits associated with AMT adoption by combining both formal and informal evaluation procedures.' Formal appraisal methods may be of limited practical use when considering the acquisition of AMT, because of the strategic (often non-quantifiable) issues involved.

> **KEY TERM**
>
> **Strategic investment appraisal** is a method of investment appraisal which allows the inclusion of both financial and non-financial factors. Project benefits are appraised in terms of their contribution to the strategies of the organisation, either by their financial contribution or, for non-financial benefits, by the use of index numbers or other means.
>
> *(OT 2000)*

2.7 Management accountants are beginning to accept the need for a more external orientation and a consideration of the longer-term effects in investment appraisal generally, particularly in those organisations which operate in rapidly changing markets with a high level of uncertainty. You should by now be aware of the importance of combining formal and informal procedures, as well as short-term and long-term considerations, in effective capital investment appraisal.

3   ALLOWING FOR INFLATION IN DCF   5/01

3.1   In our revision of the DCF approach to investment appraisal so far we have not considered the effect of inflation. Inflation may affect both the cash flows of the project and the rate at which they are discounted – the higher the expected rate of inflation, the higher will be the required return to compensate.

3.2   The incorporation of inflation into DCF computations was covered in your studies of Paper 9; we now briefly revise this.

Knowledge brought forward from Paper 9 (IDEC)

DCF and inflation

- In an inflationary environment, cash flows in a project may be given in **money terms** (the actual cash that will arise) or **real terms** (in today's pounds).

- Similarly, the required rate of return on an investment may be given as a *money* rate of return (including an allowance for a general rate of inflation) or as a **real** rate of return (the return required over and above inflation).

- The two rates of return and the inflation rate are linked by the equation:

  1 + money (nominal) rate of return = (1 + real rate)(1 + inflation rate)

  If cash flows are given in money terms, the money rate should be used to discount them; if the flows are in real terms, the real rate of return may be used to discount them, although this may not always result in the same answer (see next point).

- If some of the cost or revenues relating to the project **inflate at rates different from the general rate of inflation** that is built into the money required return, it is **not** appropriate to discount real flows at the real rate. Instead, **money flows must be computed**, by applying the relevant rates of inflation to the real flows, which must then be discounted at the money required return.

Question 5

Rice Ltd is considering a project which would cost £5,000 now. The annual benefits, for four years, would be a fixed income of £2,500 a year, plus other savings of £500 a year in year 1, rising by 5% each year because of inflation. Running costs will be £1,000 in the first year, but would increase at 10% each year because of inflating labour costs. The general rate of inflation is expected to be 7½% and the company's required money rate of return is 16%. Is the project worthwhile? (Ignore taxation.)

Answer

The cash flows at inflated values are as follows.

Year	Fixed income £	Other savings £	Running costs £	Net cash flow £
1	2,500	500	1,000	2,000
2	2,500	525	1,100	1,925
3	2,500	551	1,210	1,841
4	2,500	579	1,331	1,748

The NPV of the project is as follows.

Year	Cash flow £	Discount factor 16%	PV £
0	(5,000)	1.000	(5,000)
1	2,000	0.862	1,724
2	1,925	0.743	1,430
3	1,841	0.641	1,180
4	1,748	0.552	965
			+ 299

The NPV is positive and the project would appear to be worthwhile.

Expectations of inflation and the effects of inflation

3.3 When managers evaluate a particular project, or when shareholders evaluate their investments, they can only guess at what the rate of inflation is going to be. Their expectations will probably be wrong, at least to some extent, because it is extremely difficult to forecast the rate of inflation accurately. The only way in which uncertainty about inflation can be allowed for in project evaluation is by risk and uncertainty analysis.

3.4 We stated earlier that costs and benefits may rise at levels different from the general rate of inflation: inflation may be **general,** affecting prices of all kinds, or **specific** to particular prices. Generalised inflation has the following effects.

(a) Since fixed assets, stocks and other working capital will increase in money value, the same quantities of assets or working capital must be financed by increasing amounts of capital.

(i) If the future rate of inflation can be predicted, management can work out how much extra finance the company will need, and take steps to obtain it (for example by increasing retentions of earnings, or borrowing).

(ii) If the future rate of inflation cannot be predicted with accuracy, management should guess at what it will be and plan to obtain extra finance accordingly. However, plans should also be made to obtain 'contingency funds' if the rate of inflation exceeds expectations. For example, a higher bank overdraft facility might be negotiated, or a provisional arrangement made with a bank for a loan.

(b) Inflation means higher costs and higher selling prices. The effect of higher prices on demand is not necessarily easy to predict. A company that raises its prices by 10% because the general rate of inflation is running at 10% might suffer a serious fall in demand.

(c) Inflation, because it affects financing needs, is also likely to affect gearing, and so the cost of capital.

4 ALLOWING FOR TAXATION IN DCF

4.1 So far, in looking at project appraisal, we have also ignored **taxation**. However, payments of tax, or reductions of tax payments, are cash flows and ought to be considered in DCF analysis. Again the basics were covered in Paper 9, and you may only need to skim through the next few sections of text to remind yourself.

Exam focus point

The tax rules might be simplified for an examination question and, as mentioned earlier, you should read any question carefully to establish what tax rules and rates to use.

4.2   **Typical assumptions** which may be stated in questions are as follows.

   (a)   An assumption about the timing of payments will have to be made.

      (i)   Half the corporation tax is **payable** in the **same year** in which the **profits are earned** and **half in the following year.** This reflects the fact that large companiees have to pay tax **quarterly**.

      (ii)   Corporation tax is payable in the **year following** the one in which the taxable profits are made. Thus, if a project increases taxable profits by £10,000 in year 2, there will be a tax payment, assuming tax at (say) 30%, of £3,000 in year 3.

      (iii)   Corporation tax is payable in the **same year** that the **profits arise.**

      The question should make clear what assumptions you should use.

   (b)   Net cash flows from a project should be considered as the taxable profits arising from the project (unless an indication is given to the contrary).

Capital allowances

4.3   Capital allowances are used to reduce taxable profits, and the consequent reduction in a tax payment should be treated as a cash saving arising from the acceptance of a project.

4.4   Writing down allowances are allowed on the cost of **plant and machinery** at the rate of 25% on a **reducing balance** basis. Thus if a company purchases plant costing £80,000, the subsequent writing down allowances would be as follows.

Year		Capital allowance £	Reducing balance £
1	(25% of cost)	20,000	60,000
2	(25% of RB)	15,000	45,000
3	(25% of RB)	11,250	33,750
4	(25% of RB)	8,438	25,312

When the plant is eventually sold, the difference between the sale price and the reducing balance amount at the time of sale will be treated as:

   (a)   A taxable profit if the sale price exceeds the reducing balance, and
   (b)   A tax-allowable loss if the reducing balance exceeds the sale price

Exam focus point

Examination questions often assume that this loss will be available immediately, though in practice the balance less the sale price continues to be written off at 25% a year as part of a pool balance unless the asset has been de-pooled.

The cash saving on the capital allowances (or the cash payment for the charge) is calculated by multiplying the allowance (or charge) by the corporation tax rate.

4.5   Assumptions about capital allowances could be simplified in an exam question. For example, you might be told that capital allowances can be claimed at the rate of 25% of cost on a straight line basis (that is, over four years), or a question might refer to 'tax allowable depreciation', so that the capital allowances equal the depreciation charge.

4.6 There are two possible assumptions about the time when capital allowances start to be claimed.

(a) It can be assumed that the first claim for capital allowances occurs at the start of the project (at year 0).

(b) Alternatively it can be assumed that the first claim for capital allowances occurs later in the first year.

4.7 You should state clearly which assumption you have made. Assumption (b) is more prudent, but assumption (a) is also perfectly feasible. It is very likely, however that an examination question will indicate which of the two assumptions is required.

4.8 EXAMPLE: TAXATION

A company is considering whether or not to purchase an item of machinery costing £40,000 in 20X5. It would have a life of four years, after which it would be sold for £5,000. The machinery would create annual cost savings of £14,000.

The machinery would attract writing down allowances of 25% on the reducing balance basis which could be claimed against taxable profits of the current year, which is soon to end. A balancing allowance or charge would arise on disposal. The rate of corporation tax is 30%. Tax is payable half in the current year, half one year in arrears. The after-tax cost of capital is 8%.

Should the machinery be purchased?

4.9 SOLUTION

The first capital allowance is claimed against year 0 profits.

Cost: £40,000

Year	Allowance		Reducing balance (RB)	
	£		£	
(0) 20X5 (25% of cost)	10,000		30,000	(40,000 – 10,000)
(1) 20X6 (25% of RB)	7,500		22,500	(30,000 – 7,500)
(2) 20X7 (25% of RB)	5,625		16,875	(22,500 – 5,625)
(3) 20X8 (25% of RB)	4,219		12,656	(16,875 – 4,219)
(4) 20X9 (25% of RB)	3,164		9,492	(12,656 – 3,164)

	£
Sale proceeds, end of fourth year	5,000
Less reducing balance, end of fourth year	9,492
Balancing allowance	4,492

4.10 Having calculated the allowances each year, the tax savings can be computed. The year of the cash flow is one year after the year for which the allowance is claimed.

Year of claim	Allowance	Tax saved	Year of tax payment/saving
	£	£	(50% in each)
0	10,000	3,000	0/1
1	7,500	2,250	1/2
2	5,625	1,688	2/3
3	4,219	1,266	3/4
4	7,656	2,297	4/5
	35,000 ★		

295 **BPP**
PUBLISHING

* Net cost £(40,000 – 5,000) = £35,000

These tax savings relate to capital allowances. We must also calculate the extra tax payments on annual savings of £14,000.

4.11 The net cash flows and the NPV are now calculated as follows.

Year	Equipment £	Savings £	Tax on savings £	Tax saved on capital allowances £	Net cash flow £	Discount factor 8%	Present value of cash flow £
0	(40,000)			1,500	(38,500)	1.000	(38,500)
1		14,000	(2,100)	2,625	14,525	0.926	13,450
2		14,000	(4,200)	1,969	11,769	0.857	10,086
3		14,000	(4,200)	1,477	11,277	0.794	8,954
4	5,000	14,000	(4,200)	1,782	16,582	0.735	12,188
5			(2,100)	1,148	(952)	0.681	(648)
							5,530

The NPV is positive and so the purchase appears to be worthwhile.

An alternative and quicker method of calculating tax payments or savings

4.12 In the above example, the tax computations could have been combined, as follows.

Year	0 £	1 £	2 £	3 £	4 £
Cost savings	0	14,000	14,000	14,000	14,000
Capital allowance	10,000	7,500	5,625	4,219	7,656
Taxable profits	(10,000)	6,500	8,375	9,781	6,344
Tax at 30%	3,000	(1,950)	(2,512)	(2,934)	(1,903)

4.13 The net cash flows would then be as follows.

Year	Equipment £	Savings £	Tax £	Net cash flow £
0	(40,000)		1,500	(38,500)
1		14,000	525	14,525
2		14,000	(2,231)	11,769
3		14,000	(2,723)	11,277
4	5,000	14,000	(2,418)	16,582
5			(952)	(952)

The net cash flows are exactly the same as calculated previously in Paragraph 4.11.

Taxation and DCF

4.14 The effect of taxation on capital budgeting is theoretically quite simple. Organisations must pay tax, and the effect of undertaking a project will be to increase or decrease tax payments each year. These incremental tax cash flows should be included in the cash flows of the project for discounting to arrive at the project's NPV.

4.15 When taxation is ignored in the DCF calculations, the discount rate will reflect the pre-tax rate of return required on capital investments. When taxation is included in the cash flows, a post-tax required rate of return should be used.

4.16 If there is inflation and tax in a question, remember that tax flows do not get inflated by an extra year even though they may be paid one year later.

Question 6

A project requires an initial investment in machinery of £300,000. Additional cash inflows of £120,000 at current price levels are expected for three years, at the end of which time the machinery will be scrapped. The machinery will attract writing down allowances of 25% on the reducing balance basis, which can be claimed against taxable profits of the current year, which is soon to end. A balancing charge or allowance will arise on disposal.

The rate of corporate tax is 50% and tax is payable 50% in the current year, 50% one year in arrears. The pre-tax cost of capital is 22% and the rate of inflation is 10%. Tax payments occur in the year following the transactions. Assume that the project is 100% debt financed.

Required

Assess whether the project should be undertaken.

Answer

Post-tax: Year	Purchase £	Inflation factor	Cash flow after inflation £	Tax on cash inflow £	(W1-3) Tax saved on capital allowances £	Net cash flow £	Discount factor 11%	Present value £
0	(300,000)	1.000	(300,000)		18,750	(281,250)	1.000	(281,250)
1		1.100	132,000	(33,000)	32,813	131,813	0.901	118,764
2		1.210	145,200	(69,300)	24,609	100,509	0.812	81,613
3		1.331	159,720	(76,230)	42,187	125,677	0.731	91,870
4				(39,930)	31,640	(8,290)	0.659	(5,463)
							NPV =	5,534

The project should be undertaken at least from the financial viewpoint.

Workings

1 **Writing down allowance** (Initial cost £300,000)

Year		WDA £	Reducing balance (RB) £
0	(25% at cost)	75,000	225,000
1	(25% of RB)	56,250	168,750
2	(25% of RB)	42,188	126,562
3	(25% of RB)	31,641	94,921

2 **Balancing allowance**

	£
Sale proceeds, end of third year	-
RB, end of third year	94,921
Balancing allowance	94,921

3 **Tax saved on capital allowances**

Year of claim	Allowance claimed £	Tax saved £	Year of tax saving
0	75,000	37,500	0/1
1	56,250	28,125	1/2
2	42,188	21,094	2/3
3	126,562	63,281	3/4
	300,000		

5   PROJECT CONTROL

> ### KEY TERM
>
> **Project management** is the integration of all aspects of a project, ensuring that the proper knowledge and resources are available when and where needed, and above all to ensure that the expected outcome is produced in a timely, cost-effective manner. The primary function of a project manager is to manage the trade-offs between performance, timeliness and cost.
>
> *(OT 2000)*

5.1   Once a capital project has been evaluated and given the go-ahead, as part of the process of **project management**, project controls should be applied to ensure through a process of **continuous evaluation** that:

(a)   Capital spending does not exceed the amount authorised
(b)   Implementation of the project is not delayed
(c)   Anticipated benefits are eventually obtained

5.2   Items (a) and (b) are probably easier to control than (c), because the controls can normally be applied soon after the capital expenditure has been authorised, whereas monitoring the benefits will span a longer period.

Controls over excess spending

5.3   Controls over capital expenditure can be applied as follows.

(a)   The **authority** to make capital expenditure decisions must be formally assigned. There should be a proposer for the project who applies for approval of the spending.

   (i)   All spending over (for example) £250,000 must be authorised by the holding company's board. The spending would be proposed by a member of the board, or by another manager who is asked to make a submission to the board asking for approval of the spending.

   (ii)   Spending over (for example) £100,000 and up to (for example) £250,000 can be authorised by the subsidiary company's board. In the same way, the capital project would be proposed by a member of the board, or by another manager who is asked to make a submission to the board asking for approval of the project.

   (iii) Spending over (for example) £10,000 and up to (for example) £100,000 can be authorised by heads of departments. Once again, a junior manager should submit a proposal for approval of the project, which the head of department would be asked to authorise.

(b)   Capital expenditure decisions should be **documented**. The approval of the project should specify:

   (i)   Which manager has been authorised to carry out the expenditure. (The manager will be responsible for the successful implementation of the project.)

   (ii)   How much expenditure has been authorised

   (iii) Within what period of time the expenditure should take place

(c)   Some overspending above the amount authorised, say 5% or 10%, might be allowed. If the required expenditure exceeds the amount authorised by more than this amount, a fresh submission for **re-authorisation** of the project should be required.

(d) There should be a **total capital budget**, and the authorisation of any capital expenditure which would take total spending above the budget should be referred to board level for approval.

Control over the anticipated benefits

5.4 When a capital project has clearly defined costs, and clearly identifiable benefits, further control can be exercised over capital projects by monitoring the progress of the projects to ensure that the following occur.

(a) The anticipated benefits do actually materialise.
(b) The benefits are as big as anticipated.
(c) Running costs do not exceed expectation.

5.5 A difficulty with control of capital projects is that most projects are **unique** with no standard or yardstick to judge them against, and so if actual costs were to exceed the estimated costs, it might be impossible to tell just how much of the variance is due to **bad estimating** and how much is due to **inefficiencies** and **poor cost control.** In the same way, if benefits are below expectation, this might be because the original estimates were optimistic, or because management has been inefficient and failed to get the benefits they should have done.

5.6 Many capital projects do not have such clearly identifiable costs and benefits, for example decisions to purchase replacement assets or to acquire a new office building. The incremental benefits and costs of such schemes can be estimated for the purpose of the project evaluation, but it would need a very sophisticated management accounting system to be able to measure the actual benefits and many of the costs. Even so, some degree of monitoring and control can still be exercised by means of a post audit.

Post audits

5.7 A **post audit** or a **post-completion audit** is a review of the cash inflows to and outflows from a project after it has reached the end of its life, or at least some years after it began. As far as possible, the actual cash flows should be measured and compared with the estimates contained in the original capital expenditure appraisal. The manager responsible for the project should be asked to explain any significant variances.

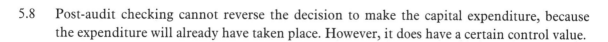

KEY TERM

Post-completion audit is an objective and independent appraisal of the measure of success of a capital expenditure project in progressing the business as planned.

(OT 2000)

5.8 Post-audit checking cannot reverse the decision to make the capital expenditure, because the expenditure will already have taken place. However, it does have a certain control value.

(a) If a manager asks for and gets approval for a capital project, and knows that in due course the project will be subject to a post audit, then the manager will be more likely to pay attention to the **benefits** and the **costs** than if no post audit were threatened.

(b) If the post audit takes place before the project life ends, and if it finds that the benefits have been less than expected because of management inefficiency, steps can be taken to **improve efficiency** and earn greater benefits over the remaining life of the project.

Alternatively, the post audit may highlight those projects which should be discontinued.

(c) A post audit can help to identify managers who have been **good performers** and those who have been poor performers.

(d) A post audit might **identify weaknesses** in the forecasting and estimating techniques used to evaluate projects, and so should help to improve the quality of forecasting for future investment decisions.

(e) A post audit might reveal areas where **improvements** can be made in methods so as to achieve better results from capital investments in general.

(f) The **original estimates** may be **more realistic** if managers are aware that they will be monitored, but post audits should not be unfairly critical.

5.9 It may be too expensive to post audit all capital expenditure projects, therefore managers may need to select a sample for a post audit. The selection will depend on the probability that the audit of any particular project will produce benefits, which is obviously difficult to determine. A reasonable guideline might be to audit all projects above a certain size, and a random sample of smaller projects.

5.10 **Problems with post audits**

(a) There are **many uncontrollable factors** in long-term investments such as environmental changes. Since such factors are outside management control there may be little to gain by identifying the resulting variances.

(b) This means that it **may not be possible** to **identify separately the costs and benefits** of any particular project or, due to uncertainty, to identify the costs and benefits at all.

(c) Post audit can be a **costly and time-consuming exercise**. Labour, which maybe a scarce resource, is required to undertake the task.

(d) Applied punitively, post audit exercises may lead to **managers becoming over cautious** and unnecessarily risk averse.

(e) The **strategic effects** of a **capital investment project** may take years to materialise and it may never be possible to identify or quantify them effectively.

5.11 It has been found that 67% of companies carry out post audits in the UK (Pike and Wolfe, 1988) and 79% of quoted firms carry out post audit to some extent (Neal, 1990). Despite the growth in popularity of post audits, you should bear in mind the possible alternative control processes.

(a) Teams could be set up to manage a project from beginning to end, control being used before the project is started and during its life, rather than at the end of its life.

(b) More time could be spend choosing projects rather than checking completed projects.

Chapter roundup

- This chapter has provided some revision of the techniques for **evaluating capital expenditure decisions**.

- Of greatest significance is the **DCF** approach, including the effects of **taxation** and **inflation**.

- Your examination will call for some **advanced applications** of the techniques and with this in mind the next chapter will build on this introduction.

Quick quiz

1   Identify the steps involved in a new programme of capital investment.

2   What is defined as 'the time required for the cash inflows from a capital investment project to equal the cash outflows' *(OT 2000)*?

3   What is defined as 'a periodic payment continuing for a limitless period' *(OT 2000)*?

4   Match up each term with the appropriate definition.

Terms

| (A)   Net terminal value |

| (B)   Net present value |

| (C)   Present value |

Definitions

| (1)   The value obtained by discounting all cash outflows and inflows of a capital investment project at a chosen target rate of return or cost of capital. |

| (2)   The cash equivalent now of a sum of money receivable or payable at a stated future date, discounted at a specified rate of return. |

| (3)   The cash surplus remaining at the end of a project after taking account of interest and capital repayments. |

Answers to quick quiz

1   (a)   Identification of an investment opportunity
    (b)   Consideration of the alternatives to the project being evaluated
    (c)   Acquiring relevant information
    (d)   Detailed planning
    (e)   Taking the investment decision

2   The payback period.

3   A perpetuity.

4   (A)   (3)
    (B)   (1)
    (C)   (2)

Now try the question below from the Exam Question Bank

Number	Level	Marks	Time
14	Introductory	n/a	35 mins

Chapter 15

APPLICATIONS OF DISCOUNTED CASH FLOW

Topic list	Syllabus reference	Ability required
1 Capital rationing	(iv)	Evaluation
2 The annualised cost of a capital item	(iv)	Evaluation
3 Capital investment real options	(iv)	Evaluation

Introduction

In this chapter, we examine some **applications of discounted cash flow (DCF)** techniques revised in the previous chapter. An enterprise may be faced with more investment opportunities than it can finance, and we look first at how capital rationing may affect the investment decision.

Later in this chapter we look at ways of assessing the **social costs** and **social benefits** of investment decisions.

Learning outcomes covered in this chapter

- Evaluate investment proposals (domestic and international)
- Calculate and interpret real options (abandonment, follow-on, deferment)
- Recommend investment decisions when capital is rationed

Syllabus content covered in this chapter

- Single period capital rationing for divisible and non-divisible projects (multi-period capital rationing will not be tested)

- Capital investment real options (ie the option to make follow-on investment, the option to abandon and the option to wait)

1   CAPITAL RATIONING

5/01

1.1   We saw in the last chapter that the decision rule with DCF techniques is to accept all projects which result in positive NPVs when discounted at the company's cost of capital. If a business suffers **capital rationing,** it will not be able to enter into all projects with positive NPVs because there is not enough capital for all the investments.

> **KEY TERM**
>
> **Capital rationing** is a restriction on an organisation's ability to invest capital funds, caused by an internal budget ceiling being imposed on such expenditure by management (**soft capital rationing**), or by external limitations being applied to the company, as when additional borrowed funds cannot be obtained (**hard capital rationing**). *(OT 2000)*

1.2   Managers are therefore faced with the problem of deciding which projects to invest in. The decision technique to be applied will depend on the type of capital rationing. **Single period capital rationing** is where capital is limited for the current period only but will be freely available in the future. **Multi-period capital rationing** is where capital will be limited for several periods.

> ### Exam focus point
>
> Multi period capital rationing is excluded from your syllabus.

1.3   Before we look at some examples of single period capital rationing we need to distinguish between divisible projects and non-divisible projects. **Divisible projects** are those which can be undertaken completely or in fractions. Suppose that project A is divisible and requires the investment of £15,000 to achieve an NPV of £4,000. £7,500 invested in project A will earn an NPV of ½ × £4,000 = £2,000. **Indivisible projects** are those which must be undertaken completely or not at all. It is not possible to invest in a fraction of the project.

Single period rationing with divisible projects

1.4   With **single period capital rationing**, investment funds are a limiting factor in the current period. The total return will be maximised if management follows the decision rule of maximising the return per unit of the limiting factor. They should therefore **select those projects whose cash inflows have the highest present value per £1 of capital invested.** In other words , rank the projects according to their **profitability index.**

> ### KEY TERM
>
> **Profitability index** $= \dfrac{\text{Present value of cash inflow}}{\text{Initial investment}}$ *(OT 2000)*

1.5   Note that the same rankings will result from the use of the ratio of **net present value** of the project (ie after deducting the initial investment) to the initial investment, which may be referred to as the **benefit-cost ratio.**

1.6   Note that the use of the PI assumes a 'standard' project, with one initial outlay, followed by a series of inflows.

1.7   EXAMPLE: SINGLE PERIOD RATIONING WITH DIVISIBLE PROJECTS

Short O'Funds Ltd has capital of £130,000 available for investment in the forthcoming period, at a cost of capital of 20%. Capital will be freely available in the future. Details of six projects under consideration are as follows. All projects are independent and divisible. Which projects should be undertaken and what NPV will result?

Project	Investment required	Present value of inflows at 20%
	£'000	£'000
P	40	56.5
Q	50	67.0
R	30	48.8
S	45	59.0
T	15	22.4
U	20	30.8

1.8 SOLUTION

The first step is to rank the projects according to the return achieved from the limiting factor of investment funds.

Project	PV inflows £'000	Investment £'000	PV per £1 invested £	Ranking
P	56.5	40	1.41	4
Q	67.0	50	1.34	5
R	48.8	30	1.63	1
S	59.0	45	1.31	6
T	22.4	15	1.49	3
U	30.8	20	1.54	2

The available funds of £130,000 can now be allocated.

Project	Investment £'000		PV £'000
R	30		48.8
U	20		30.8
T	15		22.4
P	40		56.5
Q (balance)	25	(½)	33.5
	130	Maximum PV =	192.0

Project S should not be undertaken and only half of project Q should be undertaken.

The resulting total NPV generated will be 192.0 – 130 = £62,000.

1.9 Note that the PI can be used as a project appraisal method in its own right. The decision rule to apply will be to accept all projects with a PI greater than one (in which case, PV inflows > initial investment, ie NPV > 0).

1.10 **Advantages of the PI method**

(a) Similar to the NPV method, usually giving the same result on individual projects

(b) Can be used to rank divisible projects in conditions of **capital rationing**

Disadvantages of the PI method

(a) PI indicates relative returns and is not an absolute measure

(b) The PI method may rank projects incorrectly (If cash is not rationed, it is preferable to look at the NPV, which is an absolute measure.)

(c) Establishing what is the initial investment may not be straightforward (The PI method works well only if the project has an outflow of cash at time 0, followed by cash inflows which may be at various times.)

Single period rationing with indivisible projects

1.11 If the projects are **not divisible** then the method shown in the last paragraph may not result in the optimal solution. Another complication which arises is that there is likely to be a small amount of **unused capital** with each combination of projects. The best way to deal with this situation is to use **trial and error** and test the NPV available from different combinations of projects. This can be a laborious process if there are a large number of projects available. We will continue with the previous example to demonstrate the technique.

1.12 EXAMPLE: SINGLE PERIOD RATIONING WITH INDIVISIBLE PROJECTS

Short O'Funds Ltd now discovers that funds in the forthcoming period are actually restricted to £95,000. The directors decide to consider projects P, Q and R only. They wish to invest only in whole projects, but surplus funds can be invested to earn 25% per annum in perpetuity. Which combination of projects will produce the highest NPV at a cost of capital of 20%?

1.13 SOLUTION

The investment combinations we need to consider are the various possible pairs of projects P, Q and R **plus** the investment of the surplus at 25%. Dealing with the latter first:

The cumulative PV of £1 received per annum in perpetuity is £1/r. Therefore at a cost of capital of 20% the PV of the interest on £1 invested in perpetuity at 25% is $\dfrac{£1 \times 0.25}{0.20} = £1.25$

The net present value per pound invested is £1.25 less the original investment of £1. Therefore the NPV per pound invested is £0.25. The NPVs from all possible combinations of investments can now be tested.

Projects	Required investment £'000	Funds remaining for external investment £'000		NPV of external investment £'000		NPV from projects £'000	Total NPV £'000
P and Q	90	5	(× 0.25)	1.25	(16.5 + 17.0)	33.5	34.75
P and R	70	25		6.25	(16.5 + 18.8)	35.3	41.55
Q and R	80	15		3.75	(17.0 + 18.8)	35.8	39.55

The highest NPV will be achieved by undertaking projects P and R and investing the unused funds of £25,000 externally.

Question

Bijoux Ltd is choosing which investment to undertake during the coming year. The following table has been prepared, summarising the main features of available projects.

	Cash outlays		Cash receipts	
	Time 0	Time 1	Time 1	Time 2
Project	£'000	£'000	£'000	£'000
Diamond	24	60	24	96
Sapphire	48	42	48	66
Platinum	60	42	12	138
Emerald	48	18	12	90
Quartz	36	48	24	96

There will be no cash flows on any of the projects after time 2. All projects are regarded as being of equal risk. Bijoux uses only equity sources of finance at an estimated cost of 20% per annum.

The cash flows given above represent estimated results for maximum possible investment in each project; lower levels of investment may be undertaken, in which case all cash flows will be reduced in proportion.

Required

Prepare calculations to identify the optimal set of investment assuming that capital available is limited to £120,000 at time 0, and £240,000 at time 1; assume that the Platinum project and the Emerald project are mutually exclusive (*Hint:* firstly check in which years capital rationing occurs).

Answer

Optimal investments for Bijoux

First we need to determine in which year(s) capital is rationed, taking account of the fact that only one of the Platinum and Emerald projects will be undertaken.

Project	Cash flows with Platinum		Cash flows with Emerald	
	Time 0	Time 1	Time 0	Time 1
	£'000	£'000	£'000	£'000
Diamond	(24)	(36)	(24)	(36)
Sapphire	(48)	6	(48)	6
Platinum	(60)	(30)		
Emerald			(48)	(6)
Quartz	(36)	(24)	(36)	(24)
Total	(168)	(84)	(156)	(60)
Capital available	120	240	120	240

To rank the projects the basic PI as previously defined cannot be used as this would ignore outlays at time 1. One option would be to use a PI defined as $\dfrac{\text{PV of inflows}}{\text{PV of outlays}}$ but this is not entirely appropriate as capital is not rationed at Time 1.

An alternative, used here, is to use a PI defined as $\dfrac{\text{NPV project}}{\text{Initial capital invested}}$

It is therefore concluded that effective capital rationing exists only at Time 0 ie a single period of capital rationing situation.

Project	Cash flows			PV of cash flows @ 20%					Rank
	0)	1	2	0	1	2	NPV		
	£'000	£'000	£'000	£'000	£'000	£'000	£'000	£'000	
Diamond	(24)	(36)	96	(24)	(30.0)	66.6	12.6	0.525	1
Sapphire	(48)	6	66	(48)	5.0	45.8	2.8	0.058	5
Platinum	(60)	(30)	138	(60)	(25.0)	95.8	10.8	0.180	4
Emerald	(48)	(6)	90	(48)	(5.0)	62.5	9.5	0.198	3
Quartz	(36)	(24)	96	(36)	(20.0)	66.6	10.6	0.294	2

In time 0 with only £100,000 available projects would be introduced in order of profitability as shown.

Platinum without Emerald

Project	Proportion accepted	Funds used at Time 0	Total NPV
	%	£'000	£'000
Diamond	100	24	12.6
Quartz	100	36	10.6
Platinum	100	60	10.8
Sapphire	Nil	Nil	Nil
Funds utilised and available		120	34.0

Emerald without Platinum

Project	Proportion accepted	Funds used at Time 0	Total NPV
	%	£'000	£'000
Diamond	100	24	12.6
Quartz	100	36	10.6
Emerald	100	48	9.5
Sapphire	25	12	0.7
Funds utilised and available		120	33.4

Platinum without Emerald is to be preferred as it yields a higher NPV.

Note. Platinum is selected in preference to Emerald even though it has a lower profitability index.

This is because the choice is effectively between investing £60,000 in Platinum with an NPV of £10,800 (PI = 0.18) or a package containing a £48,000 investment in Emerald and a £12,000 investment in Sapphire with a combined NPV of £10,200. This package has a profitability index of only 0.17 and is therefore rejected.

Soft and hard capital rationing

1.14 Capital rationing may be necessary in a business due to internal factors (soft capital rationing) or external factors (hard capital rationing).

1.15 **Soft capital rationing** may arise for one of the following reasons.

(a) Management may be reluctant to issue additional share capital because of concern that this may lead to outsiders gaining control of the business.

(b) Management may be unwilling to issue additional share capital if it will lead to a dilution of earnings per share.

(c) Management may not want to raise additional debt capital because they do not wish to be committed to large fixed interest payments.

(d) There may be a desire within the organisation to limit investment to a level that can be financed solely from retained earnings.

(e) Capital expenditure budgets may restrict spending.

1.16 Note that whenever an organisation adopts a policy that restricts funds available for investment, such a policy may be less than optimal as the organisation may reject projects with a positive net present value and forgo opportunities that would have enhanced the market value of the organisation.

1.17 **Hard capital rationing** may arise for one of the following reasons.

(a) Raising money through the stock market may not be possible if share prices are depressed.

(b) There may be restrictions on bank lending due to government control.

(c) Lending institutions may consider an organisation to be to risky to be granted further loan facilities.

(d) The costs associated with making small issues of capital may be too great.

2 THE ANNUALISED COST OF A CAPITAL ITEM

2.1 When an investment is being evaluated in terms of annual running costs, it may be appropriate to convert the capital cost into an annualised cost at the company's cost of capital. For example, when the capital expenditure is only a relatively small feature of a project and annual running costs are a much more significant item, annual profitability is the key factor in the decision.

EXAM FORMULA

$$\text{Equivalent annual cost} = \frac{\text{PV of costs over n years}}{\text{n year annuity factor}}$$

(a) 'PV of costs' is the purchase cost, minus the present value of any subsequent disposal proceeds at the end of the item's life.

(b) The n-year annuity factor is at the company's cost of capital, for the number of years of the item's life.

2.2 EXAMPLE: ANNUALISED COST

A project is being considered which would involve a capital expenditure of £500,000 on equipment. The annual running costs and benefits would be as follows.

	£	£
Revenues		450,000
Costs		
Depreciation	100,000	
Other	300,000	
		400,000
Profit		50,000

The equipment would have a five year life, and no residual value, and would be financed by a loan at 12% interest per annum. Using annualised figures, assess whether the project is a worthwhile undertaking. Ignore risk and taxation.

2.3 SOLUTION

The annualised capital cost of the equipment is as follows.

$$\frac{£500,000}{\text{PV of £1 pa yrs 1}-5 \text{ at } 12\%} = \frac{£500,000}{3.605} = £138,696$$

Annual profit = £450,000 − £138,696 − £300,000 = £11,304

Depreciation is ignored because it is a notional cost and has already been taken into account in the annualised cost.

The project is a worthwhile undertaking, but only by about £11,000 a year for five years.

3 CAPITAL INVESTMENT REAL OPTIONS

Exam focus point

Be prepared for this topic to be examined fairly early in the life of the new syllabus.

3.1 The application of option theory in the appraisal of capital investments is a relatively new development. To give one type of example, a business decision may amount to paying a specified price now - say, to develop a new production system - which gives the business wider flexibility in the future. Such a decision gives the business more **options** to exploit wider follow-on opportunities.

3.2 **Common types of 'real option' found in capital projects**

- The **option to make follow-on investments**: this is equivalent to a call option
- The **option to abandon** a project: equivalent to a put option
- The **option to wait** before making an investment: equivalent to a call option

Each of these types of scenario is discussed further below.

The value of follow-on investments

3.3　　The discounted cash flow technique was originally developed for holdings of stocks and shares before being developed as a technique for investment appraisal. An investor in stocks and shares is usually a passive holder of assets, with no real influence over the interest or dividends paid on the asset. The managers of a business enterprise do not however 'hold' investment projects passively. Investing in a particular project may lead to other possibilities or options which managers can take advantage of, and which will not have been reflected in a conventional NPV analysis.

3.4　EXAMPLE: FOLLOW-ON INVESTMENTS AS OPTIONS

Cornseed Publishing Ltd is a publisher of study guides in a sector of the professional training market. Over the last ten years, it has built up a share of approximately 30% of its target market. The directors of the company are now considering a project which would involve producing its study guides on CD-ROM, to be called *CD Guides*. The new CD-ROMs would not simply duplicate the material in the study guides as they would involve some interactive features. However it is thought that in the future, *CD Guides* might be developed into a more innovative fully interactive format - provisionally called *CD Tutor* - which makes fuller use of the advantages of the CD-ROM format, but this would take much more time and would require greater software know-how than is currently available. The *CD Guides* project would involve employing additional staff to develop the CD-ROM material. It is thought that Cornseed's competitors are probably considering similar CD-ROM projects.

3.5　　One of the directors, Mark Cornseed, has questioned whether the project is worthwhile. It has been calculated, using the NPV method, that the *CD Guides* project as proposed has a negative net present value of £50,000. 'Why invest in a negative NPV project?', he asks. 'CD-ROMs which are not fully interactive are not likely to be a success. Just because our competitors are putting money into them doesn't mean we should make the same mistake.'

3.6　　Another director, Julia Cornseed, points out that if the project does not go ahead, Cornseed may be missing out on the opportunity to develop *CD Tutor*. If the *CD Guides* are developed, she argues, with the added expertise gained Cornseed will be able to pursue this follow-on option. It will have a 'call' on this follow-on investment: the option to 'buy' it at a future date, or alternatively not to buy it. The only downside is that the company, assuming it allows the option to lapse, is committing itself to a project with a negative NPV of £50,000. The possible upside is that, if conditions seem right at a future date for the *CD Tutor* option to be taken up, this follow-on project could be a great success.

3.7　　The problem which now must be faced is that of putting a value on the option. In Chapter 13, we identified determinants of the value of a share option. Counterparts can be identified in valuing this follow-on investment, so that we could value the option in terms of:

(a)　The present value of the future benefit streams of the follow-on project (counterpart to: the current value of the share)

(b)　The initial cost of the follow-on project (counterpart to: the exercise price)

(c)　The time within which the option must be exercised

(d)　The variability of expected project returns (counterpart to: variability of the share price)

(e)　The risk-free rate of interest

3.8 The formulae used to value options (such as the 'Black-Scholes model') are complex and you do not need to be able to use such formulae for the *Financial Strategy* exam. For our purposes, assume that a computer model shows that the follow-on investment *(CD Tutor)* has a value of £125,000. This reflects the fact that the project could be very profitable, but the company will not know if it is likely to be until the outcome of the *CD Guides* project is known. The *CD Guides* project carries an option value of £125,000 for an option 'premium' of £50,000 - the NPV of the initial project.

3.9 Quantifying the variables in valuing such investment options is not easy to do objectively. However, viewing strategic investment decisions from the 'options' perspective can offer insights to decision-makers. If the follow-on project is high-risk, this will **increase** the value of the call option. Analogously, the value of a share option is higher if the volatility of the share price is high.

The option to abandon

3.10 In the example above (Cornseed Publishing Ltd), we were looking at the valuation of an option to expand a business. Sometimes there is the converse problem - the value of an option to abandon a project.

3.11 It may be that a major capital investment cannot be abandoned. Once the initial investment is made, it may be impossible to do things differently. If the benefit streams from a project are highly uncertain, an option to abandon the project if things go wrong could be of great value.

3.12 The possibility of putting a value on the 'put' option of abandonment highlights the value of pursuing investments which offer flexibility. For example, a company may face a choice between:

- Developing custom-designed plant to produce a single type of product, and
- Buying lower-technology machine tools to produce the same product

The NPV of Proposal (a) may be greater than the NPV for (b). But what if the product fails to sell? Abandonment in case (b) carries the value of a 'put' option, in that the company has the flexibility of using the low-technology equipment for other purposes.

The option to wait

3.13 A third type of option associated with investment decisions is the option to 'wait and see' in the expectation of gaining more relevant information before making a decision. This might seem like a justification for indefinite procrastination. The point to note is that, if we can make reasonable estimates of the determinants of the value of the option, then this could aid our strategic decision-making. Investments are rarely 'now-or-never' opportunities. More usually, there is some time period over which a project can be postponed, which corresponds to the period in which the option to invest can be exercised. During this period, new market information could emerge.

3.14 Against this, we need to consider the cash inflows forgone in the period of postponement. Managers will need to balance this cost against the value of waiting.

Using computer models for practical option problems

3.15 As already mentioned, most practical option problems require the use of a computer model; using such a model effectively demands informed judgement. The binomial model for option valuation, for example, provides a basis for such a task and is basically a method of solving decision trees. The model involves starting at a future date and working back through the tree to the present time, determining the best future action at each decision point. Eventually, the various possible cash flows generated by future events are related back to establish a present value. In practice, such decision trees tend to be extremely complex: hence the need for computer power to solve them.

3.16 The application of option pricing theory such as the binomial model allows discounting to be carried out within decision trees. Standard discounted cash flow methods do not work within decision trees: there can be no single constant discount rate for options because the risk of the option changes as time progresses and the price of underlying assets change. Therefore, the market value of the future cash flows described by the decision tree needs to be calculated by option pricing methods.

CASE STUDY LINK

Consideration of investment options may be a significant part of the case study requirements.

Chapter roundup

- The **application of basic DCF techniques** and other investment evaluation techniques to particular situations should not pose any particular difficulties provided that you learn the basic techniques thoroughly. Then, apply clear, sensible and logical reasoning to a problem, and state all your assumptions.

- As with all decision making problems, your recommendations should recognise the qualitative factors in the decision.

- **Options theory** can be applied to capital investments.

Quick quiz

1   *Hard capital rationing* occurs when a restriction on an organisation's ability to invest capital funds is caused by an internal budget ceiling imposed by management.

   True ☐

   False ☐

2   According to *CIMA Official Terminology*,

   Profitability Index (PI) = $\dfrac{(1)}{(2)}$

   What are (1) and (2)?

3   Equivalent annual cost = $\dfrac{\text{PV of costs over n years}}{\text{n year annuity factor}}$

   Explain briefly what is meant by:

   (a) PV of costs
   (b) n year annuity factor

4   Identify three common types of 'real option' found in relation to capital projects.

Answers to quick quiz

1   False. This describes *soft* capital rationing.

2   (1)   Present value of cash inflows
     (2)   Initial investment

3   (a)   The purchase cost, minus the present value of any subsequent disposal proceeds at the end of the item's life

     (b)   The company's cost of capital, for the number of years of the item's life.

4   (a)   The option to make follow-on investments
     (b)   The option to abandon a project
     (c)   The option to wait before making an investment

Now try the question below from the Exam Question Bank

Number	Level	Marks	Time
15	Examination	25	45 mins

Chapter 16

INTERNATIONAL OPERATIONS AND INVESTMENT

Topic list	Syllabus reference	Ability required
1 Multinational operations	(iv)	Analysis
2 Financing investments	(iv)	Analysis
3 Returns from overseas investments and their tax implications	(iv)	Analysis
4 International investment appraisal	(iv)	Application

Introduction

In this chapter, we consider the particular issues relating to **international operations and investments**. We look at the **different forms** of such activities may take, the **risks** involved, how they may be **financed**, and how the **returns** may be remitted back to the home country. We then go on to look at the application of **DCF techniques** in an international environment, and the **taxation** issues that arise.

Learning outcomes covered in this chapter

- Evaluate investment proposals (international)
- Recommend methods of funding investments
- Interpret the impact of changing exchange rates and inflation rates on the investment

Syllabus content covered in this chapter

- Calculate the net present value and internal rate of return by either converting the foreign currency cash flows into sterling and discounting at a sterling discount rate, or discounting the cash flows in the host country's currency using an adjusted discount rate

- The effect of taxation, including differential tax rates and double tax relief

- The effect of restrictions on remittances

- The benefits of finance drawn from the foreign environment

- The sources of long term finance including Euro currency and Eurodebt markets

- Weighted average cost of capital (WACC) and when it is appropriate to use WACC

1 MULTINATIONAL OPERATIONS

1.1 A **multinational company** or enterprise is one which owns or controls production facilities or subsidiaries or service facilities outside the country in which it is based. Thus, a company does not become 'multinational' simply by virtue of exporting or importing products: **ownership and control of facilities abroad** is involved.

The size and significance of multinationals

1.2 Multinational enterprises range from **medium-sized companies** having only a few facilities (or 'affiliates') abroad to **giant companies** having an annual turnover larger than the gross national product (GNP) of some smaller countries of the world. Indeed, the largest (the US multinationals Ford, General Motors and Exxon) each have a turnover larger than the GNPs of all but 14 countries of the world.

1.3 The extensive activities of multinational enterprises, particularly the larger ones, raises questions about the problems of **controlling** them. Individual governments may be largely powerless if multinationals are able to exploit the tax regimes of 'tax haven' countries through transfer pricing policies or if the multinationals' production is switched from one country to another.

1.4 Most of the two-way traffic in investment by multinational companies (**foreign direct investment** or FDI) is between the developed countries of the world such as the USA, European countries and Japan.

> ### KEY TERM
>
> **Foreign direct investment (FDI)** is the establishment of new overseas facilities or the expansion of existing overseas facilities, by an investor. FDI may be *inward* (domestic investment by overseas companies) or *outward* (overseas investment by domestic companies). *(OT 2000)*

Globalisation

1.5 Developments in international capital markets have provided an environment conducive to FDI. **Globalisation** describes the process by which the capital markets of each country have become internationally integrated. The process of integration is facilitated by improved telecommunications and the deregulation of markets in many countries (for example, the UK stock market's so-called Big Bang of 1986).

1.6 Securities issued in one country can now be traded in capital markets around the world. For example, shares in UK companies are traded in the USA via US banks.

1.7 For companies planning international investment activities, easy access to large amounts of **funds denominated in foreign currencies** can be very useful. Such funds are available in the **eurocurrency markets**, which can also help to bypass official constraints on international business activities.

Reasons for undertaking FDI

1.8 FDI provides an alternative to growth restricted to a firm's domestic market. A firm might develop **horizontally** in different countries, replicating its existing operations on a global basis. **Vertical** integration might have an international dimension through FDI to acquire raw material or component sources overseas (**backwards integration**) or to establish final production and distribution in other countries (**forward integration**). **Diversification** might alternatively provide the impetus to developing international interests.

1.9 FDI is likely to take place in the context of a **worldwide corporate strategy** which takes account of relative costs and revenues, tax considerations and **process specialisation**

(specialisation of processes within particular production facilities). For example, some motor vehicle manufacturers locate labour-intensive processes in lower wage countries, leaving the final stage of the production process to be located nearer the intended market.

Forms of overseas operations

1.10 Different forms of expansion overseas are available to meet various strategic objectives.

   (a) Firms may expand by means of new '**start-up' investments**, for example the setting up of an **overseas subsidiary** to operate a manufacturing plant. This does allow flexibility, although it may be slow to achieve, expensive to maintain and slow to yield satisfactory results.

   (b) A firm might **take over or merge with established firms abroad**. This provides a means of purchasing market information, market share and distribution channels. If speed of entry into the overseas market is a high priority, then acquisition may be preferred to start-up. However, enterprises available for takeover tend to be those which have high debt gearing, poor market performance and poor management. The better acquisitions will only be available at a premium.

   (c) A **joint venture** with a local overseas partner might be entered into.

Joint ventures

> **KEY TERMS**
>
> **Joint venture** is a project undertaken by two or more persons/entities joining together with a view to profit, often in connection with a single operation.   *(OT 2000)*

1.11 The two distinct types of joint venture are **industrial co-operation (contractual)**, and **joint-equity**. A contractual joint venture is for a fixed period and the duties and responsibility of the parties are contractually defined. A joint-equity venture involves investment, is of no fixed duration and continually evolves.

1.12 There is a growing trend towards a contractual form of joint venture as a consequence of the **high research and development costs** and the '**critical mass**' necessary to take advantage of economies of scale in industries such as automobile engineering. **Contractual joint ventures** have become a common means of establishing a presence in the newly emerging mixed economies of Eastern Europe. As well as in the car industry, this form of joint venture is common in the aerospace industry. A **joint-equity** venture may however be the only way of establishing a presence in countries where full foreign ownership is discouraged, such as Nigeria, Japan and some Middle Eastern countries.

Foreign subsidiaries

1.13 The basic structure of many multinationals consists of a parent company (a holding company) with subsidiaries in several countries. The subsidiaries may be wholly owned or just partly owned, and some may be owned through other subsidiaries. For example a UK parent company could own the holding company of a US group. Large multinationals have many subsidiaries in a large number of different countries and many of them are household names, for example Ford and Unilever.

The purpose of setting up subsidiaries abroad

1.14 The following are some reasons why a parent company might want to set up subsidiary companies in other countries.

(a) **The location of markets.** If, say, there is a big market in Australia for the products of a UK company, it might be cheaper for the UK company to establish a manufacturing subsidiary in Australia, in order to save the costs of shipping finished goods from the UK to Australia.

(b) **The need for a sales organisation.** Some subsidiaries are not manufacturing subsidiaries, but provide a sales and marketing organisation in their country for the parent company's goods. For example, a US parent company might set up a subsidiary in the UK, in order to sell goods in the UK which are shipped over from the USA.

(c) **The opportunity to produce goods more cheaply.** If labour costs are much lower in one country than in another, it might be profitable for a multinational to set up a manufacturing subsidiary in the low-cost country, provided that the labour force in that country has the skills that are needed to produce good quality output. For example, a UK company might design a new type of computer and set up a subsidiary in the Far East, where labour costs are lower, to manufacture the computers. They would then be shipped to the UK for sale in the UK market.

(d) **The need to avoid import controls.** When a country has regulations which restrict the import of certain goods, or impose high tariffs on imports, a multinational might decide to set up a manufacturing subsidiary in that country.

(e) **The need to obtain access to raw materials,** particularly in less developed countries (LDCs).

(f) **The availability of grants and tax concessions.**

1.15 Whatever the reason for setting up subsidiaries abroad, the aim is to increase the profits of the multinational's parent company. However there are different approaches to increasing profits that the multinational might take.

(a) At one extreme, the parent company might choose to get as much money as it can from the subsidiary, and as quickly as it can. This would involve the transfer of all or most of the subsidiary's profits to the parent company.

(b) At the other extreme, the parent company might encourage a foreign subsidiary to develop its business gradually, to achieve long-term growth in sales and profits. To encourage growth, the subsidiary would be allowed to retain a large proportion of its profits, instead of remitting the profits to the parent company. A further consequence is that the economy of the country in which the subsidiary operates should be improved, with higher output adding to the country's gross domestic product and increasing employment.

Case example

In its annual report 2000, **Tate and Lyle** disclosed 24 joint ventures, of which two were in the UK and the rest in countries such as the Czech Republic, Hungary, Namibia, Romania and Slovakia. Examples of the activities of these joint ventures include the sourcing of molasses through purchase contracts, the operation of sugar beet processing plants and the manufacture of cereal sweeteners.

Alternatives to FDI

1.16 **Exporting** and **licensing** stand as alternatives to FDI. **Exporting** may be direct selling by the firm's own export division into the overseas markets, or it may be indirect through agents, distributors, trading companies and various other such channels. **Licensing** involves conferring rights to make use of the licensor company's production process on producers located in the overseas market in return for royalty payments.

1.17 Exporting may be unattractive because of tariffs, quotas or other import restrictions in overseas markets, and local production may be the only feasible option in the case of bulky products such as cement and flat glass. Licensing can allow fairly rapid penetration of overseas markets and has the advantage that substantial financial resources will not be required. Many multinationals use a combination of various methods of servicing international markets, depending on the particular circumstances.

Countertrade

1.18 **Countertrade** is a general term used to describe a variety of commercial arrangements for reciprocal international trade or barter between companies or other organisations (eg state controlled organisations) in two or more countries.

KEY TERM

Countertrade is a form of trading activity based on other than an arm's-length goods for cash exchange. A types of countertrade include:

- **Barter**: the direct exchange of goods and services between two parties without the use of money

- **Counterpurchase**: a trading agreement in which the primary contract vendor agrees to make purchases of an agreed percentage of the primary contract value, from the primary contract purchaser, through a linked counterpurchase contract

- **Offsets**: a trading agreement in which the purchaser becomes involved in the production process, often acquiring technology supplied by the vendor

(OT 2000)

1.19 Countertrade involving exchange of **petroleum and manufacturing goods** became popular in the early 1980s as such deals provided a way of avoiding OPEC export quotas for oil-producing countries. It is also common in deals with East European countries which are **short of foreign exchange**. The huge debts of many Third World and Eastern European countries have contributed to the growth of countertrade as the only way of arranging international trade in the absence of cash or credit facilities to finance imports. It is now estimated that around 10% - 15% of international trade is conducted by some means of countertrade.

1.20 Countertrade is **costly for the exporter**; it creates lengthy and cumbersome **administrative problems**, just to set up a countertrade arrangement. It is fraught with **uncertainty**, and deals can easily collapse or go wrong. Small and medium-sized firms might be unable and unwilling to accept the costs and administrative burdens of exporting by means of countertrade arrangements. However, in some situations, countertrade might be the **only way of securing export orders**.

The risks of multinationals

1.21 Multinational companies, like any other companies, must accept the normal risks of business. However, compared with companies that trade entirely within one country, and even with companies that export from their base in one country, multinationals face additional risks, some of which we have already examined in earlier chapters of this Study Text.

1.22 The risks include the following.

(a) **Foreign exchange risks.** As we have already seen, any company that exports or imports faces the risk of higher costs or lower revenues because of adverse movements in foreign exchange rates. Multinationals that trade between one country and another therefore face this risk. A company that owns assets in different countries (subsidiaries abroad) faces the risk of accounting losses due to adverse movements in exchange rates causing a fall in the value of those assets, as expressed in domestic currency.

(b) **Political risks and country risks.** A multinational can face risks of economic or political measures being taken by governments, affecting the operations of its subsidiaries abroad. An example was the import restrictions imposed by the USA on the British cashmere industry during 1999, in retaliation for EU restrictions on banana imports. Political risk is discussed further below.

(c) **Geographical separation.** The geographical separation of the parent company from its subsidiaries adds to the problems of management control of the group of companies as a whole.

(d) **Litigation risk.** The risk of litigation varies in different countries and to minimise this risk, attention should be paid to legislation and regulations covering the products sold in different countries. Care should be taken to comply with contract terms.

(e) **Risk of loss of goods in transit.** It may be possible to insure against this risk.

Political risk

> **KEY TERM**
>
> **Political risk** is the risk that political action will affect the position and value of a company.

1.23 As stated above, when a multinational company invests in another country, by setting up a subsidiary, it may face a **political risk** of action by that country's government which restricts the multinational's freedom. The government of a country will almost certainly want to encourage the development and growth of commerce and industry, but it might also be suspicious of the motives of multinationals which set up subsidiaries in their country, perhaps fearing exploitation.

1.24 The government might offer **incentives** to encourage new investment from abroad, for example by offering cash grants towards the building of factories or the purchase of equipment.

1.25 On the other hand, the government might try to **prevent the exploitation of the country by multinationals,** and the various measures it might take include the following.

(a) **Import quotas** could be used to limit the quantities of goods that a subsidiary can buy from its parent company and import for resale in its domestic markets.

(b) **Import tariffs** could make imports (such as from parent companies) more expensive and domestically produced goods therefore more competitive.

(c) **Legal standards of safety or quality** could be imposed on imported goods to prevent multinationals from selling goods through their subsidiary which have been banned as dangerous in other countries.

(d) **Exchange control regulations** could be applied (see below).

(e) A government could **restrict the ability of foreign companies to buy domestic companies**, especially those that operate in politically sensitive industries such as defence contracting, communications, energy supply and so on.

(f) A government could **nationalise** foreign-owned companies and their assets (with or without compensation to the parent company).

(g) A government could insist on a **minimum shareholding in companies by residents**. This would force a multinational to offer some of the equity in a subsidiary to investors in the country where the subsidiary operates.

Exchange controls

1.26 Exchange controls **restrict the flow of foreign exchange** into and out of a country, usually to defend the local currency or to protect reserves of foreign currencies. Exchange controls are generally more restrictive in developing and less developed countries although some still exist in developed countries. Typically, a government might enforce regulations:

(a) Rationing the supply of foreign exchange. Anyone wishing to make payments abroad in a foreign currency will be restricted by the limited supply, which stops them from buying as much as they want from abroad.

(b) Restricting the types of transaction for which payments abroad are allowed, for example by suspending or banning the payment of dividends to foreign shareholders, such as parent companies in multinationals, who will then have the problem of **blocked funds**.

KEY TERM

Blocked funds are funds affected by government regulations restricting flows of money out of a country.

2 FINANCING INVESTMENTS

2.1 **Sources of finance** were covered in depth in your previous studies (Paper 9); whilst knowledge of these may be required for a general investment appraisal question, we shall concentrate here on the sources of particular relevance to a company with international operations and investment.

2.2 We shall first consider the various types of international long term funding sources available to multinationals, and then discuss the particular question of funding an overseas subsidiary.

International borrowing and equity markets

2.3 Borrowing and equity markets are becoming increasingly internationalised, particularly for larger companies. Companies are able to borrow long-term funds on the **eurocurrency** (money) markets and on the markets for **eurobonds**. These markets are collectively called **'euromarkets'**.

Eurocurrency markets

2.4 A UK company might borrow money from a bank or from the investing public, in sterling. But it might also borrow in a foreign currency, especially if it trades abroad, or if it already has assets or liabilities abroad denominated in a foreign currency. When a company borrows in a foreign currency, the loan is known as a **eurocurrency loan**. (It is not only European foreign currencies which are involved, and so the 'euro-' prefix is a misnomer.) For example, if a UK company borrows US $50,000 from its bank, the loan will be a 'eurodollar' loan. London is a centre for eurocurrency lending and companies with foreign trade interests might choose to borrow from their bank in another currency.

2.5 The eurocurrency markets involve the depositing of funds with a bank outside the country of the currency in which the funds are denominated and re-lending these funds for a fairly short term, typically three months, normally at a floating rate of interest. **Eurocredits** are medium to long-term international bank loans which may be arranged by individual banks or by syndicates of banks.

Eurobonds

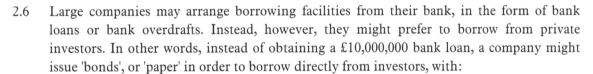

KEY TERM

A **eurobond** is a bearer bond, issued in a eurocurrency, usually eurodollars.   *(OT 2000)*

2.6 Large companies may arrange borrowing facilities from their bank, in the form of bank loans or bank overdrafts. Instead, however, they might prefer to borrow from private investors. In other words, instead of obtaining a £10,000,000 bank loan, a company might issue 'bonds', or 'paper' in order to borrow directly from investors, with:

(a) The bank merely arranging the transaction, finding investors who will take up the bonds or paper that the borrowing company issues

(b) Interest being payable to the investors themselves, not to a bank

2.7 In recent years, a strong market has built up which allows very large companies to borrow in this way, long-term or short-term.

2.8 Eurobonds are long-term loans raised by international companies or other institutions and sold to investors in several countries at the same time. Such bonds can be sold by one holder to another. The term of a eurobond issue is typically 10 to 15 years. Although eurobond funds may be raised at lower cost than direct borrowing from banks, issue costs are generally higher than the costs of using the eurocurrency markets. Eurobonds may be the most suitable source of finance for a large organisation with an excellent credit rating, such as a large successful multinational company, which:

(a) Requires a long-term loan to finance a big capital expansion programme (with a loan for at least 5 years and up to 20 years)

(b) Requires borrowing which is not subject to the national exchange controls of any government (A company in country X could raise funds in the currency of country Y by means of a eurobond issue, and thereby avoid any exchange control restrictions which might exist in country X. In addition, domestic capital issues may be regulated by the government or central bank, with an orderly queue for issues. In contrast, eurobond issues can be made whenever market conditions seem favourable.)

2.9 The interest rate on a bond issue may be fixed or variable. Many variable rate issues have a minimum interest rate which the bond holders are guaranteed, even if market rates fall even lower. These bonds convert to a fixed rate of interest when market rates do fall to this level. For this reason, they are called 'drop lock' floating rate bonds.

Eurobond issues and foreign exchange risk

2.10 A borrower contemplating a eurobond issue must consider the **foreign exchange risk** of a long-term foreign currency loan. If the money is to be used to purchase assets which will earn revenue in a currency different to that of the bond issue, the borrower will run the risk of exchange losses if the currency of the loan strengthens against the currency of the revenues out of which the bond (and interest) must be repaid. If the money is to be used to purchase assets which will earn revenue in the same currency, the borrower can match these revenues with payments on the bond, and so remove or reduce the exchange risk.

Euro-equity issues

2.11 A **euro-equity issue** may be defined as an issue of equity in a market outside the company's own domestic market. The euro-equity (international equity) market has not developed to such an extent as the comparable eurobond market. The market started in 1965 when bonds were issued with the option to convert them into equity. Later, bonds were issued with warrants attached, meaning that the bond does not have to be surrendered if the warrant is used to obtain shares. Furthermore, the warrant can be traded separately from the bond.

2.12 Conventional share issues have also been made on the euro-equity markets, as for example when there were attempts to place large numbers of shares of US corporations and of Japanese companies in Europe. These attempts were largely unsuccessful: the absence of a sufficiently liquid after-market or secondary market in such shares is the main limitation on such euro-equity issues.

2.13 'Sweeteners' are often added to the shares issued on the market, to make the issue more attractive to investors. For example, a 'rolling put option' might be added to a convertible preference share, giving the purchaser the right to sell the convertible preference share back to the company at any time between, say, five and ten years after the issue.

2.14 A company may find it appropriate to raise funds by selling shares outside its domestic capital market if this is too small for its needs. Another reason why a company may seek a euro-equity issue is to attract shareholders based in the markets in which it trades overseas. The liquidity of the company's shares and the international standing of the firm can be improved. The wider spread of shareholdings which might be achieved could act as a defence against hostile takeovers. An issue overseas may also be convenient if compliance with domestic capital market listing requirements is a complex or lengthy process.

Case example

To give one example of the sale of shares in overseas markets, the flotation of British Telecom involved an international issue alongside the main issue of shares on the UK stock market.

Should a company borrow on the euromarkets or domestic markets?

Question 1

See if you can identify the main issues which will be relevant to this question before reading the following paragraph.

2.15 The following factors are relevant to choosing between borrowing on euromarkets or domestic markets.

(a) Spreads between borrowing and lending rates are likely to be lower on the euromarket, because domestic banking systems are generally subject to tighter regulation and more stringent reserve requirements.

(b) Euromarket loans generally require no security, while borrowing on domestic markets is quite likely to involve fixed or floating charges on assets as security.

(c) Availability of euromarket funds is enhanced by the fact that euromarkets are attractive to investors as interest is paid gross without the deduction of withholding tax which occurs in many domestic markets.

(d) With interest normally at floating rates on euromarkets, draw-down dates can be flexible, although there may be early redemption penalties, and commitment fees to pay if the full amount of the loan is not drawn down.

(e) It is often easier for a large multinational to raise very large sums on the euromarkets than in a domestic financial market.

Financing a domestic investment in a foreign currency

2.16 A UK company could borrow in a foreign currency to finance an investment in sterling. For example, a company could finance a project in the UK by borrowing in US dollars. The loan could be raised as a **eurocurrency loan** from a bank or, in the case of very large companies, as a eurobond issue.

2.17 The **reason** for financing a project in a foreign currency would be the availability of a lower interest rate than the current market rate for sterling loans. However, it is easy to be deceived by lower interest rates on eurocurrency loans, and foreign currency loans at a low interest rate could prove more expensive than a loan in domestic currency at a higher interest rate. Companies need to beware of this 'interest rate trap'. The project will pay back returns in sterling, but the loan, and interest on the loan, must be paid in the foreign currency. If the currency of the loan strengthens against sterling, the **sterling cost** of the loan interest and the loan repayment will increase.

2.18 For example, suppose that a UK company borrows $6,000,000 at an interest rate of 7%, when the exchange rate is $2 = £1. The loan would finance a UK investment costing £3,000,000. Annual interest on the loan would be $420,000, which would cost £210,000 if the exchange rate does not change. But if sterling falls in value against the dollar, to say $1.50 =

£1, the loan interest will cost £280,000 a year, and the capital sum needed to repay the loan at the end of its term will be £4,000,000.

2.19 The need to finance a **foreign subsidiary** raises the following questions.

(a) How much equity capital should the parent company put into the subsidiary?

(b) Should the subsidiary be allowed to retain a large proportion of its profits, to build up its equity reserves, or not?

(c) Should the parent company hold 100% of the equity of the subsidiary, or should it try to create a minority shareholding, perhaps by floating the subsidiary on the country's domestic stock exchange?

(d) Should the subsidiary be encouraged to borrow as much long term debt as it can, for example by raising large bank loans? If so, should the loans be in the domestic currency of the subsidiary's country, or should it try to raise a foreign currency loan?

(e) Should the subsidiary be encouraged to minimise its working capital investment by relying heavily on trade credit?

2.20 The **method** of financing a subsidiary will give some indication of the nature of the investment that the parent company is prepared to make. A sizeable equity investment (or long-term loans from the parent company to the subsidiary) would indicate a **long-term investment** by the parent company. In contrast, when a subsidiary is financed largely by debt capital and short-term liabilities (even if the trade creditor is the parent company, for goods supplied by the parent to the subsidiary), this would indicate a **short-term investment** policy.

2.21 When a UK company wishes to finance operations overseas, there may be a **currency (foreign exchange) risk** arising from the method of financing used. For example, if a UK company decides on an investment in the USA, to be financed with a sterling loan:

(a) The investment will provide returns in US dollars.
(b) The investors (the lenders) will want returns paid in sterling.

If the US dollar falls in value against sterling, the sterling value of the project's returns will also fall.

2.22 To reduce or eliminate the currency risk of an overseas investment, a company might **finance it with funds in the same currency as the investment**. The advantages of borrowing in the same currency as an investment are as follows.

(a) Assets and liabilities in the same currency can be matched, thus avoiding exchange losses on conversion in the group's annual accounts.

(b) Revenues in the foreign currency can be used to repay borrowings in the same currency, thus eliminating losses due to fluctuating exchange rates.

3 RETURNS FROM OVERSEAS INVESTMENTS AND THEIR TAX IMPLICATIONS

Obtaining cash returns from an overseas subsidiary

3.1 If a subsidiary earns a profit, but then retains and reinvests the profits, the parent company will not get any cash at all. Various ways of obtaining a cash return are as follows.

(a) The subsidiary could make a profit and pay a **dividend** out of profits.

(b) The parent company could sell goods or services to the subsidiary and obtain payment. The amount of this payment will depend on the volume of sales and also on the **transfer price** for the sales.

(c) A parent company which grants a subsidiary the right to make goods protected by patents can charge a **royalty** on any goods that the subsidiary sells. The size of any royalty can be adjusted to suit the wishes of the parent company's management.

(d) If the parent company makes a **loan** to a subsidiary, it can set the interest rate high or low, thereby affecting the profits of both companies. A high rate of interest on a loan, for example, would improve the parent company's profits to the detriment of the subsidiary's profits.

(e) **Management charges** may be levied by the parent company for costs incurred in the management of international operations.

When the subsidiary is in a country where there are exchange control regulations, the parent company may have difficulty getting cash from the subsidiary.

Transfer pricing

3.2 When a foreign subsidiary makes a profit from goods/services supplied by its parent company, the profit will be included in the total profits of the multinational group. The management of the parent company must decide, however how the total profit of the group should be **divided** between the parent company and each of its subsidiaries, which is likely to depend on the **transfer prices** adopted

3.3 An example will show how shares of profits can be manipulated by accounting methods.

(a) Suppose that a US parent company ships some goods to a UK subsidiary. The goods cost US$40,000 to make, and they are sold in the UK by the subsidiary for £50,000, which is the equivalent, say, of US$75,000. The US multinational group will make a total profit of US$35,000. So how much profit from the US$35,000 has been earned by the US parent company, and how much has been earned by the UK subsidiary?

The answer depends on the transfer price at which the US parent sells the goods to its UK subsidiary.

(i) If the transfer price is US$45,000, the US parent company would make a profit of $5,000, leaving a profit of $30,000 for the UK subsidiary.

(ii) If the transfer price is US$70,000, the US parent company would make a profit of $30,000, leaving only a $5,000 profit for the UK subsidiary.

The transfer price will be set by management decision, so that the share of total profit between parent company and subsidiary can be manipulated to suit the preferences of management.

(b) The same choice of how to share total profits can be made in fixing a transfer price for goods made by a subsidiary and sold to the parent company or to another subsidiary.

Tax implications of international investment

3.4 If a UK resident company makes investments abroad it will be liable to corporation tax on the profits made, the taxable amount being before the deduction of any foreign taxes. The profits may be any of the following.

(a) Profits of an overseas branch or agency

(b)   Income from foreign securities, for example debentures in overseas companies

(c)   Dividends from overseas subsidiaries

(d)   Capital gains on disposals of foreign assets

3.5   In many instances, a company will be potentially subject to overseas taxes as well as to UK corporation tax on the same profits. There are however various ways that this may be avoided partly or wholly.

Foreign tax credits

3.6   In order to prevent the same income being taxed twice **(double taxation),** most countries give a tax credit for taxes on income paid to the host country. For example, a Japanese subsidiary of a US firm earns the equivalent of $500,000 in yen. The subsidiary pays 40% income tax ($200,000) in Japan. The US parent can claim a credit against US taxes of $200,000 when the earnings are remitted to the parent company. Foreign tax credits are also available for withholding taxes on sums paid to other countries as dividends, interest, royalties and in other forms.

Double taxation relief (DTR)

3.7   UK tax applies to the worldwide income of UK residents and the UK income of non-residents. When other countries adopt the same approach it is clear that some income may be taxed twice:

(a)   Firstly in the country where it arises

(b)   Secondly in the country where the taxpayer resides

3.8   Double taxation relief (DTR) as a result of international agreements may avoid the problem, or at least diminish its impact.

Double taxation agreements

> ### KEY TERM
>
> A **double taxation agreement** is an agreement between two countries intended to avoid the double taxation of income which would otherwise be subject to taxation in both.
>
> *(OT 2000)*

3.9   Typical provisions of double taxation agreements based on the OECD Model Agreement are as follows.

(a)   Total exemption from tax is given in the country where income arises in the hands of, for example:

(i)   Visiting diplomats

(ii)   Teachers on exchange programmes

(b)   Preferential rates of withholding tax are applied to, for example, payments of rent, interest and dividends. The usual rate is frequently replaced by 15% or less.

(c)   DTR is given to taxpayers in their country of residence by way of a credit for tax suffered in the country where income arises. This may be in the form of relief for withholding tax only or, given a holding of specified size in a foreign company, for the underlying tax on the profits out of which dividends are paid.

(d) There are exchange of information clauses so that tax evaders can be chased internationally.

(e) There are rules to determine a person's residence and to prevent dual residence (tie-breaker clauses).

(f) There are clauses which render certain profits taxable in only one rather than both of the contracting states.

(g) There is a non-discrimination clause so that a country does not tax foreigners more heavily than its own nationals.

Unilateral relief

3.10 If no relief is available under a double taxation agreement, UK legislation provides for unilateral relief. Foreign income must be included gross of any foreign tax in the UK tax computation. The foreign tax is deducted from the UK tax liability (this is credit relief) but the relief cannot exceed the UK tax on the foreign income. This means the taxpayer bears the higher of:

(a) The UK tax
(b) The foreign tax

3.11 The UK tax on the foreign income is the difference between:

(a) The UK tax before DTR on all income including the foreign income
(b) The UK tax on all income except the foreign income

Other ways of minimising taxation

Controlling foreign companies (CFCs)

3.12 A UK resident company may choose to trade abroad through an investment in a local company. Providing there are no exchange control problems and cash flow requirements do not call for the repatriation of all profits to the UK, there will generally be a tax benefit in accumulating income in a foreign company whose effective tax rate is lower than that of the UK company. (To prevent undue tax avoidance through the use of **tax havens** in this way, there are complex tax rules for **controlled foreign companies (CFCs)**.)

The migration of companies

3.13 Because the overseas profits of a UK resident company are chargeable to corporation tax whereas the overseas profits of a non-UK resident company are not, UK companies might wish to transfer their residence in order to avoid paying UK corporation tax. A company may freely transfer its residence out of the UK provided that it gives notice to the Inland Revenue and pays an exit charge based on unrealised capital gains on its assets. Only companies incorporated abroad can emigrate, as companies incorporated in the UK are automatically UK resident.

Sales at artificial transfer prices

3.14 Where sales are made to a non-resident fellow group company at an undervalue, or purchases are made from such a company at an overvalue, the Inland Revenue will substitute a market price in computing the profits chargeable to corporation tax. However, no corresponding relief is given for sales at overvalue or purchases at undervalue by the UK company.

Trading abroad

3.15 The controlled foreign companies legislation may reduce the attractiveness of setting up a subsidiary in a tax haven, as opposed to a branch of the UK company. However, a bona fide group structure may still be designed, avoiding the CFC rules, with the result that UK tax can be minimised by controlling the timing and amounts of dividends paid by the foreign subsidiary. At worst, a trading company treated as a CFC would have to distribute half of its profits to avoid an apportionment. Where dividends are paid to the UK, there may be a cashflow advantage in that dividends will, if correctly timed, be assessed in a later accounting period than trading profits would have been.

3.16 If an overseas operation is expected to make losses at first and then become profitable, it may be sensible to start with a branch and then transfer the trade to a subsidiary. Provided all the assets (or all except cash) are transferred, and the consideration is in the form of shares, gains on the transfers of assets can be deducted from the value of the shares instead of being immediately taxable in the UK. Where the overseas country is a member state of the European Union, an alternative is to allow the gains to be taxable but to claim relief for tax which would have been payable overseas but for the EU Mergers Directive (which gives certain reliefs from tax).

4 INTERNATIONAL INVESTMENT APPRAISAL

4.1 Multinational capital budgeting can be based on similar concepts to those used in the purely domestic case which we have examined earlier in this Study Text using:

   (a) **Net present value (NPV) analysis**, discounting project cash flows using the firm's weighted average cost of capital, or

   (b) The **internal rate of return method**, by which the discount rate which equates project cash inflows with project costs is found.

4.2 Before looking at the techniques of foreign project appraisal, we will first consider the most appropriate cost of capital to be used as a basis for the discount rate.

The international cost of capital

4.3 The **weighted average cost of capital** (WACC) of a firm is the weighted average of the costs to the firm of providing the returns **currently** required by its investors, the shareholders and debt holders. Whilst this is very often used as the discount rate for DCF appraisals of new projects, we have already noted that this may not always be appropriate.

The investment decision

4.4 It will be appropriate to adopt the firm's WACC as a discount rate if the following two conditions are satisfied.

   (a) The systematic risk associated with the investment should be similar to that of the firm's other investments. In this context, we assume that the company's shareholders hold the shares within a well diversified portfolio.

(b) The method of financing of the project should not affect the level of gearing of the company.

4.5 An overseas project may alter the firm's total risk. Political risk and currency risk, both of which are unsystematic, are likely to increase. Total risk may be allowed for by:

(a) Adjusting the discount rate for total risk, or

(b) Accounting for risk in projected cash flows, using a discount rate adjusted for systematic business risk and financial risk as in the case of a domestic project

4.6 In practice, it is common for firms to add a premium to the discount rate to account for risk. In comparing different approaches to adjusting for risk, the different characteristics of the special risks involved in international investment should be noted.

(a) **Political risk** is generally the risk of an adverse outcome in the form of possible expropriation of assets resulting from currently unforeseen changes in the political climate which may occur in the future. Since the risks cannot currently be foreseen, the effect is likely to be on future cash flows. If political risk were to be adjusted for through the discount rate, all cash flows would be affected.

(b) **Currency risk** can have either favourable or adverse effects on the project cashflows. Whether the effect is favourable or adverse depends on the direction of change in exchange rates and on whether the cash flows concerned are inflows or outflows. Instead of adjusting the discount rate, it is more appropriate to adjust for this 'two-way' risk by reflecting alternative outcomes in the cash flow forecasts themselves.

Effects of international portfolio diversification

4.7 As already discussed, internationalisation of a portfolio provides a means of reducing the risk of the portfolio. For a firm contemplating a foreign investment, the degree of correlation between returns on the stock markets of the two countries involved provides an indication of the level of systematic risk associated with the investment: the lower is the correlation coefficient, the lower is the likely level of **systematic risk**.

4.8 The possibility of lowering systematic risk through international investment suggests that a lower discount rate is appropriate for overseas investments. However, whether this is reasonable depends upon whether it is true that shareholders will accept a lower return on their equity in an internationally diversified firm for the reason that there is a **reduction in the domestic (home-country) systematic risk**. This is likely to be the case if the multinational firm is enabling shareholders to achieve international diversification that they would **not otherwise be able to achieve**, perhaps because of regulatory restrictions.

4.9 If the multinational firm is investing in countries in which shareholders **can readily invest themselves** directly, or via a managed investment fund such as a unit trust or investment trust, then there is no reason to suppose that shareholders will gain from the diversification within the multinational firm. In this case, there would seem to be no reason for the firm to use a lower discount rate for the overseas investment.

4.10 In the next chapter we shall be looking at the various ways that costs of capital and thus discount rates can be adjusted to take account of differing risks, including those particularly associated with international investment as discussed above.

The techniques for foreign project appraisal 5/01

4.11 Depending upon the information which is available, two alternative NPV methods are available. Both methods produce the NPV in domestic currency terms. For a UK company investing overseas, we can:

(a) Convert the project cash flows into sterling and then discount at a sterling discount rate to calculate the NPV in sterling terms, or

(b) Discount the cash flows in the host country's currency from the project at an adjusted discount rate for that currency and then convert the resulting NPV at the spot exchange rate.

4.12 There are, however, some special considerations in the international case, including the following.

(a) For the purpose of assessing how expected **performance** compares with potential performance, it is necessary to compare the project's net present value with those of similar host country projects. This involves measuring the cash flows in terms of the **currency of the host country**.

(b) A foreign project also needs to be evaluated on its net present value in respect of the **funds which can be remitted to the parent**. The purpose of this second stage is to evaluate whether the cash flow remitted justifies the cash invested from the home country.

(c) Cash flows from the subsidiary may come about through a variety of means, including **licensing fees** and **payments for imports** from the parent company.

(d) The possibility of **differing national rates of inflation** needs to be taken into account.

4.13 EXAMPLE: OVERSEAS INVESTMENT APPRAISAL

Bromwich plc, a UK company, is considering undertaking a new project in Horavia. This will require initial capital expenditure of H$1, 250m, with no scrap value envisaged at the end of the five year lifespan of the project. There will also be an initial working capital requirement of H$500m, which will be recovered at the end of the project. Pre-tax net cash inflows of H$800m are expected to be generated each year from the project.

Company tax will be charged in Horavia at a rate of 40%, with depreciation on a straight-line basis being an allowable deduction for tax purposes. Horavian tax is paid at the end of the year following that in which the taxable profits arise.

There is a double taxation agreement between the UK and Horavia, which means that no UK tax will be payable on the project profits.

The current H$/£ spot rate is 336, and the Horavian dollar is expected to appreciate against the £ by 5% per year.

A project of similar risk recently undertaken by Bromwich plc in the UK had a required post-tax rate of return of 16%.

Should the Horavian project be undertaken?

4.14 SOLUTION

Method 1 – conversion of flows into sterling and discounting at sterling discount rate

Time	0	1	2	3	4	5	6
H$M flows							
Capital	(1,750)					500	
Net cash inflows		800	800	800	800	800	
Taxation (W1)			(220)	(220)	(220)	(220)	(220)
	(1,750)	800	580	580	580	1,080	(220)
Exchange rate (W2)	336	319	303	288	274	260	247
£m flows	(5.21)	2.51	1.91	2.01	2.12	4.15	(0.89)
16% df	1	0.862	0.743	0.641	0.552	0.476	0.410
PV	(5.21)	2.16	1.42	1.29	1.17	1.98	(0.36)

NPV = £2.45m

Workings

1   *Taxation*

	H$m
Net cash inflow	800
Less: depreciation (1,250/5)	(250)
	550 @ 405% = H$220m

2   *Exchange rate*

Current spot = H$336/£. If the H$ is *appreciating* against the £, this means that the H$ is getting more valuable in terms of £, ie there will be more £ per H$ or *less H$ per £*.

Thus in one year's time the H$/£ rate will fall by 5%, to 95% × 336 = 319, etc.

Method 2 – discounting foreign cash flows at an adjusted discount rate

If we are to keep the cash flows in H$, and they need to be discounted at a rate that takes account of both the domestic discount rate (16%) and the rate at which the exchange rate is expected to decrease (5%). This is in fact an application of the **interest rate parity theorem.**

$$\text{Forward rate H\$/£} = \text{Spot H\$/£} \times \frac{1+\text{Hovarian interest rate}}{1+\text{UK interest rate}}$$

$$319 = 336 \times \frac{1+i_H}{1.16}$$

$$1 + I_H = \frac{319}{336}(=0.95) \times 1.16 = 1.10$$

Thus the adjusted discount rate is 10%.

Discounting the H$ flows at this rate:

Time	0	1	2	3	4	5	6
H$M flows							
Capital	(1,750)	800	580	580	580	1,080	(220)
10% df	1	0.909	0.826	0.751	0.683	0.621	0.564
PV	(1,750)	727.1	479.1	435.6	396.1	670.7	(124.1)

NPV = H$834.6

Translating this present value at the spot rate gives H$834.6/336 = **£2.48m**

This method is useful if the currency flows are annuities and the adjusted discount rate is a round number, as the computation can be reduced by the use of annuity tables.

Question 2

Donegal plc is considering whether to establish a subsidiary in Ruritania, at a cost of Ruritanian $2,400,000. This would be represented by fixed assets of $2,000,000 and working capital of $400,000. The subsidiary would produce a product which would achieve annual sales of $1,600,000 and incur cash expenditures of $1,000,000 a year.

The company has a planning horizon of four years, at the end of which it expects the realisable value of the subsidiary's fixed assets to be $800,000. It expects also to be able to sell the rights to make the product for $500,000 at the end of four years.

It is the company's policy to remit the maximum funds possible to the parent company at the end of each year.

Tax is payable at the rate of 35% in Ruritania and is payable one year in arrears.

Tax allowable depreciation is at a rate of 25% on a straight line basis on all fixed assets.

Administration costs of £100,000 per annum will be incurred each year in the UK over the expected life of the project.

The UK taxation rate on taxable profits made in Ruritania and remitted to the UK, and on UK income and expenditure is 30%, payable one year in arrears.

The Ruritanian $:£ exchange rate is 5:1.

The company's cost of capital for the project is 10%.

Calculate the NPV of the project.

Answer

				Time			
$000 cash flows	0	1	2	3	4	5
Sales receipts		1,600	1,600	1,600	1,600	
Costs		(1,000)	(1,000)	(1,000)	(1,000)	
Tax allowable depreciation		(500)	(500)	(500)	(500)	
$ taxable profit		100	100	100	100	
Taxation			(35)	(35)	(35)	(35)
Add back tax allowable depreciation		500	500	500	500	
Capital expenditure	(2,000)					
Scrap value					800	
Tax on scrap value (W1)						(280)
Terminal value					500	
Tax on terminal value						(175)
Working capital	(400)				400	
	(2,400)	600	565	565	2,265	(490)
Exchange rates	5:1	5:1	5:1	5:1	5:1	5:1
£000 cash flows						
From/(to) Ruritania	(480)	120	113	113	453	(98)
Additional UK tax (W2)			(6)	(6)	(6)	(84)
Additional UK expenses/income		(100)	(100)	(100)	(100)	
UK tax effect of UK expenses/income			30	30	30	30
Net sterling cash flows	(480)	20	37	37	377	(152)
UK discount factors	1	0.909	0.826	0.751	0.683	0.621
Present values	(480)	18	31	28	257	(94)

NPV = (£240,000), therefore the company should not proceed.

Working 1

Tax is payable on $800,000 as tax written down = $2,000,000 – (4 × $500,000) = 0

Working 2

Years 1-3

$ taxable profit	= $100,000
At 5:1 exchange rate	= £20,000

Tax at 30%   = £6,000

Year 4

$ taxable profit   = $100,000 + $800,000 + $500,000
                             = $1,400,000

At 5:1 exchange rate   = £280,000

Tax at 30%   = £84,000

Chapter round up

- In this chapter we have looked at the issues specific to **multinational operations** and **international investment.**

- **Foreign direct investment (FDI)** will generally be undertaken if exporting is more costly than overseas production. However, difficulties in **repatriating profits** and other **political risk** factors complicate the issue.

- Multinational companies will have greater access to **international sources of finance**, such as **eurocurrencies** and **eurodebt** markets.

- The financing of an **overseas subsidiary** needs careful consideration to minimise risks whilst remaining cost-effective.

- **Taxation issues** can influence the manner in which the foreign investment is set up and returns received by the parent company (eg by **transfer pricing).**

- **International portfolio diversification** can bring advantages resulting from differences in country economies, although whether this affects the choice of **appropriate discount rate** for overseas projects will depend upon the extent to which investors have access to international investment opportunities themselves.

- **DCF appraisals** of foreign investments may be carried out in the usual way, taking account of **changing exchange rates** and **taxation arrangements** where necessary.

Quick quiz

1   Identify the various types of risk affecting a typical multinational manufacturing company.

2   What are defined as 'funds affected by government regulations restricting flows of money out of a country'?

3   What is the term for 'a form of trading activity based on other than an arm's-length goods for cash exchange' *(OT 2000)*?

4   Why might a company undertake a foreign joint venture?

5   Why is it not necessarily cheaper to finance a domestic investment with a foreign loan at a lower interest rate than the domestic rate?

6   What is a double taxation agreement?

7   How should the domestic discount rate be adjusted if the foreign project flows are to be discounted?

Answers to quick quiz

1   (a)   Currency risk (or foreign exchange risk)
    (b)   Political risk
    (c)   Country risk
    (d)   Geographical separation risk
    (e)   Litigation risk
    (f)   Risk of loss of goods in transit

2   Blocked funds

3   Countertrade

4   As a means of expanding a business overseas, particularly when it is difficult or expensive to takeover an existing business or to set up from scratch

5   The domestic cost of a foreign loan will be affected by exchange rates as well as foreign interest rates.

6   An agreement between countries to avoid or minimise double taxation on profits earned abroad which are also taxable in the investor's home country

7   1 + adjusted discount rate = (1 + domestic discount rate)(*1 + expected rate at which the foreign exchange rate is expected to change)

Now try the question below from the Exam Question Bank

Number	Level	Marks	Time
16	Examination	25	45 mins

Chapter 17

INVESTMENT APPRAISAL: CHANGING RISKS

Topic list	Syllabus reference	Ability required
1 The cost of capital, the NPV of new projects and the value of shares	(iv)	Analysis
2 The adjusted present value method of project evaluation	(iv)	Analysis
3 Adjusted cost of capital	(iv)	Analysis
4 The capital asset pricing model (CAPM)	(iv)	Analysis
5 The arbitrage pricing model	(iv)	Analysis
6 CAPM and MM combined – geared betas	(iv)	Analysis
7 The certainty equivalent approach	(iv)	Analysis

Introduction

The prime objective of financial managers is generally assumed to be that of maximisation of shareholders' wealth. So far, we have looked at the appraisal of projects in isolation; here we will be considering their **impact on the value of the investing firm.** We shall first consider the case when **risks (financial and business) are unchanged**, when the current WACC may be used. We then go on to consider the **alternative approaches** that may be used when one or both types of risk are potentially altered by the project or its finance.

Learning outcomes covered in this chapter

- Interpret the risks facing an organisation
- Evaluate investment proposals (domestic and international)
- Calculate the tax shield of debt finance on an investment

Syllabus content covered in this chapter

- Adjusting the WACC for changes in capital structure. Knowledge of the use of $r^* = r(1 - T^*L)$ will be expected.

- Adjusted present value (APV). The two step method of APV will be tested for debt introduced permanently and debt in place for the duration of the project.

- Capital Asset Pricing Model (CAPM). The ability to gear and ungear betas will be tested (candidates will not be asked to calculate a beta value from raw data using regression or other methods).

- Arbitrage pricing theory. The main principles of this theory will be tested and its advantages and disadvantages compared with the CAPM.

- Risk adjustment using the certainty equivalent method when given a risk free rate and certainty equivalent values.

BPP
PUBLISHING

1 THE COST OF CAPITAL, THE NPV OF NEW PROJECTS AND THE VALUE OF SHARES

1.1 Using the **dividend valuation model**, it can be argued that the total value of a company's shares will increase by the NPV of any project that is undertaken, provided that there is no change in the company's WACC. We shall begin by considering this argument for companies financed entirely by equity, so that the WACC and the cost of equity are the same.

1.2 Suppose that a company relying on equity as its only source of finance wishes to invest in a new project. If the money is raised by issuing new share capital to the existing shareholders and the inflows generated by the new project are used to increase dividends, then the **project will have to show a positive net present value (NPV) at the shareholders' required rate of return**, because otherwise the shareholders would not agree to provide the new capital.

1.3 The **gain to the shareholders** after acceptance of the new project will be the **increase** in the market value of the company after acceptance of the new project **less** the amount of funds raised from the shareholders to finance the project.

The market value of the shares will increase by:

$$\frac{A_1}{(1+r)} + \frac{A_2}{(1+r)^2} + \frac{A_3}{(1+r)^3} + \ldots - (\text{Cost of project})$$

where $A_1, A_2 \ldots$ are the additional dividends at years 1, 2 and so on

r is the shareholders' required return $(= \text{cost of equity})$

This is the NPV of the project at the WACC of the company (which is simply the cost of equity.

Investments financed by retained profits

1.4 If for some reason there is a limit to the number of new shares that a company can issue to its shareholders and a company could undertake many projects with positive net present values, then reducing its dividend payment would increase the supply of capital available. Even though in the short term dividends will be reduced, this will be more than compensated for in the long term by the fact that extra cash inflows generated by the investments will increase dividends in the future. Indeed, it can be argued that no dividends should be paid until all projects with positive net present values have been financed.

1.5 EXAMPLE: INCREASE IN THE MARKET VALUE OF SHARES

Hubble plc, which has just paid its current dividend, expects to pay dividends of £8,000 a year into the foreseeable future.

A new project has just been discovered which will require an outlay of £3,000 at year 1 and will yield cash inflows of £2,000 each year for two years. If the project is accepted, dividends will be adjusted accordingly. The shareholders' cost of capital is estimated at 15%.

If the shareholders were told at time 0 that the project was going to be accepted and they were given full information about the project, what should be the theoretical increase in the market value of the company's shares?

1.6 SOLUTION

(a) The market value of company at time 0 before acceptance of the new project is:

$$\frac{£8,000}{0.15} = £53,333$$

(b) The market value of the company at time 0 after acceptance of the new project is:

$$\frac{£5,000}{1.15} + \frac{£10,000}{1.15^2} + \frac{£10,000}{1.15^3} + \frac{£8,000}{1.15^4} + .(£8,000 \text{ pa in perpetuity})$$

The year 1 dividend will be £3,000 lower than before and the years 2 and 3 dividends will be £2,000 higher than before.

At time 3 the PV of £8,000 receivable from time 4 onwards is $\frac{8,000}{0.15} = 53,333$, thus the

market value at time 0 is $\frac{5,000}{1.15} + \frac{10,000}{1.15^2} + \frac{10,000}{1.15^3} + \frac{53,333}{1.15^3} = 53,552$

(c) The market value of the company at year 0 would increase by £219 (£53,552 – £53,333) after acceptance of the project. The £219 can be proved as follows.

(i) NPV of the project at year 1 $= \frac{£2,000}{1.15^2} + \frac{£2,000}{1.15} - £3,000$

$$= £(1,512 + 1,739 - 3,000) = £251$$

(ii) NPV at year 0 of £251 receivable at the end of year 1

$$= \frac{£251}{1.15} = £218$$

This NPV of £218 is the same as the increase in the market value of £219, allowing for a rounding error of £2.

1.7 In the example above the shareholders would in theory benefit from a sudden rise in the price equal to the net present value of the new project as soon as the project was accepted. In practice, however, this is unlikely to happen for the following reasons.

(a) It would only happen if there is a strong form efficient market, or if dividend forecasts are published and are believed.

(b) Shareholders do not necessarily make rational decisions, so market values may not in practice respond to changes in future dividend expectations.

Conclusions for ungeared companies

1.8 If an **all equity** company undertakes a project, and it is financed in such a way that **its cost of capital remains unchanged, the total market value of ordinary shares will increase by the amount of the NPV of the project.**

1.9 If the market has strong form efficiency the shares will increase in value as soon as details of the intended project become available in advance of extra profits actually being earned and extra dividends actually being received from the project.

Geared companies

1.10 The situation is the same if a company has debt capital in its capital structure.

1.11 EXAMPLE: GEARED COMPANY

Trubshaw plc is financed 50% by equity and 50% by debt capital. The cost of equity is 20% and the cost of debt is 14%. Ignoring tax, this means that Trubshaw's WACC is 17%.

The company currently pays out all its profits as dividends, and expected dividends are £800,000 a year into the indefinite future.

A project is under consideration which would cost £1,200,000, to be financed half by a new issue of equity and half by a new loan. It would increase annual profits before interest by £340,000. The costs of equity and debt capital would be unchanged.

(a) What is the NPV of the project?

(b) By how much would the value of equity increase if the project is undertaken?

(c) How should this project be financed, such that the debt/equity ratio of the company remains at 50%:50%?

1.12 SOLUTION

(a) The NPV of the project is as follows.

Year	Cash flow £	Discount factor 17%	Present value £
0	(1,200,000)	1.0	(1,200,000)
1 - ∞	340,000	1/0.17	2,000,000
		NPV	800,000

(b) The market value of the company as a whole will increase by £2,000,000, which is the project's NPV plus the cost of the investment. Of this, £1,000,000 will be debt capital and £1,000,000 will be equity.

(c) To maintain the 50:50 debt:equity ratio, the cost of the investment will be financed by £1,000,000 debt capital and £200,000 equity. It would not be financed by £600,000 of each. This is because the NPV of £800,000 will add to the value of equity **only**, not to the value of the debt capital. If new equity of £200,000 is issued, the NPV of £800,000 will increase the market value of equity by £1,000,000 in total, which matches the new loan capital of £1,000,000.

The increased value of equity can be proved as follows.

	£
Annual profit from project, before interest	340,000
Less interest cost (£1,000,000 × 14%)	140,000
Increase in annual profits and dividends	200,000
Cost of equity	÷20%
Increase in the market value of equity	£1,000,000

1.13 This example illustrates that **given an unchanged WACC**, the value of equity will be increased by the NPV of any project which is undertaken (plus the extra funds invested in equity, in this case £200,000) with the NPV calculated using a discount rate equal to the WACC.

Arguments against using the current WACC in investment appraisal

1.14 The circumstances under which using the existing WACC as the cost of capital for new investment appraisal may not be appropriate are as follows.

(a) New investments undertaken by a company might have different **business risk** characteristics from the company's existing operations. As a consequence, the return required by investors might go up (or down) if the investments are undertaken, because their business risk is perceived to be higher (or lower).

(b) The finance that is raised to fund a new investment might substantially change the capital structure and the perceived **financial risk** of investing in the company. Depending on whether the project is financed by equity or by debt capital, the perceived financial risk of the entire company might change. This must be taken into account when appraising investments.

(c) Many companies raise **floating rate** debt capital as well as fixed interest debt capital. With floating rate debt capital, the interest rate is variable, and is altered every three or six months or so in line with changes in current market interest rates. The cost of debt capital will therefore fluctuate as market conditions vary. Floating rate debt is difficult to incorporate into a WACC computation, and the best that can be done is to substitute an 'equivalent' fixed interest debt capital cost in place of the floating rate debt cost.

Alternative approaches to investment appraisal when risks are changing

1.15 So how do we appraise investments when the business risk or the finance risk (or both) may change as a result of the project? The rest of the chapter addresses this question, by looking at the following techniques.

Changing capital structure

(a) The **adjusted present value (APV)** approach
(b) The recognition of an **adjusted cost of capital (r★)**

Changing business risk

(c) The **Capital Asset Pricing Model (CAPM)**
(d) **Arbitrage pricing theory**

Both capital structure and business risk changing

(e) The CAPM with **geared betas**

Finally, we shall consider the use of **certainty equivalents** in investment appraisal.

2 THE ADJUSTED PRESENT VALUE METHOD OF PROJECT EVALUATION

5/01

> **KEY TERM**
>
> **Adjusted present value method (APV)** is where the capital structure of a company is complex, or expected to vary over time. Discounted cash flows may be separated into:
>
> (a) Those which relate to operational items, and
> (b) Those associated with financing.
>
> This treatment enables assessment to be made of the separate features of each area.
>
> *(OT 2000)*

2.1 We have seen that a company's gearing level has implications for both the value of its equity shares and its WACC. The viability of an investment project will depend partly on how the investment is financed, and how the method of finance affects gearing.

2.2 The net present value method of investment appraisal is to discount the cash flows of a project at a cost of capital. This cost of capital might be the WACC, but it could also be another cost of capital, perhaps one which allows for the risk characteristics of the individual project (as we shall see later).

2.3 An alternative method of carrying out project appraisal is to use the **adjusted present value (APV) method**. The APV method involves two stages.

Step 1. Evaluate the project first of all as if it were all equity financed, and so as if the company were an all equity company to find the 'base case NPV'

Step 2. Make adjustments to allow for the effects of the method of financing that has been used

2.4 EXAMPLE: APV METHOD

A company is considering a project that would cost £100,000 to be financed 50% by equity (cost 21.6%) and 50% by debt (pre-tax cost 12%). The financing method would maintain the company's WACC unchanged. The cash flows from the project would be £36,000 a year in perpetuity, before interest charges. Corporation tax is at 30%.

Appraise the project using firstly the NPV method and secondly the APV method.

2.5 SOLUTION

We can use the **NPV method** because the company's WACC will be unchanged.

	Cost %	Weighting	Product %
Equity	21.6	0.5	10.8
Debt (70% of 12%)	8.4	0.5	4.2
		WACC	15.0

Annual cash flows in perpetuity from the project are as follows.

	£
Before tax	36,000
Less tax (30%)	10,800
After tax	25,200

NPV of project = − £100,000 + (25,200 ÷ 0.15)

= − £100,000 + £168,000

= + £68,000

Note that the tax relief that will be obtained on debt interest is taken account of in the WACC *not* in the project cash flows.

2.6 Since £100,000 of new investment is being created, the value of the company will increase by £100,000 + £68,000 = £168,000, of which 50% must be debt capital.

The company must raise 50% × £168,000 = £84,000 of 12% debt capital, and (the balance) £16,000 of equity. The NPV of the project will raise the value of this equity from £16,000 to £84,000 thus leaving the gearing ratio at 50:50.

2.7 The **APV approach** to this example is as follows.

(a) First, we need to know the **cost of equity in an equivalent ungeared company**. The MM formula we can use to establish this is as follows (given earlier in Chapter 8).

EXAM FORMULA

Cost of ordinary (equity) share capital in a geared firm (with tax):

$$k_{eg} = k_{eu} + [k_{eu} - k_d]\frac{V_D(1-t)}{V_E}$$

Remember k_d is the **pre-tax** cost of debt using the information from the question, Paragraph 2.4,

$$21.6\% = k_{eu} + \left[(k_{eu} - 12\%) \times \frac{50 \times 0.7}{50}\right]$$

$$21.6\% = k_{eu} + 0.70k_{eu} - 8.4\%$$

$$1.70k_{eu} = 30\%$$

$$k_{eu} = 17.647\%$$

(b) Next, we calculate the **NPV of the project as if it were all equity financed**. The cost of equity would be 17.647%

$$NPV = \frac{£25,200}{0.17647} - £100,000 = +£42,800$$

(c) Next, we can use an MM formula for the relationship between the value of geared and ungeared companies, to establish **the effect of gearing on the value of the project**. £84,000 will be financed by debt.

$$V_g \text{ (APV)} = V_u + DT_C$$
$$= + £42,800 + (£84,000 \times 0.30) = £25,200$$
$$= £68,000$$

2.8 The value DT_C (value of debt × corporate tax rate) represents the **present value of the tax shield on debt interest,** that is the present value of the savings arising from tax relief on debt interest. This can be proved as follows.

Annual interest charge = 12% of £84,000	=	£10,080
Tax saving (30% × £10,080)	=	£3,024.00
Cost of debt (pre-tax)	=	12%
PV of tax savings in perpetuity	=	$\frac{£3,024}{0.12}$
	=	£25,200 (by coincidence only this equals the project net of tax cash flows)

2.9 $DT_C = £84,000 \times 0.30 = £25,200$ is a quicker way of deriving the same value. Note, however, this only works where the interest is payable in **perpetuity.** If not the PV of the tax shield will need to be computed by the 'long hand' method above, using an appropriate annuity factor.

2.10 The APV and NPV approaches produce the same conclusion. However, the APV method can also be adapted to allow for financing which **changes the gearing structure** and the WACC.

2.11   In this respect, it is superior to the NPV method. Suppose, for example, that in the previous example, the **entire project were to be financed by debt**. The APV of the project would be calculated as follows.

(a)   The NPV of project if all equity financed is:

$$\frac{£25,200}{0.17647} - £100,000$$

$$=\quad + £42,800 \text{ (as before)}$$

(b)   The adjustment to allow for the method of financing is the present value of the tax relief on debt interest in perpetuity.

$$DT_C\quad=\quad £100,000 \times 0.30 = £30,000$$

(c)   APV   =   £42,800 + £30,000 = +£72,800

The project would increase the value of equity by £72,800.

Question 1

A project costing £100,000 is to be financed by £60,000 of irredeemable 12% debentures and £40,000 of new equity. The project will yield an annual cash flow of £21,000 in perpetuity. If it were all equity financed, an appropriate cost of capital would be 15%. The corporation tax rate is 30%. What is the project's APV?

Answer

	£
NPV if all equity financed: £21,000/0.15 – £100,000	40,000
PV of the tax shield: £60,000 × 12% × 30%/0.12	18,000
APV	58,000

The advantages and disadvantages of the APV method

2.12   The main advantage of the APV method is that it can be used to evaluate all the effects of the method of financing a project. The NPV technique can allow for the financing side-effects implicitly, by adjusting the discount rate used. In contrast, the APV technique allows for the financing side-effects explicitly.

2.13   The main difficulties with the APV technique are:

(a)   Establishing a suitable cost of equity, for the initial DCF computation as if the project were all-equity financed

(b)   Identifying all the costs associated with the method of financing

3   ADJUSTED COST OF CAPITAL

3.1   As well as reflecting how the net present value of a project can be increased or decreased by the effects of how the project is financed, the APV approach suggests that it is possible to calculate an **adjusted cost of capital** for use in specific circumstances.

3.2   First of all, we can distinguish the opportunity cost of capital and the adjusted cost of capital.

(a)   The **opportunity cost of capital** (r) is the expected rate of return available in capital markets on assets of equivalent risk. This depends on the risk of the project cash flows, and should be used if there are no significant side-effects arising from the method of financing.

(b) The **adjusted cost of capital** (r*) is an adjusted opportunity cost which reflects the financing side-effects of the project. A firm should accept projects which have a positive net present value (NPV) at the adjusted cost of capital r*.

MM formula

3.3 The following is the formula for the adjusted cost of capital (r*) suggested by the work of Modigliani and Miller.

> **EXAM FORMULA**
>
> $r^* = r(1 - T^*L)$, or $k_{adj} = k_{eu}(1 - tL)$

where T* is the net tax saving, expressed in pounds, of £1 of future debt interest payments

L is the marginal contribution of the project to the debt capacity of the firm, expressed as a proportion of the **present value of the project**. This is basically equivalent to $\dfrac{V_D}{V_D + V_E}$ for the project ($V_D + V_E$ = total market value of project = PV of project returns)

3.4 EXAMPLE: MM FORMULA

Project X, requiring an investment of £1,000,000, adds £300,000 to a firm's debt capacity. The project leads to a constant annual saving of £300,000 indefinitely. The opportunity cost of capital is 20%. Assume that the tax shield on interest payments is T* = 0.30 (30 per cent). What is the adjusted cost of capital?

3.5 SOLUTION

First we compute the APV of the project:

$$\text{Base case NPV} = \frac{£300,000 \times 0.7}{0.2} - £1m = £50,000$$

PV of tax shield = $0.3 \times £300,000 = 90,000$

APV = £50,000 + 90,000 = £140,000

Next we use this to computer L: V_D = 300,000

V_E = £700,000 + £140,000 = £840,000

$V_E + V_D$ = £1,140,000

So L = $\dfrac{300}{1,140}$

Finally we apply the MM formula:

$$r^* = 0.2 \left[1 - 0.3\left(\frac{300}{1,140}\right)\right] = \mathbf{18.42\%}$$

3.6 In what circumstances may the MM formula be used? The MM formula works exactly for any project which is expected to generate a level cash flow in perpetuity and to support permanent debt. The formula also works as a reasonable approximation for projects with limited lives or irregular cash flow streams.

4 THE CAPITAL ASSET PRICING MODEL (CAPM)

> ## KEY TERMS
>
> The **capital asset pricing model** is a theory which predicts that the expected risk premium for an individual stock will be proportional to its beta, such that:
>
> Expected risk premium = Beta factor (β) × Expected risk premium in
> on a stock   the market
>
> **Risk premium** is defined as the expected incremental return for making a risky investment rather than a safe one.
>
> **Beta factor** (β) is the measure of the volatility of the return on a share relative to the market. It is defined mathematically as a share's covariance with the market portfolio divided by the variance of the market portfolio.   *(OT 2000)*

4.1 The CAPM is a model whereby a required rate of return for an investment may be computed for **its particular level of risk,** based upon prevailing risk-free and market rates of return. This is very useful for project appraisal where the business risk of its returns differs from that of the investing company's operations, so that **existing company required rates of return are inappropriate for use in the project appraisal.**

4.2 As we shall see, we can combine the CAPM theory with that of MM to arrive at an appropriate appraisal method for a project which has both a **different business risk** and a **different capital structure** from that of the investing company.

4.3 First, however, we shall briefly revise the basics of the CAPM, which you studied in Paper 4. Remember, it is derived from the principles of portfolio theory, which was revised earlier.

Knowledge brought forward from Paper 4 (IFIN)

The capital asset pricing model

- The CAPM assumes that investors (eg shareholders in a company that is considering a new investment) are **well diversified** – their portfolio of risky securities is spread across the market such that the unsystematic (or specific) risk elements of the individual securities are diversified away, leaving only the **systematic risk** elements to contribute to their overall risk. This is known as the **market portfolio.**

- An individual investor can **dilute the risk** of his portfolio by combining the market portfolio with **risk-free** securities (such as Government gilts), giving a return of R_f.

- Any new investment introduced into the portfolio will introduce an extra element of systematic risk (the unsystematic risk having been diversified away) for which the investor will require an **appropriate level of return.**

- The appropriate level of return is determined by measuring the new investment's systematic risk relative to overall market risk – this is its **beta factor,** β.

- A **beta factor of more than 1** means that the investment is systematically more risky than the market on average – its share price will move more than the market as a whole in reaction to changes in market-wide conditions. Investors will therefore require a **greater return than the average market return (R_m)** (measured by, for example the FTSE all-share index). Conversely, an investment with β **of less than one** will be less risky than the market on average, and will thus require a **lower return than R_m.**

- The CAPM model thus gives a required return from an investment, R_i, as

  $R_i = R_f + \beta_i(R_m - R_f)$

- $R_m - R_f$ is the **market risk premium,** being the excess return over risk-free rate offered by the market as a whole as compensation for undertaking an investment with market level of risk.

- In practice, β **values** may be estimated for individual shares on the market from a regression exercise, plotting the share price movements over time against those of the market as a whole.

- In exam questions, you may be required to use a formula to calculate the beta factor:

  $$\beta = \frac{\text{Covariance between the investment returns and market returns}}{\text{Variance of the market return}}$$

- R_i may be used as a discount rate for the appraisal of a new investment with a level of systematic risk represented by β_i.

The CAPM and project appraisal

4.4   The CAPM can be used instead of the dividend valuation model to establish an **equity cost of capital** to use in project appraisal.

EXAM FORMULA

$k_e = R_f + [R_m - R_f]\,\beta$

where β is the beta value for the company's equity capital.

4.5   EXAMPLE: CAPM AND PROJECT APPRAISAL (1)

A company is financed by a mixture of equity and debt capital, whose market values are in the ratio 3:1. The debt capital, which is considered risk-free, yields 10% before tax. The average stock market return on equity capital is 16%. The beta value of the company's equity capital is estimated as 0.95. The tax rate is 30%.

What would be an appropriate cost of capital to be used for investment appraisal of new projects with the same systematic risk characteristics as the company's current investment portfolio?

4.6   SOLUTION

An appropriate cost of capital to use, assuming no change in the company's financial gearing, is its WACC. However, the CAPM can be used to estimate the cost of the company's equity.

$r_e = 10\% + (16 - 10) \times 0.95\% = 15.7\%$

The after tax cost of debt is $0.70 \times 10\% = 7\%$.

The WACC is therefore:

(¾ × 15.7%) + (¼ × 7.0%) = 13.525%.

The cost of capital to use in project appraisal is 13.525%.

How is the WACC different using the CAPM?

4.7 You might be wondering how the weighted average cost of capital (WACC) is different when we use the CAPM compared to the method of calculating the WACC which was described in the earlier chapter on the cost of capital. The only difference, in fact, is the method used to calculate the cost of the firm's equity: the dividend valuation model or the CAPM.

Question 2

See if you can explain why you think the two methods will produce different values, before reading the next paragraph.

4.8 Using the different techniques for measuring the cost of equity will produce two different values for these reasons.

(a) The dividend valuation model uses expectations of actual dividends and current share values. Dividends may include extra or lower returns caused by unsystematic risk variations, as well as systematic risk. Share prices might not be in equilibrium.

(b) The CAPM considers systematic risk only, and assumes equilibrium in the stock market.

4.9 If dividends reflect systematic risk only, and if stock market prices are in equilibrium, the dividend valuation model and the CAPM should produce roughly the same estimates for the cost of a firm's equity and for its WACC.

The use of the CAPM for capital investment decisions

4.10 The CAPM produces a required return based on the expected return of the market (R_m), the risk-free interest rate (R_f) and the variability of project returns relative to the market returns (β). Its main advantage when used for investment appraisal is that it produces a discount rate which is based on the **systematic** risk of the individual investment. It can be used to **compare projects of all different risk classes** and is therefore superior to an NPV approach which uses only one discount rate for all projects, regardless of their risk.

4.11 The model was developed with respect to securities; by applying it to an investment within the firm, the company is assuming that the shareholder wishes investments to be evaluated as if they were securities in the capital market and thus assumes that all shareholders will hold diversified portfolios and will not look to the company to achieve diversification for them.

4.12 The greatest practical problems with the use of the CAPM in capital investment decisions are as follows.

(a) It is **hard to estimate** returns on projects under different economic environments, market returns under different economic environments and the probabilities of the various environments.

(b) The CAPM is really just a **single period model**. Few investment projects last for one year only and to extend the use of the return estimated from the model to more than one time period would require both project performance relative to the market and the economic environment to be reasonably stable.

In theory, it should be possible to apply the CAPM for each time period, thus arriving at successive discount rates, one for each year of the project's life. In practice, this would exacerbate the estimation problems mentioned above and also make the discounting process much more cumbersome.

(c) It may be **hard to determine the risk-free rate of return**. Government securities are usually taken to be risk-free, but the return on these securities varies according to their term to maturity.

Question 3

Company X and company Y both pay an annual cash return to shareholders of 34.048 pence per share and this is expected to continue in perpetuity. The risk-free rate of return is 8% and the current average market rate of return is 12%. Company X's β coefficient is 1.8 and company Y's is 0.8. What is the expected return from companies X and Y respectively, and what would be the predicted market value of each company's shares?

Answer

(a) The expected return for X is 8% + (12% – 8%) × 1.8 = 15.2%
(b) The expected return for Y is 8% + (12% – 8%) × 0.8 = 11.2%

The dividend valuation model can now be used to derive expected share prices.

(c) The predicted value of a share in X is $\dfrac{34.048p}{0.152}$ = 224 pence

(d) The predicted value of a share in Y is $\dfrac{34.048p}{0.112}$ = 304 pence

The actual share prices of X and Y might be higher or lower than 224p and 304p. If so, CAPM analysis would conclude that the share is currently either overpriced or underpriced.

Question 4

The risk-free rate of return is 7%. The average market return is 11%.

(a) What will be the return expected from a share whose β factor is 0.9?

(b) What would be the share's expected value if it is expected to earn an annual dividend of 5.3p, with no capital growth?

Answer

(a) 7% + (11% – 7%) × 0.9 = 10.6%
(b) $\dfrac{5.3p}{10.6\%}$ = 50 pence

Question 5

The standard deviation of market returns is 50%, and the expected market return (R_m) is 12%. The risk-free rate of return is 9%. The covariance of returns for the market with returns on shares in Anxious plc has been 20%. Calculate a beta value and a cost of capital for Anxious plc equity.

Answer

(a)   The variance of market returns is $0.50^2 = 0.25$.

$$\beta = \frac{0.20}{0.25} = 0.8$$

(b)   Cost of Anxious equity $= 9\% + (12 - 9) \times 0.8\% = 11.4\%$

5   THE ARBITRAGE PRICING MODEL

Exam focus point

What is important here is to be aware that there are other models apart from the CAPM, and to know the benefits and limitations of the arbitrage pricing model (APM) relative to the CAPM. *Detailed* knowledge of the APM and calculations based on it will not be required.

5.1   The CAPM is seen as a useful analytical tool by financial managers as well as by financial analysts. However, critics suggest that the relationship between risk and return is more complex than is assumed in the CAPM. One model which could replace the CAPM in the future is the **arbitrage pricing model (APM)**.

5.2   Unlike the CAPM, which analyses the returns on a share as a function of a single factor - the return on the market portfolio - the APM assumes that the return on each security is based on a number of independent macroeconomic factors. The actual return r on any security is shown as:

$$r = E(r_j) + \beta_1 F_1 + \beta_2 F_2 \dots + e$$

where $E(r_j)$ is the expected return on the security
β_1 is the sensitivity to changes in factor 1
F_1 is the difference between actual and expected values of factor 1
β_2 is the sensitivity to changes in factor 2
F_2 is the difference between actual and expected values of factor 2
e is a random term

KEY TERM

Arbitrage pricing theory is a model which assumes that the return on a security is based on a number of independent factors, to each of which a particular risk premium is attached.

5.3   Factor analysis is used to ascertain the factors to which security returns are sensitive. Four key factors identified by researchers have been:

- Unanticipated inflation
- Changes in the expected level of industrial production
- Changes in the risk premium on bonds (debentures)
- Unanticipated changes in the term structure of interest rates

5.4   If a certain combination of securities is expected to produce higher returns than is indicated by its risk sensitivities, then traders will engage in arbitrage trading to improve the expected returns. It has been demonstrated that when no further arbitrage opportunities exist, the expected return $E(r_j)$ can be shown as:

$$E(r_j) = R_f + \beta_1(R_1 - R_f) + \beta_2(R_2 - R_f) \ldots$$

where R_f is the risk-free rate of return

R_1 is the expected return on a portfolio with unit sensitivity to factor 1 and no sensitivity to any other factor

R_2 is the expected return on a portfolio with unit sensitivity to factor 2 and no sensitivity to any other factor

5.5 This implies that the expected rate of return on a security is a function of the risk-free rate of return plus risk premiums $((R_1 - R_f), (R_2 - R_f)$ etc) depending on the sensitivity of the security to various factors such as the four factors identified in Paragraph 6.3 above.

5.6 With the APM, the CAPM's problem of identifying the market portfolio is avoided, but this is replaced with the problem of identifying the macroeconomic factors and their risk sensitivities. As with the CAPM, the available empirical evidence is inconclusive and neither proves nor disproves the theory of the APM. Both the CAPM and the APM do however provide a means of analysing how risk and return may be determined in conditions of competition and uncertainty.

6   CAPM AND MM COMBINED – GEARED BETAS

6.1 The gearing of a company will affect the risk of its equity. If a company is geared and its **financial risk is therefore higher** than the risk of an all-equity company, then the β value of the geared company's equity will be higher than the β value of a similar ungeared company's equity.

6.2 The CAPM is consistent with the propositions of Modigliani and Miller. MM argue that as gearing rises, the cost of equity rises to compensate shareholders for the extra financial risk of investing in a geared company. This financial risk is an aspect of systematic risk, and ought to be reflected in a company's beta factor.

Beta values and the effect of gearing: geared betas and ungeared betas

6.3 The connection between MM theory and the CAPM means that it is possible to establish a mathematical relationship between the β value of an ungeared company and the β value of a similar, but geared, company. The β value of a geared company will be higher than the β value of a company identical in every respect except that it is all-equity financed. This is because of the extra financial risk. The mathematical relationship between the 'ungeared' and 'geared' betas is as follows.

$$\beta_u = \beta_g \frac{V_E}{V_E + V_D(1-t)} + \beta_d \frac{V_D(1-t)}{V_E + V_D(1-t)}$$

where β_u is the beta factor of an ungeared company: the ungeared beta

β_g is the beta factor of equity in a similar, but geared company: the geared beta

β_d is the beta factor of debt in the geared company

V_D is the market value of the debt capital in the geared company

V_E is the market value of the equity capital in the geared company

t is the rate of corporate tax

6.4 Debt is often assumed to be risk-free and its beta (β_d) is then taken as zero, in which case the formula above reduces to the following form.

EXAM FORMULA

$$\beta_u = \beta_g \times \frac{V_E}{V_E + V_D(1-t)} \quad \text{or, without tax,} \quad \beta_u = \beta_g \times \frac{V_E}{V_E + V_D}$$

6.5 EXAMPLE: CAPM (7)

Two companies are identical in every respect except for their capital structure. Their market values are in equilibrium, as follows.

	Geared plc £'000	Ungeared plc £'000
Annual profit before interest and tax	1,000	1,000
Less interest $(4,000 \times 8\%)$	320	0
	680	1,000
Less tax at 30%	204	300
Profit after tax = dividends	476	700
Market value of equity	3,900	6,600
Market value of debt	4,180	0
Total market value of company	8,080	6,600

The total value of Geared plc is higher than the total value of Ungeared plc, which is consistent with MM's proposition that $V_g = V_u + V_D t$.

All profits after tax are paid out as dividends, and so there is no dividend growth. The beta value of Ungeared plc has been calculated as 1.0. The debt capital of Geared plc can be regarded as risk-free.

Calculate:

(a) The cost of equity in Geared plc
(b) The market return R_m
(c) The beta value of Geared plc

6.6 SOLUTION

(a) Since its market value (MV) is in equilibrium, the cost of equity in Geared plc can be calculated as:

$$\frac{d}{MV} = \frac{476}{3,900} = 12.20\%$$

(b) The beta value of Ungeared plc is 1.0, which means that the expected returns from Ungeared plc are exactly the same as the market returns, and $R_m = 700/6,600 = 10.6\%$.

(c) $\beta_g = \beta_u \times \dfrac{V_E + V_D(1-t)}{V_E}$

$$= 1.0 \times \frac{3,900 + (4,180 \times 0.70)}{3,900} = 1.75$$

The beta of Geared plc, as we should expect, is higher than the beta of Ungeared plc.

Using the geared and ungeared beta formula to estimate a beta factor for a company

6.7 Another way of estimating a beta factor for a company's equity is to use data about the returns of other quoted companies which have similar operating characteristics: that is, to use the beta values of other companies' equity to estimate a beta value for the company under consideration. The beta values estimated for the firm under consideration must be adjusted to allow for differences in gearing from the firms whose equity beta values are known. The formula for geared and ungeared beta values can be applied.

6.8 EXAMPLE: CAPM

The management of Crispy plc wish to estimate their company's equity beta value. The company, which is an all-equity company, has only recently gone public and insufficient data is available at the moment about its own equity's performance to calculate the company's equity beta. Instead, it is thought possible to estimate Crispy's equity beta from the beta values of quoted companies operating in the same industry and with the same operating characteristics as Crispy.

Details of three similar companies are as follows. The tax rate is 30%.

(a) Snapp plc has an observed equity beta of 1.15. Its capital structure at market values is 70% equity and 30% debt. Snapp plc is very similar to Crispy plc except for its gearing.

(b) Crackle plc is an all-equity company. Its observed equity beta is 1.25. It has been estimated that 40% of the current market value of Crackle is caused by investment in projects which offer high growth, but which are more risky than normal operations and which therefore have a higher beta value. These investments have an estimated beta of 1.8, and are reflected in the company's overall beta value. Crackle's normal operations are identical to those of Crispy.

(c) Popper plc has an observed equity beta of 1.35. Its capital structure at market values is 60% equity and 40% debt. Popper has two divisions, X and Y. The operating characteristics of X are identical to those of Crispy but those of Y are thought to be 50% more risky than those of X. It is estimated that X accounts for 75% of the total value of Popper, and Y for 25%.

Required

(a) Assuming that all debt is virtually risk-free, calculate three estimates of the equity beta of Crispy, from the data available about Snapp, Crackle and Popper respectively.

(b) Now assume that Crispy plc is not an all-equity company, but instead is a geared company with a debt:equity ratio of 2:3 (based on market values). Estimate the equity beta of Crispy from the data available about Snapp.

6.9 SOLUTION

(a) **Snapp plc - based estimate**

$$\beta_g = \beta_u \times \frac{V_E + V_D(1-t)}{V_E}$$

$$1.15 = \beta_u \times \frac{70 + 30(1-0.30)}{70}$$

$$1.15 = 1.3\beta_u$$

$$\beta_u = 0.88$$

(b) **Crackle plc - based estimate**

If the beta value of normal operations of Crackle is β_n, and we know that the high-risk operations have a beta value of 1.8 and account for 40% of Crackle's value, we can estimate a value for β_n.

Overall beta	=	0.4(high risk beta) + 0.6(normal operations beta)
1.25	=	$0.4(1.8) + 0.6\,\beta_n$
β_n	=	0.88

Since Crackle is an all-equity company, this provides the estimate of Crispy's equity beta.

(c) **Popper plc - based estimate**

It is easiest to arrive at an estimate of Crispy's equity beta by calculating the equity beta which Popper would have had if it had been an all-equity company instead of a geared company.

$$\beta_g = \beta_u \times \frac{V_E + V_D(1-t)}{V_E}$$

$$1.35 = \beta_u \times \frac{0.6 + 0.4(1-0.30)}{0.6}$$

$$\beta_u = \frac{1.35}{1.47} = 0.92$$

This equity beta estimate for Popper plc is a weighted average of the beta values of divisions X and Y, so that:

$$0.92 = 0.75\beta_x + 0.25\beta_y$$

where β_x and β_y are the beta values for divisions X and Y respectively. We also know that Y is 50% more risky than X, so that $\beta_y = 1.5\beta_x$.

$$0.92 = 0.75\beta_x + 0.25(1.5\beta_x)$$

$$\beta_x = 0.82$$

Since Crispy plc is similar in characteristics to division X, the estimate of Crispy's equity beta is 0.82.

6.10 If Crispy plc is a geared company with a market-value based gearing ratio of 2:3, we can use the geared and ungeared beta formula again. The ungeared beta value, based on data about Snapp, was 0.88. The geared beta of Crispy would be estimated as:

$$\beta_g = 0.88 \times \frac{3 + 2(1-0.30)}{3} = 1.29$$

Weaknesses in the formula

6.11 The problems with using the geared and ungeared beta formula for calculating a firm's equity beta from data about other firms are as follows.

(a) It is difficult to identify other firms with identical operating characteristics.

(b) Estimates of beta values from share price information are not wholly accurate. They are based on statistical analysis of historical data, and as the previous example shows, estimates using one firm's data will differ from estimates using another firm's data. The beta values for Crispy estimated from Snapp, Crackle and Popper are all different.

(c) There may be differences in beta values between firms caused by:

   (i)   Different cost structures (eg, the ratio of fixed costs to variable costs)

   (ii)   Size differences between firms

   (iii) Debt capital not being risk-free

(d) If the firm for which an equity beta is being estimated has opportunities for growth that are recognised by investors, and which will affect its equity beta, estimates of the equity beta based on other firms' data will be inaccurate, because the opportunities for growth will not be allowed for.

6.12 Perhaps the most significant simplifying assumption is that to link MM theory to the CAPM, it must be assumed that the cost of debt is a risk-free rate of return. This could obviously be unrealistic. Companies may default on interest payments or capital repayments on their loans. It has been estimated that corporate debt has a beta value of 0.2 or 0.3.

6.13 The consequence of making the assumption that debt is risk-free is that the formulae tend to **overstate** the financial risk in a geared company and to **understate** the business risk in geared and ungeared companies by a compensating amount. In other words, β_u will be slightly higher and β_g will be slightly lower than the formulae suggest.

7 THE CERTAINTY EQUIVALENT APPROACH

7.1 Another, simpler method of allowing for risk in investment appraisal is the **certainty equivalent approach**. By this method, the expected cash flows of the project are converted to equivalent riskless amounts. The greater the risk of an expected cash flow, the smaller the certainty equivalent value (for receipts) or the larger the certainty equivalent value (for payments). The disadvantage of the certainty equivalent approach is that the amount of the adjustment to each cash flow is decided subjectively by management.

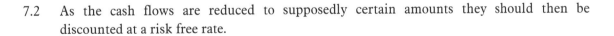

KEY TERM

Certainty equivalent method is an approach to dealing with risk in a capital budgeting context. It involves expressing risky future cash flows in terms of the certain cash flow which would be considered, by the decision-maker, as their equivalent, ie the decision-maker would be indifferent between the risky amount and the (lower) riskless amount considered to be its equivalent. *(OT 2000)*

7.2 As the cash flows are reduced to supposedly certain amounts they should then be discounted at a risk free rate.

7.3 EXAMPLE: CERTAINTY EQUIVALENTS

Dark Ages Ltd, whose cost of capital is 10%, is considering a project with the following expected cash flows.

Year	Cash flow £	Discount factor 10%	Present value £
0	(9,000)	1.000	(9,000)
1	7,000	0.909	6,363
2	5,000	0.826	4,130
3	5,000	0.751	3,755
		NPV	5,248

BPP PUBLISHING

The project would seem to be worthwhile. However, because of the uncertainty about the future cash flows, the management decides to reduce them to certainty equivalents by taking only 70%, 60% and 50% of the years 1, 2 and 3 cash flows respectively. (Note that this method of risk adjustment allows for different risk factors in each year of the project.) Is the project worthwhile?

7.4 SOLUTION

The risk-adjusted NPV of the project would be as follows.

Year	Cash flow	PV factor	PV
	£		£
0	(9,000)	1.000	(9,000)
1	4,900	0.909	4,454
2	3,000	0.826	2,478
3	2,500	0.751	1,878
		NPV	(190)

The project is too risky and should be rejected although this has ignored any potential adjustment to the discount rate as a result of the 'certainty' of the cash flows.

Chapter roundup

- Managers need to know the **cost of capital** for their company for several reasons. Of particular interest to the management accountant is the cost of capital to be used **for the purposes of investment appraisal**.

- The **risk** associated with a project must be taken into account when appraising that project.

- The **APV** method suggests that it is possible to calculate an **adjusted cost of capital** for use in project appraisal, as well as indicating how the net present value of a project can be increased or decreased by project financing effects

- The **CAPM** assumes that the investor is only interested in being compensated for the systematic risk of the project.

- The **beta factor** used in the CAPM allows for systematic risk. It is a measure of the importance of **systematic risk** to the **required return** on an investment.

- In the future the **arbitrage pricing model** could replace the CAPM as a tool for analysing the determination of risk and returns.

- When an investment has differing business and finance risks from the existing business suitably computed **geared betas** may be used to get a appropriate required return.

- Project cash flows are converted to equivalent riskless amounts under the **certainly equivalent** approach.

Quick quiz

1   Identify the two aspects of the cost of capital

     It is (A) ……………………………………..

     It is (B) ……………………………………..

2   Which type of risk is reflected by which model? (Answer Yes/No in each case.)

	Systematic risk	*Unsystematic risk*
Dividend valuation model	(1) Y/N?	(2) Y/N?
CAPM	(3) Y/N?	(4) Y/N?

3   Which method of project appraisal involves making adjustments for the effects of the method of financing that has been used?

4   What are the main difficulties with the technique identified in Quick quiz question 3 above?

5   Identify r*, r, T* and L in the following MM formula for the adjusted cost of capital.

     r* = r [1 – T*L]

Answers to quick quiz

1   (A)   The cost of funds a company uses.
     (B)   The minimum return a company should be making on its investments.

2   (1) Y (2) Y (3) Y (4) N

3   The adjusted present value (APV) method.

4   (a)   Establishing a suitable cost of equity as if the project were all equity financed.
     (b)   Identifying all costs associated with the method of financing.

5   r is the opportunity cost of capital

     r* is the adjusted cost of capital, reflecting financing side-effects

     T* is the net tax saving in pounds of £1 of future debt interest payments

     L is the marginal contribution of the project to the debt capacity of the firm, expressed as a proportion of the present value of the project

Now try the question below from the Exam Question Bank

Number	Level	Marks	Time
17	Examination	35	63 mins

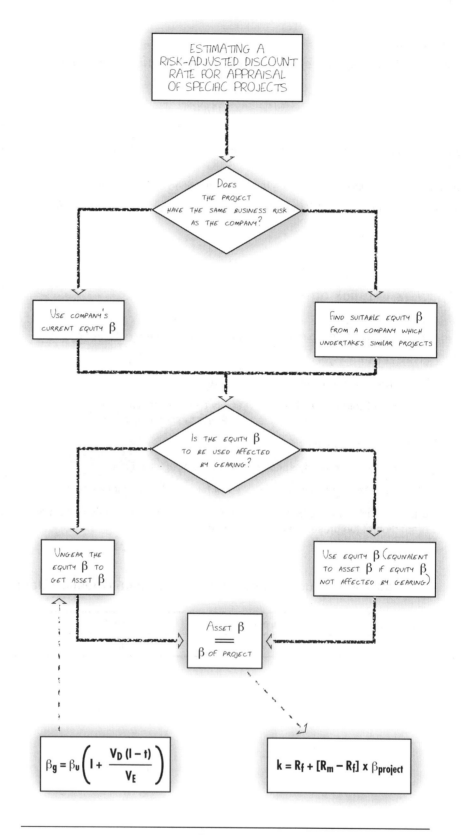

ESTIMATING A
RISK-ADJUSTED DISCOUNT
RATE FOR APPRAISAL
OF SPECIFIC PROJECTS

DOES
THE PROJECT
HAVE THE SAME BUSINESS RISK
AS THE COMPANY?

USE COMPANY'S
CURRENT EQUITY β

FIND SUITABLE EQUITY β
FROM A COMPANY WHICH
UNDERTAKES SIMILAR PROJECTS

IS THE EQUITY β
TO BE USED AFFECTED
BY GEARING?

UNGEAR THE
EQUITY β TO
GET ASSET β

USE EQUITY β (EQUIVALENT
TO ASSET β IF EQUITY β
NOT AFFECTED BY GEARING)

ASSET β
=
β OF PROJECT

$$\beta_g = \beta_u \left(1 + \frac{V_D (1 - t)}{V_E} \right)$$

$$k = R_f + [R_m - R_f] \times \beta_{project}$$

FINANCIAL STRATEGY: GEARING/UNGEARING BETAS

Appendix: Mathematical tables and exam formulae

PRESENT VALUE TABLE

Present value of £1 ie $(1+r)^{-n}$ where r = interest rate, n = number of periods until payment or receipt.

Periods					Interest rates (r)					
(n)	1%	2%	3%	4%	5%	6%	7%	8%	9%	10%
1	0.990	0.980	0.971	0.962	0.952	0.943	0.935	0.926	0.917	0.909
2	0.980	0.961	0.943	0.925	0.907	0.890	0.873	0.857	0.842	0.826
3	0.971	0.942	0.915	0.889	0.864	0.840	0.816	0.794	0.772	0.751
4	0.961	0.924	0.888	0.855	0.823	0.792	0.763	0.735	0.708	0.683
5	0.951	0.906	0.863	0.822	0.784	0.747	0.713	0.681	0.650	0.621
6	0.942	0.888	0.837	0.790	0.746	0.705	0.666	0.630	0.596	0.564
7	0.933	0.871	0.813	0.760	0.711	0.665	0.623	0.583	0.547	0.513
8	0.923	0.853	0.789	0.731	0.677	0.627	0.582	0.540	0.502	0.467
9	0.914	0.837	0.766	0.703	0.645	0.592	0.544	0.500	0.460	0.424
10	0.905	0.820	0.744	0.676	0.614	0.558	0.508	0.463	0.422	0.386
11	0.896	0.804	0.722	0.650	0.585	0.527	0.475	0.429	0.388	0.350
12	0.887	0.788	0.701	0.625	0.557	0.497	0.444	0.397	0.356	0.319
13	0.879	0.773	0.681	0.601	0.530	0.469	0.415	0.368	0.326	0.290
14	0.870	0.758	0.661	0.577	0.505	0.442	0.388	0.340	0.299	0.263
15	0.861	0.743	0.642	0.555	0.481	0.417	0.362	0.315	0.275	0.239
16	0.853	0.728	0.623	0.534	0.458	0.394	0.339	0.292	0.252	0.218
17	0.844	0.714	0.605	0.513	0.436	0.371	0.317	0.270	0.231	0.198
18	0.836	0.700	0.587	0.494	0.416	0.350	0.296	0.250	0.212	0.180
19	0.828	0.686	0.570	0.475	0.396	0.331	0.277	0.232	0.194	0.164
20	0.820	0.673	0.554	0.456	0.377	0.312	0.258	0.215	0.178	0.149

Periods					Interest rates (r)					
(n)	11%	12%	13%	14%	15%	16%	17%	18%	19%	20%
1	0.901	0.893	0.885	0.877	0.870	0.862	0.855	0.847	0.840	0.833
2	0.812	0.797	0.783	0.769	0.756	0.743	0.731	0.718	0.706	0.694
3	0.731	0.712	0.693	0.675	0.658	0.641	0.624	0.609	0.593	0.579
4	0.659	0.636	0.613	0.592	0.572	0.552	0.534	0.516	0.499	0.482
5	0.593	0.567	0.543	0.519	0.497	0.476	0.456	0.437	0.419	0.402
6	0.535	0.507	0.480	0.456	0.432	0.410	0.390	0.370	0.352	0.335
7	0.482	0.452	0.425	0.400	0.376	0.354	0.333	0.314	0.296	0.279
8	0.434	0.404	0.376	0.351	0.327	0.305	0.285	0.266	0.249	0.233
9	0.391	0.361	0.333	0.308	0.284	0.263	0.243	0.225	0.209	0.194
10	0.352	0.322	0.295	0.270	0.247	0.227	0.208	0.191	0.176	0.162
11	0.317	0.287	0.261	0.237	0.215	0.195	0.178	0.162	0.148	0.135
12	0.286	0.257	0.231	0.208	0.187	0.168	0.152	0.137	0.124	0.112
13	0.258	0.229	0.204	0.182	0.163	0.145	0.130	0.116	0.104	0.093
14	0.232	0.205	0.181	0.160	0.141	0.125	0.111	0.099	0.088	0.078
15	0.209	0.183	0.160	0.140	0.123	0.108	0.095	0.084	0.074	0.065
16	0.188	0.163	0.141	0.123	0.107	0.093	0.081	0.071	0.062	0.054
17	0.170	0.146	0.125	0.108	0.093	0.080	0.069	0.060	0.052	0.045
18	0.153	0.130	0.111	0.095	0.081	0.069	0.059	0.051	0.044	0.038
19	0.138	0.116	0.098	0.083	0.070	0.060	0.051	0.043	0.037	0.031
20	0.124	0.104	0.087	0.073	0.061	0.051	0.043	0.037	0.031	0.026

CUMULATIVE PRESENT VALUE TABLE

This table shows the present value of £1 per annum, receivable or payable at the end of each year for n years $\dfrac{1-(1+r)^{-n}}{r}$.

Periods					Interest rates (r)					
(n)	1%	2%	3%	4%	5%	6%	7%	8%	9%	10%
1	0.990	0.980	0.971	0.962	0.952	0.943	0.935	0.926	0.917	0.909
2	1.970	1.942	1.913	1.886	1.859	1.833	1.808	1.783	1.759	1.736
3	2.941	2.884	2.829	2.775	2.723	2.673	2.624	2.577	2.531	2.487
4	3.902	3.808	3.717	3.630	3.546	3.465	3.387	3.312	3.240	3.170
5	4.853	4.713	4.580	4.452	4.329	4.212	4.100	3.993	3.890	3.791
6	5.795	5.601	5.417	5.242	5.076	4.917	4.767	4.623	4.486	4.355
7	6.728	6.472	6.230	6.002	5.786	5.582	5.389	5.206	5.033	4.868
8	7.652	7.325	7.020	6.733	6.463	6.210	5.971	5.747	5.535	5.335
9	8.566	8.162	7.786	7.435	7.108	6.802	6.515	6.247	5.995	5.759
10	9.471	8.983	8.530	8.111	7.722	7.360	7.024	6.710	6.418	6.145
11	10.368	9.787	9.253	8.760	8.306	7.887	7.499	7.139	6.805	6.495
12	11.255	10.575	9.954	9.385	8.863	8.384	7.943	7.536	7.161	6.814
13	12.134	11.348	10.635	9.986	9.394	8.853	8.358	7.904	7.487	7.103
14	13.004	12.106	11.296	10.563	9.899	9.295	8.745	8.244	7.786	7.367
15	13.865	12.849	11.938	11.118	10.380	9.712	9.108	8.559	8.061	7.606
16	14.718	13.578	12.561	11.652	10.838	10.106	9.447	8.851	8.313	7.824
17	15.562	14.292	13.166	12.166	11.274	10.477	9.763	9.122	8.544	8.022
18	16.398	14.992	13.754	12.659	11.690	10.828	10.059	9.372	8.756	8.201
19	17.226	15.679	14.324	13.134	12.085	11.158	10.336	9.604	8.950	8.365
20	18.046	16.351	14.878	13.590	12.462	11.470	10.594	9.818	9.129	8.514

Periods									Interest rates (r)	
(n)	11%	12%	13%	14%	15%	16%	17%	18%	19%	20%
1	0.901	0.893	0.885	0.877	0.870	0.862	0.855	0.847	0.840	0.833
2	1.713	1.690	1.668	1.647	1.626	1.605	1.585	1.566	1.547	1.528
3	2.444	2.402	2.361	2.322	2.283	2.246	2.210	2.174	2.140	2.106
4	3.102	3.037	2.974	2.914	2.855	2.798	2.743	2.690	2.639	2.589
5	3.696	3.605	3.517	3.433	3.352	3.274	3.199	3.127	3.058	2.991
6	4.231	4.111	3.998	3.889	3.784	3.685	3.589	3.498	3.410	3.326
7	4.712	4.564	4.423	4.288	4.160	4.039	3.922	3.812	3.706	3.605
8	5.146	4.968	4.799	4.639	4.487	4.344	4.207	4.078	3.954	3.837
9	5.537	5.328	5.132	4.946	4.772	4.607	4.451	4.303	4.163	4.031
10	5.889	5.650	5.426	5.216	5.019	4.833	4.659	4.494	4.339	4.192
11	6.207	5.938	5.687	5.453	5.234	5.029	4.836	4.656	4.486	4.327
12	6.492	6.194	5.918	5.660	5.421	5.197	4.988	4.793	4.611	4.439
13	6.750	6.424	6.122	5.842	5.583	5.342	5.118	4.910	4.715	4.533
14	6.982	6.628	6.302	6.002	5.724	5.468	5.229	5.008	4.802	4.611
15	7.191	6.811	6.462	6.142	5.847	5.575	5.324	5.092	4.876	4.675
16	7.379	6.974	6.604	6.265	5.954	5.668	5.405	5.162	4.938	4.730
17	7.549	7.120	6.729	6.373	6.047	5.749	5.475	5.222	4.990	4.775
18	7.702	7.250	6.840	6.467	6.128	5.818	5.534	5.273	5.033	4.812
19	7.839	7.366	6.938	6.550	6.198	5.877	5.584	5.316	5.070	4.843
20	7.963	7.469	7.025	6.623	6.259	5.929	5.628	5.353	5.101	4.870

EXAM FORMULAE

Valuation models

(i) Irredeemable preference share, paying a constant annual dividend, d, in perpetuity, where P_0 is the ex-div value:

$$P_0 = \frac{d}{k_{pref}}$$

(ii) Ordinary (equity) share, paying a constant annual dividend, d, in perpetuity, where P_0 is the ex-div value:

$$P_0 = \frac{d}{k_e}$$

(iii) Ordinary (equity) share, paying an annual dividend, d, growing in perpetuity at a constant rate, g, where P_0 is the ex-div value:

$$P_0 = \frac{d_1}{k_e - g} \text{ or } P_0 = \frac{d_0[1 + g]}{k_e - g}$$

(iv) Irredeemable (undated) debt, paying annual after tax interest, $i(1 - t)$, in perpetuity, where P_0 is the ex-interest value:

$$P_0 = \frac{i[1 - t]}{k_{d\,net}}$$

or, without tax:

$$P_0 = \frac{i}{k_d}$$

(v) Total value of the geared firm, V_g (based on MM):

$$V_g = V_u + DT_c$$

(vi) Future value S, of a sum X, invested for n periods, compounded at r% interest:

$$S = X[1 + r]^n$$

(vii) Present value of £1 payable or receivable in n years, discounted at r% per annum:

$$PV = \frac{1}{[1 + r]^n}$$

(viii) Present value of an annuity of £1 per annum, receivable or payable for n years, commencing in one year, discounted at r% per annum:

$$PV = \frac{1}{r}\left[1 - \frac{1}{[1 + r]^n}\right]$$

(ix) Present value of £1 per annum, payable or receivable in perpetuity, commencing in one year, discounted at r% per annum:

$$PV = \frac{1}{r}$$

(x) Present value of £1 per annum, receivable or payable, commencing in one year, growing in perpetuity at a constant rate of g% per annum, discounted at r% per annum:

$$PV = \frac{1}{r - g}$$

Cost of capital

(i)   Cost of irredeemable preference capital, paying an annual dividend d in perpetuity, and having a current ex-div price P_0:

$$k_{pref} = \frac{d}{P_0}$$

(ii) Cost of irredeemable debt capital, paying annual net interest i(1 – t), and having a current ex-interest price P_0:

$$K_{d\,net} = \frac{i[1-t]}{P_0}$$

(iii) Cost of ordinary (equity) share capital, paying an annual dividend d in perpetuity, and having a current ex div price P_0:

$$k_e = \frac{d}{P_0}$$

(iv) Cost of ordinary (equity) share capital, having a current ex div price, P_0, having just paid a dividend, d_0, with the dividend growing in perpetuity by a constant g% per annum:

$$k_e = \frac{d_1}{P_0} + g \ \text{ or } k_e = \frac{d_0[1+g]}{P_0} + g$$

(v)   Cost of ordinary (equity) share capital, using the CAPM:

$$k_e = R_f + [R_m - R_f]\beta$$

(vi) Cost of ordinary (equity) share capital in a geared firm, (no tax):

$$k_{eg} = k_0 + [k_0 - k_d]\frac{V_D}{V_E}$$

(vii) Cost of ordinary (equity) share capital in a geared firm, (with tax):

$$K_{eg} = k_{eu} + [k_{eu} - k_d]\frac{V_D[1-t]}{V_E}$$

(viii) Weighted average cost of capital, k_0:

$$k_0 = k_{eg}\left[\frac{V_E}{V_E + V_D}\right] + k_d\left[\frac{V_D}{V_E + V_D}\right]$$

(ix) Adjusted cost of capital (MM formula)

$$k_{adj} = k_{eu}[1 - tL] \text{ or } r^\star = r[1 - T^\star L]$$

In the following formula, β_u is used for an ungeared β, and β_g is used for a geared β:

(x) β_u from β_g, taking β_d as zero, (no tax):

$$\beta_u = \beta_g\left[\frac{V_E}{V_E + V_D}\right]$$

(xi) β_u from β_g, taking β_d as zero, (with tax):

$$\beta_u = \beta_g\left[\frac{V_E}{V_E + V_D[1-t]}\right]$$

Exam formulae

Other formulae

(i)   Purchasing power parity (Law of one price)

$$\text{Forward rate US\$/£} = \text{Spot US\$/£} \times \frac{1 + \text{US inflation rate}}{1 + \text{UK inflation rate}}$$

(ii)   Interest rate parity (International Fisher effect)

$$\text{Forward rate US\$/£} = \text{Spot US\$/£} \times \frac{1 + \text{nominal US interest rate}}{1 + \text{nominal UK interest rate}}$$

(iii)   Link between nominal (money) and real interest rates

$$[1 + \text{nominal (money) rate}] = [1 + \text{real interest rate}][1 + \text{inflation rate}]$$

(iv)   Equivalent annual cost

$$\text{Equivalent annual cost} = \frac{\text{PV of costs over n years}}{\text{n year annuity factor}}$$

(v)   Theoretical ex-rights price

$$\text{TERP} = \frac{1}{N+1}[(N \times \text{rights on price}) + \text{Issue price}]$$

(vi)   Value of a right

$$\text{Value of a right} = \frac{\text{Rights on price} - \text{Issue price}}{N+1}$$

or

$$\frac{\text{Theoretical ex rights price} - \text{Issue price}}{N}$$

where N = number of rights required to buy one share.

Exam question and answer bank

Some questions of examination standard are given marks.

1   EARNINGS PER SHARE   *20 mins*

The main objective of a listed company is the maximisation of earnings per share. Discuss.

2   CORPORATE GOVERNANCE   *20 mins*

(a)   Describe the main recommendations of the final report of the Committee on the Financial Aspects of Corporate Governance (the Cadbury Report) published in December 1992.

(b)   Discuss the arguments for and against the introduction of statutory controls on corporate governance.

3   SUBSIDIARIES   *36 mins*

Your company has two subsidiaries, X Ltd and Y Ltd, both providing computer services, notably software development and implementation. The UK market for such services is said to be growing at about 20% a year. The business is seasonal, peaking between September and March.

You have available the comparative data shown in the Appendix to this question below. The holding company's policy is to leave the financing and management of subsidiaries entirely to the subsidiaries' directors.

Required

In the light of this information, compare the performance of the two subsidiaries.

It may be assumed that the difference in size of the two companies does not invalidate a comparison of the ratios provided.

Appendix

Data in this Appendix should be accepted as correct. Any apparent internal inconsistencies are due to rounding of the figures.

		X Ltd	Y Ltd
Turnover in most recent year (£'000)			
Home		2,856	6,080
Export		2,080	1,084
Total		4,936	7,164
Index of turnover 20X9			
(20X6 = 100)			
Home		190%	235%
Export		220%	150%
Total		200%	220%
Operating profit 20X9 (£'000)		840	720
Operating capital employed 20X9 (£'000)		625	1,895

Ratio analysis		X Ltd			Y Ltd		
		20X9	*20X8*	*20X7*	*20X9*	*20X8*	*20X7*
Return on operating capital employed	%	134	142	47	38	40	52
Operating profit: Sales	%	17	16	6	10	8	5
Sales: Operating capital employed	×	8	9	8	4	5	10
Percentages to sales value:							
Cost of sales	%	65	67	71	49	49	51
Selling and distribution costs	%	12	11	15	15	16	19
Administration expenses	%	6	6	8	26	27	25
Number of employees		123	127	88	123	114	91
Sales per employee	£'000	40	37	31	58	52	47
Average remuneration per employee	£'000	13	13	12	16	4	13

		X Ltd			Y Ltd		
		20X9	20X8	20X7	20X9	20X8	20X7
Tangible fixed assets							
Turnover rate	×	20	21	14	9	11	14
Additions, at cost	%	57	47	58	303	9	124
Percentage depreciated	%	45	36	20	41	60	72
Product development costs carried							
forward as a percentage of turnover	%	0	0	0	10	8	6
Debtors : Sales	%	18	18	22	61	41	39
Stocks : Sales	%	0	1	0	2	2	1
Cash : Sales	%	7	9	2	1	1	0
Trade creditors : Sales	%	2	2	3	32	21	24
Trade creditors : Debtors	%	11	14	15	53	50	62
Current ratio (:1)		1.5	1.3	1.2	1.1	1.1	0.9
Liquid ratio (:1)		1.5	1.3	1.2	1.0	1.0	0.9
Liquid ratio excluding bank overdraft		0	0	0	1.4	1.5	1.2
Total debt : Total assets	%	61	71	109	75	72	84

Total Marks = 20

4   ALMOND ARTS PLC (Pilot Paper)   *90 mins*

Scenario

Almond Arts plc manufactures and distributes paint and related products to the building trade. It has traded for over 40 years and has been listed on the UK stock market since 1968. The shares are now widely held, with approximately 75 per cent in the hands of institutional investors. Draft, abbreviated financial statements for the year to 31 December 2000 are attached. The company's directors are considering a rights issue to help finance an expansion programme. The first phase of the expansion will involve expenditure of £3 million on fixed assets and £1 million on stock in 2001. Additional capital expenditure of £2 million will be required in 2002.

Assume you are assistant to the finance director. You have been asked to provide some key financial data and supporting evidence for discussion by the board. You have so far obtained the following information based on the assumption that the expansion will go ahead. *Using the draft accounts for the year to 31 December 2000 as a base:*

- Turnover is expected to grow by 5 per cent in the financial year ending 31 December 2001. This increased level of sales is expected to be at least maintained in 2002 and beyond.

- The ratio of cost of sales excluding depreciation to sales (turnover) will improve in 2001 by 2.6 percentage points as a result of improved buying procedures.

- Operating expenses in 2001 are expected to be held constant at the year 2000 level as a result of organisational restructuring and efficiency measures. However, this will involve a one-off charge of £125,000 during the year for redundancy payments.

Other relevant information is as follows.

The company's tax accountant estimates that tax payable for 2001 will be £850,000. Assume tax is paid in the year in which the liability occurs.

The ratios of *debtors to sales* and *trade creditors to cost of sales less depreciation* are expected to remain the same in 2001 as in 2000. Operating expenses are paid in the year in which they occur.

No sales of fixed assets are planned for the next two years. Depreciation on existing and new assets will be £1.2 million in 2001.

Dividends are payable in the year after they are declared. The company plans to maintain the 2000 payout ratio in 2001.

The company's cost of equity is 14 per cent per annum. It uses this rate to evaluate new investments but a full appraisal has not yet been carried out for the expansion proposals.

Assume interest charges for 2001 will relate only to payment on existing fixed rate debt (ie no overdraft interest will be payable).

Inflation is anticipated at between 2 per cent and 3 per cent per annum for 2001. Interest rates on long-term bonds suggest that inflation is likely to rise above 3 per cent in 2002.

Financial objectives

The company's financial objectives are stated as follows.

- To earn an annual after tax return on shareholders' funds (as at the end of each financial year) of at least 25 per cent

- To increase earnings per share and dividends per share by at least 10 per cent per year

- To increase share price year on year without taking undue risk

Draft profit and loss account for the year to 31 December 2000

	£'000
Turnover	16,500
Cost of sales (note 1)	11,600
Operating expenses	1,750
Operating profit	3,150
Interest	200
Corporation tax	885
Net profit	2,065
Dividends declared	1,136
Retained profits	929

Draft balance sheet at 31 December 2000

	£'000
Fixed assets (net book value)	7,500
Current assets	
Stock	2,850
Debtors	1,675
Cash and bank	55
Less: *current liabilities*	
Trade creditors	1,750
Other creditors (dividends)	1,136
Net current assets	1,694
Amounts payable after 1 year	
10% Debentures 2005	2,000
Total assets less liabilities	7,194
Financed by	
Ordinary share capital (ordinary shares of £1)	5,000
Retained profits	2,194
Total shareholders' funds	7,194

Notes

1 Including depreciation of £925,000.

2 *Share price information (pence)*

As at 31 December 1999:	465p	Range for year (1.1.99 - 31.12.99)	425p-535p
As at today (31 December 2000):	525p	Range for year (1.1.00 - 31.12.00)	515p-565p

3 *Other financial information for 1999*

EPS	37.2p
DPS	20.5p
After tax return on shareholders' funds	26.2%

Required

Assume that today is 31 December 2000. Prepare:

(a) (i) A forecast profit and loss account for the year to 31.12.2001

(ii) A forecast balance sheet as at 31.12.2001

(iii) A cash flow forecast for 2001 (this is not an investment appraisal and you do not need to discount your cash flows)

(iv)   Calculations of after tax return on shareholders' funds, earnings per share and dividends per share for the two years 2000 and 2001

Notes

Work to the nearest £'000 for parts (i) and (ii).

Assume that the expansion is to be part-funded by a rights issue of 1 for 10 at 475 pence. Ignore issue costs.

20 Marks

(b)   Write a report to the finance director of Almond Arts plc in which you:

(i)   Discuss the key aspects and implications of the financial information you have obtained in your answer to part (a) of the question, in particular whether the company is likely to achieve its financial objectives in the years to 31 December 2000 and 2001. Include in your discussion comments on the suitability of the financial objectives for the company in its present circumstances and advise on alternative objectives which the directors could consider.

(ii)   Explain the need for financing in 2001 and discuss alternative types of finance that might be suitable for the company at the present time. Use relevant data from the scenario and your answers to part (a) of the question, plus any additional calculations you think appropriate and relevant. Make whatever assumptions you think necessary. If you have been unable to complete your calculations for part (a), use your assumptions as the basis for discussions.

(iii)   Discuss the difficulties of incorporating inflation into forecasts and comment on how a rate of inflation exceeding the 2-3 per cent anticipated for 2001 might affect the achievement of the objectives (you are not expected to rework your figures).

(iv)   Recommend a course of action for the board to consider.   **30 Marks**

Total Marks = 50

5   **ABC**   *15 mins*

The managing directors of three profitable listed companies discussed their company's dividend policies at a business lunch.

Company A has deliberately paid no dividends for the last five years.

Company B always pays a dividend of 50% of earnings after taxation.

Company C maintains a low but constant dividend per share (after adjusting for the general price index), and offers regular scrip issues and shareholder concessions.

Each managing director is convinced that his company's policy is maximising shareholder wealth.

Required

What are the advantages and disadvantages of the alternative dividend policies of the three companies? Discuss the circumstances under which each managing director might be correct in his belief that his company's dividend policy is maximising shareholder wealth. State clearly any assumptions that you make.

6   **MEDICONS PLC (Pilot Paper)**   *45 mins*

MediCons plc provides a range of services to the medical and healthcare industry. These services include providing locum (temporary) cover for healthcare professionals (mainly doctors and nurses), emergency call-out and consultancy/advisory services to government-funded health organisations. The company also operates a research division that has been successful in recent years in attracting funding from various sources. Some of the employees in this division are considered to be leading experts in their field and are very highly paid.

A consortium of doctors and redundant health-service managers started the company in 1989. It is still owned by the same people, but has since grown into an organisation employing over 100 full-time staff throughout the UK. In addition, the company uses specialist staff employed in state-run organisations on a part-time contract basis. The owners of the company are now interested in either obtaining a stock market quotation, or selling the company if the price accurately reflects what they believe to be the true worth of the business.

Summary financial statistics for MediCons plc and a competitor company, which is listed on the UK Stock Exchange, are shown below. The competitor company is broadly similar to MediCons plc but uses a higher proportion of part-time to full-time staff and has no research capability.

	MediCons plc *Last year end:* *31.3.2000*	Competitor *Last year end:* *31.3.2000*
Shares in issue (m)	10	20
Earnings per share (pence)	75	60
Dividend per share (pence)	55	50
Net asset value (£m)	60	75
Debt ratio (outstanding debt as % of total financing)	10	20
Share price (pence)	n/a	980
Beta coefficient	n/a	1.25
Forecasts:		
Growth rate in earnings and dividends (% per annum)	8	7
After tax cash flow for 2000/2001 (£m)	9.2	n/a

Notes

1   The expected post-tax return on the market for the next twelve months is 12 per cent and the post-tax risk-free rate is 5 per cent.

2   The treasurer of the company has provided the forecast growth rate for MediCons plc. The forecast for the competitor is based on published information.

3   The net assets of MediCons plc are the net book values of land, buildings, equipment and vehicles plus net working capital.

4   Sixty per cent of the shares in the competitor company are owned by the directors and their relatives or associates.

5   MediCons plc uses a 'rule-of-thumb' discount rate of 15 per cent to evaluate its investments.

6   Assume that growth rates in earnings and dividends are constant per annum.

7   The post-tax cost of debt for MediCons plc and its competitor is 7 per cent.

Required

Assume that you are an independent consultant retained by MediCons plc to advise on the valuation of the company and on the relative advantages of a public flotation versus outright sale.

Prepare a report for the directors that provides a range of share prices at which shares in MediCons plc might be issued. Use whatever information is available and relevant and recommend a course of action.

Explain the methods of valuation that you have used and comment on their suitability for providing an appropriate valuation of the company. In the report you should also comment on the difficulties of valuing companies in a service industry and of incorporating a valuation for intellectual capital.

Total Marks = 25

Note. Approximately one-third of the marks are available for appropriate calculations, and two-thirds for discussion.

7   **SHARE VALUES**   *25 mins*

(a)   Outline the fundamental analysis theory of share values, giving numerical examples.

(b)   To what extent is the validity of the fundamental analysis theory affected by the efficiency of the stock market?

8   **CASTOR AND POLLUX**   *45 mins*

(a)   Outline the Modigliani-Miller theory on the effect of gearing on the cost of capital to, and value of, the firm, in the absence of taxation. Explain how the theory is adjusted to take into account the effects of taxation. What are the principal weaknesses of this theory?   **10 Marks**

(b) Castor plc and Pollux plc are two companies, operating in the same industry, which have reported identical net operating incomes. The stock market regards the net operating incomes of the two companies as being subject to the same degree of business risk.

Castor plc is financed entirely by equity, its share capital consisting of 20 million 50p shares with a market price of £4.80 per share (ex div). The cost of equity to Castor is estimated to be 18%. Pollux plc is financed by a combination of £20,000,000 12% irredeemable debenture stock (market price £120%) and 30 million £1 ordinary shares.

The risk free rate of interest is 10%. The market prices of Castor plc's shares and Pollux plc's debentures are considered to be in equilibrium.

Required

Using (where appropriate) the Modigliani-Miller propositions, calculate:

(i)   The equilibrium market price of Pollux plc's shares
(ii)   The equilibrium cost of equity to Pollux plc
(iii) The weighted average cost of capital to Pollux plc

Assume (I) no taxation; and (II) corporation tax at 25%. (Make separate calculations for each assumption.)

Ignore dividends and accrued interest on the stocks.   **15 Marks**

Total Marks = 25

9   **KILLISICK AND HOLBECK**   *45 mins*

Killisick plc wishes to acquire Holbeck plc. The directors of Killisick are trying to justify the acquisition to the shareholders of both companies on the grounds that it will increase the wealth of all shareholders. The supporting financial evidence produced by Killisick's directors is summarised below.

	Killisick	Holbeck
	£'000	£'000
Operating profit	12,400	5,800
Less interest payable	4,431	2,200
Profit before tax	7,969	3,600
Less taxation	2,789	1,260
Earnings available to ordinary shareholders	5,180	2,340
Earnings per share (pre-acquisition)	14.80 pence	29.25 pence
Market price per share (pre-acquisition)	222 pence	322 pence
Estimated market price (post-acquisition)	240 pence	
Estimated equivalent value of one old Holbeck share (post-acquisition)		360 pence

Payment is to be made with Killisick ordinary shares, at an exchange ratio of 3 Killisick shares for every 2 Holbeck shares.

Required

(a) Show how the directors of Killisick produced their estimates of post-acquisition value and, if you do not agree with these estimates, produce revised estimates of post-acquisition values. All calculations must be shown. State clearly any assumptions that you make.   **10 Marks**

(b) If the acquisition is contested by Holbeck plc, using Killisick's estimate of its post-acquisition market price calculate the maximum price that Killisick could offer without reducing the wealth of its existing shareholders.   **3 Marks**

(c) The board of directors of Holbeck plc later informally indicate that they are prepared to recommend to their shareholders a 2 for 1 share offer.

   Further information regarding the effect of the acquisition on Killisick is given below.

   (i)   The acquisition will result in an increase in the total pre-acquisition after tax operating cash flows of £2,750,000 a year indefinitely.

   (ii)   Rationalisation will allow machinery with a realisable value of £7,200,000 to be disposed of at the end of the next year.

   (iii) Redundancy payments will total £3,500,000 immediately and £8,400,000 at the end of the next year.

   (iv)   Killisick's cost of capital is estimated to be 14% a year.

   All values are after any appropriate taxation. Assume that the pre-acquisition market values of Killisick and Holbeck shares have not changed.

Recommend, using your own estimates of post-acquisition values, whether Killisick should be prepared to make a 2 for 1 offer for the shares of Holbeck. **6 Marks**

(d) Disregarding the information in (c) above and assuming no increase in the total post-acquisition earnings, assess whether this acquisition is likely to have any effect on the value of debt of Killisick plc. **6 Marks**

Total Marks = 25

---

10   NEWBEGIN ENTERPRISES LTD
45 mins

Newbegin Enterprises Ltd is considering whether to invest in a project which would entail immediate expenditure on capital equipment of £40,000. Expected sales from the project are as follows.

Probability	Sales volume (*Units*)
0.10	2,000
0.25	6,000
0.40	8,000
0.15	10,000
0.10	14,000

Once sales are established at a certain volume in the first year, they will continue at that same volume in later years. The unit price will be £10, the unit variable cost will be £6 and additional fixed costs will be £20,000. The project would have a life of six years, after which the equipment would be sold for scrap to earn £3,000. The company's cost of capital is 10%.

Required

(a) What is the expected value of the NPV of the project? **5 Marks**

(b) What is the minimum annual volume of sales required to justify the project? **5 Marks**

(c) Making whatever assumptions are necessary, describe (giving calculations) several different methods of analysing the risk or uncertainty in the project. **15 Marks**

Total Marks = 25

---

11   QW PLC (Pilot Paper)
45 mins

Assume that you are treasurer of QW plc, a company with diversified, international interests. The company wishes to borrow £10 million for a period of three years. Your company's credit rating is good and current market data suggests that you could borrow at a fixed rate of interest at 8 per cent per annum or at a floating rate of LIBOR + 0.2 per cent per annum. You believe that interest rates are likely to fall over the next three years, and favour borrowing at a floating rate.

Your company's bankers are currently working on raising a three-year loan for another of their customers, ER plc. This company is smaller and less well known than QW plc, and its credit rating is not as high. ER plc could borrow at a fixed rate of 9.5 per cent per annum or a floating rate of LIBOR + 0.5 per cent. ER plc has indicated to the bank that it would prefer a fixed-rate loan. Your bankers have suggested you engage in a swap which might benefit both companies. The bank's commission would be 0.2 per cent of the benefits to the two parties. Your counterpart in ER plc suggests that the commission fees and swap benefits should be shared equally.

Assume that interest is paid at the end of each twelve-month period of the loan's duration and that the principal is repaid on maturity (ie at the end of three years).

You have been in post for twelve months, having been recruited from a large financial institution. You have a keen interest in using financial derivatives (such as futures and options) to both manage risk and generate revenue. Some board members have expressed concern that your activities may be involving the company in unnecessary risk.

Required

Write a report to the board which:

(a) Explains the meaning and use of financial derivatives, in general terms, and the advantages and disadvantages of their use for companies such as QW plc **8 Marks**

(b)   Describes the characteristics and benefits of interest rate swaps compared with other forms of interest-rate-risk management, such as forward rate agreements and interest rate futures

8 Marks

(c)   Explains the course of action necessary to implement the swap being considered with ER plc, and calculates and comments on the financial benefits to be gained from the operation   **9 Marks**

Total Marks = 25

12   OXLAKE PLC   *45 mins*

Oxlake plc has export orders from a company in Singapore for 250,000 china cups, and from a company in Indonesia for 100,000 china cups. The unit variable cost to Oxlake of producing china cups is 55. The unit sales price to Singapore is Singapore $2.862 and to Indonesia, 2,246 rupiahs. Both orders are subject to credit terms of 60 days, and are payable in the currency of the importers. Past experience suggests that there is 50% chance of the customer in Singapore paying 30 days late. The Indonesian customer has offered to Oxlake the alternative of being paid US $125,000 in 3 months time instead of payment in the Indonesian currency. The Indonesian currency is forecast by Oxlake's bank to depreciate in value during the next year by 30% (from an Indonesian viewpoint) relative to the US dollar.

Whenever appropriate, Oxlake uses option forward foreign exchange contracts.

Foreign exchange rates (mid rates)

	$Singapore/$US	$US/£	Rupiahs/£
Spot	2.1378	1.4875	2,481
1 month forward	2.1132	1.4963	No forward
2 months forward	2.0964	1.5047	market exists
3 months forward	2.0915	1.5105	

Assume that any foreign currency holding in the UK will be immediately converted into sterling.

	Money market rates (% per year)	
	Deposit	Borrowing
UK clearing bank	6	11
Singapore bank	4	7
Euro-dollars	7½	12
Indonesian bank	15	Not available
Euro-sterling	6½	10½
US domestic bank	8	12½

These interest rates are fixed rates for either immediate deposits or borrowing over a period of two or three months, but the rates are subject to future movement according to economic pressures.

Required

(a)   Using what you consider to be the most suitable way of protecting against foreign exchange risk, evaluate the sterling receipts that Oxlake can expect from its sales to Singapore and to Indonesia, without taking any risks.

All contracts, including foreign exchange and money market contracts, may be assumed to be free from the risk of default. Transactions costs may be ignored.   **13 Marks**

(b)   If the Indonesian customer offered another form of payment to Oxlake, immediate payment in US dollars of the full amount owed in return for a 5% discount on the rupiah unit sales price, calculate whether Oxlake is likely to benefit from this form of payment.   **7 Marks**

(c)   Discuss the advantages and disadvantages to a company of invoicing an export sale in a foreign currency.   **5 Marks**

Total Marks = 25

13   BAILEY SMALL (Pilot Paper)   *45 mins*

Bailey Small plc is an importer/exporter of heavy machinery for a variety of industries. It is based in the UK but trades extensively with the USA. Assume that you are a newly appointed management accountant with Bailey Small plc. The company does not have a separate treasury function and it is part of your duties to assess and manage currency risks. You are concerned about the recent fluctuations in the exchange rate between US$ and sterling and are considering various methods of hedging the exchange risk involved. Assume it is now the end of March. The following transactions are expected on 30 June.

Sales receipts	$450,000
Purchases payable	$250,000

Economic data

- The spot rate of exchange is US$41.6540-1.6590 to the £.

- The US$ premium on the three-month forward rate of exchange is 0.82-0.77 cents.

- Annual interest rates for three months' borrowing are: USA 6 per cent; UK 9 per cent.

- Annual interest rates for three months' lending are: USA 4 per cent; UK 6.5 per cent.

- Option prices (cents per £, contract size £12,500):

	Calls		Puts	
Exercise price $	June	September	June	September
1.60	-	15.20	-	-
1.65	2.65	7.75	-	3.45
1.70	1.70	3.60	-	9.32

Assume that there are three months from now to expiry of the June contracts.

Required

(a) Calculate the net sterling receipts that Bailey Small plc can expect from its transactions if the company hedges the exchange risk using each of the following alternatives:

    (i)   The forward foreign exchange market
    (ii)   The money market

Accompany your calculations with brief explanations of your approach and recommend the most financially advantageous alternative for Bailey Small plc. Assume transaction costs would be 0.2 per cent of the US$ transaction value under either method, paid at the beginning of the transaction (ie now). **8 Marks**

(b) Explain the factors the company should consider before deciding to hedge the risk using the foreign currency markets, and identify any alternative actions available to minimise risk. **5 Marks**

(c) Discuss the relative advantages and disadvantages of using foreign currency options compared with fixed forward contracts. To illustrate your arguments assume that the actual spot rate in three months' time is 1.6458-1.6513, and assess whether Bailey Small plc would have been better advised to hedge using options, rather than a fixed forward contract. **12 Marks**

Total Marks = 25

14   **DINARD PLC**   *35 mins*

(a) Explain the difference between real rates of return and money rates of return and outline the circumstances in which the use of each would be appropriate when appraising capital projects under inflationary conditions

(b) Dinard plc has just developed a new product to be called Rance and is now considering whether to put it into production. The following information is available.

    (i)   Costs incurred in the development of Rance amount to £480,000.

    (ii)   Production of Rance will require the purchase of new machinery at a cost of £2,400,000 payable immediately. This machinery is specific to the production of Rance and will be obsolete and valueless when that production ceases. The machinery has a production life of four years and a production capacity of 30,000 units per annum.

    (iii) Production costs of Rance (at year 1 prices) are estimated as follows.

	£
Variable materials	8.00
Variable labour	12.00
Variable overheads	12.00

In addition, fixed production costs (at year 1 prices), including straight line depreciation on plant and machinery, will amount to £800,000 per annum.

(iv)   The selling price of Rance will be £80.00 per unit (at year 1 prices). Demand is expected to be 25,000 units per annum for the next four years.

(v)   The retail price index is expected to increase at 5% per annum for the next four years and the selling price of Rance is expected to increase at the same rate. Annual inflation rates for production costs are expected to be as follows.

	%
Variable materials	4
Variable labour	10
Variable overheads	4
Fixed costs	5

(vi)   The company's weighted average cost of capital in money terms is expected to be 15%.

Required

Advise the directors of Dinard plc whether it should produce Rance on the basis of the information above.

Notes

Unless otherwise specified all costs revenues should be assumed to rise at the end of each year.

Ignore taxation.

15   ANTARES PLC   *45 mins*

Antares plc, a multi-product company, is considering four investment projects, details of which are given below.

Development costs already incurred on the projects are as follows.

A	B	C	D
£	£	£	£
100,000	75,000	80,000	60,000

Each project will require an immediate outlay on plant and machinery, the cost of which is estimated as follows.

A	B	C	D
£	£	£	£
2,100,000	1,400,000	2,400,000	600,000

In all four cases the plant and machinery has a useful life of five years at the end of which it will be valueless.

Unit sales per annum, for each project, are expected to be as follows.

A	B	C	D
£	£	£	£
150,000	75,000	80,000	120,000

Selling price and variable costs per unit for each project are estimated below.

	A	B	C	D
	£	£	£	£
Selling price	30.00	40.00	25.00	50.00
Materials	7.60	12.00	4.50	25.00
Labour	9.80	12.00	5.00	10.00
Variable overheads	6.00	7.00	2.50	10.50

The company charges depreciation on plant and machinery on a straight line basis over the useful life of the plant and machinery. Development costs of projects are written off in the year that they are incurred. The company apportions general administration costs to projects at a rate of 5% of selling price. None of the above projects will lead to any actual increase in the company's administration costs.

Working capital requirements for each project will amount to 20% of the expected annual sales value. In each case this investment will be made immediately and will be recovered in full when the projects end in five years time.

Funds available for investment are limited to £5,200,000. The company's cost of capital is estimated to be 18%.

Required

(a) Calculate the NPV of each project. **12 Marks**

(b) Calculate the profitability index for each project and advise the company which of the new projects, if any, to undertake. You may assume that each of the projects can be undertaken on a reduced scale for a proportionate reduction in cash flows. Your advice should state clearly your order of preference for the four projects, what proportion you would take of any project that is scaled down, and the total NPV generated by your choice.

5 Marks

(c) Discuss the limitations of the profitability index as a means of dealing with capital rationing problems. **8 Marks**

Ignore taxation. **Total Marks = 25**

---

16 DA COSTA PLC (Pilot Paper) *45 mins*

DaCosta plc is a manufacturer of expensive, built-to-order motor cars. The company has been trading for 25 years and has seen year-on-year growth of sales and profits. Whereas most of the large, mass-production motor manufacturers have experienced over-capacity and falling profit margins in recent years, DaCosta plc has a waiting list of six months for a new car. All cars are manufactured in the UK, but there are sales outlets throughout Europe and the Far East. The chief executive of the company, who is still the major shareholder, is considering extending the distributor network into the USA where there is a rising demand. At present, American customers have to order direct from the UK.

A detailed assessment of the costs and likely incremental revenues of opening distributorships into major US cities has been carried out. The initial cost of the investment is US$4.5 million. The cash flows, all positive and net of all taxes, are summarised below.

Year	1	2	3	4
Cash flow (US$million)	1.75	1.95	2.50	3.50

The following information is available.

*   The expected inflation rate in the USA is 2 per cent a year.

*   Real interest rates in the UK and USA are the same. They are expected to remain the same for the foreseeable future.

*   The current spot rate is US$1.6 per £1 sterling.

*   The risk-free rate of interest in the USA is 4 per cent per annum and in Britain 5 per cent per annum. These rates are not expected to change in the foreseeable future.

*   The company's post-tax WACC is 14 per cent per annum, which it uses to evaluate all investment decisions.

*   The company is financed by £10 million shareholders' funds (book values) and £2 million long-term debt which is due to be retired in two years' time.

The company can finance part of the investment from cash flow but, as it is also expanding operations in the UK, the chief executive would prefer external finance if this is available on acceptable terms. He has noted that borrowing rates in the euro-debt market appear very favourable at the present time. At 3 per cent they are below the rates in both the UK and the USA.

Required

(a) Calculate the *sterling* net present value of the project using both of the following methods:

(i)   By discounting annual cash flows in sterling
(ii) By discounting annual cash flows in US$ **10 Marks**

(b)   Discuss:

    (i)   The use of WACC as a discount rate in an international investment decision, in general terms and as it applies to DaCosta plc

    (ii)   The main risk to be faced by a company such as DaCosta plc when it moves into a new international market, and how it might manage those risks

    (iii)   The main methods of financing overseas operations and the factors that the company should consider before making a decision about borrowing in euro debt   **15 Marks**

Total Marks = 25

---

17   DARON   *63 mins*

The senior managers of Daron, a company located in a European country, are reviewing the company's medium-term prospects. The company is in a declining industry, and is heavily dependent on a single product. Sales volume is likely to fall for the next few years. a general election will take place in the near future and the managers believe that the future level of inflation will depend upon the result of the election. Inflation is expected to remain at approximately 5% if political party a wins the election, or will quickly move to approximately 10% per year if party b wins the election. Opinion polls suggest that there is a 40% chance of party b winning. An increase in the level of inflation is likely to reduce the volume of sales of Daron.

Projected financial data for the next five years, including expected inflation where relevant, are shown below.

Political party A wins, inflation 5% per year

			$million		
	20X7	*20X8*	*20X9*	*20Y0*	*20Y1*
Operating cash flows:					
Sales	28	29	26	22	19
Variable costs	17	18	16	14	12
Fixed costs	3	3	3	3	3
Other financial data:					
Incremental working capital*	-	(1)	(2)	(3)	(3)
Tax allowable depreciation	4	3	3	2	1

Political party B wins, inflation 10% per year

			$million		
	20X7	*20X8*	*20X9*	*20Y0*	*20Y1*
Operating cash flows:					
Sales	30	26	24	20	16
Variable costs	18	16	15	12	11
Fixed costs	3	3	4	4	4
Other financial data:					
Incremental working capital*	1	(2)	(2)	(3)	(3)
Tax allowable depreciation	4	3	3	2	1

* A bracket signifies a decrease in working capital.

Tax allowable depreciation will be negligible after 20Y1 in both cases. Cash flows after year 20Y1, excluding tax savings from tax allowable depreciation, are expected to be similar to year 20Y1 cash flows for a period of five years, after which substantial new fixed investment would be necessary in order to continue operations.

Working capital will remain approximately constant after the year 20Y1. Corporation taxation is at a rate of 30% per year, and is expected to continue at this rate. Tax may be assumed to be payable in the year that the income arises.

Daron's current ordinary share price is 92 centos. (100 centos = $1)

Summarised balance sheet of Daron as at 31 March 20X6

	$ million
Tangible fixed assets	24
Net current assets	12
Total assets less current liabilities	36
Loans and other borrowings falling due after one year	14
Capital and reserves:	
Called up share capital (25 centos par value)	5
Reserves	17
	36

The company can currently borrow long-term from its bank at an interest rate of 10% per year. This is likely to quickly rise to 15.5% per year if the political party B wins the election. The real risk free rate (ie excluding inflation) is 4% and the real market return is 10%.

Daron's equity beta is estimated to be 1.25. This is not expected to significantly change if inflation increases.

Three alternatives are available to the managers of Daron.

(i) Recommend the sale of the company now. An informal, unpublicised, offer of $20 million for the company's shares has been received from a competitor.

(ii) Continue existing operations, with negligible capital investment for the foreseeable future.

(iii) If the political party A wins the election, diversify operations by buying a going concern in the hotel industry at a cost of $9 million. The purchase would be financed by the issue of 10% convertible debentures. Issue costs are 2% of the gross sum raised. Daron has no previous experience of the hotel industry.

Financial projections for the hotel purchase

	$million				
	20X7	*20X8*	*20X9*	*20Y0*	*20Y1*
Turnover	9	10	11	12	13
Variable costs	6	6	7	7	8
Fixed costs	2	2	2	2	2
Other financial data:					
Incremental working capital	1	-	-	1	-

Tax allowable depreciation is negligible for the hotel purchase. The after tax realisable value of the hotel at the end of year 20Y1 is expected to be $10 million, including working capital. The systematic risk of operating the hotels is believed to be similar to that of the company's existing operations.

Required

Using the above data, prepare a report advising the managers of Daron which, if any, of the three alternatives to adopt. Include in your report comment on any weaknesses/limitations of your data analysis. Relevant calculations, including:

(a) Estimates of the present values of future cash flows from existing operations; and
(b) The estimated adjusted present value of diversifying into the hotel industry

should form appendices to your report.

The book value and market value of debt may be assumed to be the same. State clearly any other assumptions that you make.

Total Marks = 35

1   EARNINGS PER SHARE

Maximisation of wealth

The fundamental assumption which underlies financial theory is that the sole purpose of the existence of a company is to **increase the wealth** of its owners by the maximum amount possible. In other words, the primary purpose is to increase the wealth of the ordinary shareholders. This proposal will be investigated to determine to what extent such an aim coincides with the maximisation of earnings per share.

Maximisation means that the directors will try to obtain the **best possible results** from a given situation and will not settle for a level of performance that is merely satisfactory (satisficing). It might appear that to aim at maximising rather than satisficing earnings will be in the interests of the ordinary shareholders. However, the effects of the aim of maximisation of earnings can only be evaluated in the context of the directors' attitude to **risk**. It might mean that very risky investments are being undertaken since they yield potentially the highest returns. However, this could have the side effect of **depressing** the **share price** and thereby the **market value** of the company, which in turn represents a fall in the wealth of the shareholders. Further, if new equity needs to be raised, a larger number of shares will need to be issued if the price is depressed, and thus in the long term, earnings per share could even be reduced.

How wealth is increased

The wealth of the shareholders can be increased in two ways: by a **rise** in the **market price** of the **shares**, or by means of a **distribution of dividends**.

An **increase in earnings per share** means that there will be more profits available for distribution as dividend, and that there will be more profits that can be retained within the firm to invest in further expansion and earnings growth. This implies that the financial worth of the company will be increased, and as a result, the market price of the shares can be expected to rise. In the long term, therefore, there will be a relationship between shareholder wealth and earnings per share, since a proportion of the earnings will be paid out as dividend and the remainder reinvested to provide future growth in profits and dividends. However, there is a risk that a company may seek to increase earnings per share in the short term at the expense of **longer term development** and therefore earnings. Thus the relationship is only valid if the directors take a long term view of maximising earnings per share in setting their targets.

Other objectives

The statement in the question implies the acknowledged fact that companies do not have one single objective, but operate within a matrix of different objectives, both **financial** and **non-financial**. These other objectives are frequently formulated with the aim of assisting the achievement of the main objective, for example, a division of the company may be set the target of achieving a minimum rate of return on capital employed of 20%. However, these subsidiary targets are frequently evaluated over a short-term period, typically six months to a year. Thus they can come into **conflict** with the primary aim of maximising earnings in the long term. Other objectives may act as a **constraint on** the primary objective. For example, a financial constraint might be that a ceiling is set on the permitted level of gearing in order to limit the financial risk of the company. In a more highly geared company, the proportion of equity is lower and therefore the potential level of earnings per share is higher, albeit with a higher level of risk of annual fluctuations as the interest rate varies.

Non-financial objectives include, for example, to act scrupulously in relationships with customers and suppliers; to operate fair and generous personnel policies; to have competitive remuneration levels and good training and development programmes; and to achieve the highest standards that can reasonably be maintained in environmental policies. These policies do not necessarily run counter to the aim of maximising earnings per share, and may even enhance it by improving the image of the firm in its operating environment. However they will act as at least a short-term constraint upon the maximisation of earnings per share and shareholder wealth.

Conclusion

To conclude, it has been shown that the timescale over which decisions are evaluated is important in deciding the degree to which the maximisation of earnings per share is successful in achieving the maximisation of shareholder wealth, the two becoming increasingly similar as the timescale lengthens. However, this situation will always be subject to important constraints imposed by subsidiary financial and non-financial objectives.

2 CORPORATE GOVERNANCE

(a) The main recommendation of the Cadbury report was that the boards of all listed companies should comply with the 'Code of Best Practice' defined in the report. A 'statement of compliance' with the Code should become a listing requirement and the directors of all UK companies should use the Code for guidance. In accounts, directors should state whether the report and accounts comply with the Code and give reasons for any non-compliance.

Some of the principal items in the Code are as follows.

(i) The board of directors should **meet regularly** and monitor the performance of the executive management.

(ii) There should be a **separation of powers** at the top of the firm. This should be achieved either by a separation of the posts of chairman and chief executive, or by ensuring that there is a strong independent group present on the board.

(iii) There should be a **formal schedule of matters** that must be **referred to the board** such as material acquisitions and disposals, capital investments and borrowings.

(iv) The board should include a number of **fully independent non-executive directors**.

(v) Directors' contracts should normally be for a **maximum of three years**, and all emoluments should be fully disclosed. Directors' pay should be decided by a separate remuneration committee which, following the Greenbury Committee recommendations, should have its report included in the company's annual report and accounts.

(vi) An **audit committee** should be appointed with the authority, resources and access to investigate anything within its terms of reference. It should have at least one meeting per year with the auditors when no executive directors are present.

(vii) The directors should report on the **effectiveness** of the **internal control systems**.

(viii) The board should present a **clear and balanced assessment** of the **company's position**, together with a going concern statement supported by any necessary assumptions or qualifications.

(b) It is not totally correct to talk about the introduction of statutory control on corporate governance since there has been some degree of control for a considerable time through such instruments as the Companies Acts. An example is the regulations governing the appointment and responsibilities of directors. However, many of the controls commonly accepted by firms are not statutory in nature but are generally agreed codes of practice. An example of this is the **City Code** on Takeovers and Mergers which has no legal backing but is administered and enforced by the Takeover Panel.

Recent incidents in the City have increased the pressure for stricter statutory controls. Particular areas of concern include:

(i) **Accounting policies** which are **misleading** as to the true financial health of the company, for example in the area of the capitalisation of intangibles

(ii) The **weakness** of the **shareholders' control** over the directors' investment decisions

(iii) The **lack of clearly defined rules** for the governance and investment of pension funds

From the viewpoint of firms which try to follow the spirit of the law and abide by such regulations as do exist, further legislation will only add to the burden of overheads. There could be a large increase in the amount of litigation, some of it for unintentional breaches of detailed rules. This is happening now in the waste management industry which is subject to much more stringent statutory regulation than most other industries. However, unless all firms do comply not only with the letter but also with the spirit of the legislation it is very likely that more legislation will be introduced in the near future.

3 SUBSIDIARIES

Profitability

X Ltd is the **more profitable** company, both in **absolute terms** and in **proportion to sales** and to **operating capital employed**. This may indicate that X Ltd is much better managed than Y Ltd, but this is not the only possibility, and a study of the other data shows that Y Ltd's profitability, while at present lower, may be more sustainable.

Asset usage

While Y appears to be making worse use of its assets than X, with **asset turnover ratios** lower than X's and falling, this seems to be largely because Y has recently acquired substantial new assets. It may be that within the next few years X will have to undertake a major renewals programme, with consequent adverse effects on its asset turnover ratios.

Sales

A higher percentage of Y's sales are to the home market, while it has still achieved fairly substantial export sales. This suggests that Y could have done better in **exploiting** the **export market**, but also that Y is less exposed than X to **exchange rate fluctuations** and the possible imposition of **trade barriers**. The prospects for the home market appear good, and should give scope for adequate growth. Y has achieved higher growth in total turnover than X over the past three years.

Y is making **sales per employee** about 50% higher than X, and has consistently done so over the past three years. X shows no sign of catching up, despite the fact that its total number of employees has recently fallen slightly. The modest rises in sales per employee over the past three years in both X and Y may be due largely to inflation.

Costs

Y seems to be significantly better than X at controlling the cost of sales (49% of sales in Y, and 65% in X), though X has made improvements over the past three years while there has been little change in Y. On the other hand, X's **administration expenses** have been only 6% of sales, while Y's have been 26% of sales. This contrast between the two types of cost suggests that different categorisations of costs may have been used. If we combine the cost of sales and administration expenses, then for X they total 71% of sales and for Y they total 75% of sales. There is thus little difference between the companies, though X has shown improved cost control while Y has not. X has also had **lower selling and distribution costs**. One must however bear in mind that X will have had a lower depreciation element in its costs than Y, because Y has recently invested substantially in fixed assets. Y's costs will also be increased by its higher salaries, which may pay off in better employee motivation and hence higher sales per employee. On the other hand, Y's costs have been kept down by the carrying forward of an increasing amount of product development costs, an accounting policy which may well be imprudent.

Working capital management

In working capital management, X has the edge. Y has **very high debtors**, and these have recently risen sharply as a proportion of turnover. Y also carries rather more **stock** than X, and has very little cash. While both companies have tolerable current and liquid ratios, X's are certainly safer. Y achieves a liquid ratio of 1:1 almost entirely by relying on debtors. If it suffers substantial bad debts, or if the bank should become concerned and call in the overdraft, Y could suffer serious **liquidity problems**. It also depends heavily on trade credit to finance debtors. While it is sensible to take advantage of trade credit offered, Y may depend too much on the continued goodwill of its suppliers. This may indicate the need for a fresh injection of equity.

Conclusion

On balance, X seems to be a sounder company than Y, with better financial management.

4   **ALMOND ARTS PLC**

> **Tutorial note.** The question is divided into two parts, calculations and discussions. However, it is impossible to attempt the discussion section competently without having first completed the calculations.
>
> When attempting the calculations, be sure to take account of all the information provided in the question, since the way in which certain figures are to be calculated is actually quite closely defined.
>
> Although the majority of the calculations fall in the first part of the question, you will need to undertake further numerical analysis within the main body of the report.

(a)   (i)   **Almond Arts plc: Forecast profit and loss account for the year to 31 December 2001**

	Note	£'000
Turnover	1	17,325
Cost of sales	2	10,759
Depreciation		1,200
Operating expenses		1,750
Operating profit		3,616
Interest	3	200
Redundancy payment		125
Corporation tax		850
Net profit		2,441
Dividends declared	4	1,343

Notes

1   Turnover is expected to grow by 5% from £16,500,000 to £17,325,000.

2

	£'000
Cost of sales y/e 31.12.00	11,600
Less depreciation	925
	10,675
As a percentage of sales	64.7%
Expected reduction in percentage	2.6%
Percentage of sales for y/e 31.12.01	62.1%
Cost of sales for y/e 31.12.01	10,759

3   Debenture interest = £2,000,000 × 10%

4   The existing payout ratio is 31,136/2,065 = 55%.

      This payout ratio will be applied to the net profit for the year of £2,441,000.

(ii)   **Almond Arts plc: Forecast balance sheet as at 31 December 2001**

	Note	£'000	£'000
Fixed assets (net book value)	1		9,300
Current assets			
Stock	2		3,850
Debtors	3		1,759
Cash and bank	4		865
Less: current liabilities			
Trade creditors	5	1,764	
Other creditors (dividends)	6	1,343	
			3,107
Net current assets			3,367
Amounts falling due after 12 months			
10% debentures 2005			2,000
Total net assets			10,667

	Note	£'000	£'000
Financing			
Ordinary share capital	7		5,500
Share premium account	8		1,875
Reserves	9		3,292
Total shareholders' funds			10,667

Notes

1

	£'000
Opening fixed assets	7,500
Additions for year	3,000
Less depreciation	1,200
Closing fixed assets	9,300

2 Stock will increase by £1,000,000 on the 31.12.00 figure.

3 The ratio of debtors to sales at 31.12.00 is 1,675/16,500 = 10.15%.

If this is applied to the 2001 sales of £17,325,000, the closing debtors will be £1,759,000.

4 This can be calculated most quickly as the balancing figure:

	£'000
Shareholders' funds	10,667
Net assets excluding cash	9,802
Closing cash balance	865

Note. This figure can be cross checked once the cash flow forecast has been completed.

5 The ratio of trade creditors to cost of sales at 31.12.00 is 1,750/10,675 = 16.39%.

If this is applied to the 2001 cost of sales of £10,759,000, the closing creditors will be £1,764,000.

6 From forecast profit and loss account.

7

	£'000
Share capital at 31.12.00	5,000
1 for 10 rights issue	500
Share capital at 31.12.01	5,500

8 The rights issue will raise 500,000 × 4.75 = £2,375,000. The nominal value of the new shares is £500,000. The balance of £1,875,000 must be credited to the share premium account.

9

	£'000
Opening reserves	2,194
Add net profit for year	2,441
Less dividend	1,343
Closing reserves	3,292

(iii) **Almond Arts plc: Cashflow forecast for the year to 31.12.2001**

	Note	£'000	£'000
Income arising from operations:			
Operating profit			3,616
Add back depreciation			1,200
Increase in debtors	1		(84)
Increase in creditors	2		14
Total			4,746
Less			
Investment in fixed assets		3,000	
Investment in stock		1,000	
Interest paid		200	
Corporation tax paid		850	
Dividends paid		1,136	
Redundancy payment		125	
Total			6,311
Net cash flow from operations			(1,565)
New capital from rights issue			2,375
Total cash flow for the year			810
Opening cash balance			55
Closing cash balance			865

Notes

1 1,675 – 1,759 = (84)

2 1,750 – 1,764 = 14

3 The dividend paid in the year to 31.12.01 is the dividend declared for the previous year.

(iv) The after tax return on shareholders' funds can be found by dividing the profit available for dividend by the total shareholders' funds as at the year end.

Note: there is an argument for using the **average** level of shareholders' funds in the calculation, but the financial objective of the company defines shareholders' funds as the **year end** figure.

	2000 £'000	2001 £'000
Profit available for dividend	2,065	2,441
Shareholders' funds	7,194	10,667
Return on shareholders' funds	**28.7%**	**22.9%**

Earnings per share can be found by dividing the profit available for dividend by the total number of shares in issue at the end of the year.

	2000	2001
Profit available for dividend (£'000)	2,065	2,441
Number of shares in issue	5,000	5,500
Earnings per share	**41.3p**	**44.4p**

Dividend per share can be found by dividing the dividend declared for the year by the total number of shares in issue at the end of the year.

	2000	2001
Dividend declared (£'000)	1,136	1,343
Number of shares in issue	5,000	5,500
Dividend per share	**22.7p**	**24.4p**

(b) To: Finance Director, Almond Arts plc
From: Assistant to Finance Director
Date: 31.12.2000

Re: Review of forecast financial performance for the period 1.1.2000 - 31.12.2001

Introduction

This report is concerned with the forecast financial performance of the company for the years 2000 and 2001. There are a number of points that the board should consider in its planning for the next year, and which will be discussed in more detail below.

- The likely level of performance in relation to the stated financial objectives.
- The need for additional financing during 2001.
- The effect of inflation upon the forecast figures.
- Alternative measures of financial performance that could be introduced.

Performance against stated financial objectives

1 *After-tax return on shareholders' funds*

Almond Arts plc has the objective of earning an annual after-tax return on shareholders' funds of at least 25%. The forecasts suggest that this target will be met for the year to 31.12.2000, with a return of 28.7%. However, the forecast for 2001 indicates a rate of return of 22.9%, which is below the target level. The main reason for the shortfall is the **significant level of investment** that is planned for the year, since net profits are forecast to increase by 18% during the same period.

It is a weakness of using this type of accounting measure that the calculated returns do go down at the start of a period of investment. This can translate into a temptation to cut back on entirely necessary investment as a means of improving short-term performance.

2 *Annual 10% increase in earnings per share*

The forecast performance against this measure is as follows.

	1999	2000	2001
Earnings per share (pence)	37.2	41.3	44.4
Annual increase (pence)	4.1	3.1	
Annual increase (percent)	11.0	7.5	

This performance target should be met in 2000, but the company will fall well short of this in 2001. There are two main reasons for this:

- The **rights issue** will increase the number of shares in issue before the benefits of the new investment are reflected in the earnings figure.

- The **one-off payment** of **redundancy costs** will depress the earnings figure.

Once again, this is more a problem of the measure used than of the likely long-term performance of the company. This situation is likely to persist, even when the EPS is adjusted for comparability due to the change in the number of shares in issue, as demanded by the FRS.

3   *Annual 10% increase in dividend per share*

The forecast performance against this measure is as follows.

	1999	2000	2001
Dividend per share (pence)	20.5	22.7	24.4
Annual increase (pence)	2.2	1.7	
Annual increase (percent)	10.7	7.5	

As with EPS, this performance target should be met in 2000, but the company will fall well short in 2001. Maintenance of the **payout ratio** at 55% means that the growth in dividend per share will directly reflect the rate of growth in earnings per share. The company would need to make a significant change to the payout ratio to meet this target, largely due to the increase in the number of shares in issue. Although in theory shareholders should be indifferent between capital appreciation and dividends, in practice there is often a **preference for dividends** at the expense of capital growth. This is because investors will usually opt for certain cash now in the form of dividends, rather than waiting for capital growth to be achieved.

The payout ratio is the crux of a major tension in company investment policy. **Shareholders desire** a good level of **dividends** that increase year on year, while **companies** often prefer to **retain earnings** as a simple way of financing future investment. Restricting dividends may cause a loss of confidence by the markets and impact upon the share price, and for this reason companies will often prefer to finance new investments by means of debt.

4   *To increase share price year on year*

The share price provides a measure of the value of the company. Although in theory this is determined by the present value of future cash flows, discounted at the cost of capital, in practice other factors will also influence the share price. The overall level of **market confidence, interest rates and takeover activity** will all affect the price of the company's shares. For this reason, it would be more helpful to specify the target as the level of the share price in relation to the overall level of the market, rather than considering it in isolation.

Given these provisos, the share price at the end of 2000 is higher than that at the end of 1999 (525p as compared with 465p), and thus the company appears to have met this target for the current year. The closing share price for 2001 can be estimated using the dividend valuation model and on the basis of the P/E ratio:

Dividend valuation model:

$$P_0 = \frac{d_0(1+g)}{(k_e - g)}$$

where P_0 =   current market price of share (ex div)
        d_0 =   current net dividend per share
        k_e =   shareholders' cost of capital
        g =   expected annual rate of growth in dividends

The cost of capital is 14%, and a 10% rate of dividend growth will be assumed. The net dividend per share will be taken as the dividend forecast of £1,343,000 for 2001.

$$P = \frac{1,343(1 + 0.10)}{(14\% - 10\%)}$$

P   =   £36.9m

Price per share = £36.9m ÷ 5.5m = £6.71

P/E ratio:

The current P/E ratio can be found by dividing the share price of 525p by the EPS of 41.3p = 12.7. If this is applied to the earnings forecast for 2001 of £2,441, the estimated market capitalisation is £31m. This equates to a price per share of £5.64.

Both these approaches suggest that the share price will increase by the end of 2001, with the dividend valuation model predicting the largest increase. This is because this model incorporates the expected growth rate that is expected to result from the investment programme, whereas the P/E ratio method does not.

The need for additional financing during 2001

The cash flow forecast shows that in the absence of any additional financing, there will be a negative cash flow during the year of £1.565m. This is due to the significant investment of £4m in fixed assets and stock that will take place during the period. However, if profits growth continues at 5% per annum the cash flow for 2002 and 2003 should be roughly as follows:

	Notes	2002	2003
		£'000	£'000
Cash flow from operations	1	4,983	5,232
Less			
Interest	2	200	200
Dividends	3	1,343	1,477
Taxation	4	935	1,029
Fixed assets		2,000	
Net cash flow from operations		505	2,527
Opening cash balance		865	1,370
Closing cash balance		1,370	3,897

Notes:

1   It is assumed that the income arising from operations will continue to grow at 5% per year, and that efficiency savings will offset inflationary increases in costs.

2   It is assumed that there will be no interest payments beyond those due on the debentures.

3   The dividend for 2002 is that forecast to be declared at the end of 2001. It is assumed that dividends will increase by 10% per year in line with the performance targets.

4   It is assumed that tax will increase at 10% per year in line with earnings.

In the absence of the rights issue being made, the cash position would be as follows.

	2001	2002	2003
	£'000	£'000	£'000
Opening cash balance	55	(1,510)	(1,005)
Cash flow for year	(1,565)	505	2,527
Closing cash balance	(1,510)	(1,005)	1,522

While it is acknowledged that these figures are very rough, they do seem to indicate that the company will only have a **cash deficit** for two years, with the cash balance becoming positive during the first half of 2003. This raises the question as to whether the company should be making a **large rights issue** to finance the investment, particularly given the effect of this on the performance indicators highlighted above. If the cash shortage is only a temporary situation, the company should consider using some form of **short or medium-term finance** to cover the deficit. The issue of additional permanent capital should only be made if there are further profitable investments in the pipeline.

Alternative sources of funds in this situation include:

*   A medium-term bank loan

*   Financing the new assets by the use of hire purchase agreements or a finance lease

*   Staging the expenditure more gradually and using short-term finance

- Retaining a higher proportion of earnings for the next one or two years - this would require a significant change in the company's existing dividend policy

The effect of inflation upon the forecast figures

At present, low inflation is forecast for the period in question, and therefore the effect upon the forecast figures is likely to be low. However, this assumes that all the elements of the cost base will be subject to the general level of inflation. In practice, there is considerable variability in the level of inflation between different cost factors, and if there were to be a **significant increase** in the **cost of key raw materials** for example, this could have a major impact upon the forecasts. In addition, there are signs that **wages** are increasing at a higher level than prices, and this could have a significant impact upon a manufacturing company such as Almond Arts.

The figures in the forecasts appear to be in nominal terms, ie with an allowance for inflation. The true situation might be clearer if figures were restated in **real terms** for comparison.

If inflation began to rise at a level above the 3% forecast, the impact would depend upon the way in which the different variables were affected, and the extent to which Almond Arts would be able to recover its costs through **increases** in **selling prices**. However, higher inflation would be likely to result in an improvement in the reported ratios on which performance is judged. This is because the dividend and earnings ratios are calculated on the basis of the **book value** of the assets, and it is unlikely that the entire asset base would be revalued immediately in the event of a rise in the level of inflation.

Alternative measures of financial performance

It has become apparent throughout the foregoing discussion that there are weaknesses in the use of the current financial performance targets. The main area on which attention should be focussed is the extent to which the company is achieving an **increase** in the **level of shareholder wealth**, and the use of proxies for this such as dividend per share can be misleading. It would perhaps be more helpful to focus on the market capitalisation and P/E ratio of the company in relation to the sector as a whole.

Another approach would be to take a **wider view** of the **company's activities** and direct attention to performance against a basket of ratios that would measure performance in the key areas of:

- Profitability and return
- Liquidity and working capital management
- Debt and gearing
- Shareholders' investment ratios

Although such an approach would be less specific, it might assist the company to make better long-term decisions.

Conclusions and recommendations

The forecasts suggest that the proposed investment will be **beneficial** in terms of both **returns** and **cash flow**. However, the following issues should be addressed before final decisions are taken regarding the investment and its financing.

All new investments are evaluated at the cost of capital of 14%. Since this is a major new investment for the company, the **specific risks** attaching to the project should be investigated and compared with the risk profile of the existing operations. If necessary, the discount rate should be adjusted to reflect any significant differences.

The **sensitivity** of the project outcome to changes in the key variables should be analysed.

The **method of financing** the project should be **re-evaluated**. It appears that the company will become cash positive again within three years if no new capital is raised, and therefore the possibility of using medium-term finance rather than additional permanent capital should be investigated.

There should be a review of the company's financial objectives and the way in which they are measured.

5   **ABC**

A's policy

Company A, which has deliberately avoided paying any dividends in the last five years, is pursuing a sensible policy for a rapidly growing company. All its post-tax profits are being **reinvested** in the company's business. By adopting this strategy, Company A reduces to a minimum its need to raise new capital from the market. **Issue costs** are **reduced** or **eliminated** and the company has greater flexibility in its investment programme since decision taking is not dependent on gaining market approval. Furthermore, since the company is probably investing heavily its taxation liability may well be small.

B's policy

At first sight the policy pursued by Company B, of distributing 50% of post-tax profits, appears to offer the shareholders **predictability**. In fact, however, with changes in the company's operating profits and in the tax regime, the post-tax earnings may fluctuate considerably. **Reducing** the **dividend** of a quoted company normally causes its **share price** to **fall sharply**, since the market takes this as casting considerable doubt on its future earnings potential. But, the more **mature** and **predictable** that Company B's business is, the greater the merit in its dividend policy. A mature business usually needs less new capital investment than a growing one and so a higher level of dividend is justified. Distributing profits allows shareholders to make some adjustment to the risk and return profile of their portfolios without incurring the transaction costs of buying and selling.

C's policy

Company C's policy falls between those of A and B in that a dividend is paid, albeit a small one. The **predictability** of the dividend will be welcomed by shareholders, since it allows them to make their financial plans with more certainty than would otherwise be possible. It also gives C part of A's advantage; **retained earnings** can be used as the principal source of investment capital. To the extent that they are relevant at all, scrip issues are likely to increase a company's market value, since they are often made to increase the marketability of the shares. Shareholder concessions are simply a means of attracting the 'small' shareholder who can benefit from them personally, and have no impact on dividend policy.

Effect on shareholders

In addition to looking at the cash flows of each company, we must also consider the impact of these dividend policies on the after tax wealth of shareholders. Shareholders can be divided into groups or **'clienteles'**. Different clienteles may be attracted to invest in each of the three firms, depending on their tax situation. It is worth noting that one clientele is as good as another in terms of the valuation it implies for the firm.

Company A would be particularly attractive to individuals who do not require an income stream from their investment and prefer to obtain a **return** through **capital growth**. Company B's clientele prefer a much higher proportion of their return to be in the form of **income**, although it would not be income on which they rely since it may be very variable from year to year. **Tax exempt funds**, such as pension funds, are indifferent between returns in the form of income or capital and might well invest in B since they need a flow of income to meet their day to day obligations. A large, diversified portfolio would reduce the effect of variability in the dividend. Company C is more likely to appeal to the **private investor** since most of the return is in the form of capital growth and there are shareholder concessions too.

So, each company may maximise the wealth of its shareholders. If the theorists are right, A, B and C all **maximise shareholder wealth** because the value of the companies is unaffected by dividend policy. Alternatively, each company's group of shareholders may favour their company's policy (and so their wealth is maximised) because the dividend policy is appropriate to their tax position and so maximises their post-tax returns.

6   MEDICONS PLC

> **Tutorial note**. This is a lengthy question that addresses a number of areas of knowledge, including the valuation of intellectual capital, share valuation, and the issues surrounding a Stock Market flotation. The answer is required in a report format, and you should map out an appropriate structure that will allow you to address all the key issues.
>
> When applying the dividend valuation model to MediCons plc, there are a number of approaches that could be taken. However, the most appropriate route is to calculate the WACC for the competitor, and then to adjust for the different levels of gearing in the two companies.

To: Board of directors, MediCons plc
From: Independent consultant
Date: dd.mm.yy

Re: Valuation of MediCons plc

Introduction

This report deals with the alternative methods available for the valuation of the shares in the company. It also seeks to highlight some of the key issues to be addressed in arriving at an appropriate valuation for this type of company, and looks at the relative merits of public flotation versus an outright sale of the business.

Company valuation

There are four main valuation techniques that could be appropriate in this situation:

1   Net assets basis
2   Price/earnings ratio
3   Dividend valuation model
4   Discounting the future earnings stream

These will be discussed in more detail below.

1   Net assets basis

This method arrives at a price for the business on the basis of the **market** value of the **asset base**. It is most commonly used to arrive at a **break-up value** for businesses with a significant amount of fixed assets. However, it is less appropriate for service businesses, and in particular for those in which the majority of the value is in the form of **human** and/or **intellectual capital**. In the latter type of company, a net assets valuation can be attempted if the intangibles are included as assets in the balance sheet. However, a significant part of the value of MediCons plc resides in its research division, and this is not reflected at all in the company's present balance sheet. Although it could be argued that items such as brands should be included in the balance sheet so as to make the market more aware of the true value of the company, in reality it is extremely difficult both to arrive at and to retain an appropriate measure of these types of items. A further argument against the incorporation of this type of intangible is that if the company is publicly quoted, and if the market shows semi-strong or strong form efficiency, then the market price of the shares should reflect this information in any case.

In view of these points, there is little point in attempting a net assets valuation for MedCons plc at the present time. The inappropriateness of this can be illustrated with reference to the competitor, which would have a theoretical net assets based valuation of £75m as compared with a market capitalisation of £196m (£9.80 share price × 20m shares in issue).

2   Price/earnings ratio

This method compares the earnings information of the company with that of **other companies** of **similar size** and **characteristics** that operate in the same markets, to arrive at an appropriate market price for the shares. The information that has been provided for the quoted competitor will be used to arrive at an initial price, but this will need to be adjusted to reflect the fact that the competitor lacks MediCons' research capability.

The price/earnings (P/E) ratio is calculated by **dividing** the **market price** of the **shares** by the **earnings per share**. The competitor has a P/E ratio of 16.3 (980p/60p). Although this is above the average for quoted industrial companies as a whole, it does not appear to be unreasonably high for the medical sector. Given that MediCons plc is forecasting better growth prospects than the competitor, and also has a research capability, it seems reasonable to value the company on a P/E of around 18 times. This would value MediCons plc at £135m (18 × 75p × 10m shares in issue). However, if the shares were to be offered on the open market, it would be prudent to price them at a **discount** to this to reflect the fact that the company would be a new entrant to the stock market, despite an eleven year trading history. Pricing at a discount will also make the issue more attractive to investors and thereby help to obtain a good take-up of shares.

Valuation on a P/E of 18 implies a price of £13.50 per share. If the shares were to be offered at a discount of, say, 15%, this would result in an offer price of around £11.50 per share, and a market capitalisation of £115m.

3   **Dividend valuation model**

The dividend valuation model has the central assumption that the market value of shares is directly related to the expected future dividends on those shares. It can be expressed as:

$$P_0 \quad = \quad \frac{d_0(1+g)}{(k_e - g)}$$

where	P_0	=	current market share price (ex div)
d_0	=	current net dividend per share
k_e	=	shareholders' cost of capital
g	=	expected annual rate of growth in dividends

Since the shares are not yet quoted, it is not possible to say exactly what the shareholders' net **cost of capital** is likely to be. However, given the comments about comparability above, it might be reasonable to apply the competitor's cost of capital to provide a first estimate. In order to do this it is necessary to calculate the weighted average cost of capital (WACC) for the competitor. The first stage in this process is to calculate the cost of equity for the competitor, which can be done using the capital asset pricing model (CAPM):

$$k_e \quad = \quad R_f + (R_m - R_f)\,\beta$$

where	k_e	=	cost of equity
R_f	=	risk free rate of return
R_m	=	market rate of return
β	=	beta value

In this case:

$$k_e \quad = \quad 5\% + (12\% - 5\%)1.25$$

$$k_e \quad = \quad 13.75\%$$

Since it is known that the debt ratio of the competitor is 20%, and that the post-tax cost of debt is 7%, the WACC can now be found using the following expression:

$$\text{WACC} \quad = \quad \frac{k_e(V_E)}{(V_E + V_D)} + \frac{k_d(V_D)}{(V_E + V_D)}$$

where	k_e	=	cost of equity
k_d	=	post-tax cost of debt
V_E	=	proportion of equity in capital structure
V_D	=	proportion of debt in capital structure

In this case:

$$\text{WACC} \quad = \quad \frac{(13.75\% \times 80)}{(80 + 20)} + \frac{(7\% \times 20)}{(80 + 20)}$$

$$\text{WACC} \quad = \quad 12.4\%$$

This WACC can now be adjusted to take into account the different debt ratio in MediCons plc to provide an estimate of the cost of equity:

$$12.4\% \quad = \quad \frac{(k_e \times 90)}{(90 + 10)} + \frac{(7\% \times 10)}{(90 + 10)}$$

$$12.4\% \quad = \quad 0.9k_e + (0.1 \times 7\%)$$

$$k_e \quad = \quad \frac{12.4\% - 0.7\%}{0.9}$$

$$k_e = 13\%$$

This cost of equity can now be used in the dividend valuation model to estimate the market value of MediCons plc:

$$P_0 = \frac{d_0(1 + g)}{(k_e - g)}$$

$$P_0 = \frac{(55p \times 10m) \times (1 + 8\%)}{(13\% - 8\%)}$$

$$P_0 = £118.8m$$

The dividend valuation model values the company at £118.8m, or £11.88 per share. This assumes a growth rate of 8%. However in reality the **potential growth** rate may be **higher** since the company is currently evaluating investments at a discount rate that is above the estimated cost of capital. This means that it may be turning down investments that would in fact add value to the company.

The same method of valuation can be applied to the competitor for comparative purposes:

$$P_0 = \frac{(50p \times 20m) \times (1 + 7\%)}{(13.75\% - 7\%)}$$

$$P_0 = £158.5m \text{ or } £7.92 \text{ per share}$$

4   **Discounting the future earnings stream**

This method involves discounting the future long-term earnings stream at the shareholders' cost of capital to arrive at a value for the company. However, there is insufficient information available to use this approach here; much more information about the long-term cash flow projections and estimates of terminal values is needed before this method could be attempted.

The relative advantages of flotation and direct sale

The following points should be considered when deciding which option is to be preferred.

Flotation will **create** a **wider market** for the company's shares. This has the twin benefits that it will be easier for the company to **raise additional capital** to finance expansion, and that the existing shareholders will be able to **realise** all or part of their holding. However, if MediCons plc is to achieve a good price, the existing owners should aim to retain the major part of their holding for a reasonable period following the flotation.

Flotation will allow the company to **offer share option schemes** to its employees, which should assist in the recruitment and retention of good staff. This is particularly important in a company such as MediCons plc, where a significant part of the value in the company is linked to the knowledge base and research capability. Retaining a high proportion of the key staff will be vital to the success of any change in ownership, and must be taken into account in the structuring of either the sale or the flotation.

Flotation will be an **expensive process** and will mean that the company has to comply with the stringent **Stock Exchange regulations**. It will put extra administrative burdens on the management and will cost more to organise than would a direct sale of the business.

The aims of the existing owners are important in **determining** the best course of action. If a significant number of the existing consortium wish to maintain control over the business in the future, then they are more likely to be able to achieve this if the company is floated rather than sold.

Conclusions and recommendations

The calculations suggest that the company should achieve a **sale price** of at least £120m. This compares with a market capitalisation of the competitor of £196m. Since MediCons has better growth prospects and also has a research base, which the competitor lacks, it may be able to achieve a better price than this, but £120m should be regarded as the base price in any negotiations.

It is also recommended that the company should opt for a **Stock Market quotation** rather than for a direct sale. Given the current state of the market for this type of stock, it should be able to achieve a good price, and flotation will also give flexibility to the owners in allowing them to realise a part of their investment, while at the same time retaining control over the future direction of the business.

7 SHARE VALUES

(a) **Fundamental analysis**

The fundamental analysis theory of share values states that the value of a share is the **present value** of the **expected future dividends**. No buyer would pay more for the share than this amount, because he would only have to invest this amount elsewhere to obtain the same income stream; and no seller would accept less than this amount, as to do so would involve an avoidable loss of wealth.

The theory assumes that there is a **single discount rate** applicable to all investors and potential investors in the shares (of one class) in a given company. This rate is applied to the expected future dividends to obtain a present value.

Examples

(i) X plc is expected to pay a dividend of 30p a share each year for ever, starting one year from now. An appropriate discount rate is 25%. The current market value per share (ex div) should be 30p/0.25 = £1.20.

(ii) Y plc is expected to pay a dividend of 21p a share one year from now. Thereafter, dividends are expected to rise by 3% a year. An appropriate discount rate is 15%. The current market value (taking into account the expected dividend growth) is:

$$\frac{21}{1.15} + \frac{21 \times 1.03}{1.15^2} + \frac{21 \times 1.03^2}{1.15^3} + \ldots = \frac{21}{0.15 - 0.03} = 175p = £1.75$$

The theory can be applied to the **valuation** of **interest-bearing securities**. The income stream from such securities is usually known with certainty, whereas future dividends from shares can only be estimated. With redeemable securities, not only the interest but also the amount due on maturity must be discounted in arriving at a present value.

(b) **Efficient stock market**

In an **information-efficient stock market**, **no one investor dominates** the **market, transaction costs** are not a **significant deterrent** to dealing and the prices at which shares are bought and sold reflect all available relevant information. Share prices will therefore be set in a rational way, taking account of the prospects for companies, and one would expect the fundamental analysis theory to apply. Exactly how it would apply would depend on the level of efficiency of the stock market, which is considered below.

Inefficient stock market

If the stock market is inefficient, **share prices** may **differ significantly** and **permanently** from what the fundamental analysis theory would lead one to expect. A dominant investor or high dealing costs may distort prices; and if share prices do not reflect all available relevant information about companies, they may come to bear little relation to likely future dividends.

The level of efficiency of a stock market in this sense depends on the extent to which **market prices reflect relevant information**. Under **weak form efficiency**, only information about **past price** movements and their implications is reflected in current market prices; under **semi-strong** form efficiency, all **publicly available information** is reflected in **current market prices**; and under **strong form efficiency**, even **confidential information** (such as secret plans for new investments) is reflected in current market prices.

Information about a company, such as recent results or a proposed new investment, is normally known to only a few people at first. It is published, and after a while several investors will have dealt in the company's shares at prices which reflect the information. Thus whatever the level of efficiency of the stock market, if it is efficient at all then share prices will eventually reflect each item of relevant information about the company. Share prices should therefore be determined according to the principles of the **fundamental analysis theory**, although perhaps after some delay, even if the stock market shows only weak form efficiency.

8 CASTOR AND POLLUX

(a) **Modigliani and Miller's theory** of capital structure differs from the traditional view in its assumptions about shareholder behaviour. As a consequence they questioned the view that there is an optimal level of gearing that reduces the cost of capital and maximises the total market value of the firm. They showed that it is the **income generated** from the business activities of the firm which determines value and not the way in which this income is allocated between the providers of capital. If the shares of two firms with different levels of gearing but the same level of business risk are traded at different prices, then **shareholders** will **switch** their **investment** from the **overvalued** to the **undervalued firm**. At the same time they will **adjust** their **level of personal borrowing** through the market in order to maintain their overall level of business risk at the same level. This process which is called arbitrage will result in the firms having the same equilibrium total value.

The implications of the theory for the firm's **cost of capital** and **total market value** at different levels of gearing can best be illustrated graphically.

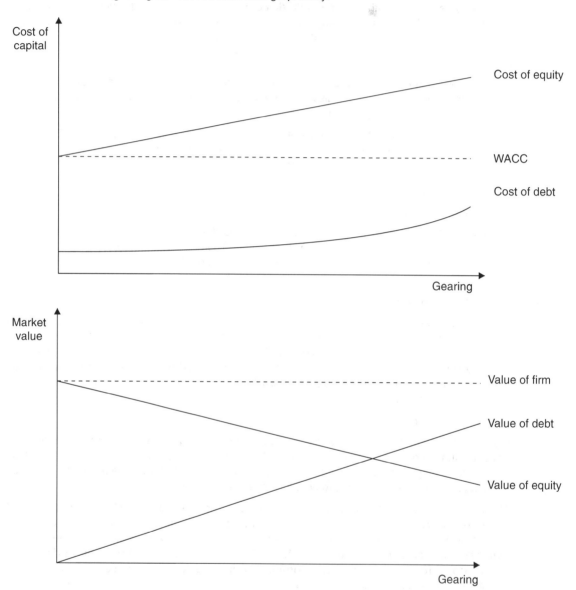

When **taxation is introduced** into the **model**, the total market value of the firm is no longer independent of its capital structure. This is because **interest on debt** is **allowable against tax**. The market value of the firm now increases with gearing, the amount of the increase being equal to the present value of the tax shield on the interest payments. This also means that the WACC declines as the gearing increases.

The main weaknesses of the theory arise from its simplifying assumptions.

(i)   In defining the arbitrage process it is assumed that **personal borrowing** is a **perfect substitute** for **corporate borrowing**. This is unlikely to be true in practice since the private investor does not have the protection of limited liability and cannot usually negotiate such good rates as the corporate borrower.

(ii)   It is assumed that **all earnings** are **paid** out as **dividend**. In practice a variable proportion of earnings is normally retained.

(iii) It is extremely **difficult** to **identify firms** with **identical business risk** and **operating profiles**.

(iv) It is assumed that **investors' only criteria** are **risk and return**. In practice, investors will also be concerned with other factors such as the ethical stance of the company, and they do not have perfect information about the market.

The theory begins to break down at very high levels of gearing since firms in this situation are normally heading for bankruptcy. For all these reasons, it has not been possible for the theory to be fully proved empirically.

(b) (i) Since the companies are identical in every respect apart from their level of gearing, in the absence of taxation their total market value will be equal.

The total market value of Castor = 20m shares × £4.80 = £96m

The total market value of Pollux is therefore also £96m. The total market value of a geared company is given by:

$$MV_p = V_E + V_D$$

where: MV_p = market value of Pollux
V_E = market value of equity
V_D = market value of debt

In the case of Pollux, V_D = £20m × 120% = £24m. The market value of the equity can now be found:

$$£96m = V_E + £24m$$
$$E = £72m$$

There are 30m shares in issue. The equilibrium share price will therefore be £72m/30m = £2.40 per share

If the rate of corporation tax is 25%, the total value of the company will be increased by the tax shield on the interest payments:

$$V_g = V_u + DT_c$$
where V_g = market value of the geared company
V_u = market value of the ungeared company
D = market value of debt
T_c = rate of corporation tax

In this case:
$$V_g = £96m + (£24m × 0.25) = £102m$$

Of this, £78m (£102m – £24m) is attributable to equity. The theoretical equilibrium share price will therefore be £78m/30m = £2.60 per share.

(ii) Since the companies are identical in every respect, in the absence of taxation they will have the same WACC.

In the case of Castor which is totally equity financed, the WACC will be the same as the cost of equity, ie 18%. The WACC for Pollux will also therefore be 18%. The cost of debt is 10% (12%/120%). The market values of debt and equity are known and therefore the cost of equity can be found using the expression:

$$WACC = k_e × \frac{V_E}{V_E + V_D} + k_d × \frac{V_D}{V_E + V_D}$$

where: k_e = cost of equity
k_d = cost of debt
$V_E/(V_E+V_D)$ = 72m/96m = 75%
$V_D/(V_E+V_D)$ = 24m/96m = 25%
18% = $(k_e × 75\%) + (10\% × 25\%)$
k_e = $(18\% – (10\% × 25\%))/75\%$ = 20.67%

If **taxation** is to be taken into account, it has been shown that the total market value of the company will rise due to the PV of the tax shield on the debt interest. This increase in value will accrue to the ordinary shareholders. The level of dividends in the absence of tax can be calculated using the dividend valuation model:

$$k_e = d/p_o$$

where: k_e = cost of equity
d = annual level of dividends
p_o = market value of equity
$20.67\% = d/£72m$
d = £14.8824m

The annual value of the **tax shield** on the **debt interest** is £0.6m (£20m × 12% × 25%). The dividend valuation model can now be used again to find the cost of equity if this amount is added to the dividend total:

$$k_e = \frac{£14.8824m + £0.6m}{£78.0m} = 19.85\%$$

(iii) In the absence of taxation, the WACC of Pollux will be identical to that of Castor, ie 18%. If taxation is to be taken into account, then the WACC can be found using the expression:

$$WACC = k_e \times \frac{V_E}{V_E + V_D} + k_d(1 - T_c) \times \frac{V_D}{V_E + V_D}$$

$$WACC = \frac{19.85\% \times 78}{78 + 24} + \frac{10\%(1 - 0.25) \times 24}{78 + 24}$$

9   KILLISICK AND HOLBECK

(a)

	Killisick plc	Holbeck plc
Earnings	£5,180,000	£2,340,000
EPS	14.8p	29.25p
Number of shares	35,000,000	8,000,000

An offer of three shares in Killisick for two shares in Holbeck would result in the equity of Killisick increasing to 47,000,000 shares.

In order to establish how the estimated post-acquisition market price of Killisick was reached, we must look at P/E ratios.

	Killisick plc	Holbeck plc
Pre-acquisition price	222	322
EPS	14.8	29.25
P/E ratio, pre-acquisition	15	11

The post-acquisition earnings, assuming no synergy or growth, would be (5,180 + 2,340) £7,520,000 or (÷ 47 million shares) 16p a share.

The estimated post-acquisition share price of Killisick plc is 240p. On the assumption that the post-acquisition EPS is 16p, the P/E ratio would be 15.

It would therefore seem that the estimated post-acquisition market price of Killisick plc shares has been derived by applying the pre-acquisition P/E ratio of Killisick to an estimated post-acquisition EPS (assuming no profits growth through synergy).

The estimated post-acquisition equivalent market value of an old Holbeck share is 1.5 times 240 pence, because three Killisick shares will be exchanged for two Holbeck shares, giving a relative value of 3:2 or 1.5.

These estimates cannot be realistic, because it is incorrect to assume that on a takeover where neither company is minuscule relative to the other, the post-acquisition P/E ratio will be the same as the pre-acquisition P/E ratio of the more highly rated company in the takeover.

Killisick is hoping to take over a public company with a **lower P/E ratio** than its own, and its directors must expect Killisick's post-acquisition P/E ratio to fall accordingly.

A better estimate of the post acquisition P/E ratio would be the *weighted average* of their pre-acquisition P/Es as follows.

	Earnings £'000		Market value £'000
Killisick	5,180	(35m × 222p)	77,700
Holbeck	2,340	(8m × 322p)	25,760
Combined	7,520		103,460

Weighted average P/E ratio $\frac{103,460}{7,520}$ = 13.758

Applying this to a post-acquisition EPS of 16p, an estimated post-acquisition market price of Killisick plc shares would be (13.758 × 16p) 220p each. This would make the post-acquisition equivalent MV of an old Holbeck share (220 × 1.5) = 330p.

There would be a very slight gain for Holbeck plc shareholders at the expense of Killisick plc shareholders, but not much. This is because the share exchange ratio of three for two reflects almost exactly the pre-acquisition market prices per share of 322:222 = 1.45 or nearly 1.50, which is 3:2.

(b)

	£'000
Value of 35 million Killisick shares:	
Estimated post-acquisition value (× 240p)	84,000
Pre-acquisition value (× 222p)	77,700
Gain to Killisick shareholders from acquisition (× 18p)	6,300

Killisick plc could raise its offer by £6,300,000 without reducing the wealth of its shareholders, but only assuming that the 240p estimate of the post-acquisition share price is correct. This extra value might be offered in cash (£0.7875 per share in Holbeck) or in more shares in Killisick.

(c) The pre-acquisition market value of Killisick plc is unchanged at 222p, and so a two-for-one share exchange offer would value each share in Holbeck at 444p as well, compared with its current 322p.

	£'000
Offer value for 8,000,000 shares in Holbeck (× 444p)	35,520
Current value of 8,000,000 shares in Holbeck (× 322p)	25,760
Excess	9,760

The revised offer would only maintain the wealth of current shareholders if the combined share values of the post-acquisition company were to increase by at least £9,760,000.

It is assumed that the value of the post-acquisition company will be increased by the NPV of the asset disposals, savings in running costs and extra redundancy costs, discounted at Killisick's cost of capital of 14% per year.

Year	Item	Amount £'000	Discount factor 14%	Present value £'000
0	Redundancy costs	(3,500)	1.000	(3,500.0)
1	Redundancy costs	(8,400)	0.877	(7,366.8)
1	Fixed asset disposals	7,200	0.877	6,314.4
1 - ∞	Savings in running costs	2,750	(1 ÷ 0.14) = 7.14	19,642.9
			Net present value	15,090.5

We might therefore conclude that because of redundancies and rationalisation, the combined value of the post-acquisition companies will increase by about £15,000,000 which is more than the £9,760,000 needed to fund the extra price being offered for their shares to Holbeck shareholders. Of the increase in share values, Holbeck shareholders would benefit by the first £9,760,000, leaving the remaining £5,240,000 to be shared between all shareholders in the post-acquisition company.

A two for one offer should therefore be made.

(d) Assuming no increase in total post-acquisition earnings, the group will have a fairly low interest cover ratio. The interest cover in the 'old' Killisick is (12,400 ÷ 4,431) 2.8 times and in the 'old' Holbeck is (5,800 ÷ 2,200) = 2.6 times. In the combined company it will be (12,400 + 5,800) ÷ (4,431 + 2,200) = 2.75 times.

Although we do not have balance sheet details, this low interest cover indicates **high gearing**, and the cost of the existing debt capital might therefore be high.

The takeover will create an **enlarged company**, and because of this, it is fairly reasonable to assume that the risk of default will be less than with either of the 'old' companies taken individually. This **reduction in default risk**, if perceived to be significant, might reduce the return that investors in debt capital seek from the company. A reduction in the required return on marketable fixed interest capital would raise its market value. In this respect, the acquisition would have some effect on the market value of Killisick's debt.

Of course, Killisick's debt might be non-marketable bank loans and overdrafts, in which case the acquisition would not have any effect on the market value of the debt, since such debt has no market value.

10 NEWBEGIN ENTERPRISES LTD

(a) The EV of annual sales volume is as follows.

Probability	Sales volume	Expected value
	Units	Units
0.10	2,000	200
0.25	6,000	1,500
0.40	8,000	3,200
0.15	10,000	1,500
0.10	14,000	1,400
		7,800

The EV of contribution will be $7,800 \times £(10 - 6) = £31,200$. The EV of additional cash profits each year will be $£31,200 - £20,000 = £11,200$.

Year	Cash flow	Discount factor	Present value of cash flow
	£	10%	£
0	(40,000)	1.000	(40,000)
1-6	11,200	4.355	48,776
6	3,000	0.564	1,692
			10,486

The expected value of the NPV of the project is £10,486.

(b) To justify the project the NPV must be at least zero. Assuming that the cost of the equipment and its residual value are known with certainty, we can calculate the minimum required PV of annual cash profits, as follows.

	Present value
	£
PV of capital outlay	40,000
Less PV of residual value	1,692
PV of annual cash profits required for NPV of zero	38,308
Discount factor of £1 pa for six years at 10%	4.355
Annual cash profit required for NPV of zero = $\dfrac{£38,308}{4.355}$ =	£8,796
Annual fixed costs	£20,000
Annual contribution required for NPV of zero	£28,796
Contribution per unit	£4

Annual sales required are $\dfrac{£28,796}{£4}$ = 7,199 units, say 7,200 units.

(c) Risk and uncertainty analysis can be carried out in several ways.

(i) Sensitivity analysis could be used to measure the percentage adverse change in estimates of cost or revenues which would make the NPV of the project negative.

The sales volume

Since the breakeven annual sales volume is about 7,200 units and expected sales are 7,800 units, the EV of sales volume could fall by 600 units or about 7.7% before the project ceases to be viable.

The price and fixed and variable costs

	£
EV of annual sales revenue (7,800 × £10)	78,000
EV of annual variable costs (7,800 × £6)	46,800
Annual fixed costs	20,000
PV of sales revenue over six years (× 4.355)	339,690
PV of variable costs over six years (× 4.355)	203,814
PV of fixed costs over six years (× 4.355)	87,100

A fall in NPV of £10,486 to £0 would occur, at an annual sales volume of 7,800 units, if:

(1)   The sales price were $\dfrac{10,486}{339,690}$ = 3.1% lower

(that is, 31 pence less per unit, a price of £9.69 per unit)

(2)   The variable costs were $\dfrac{10,486}{203,814}$ = 5.1% higher

(that is, 31 pence per unit higher, at £6.31 per unit)

(3)   Annual fixed costs were $\dfrac{10,486}{87,100}$ = 12.0% higher

(that is, £2,400 higher, at £22,400).

The capital cost of equipment

If the residual value is certain to be £3,000, the project would cease to be viable if the cost of the equipment were more than

$$\frac{10,486}{40,000}$$ or about 26.2% above the estimated cost.

(ii)   To allow for risk, we could **raise** the **discount rate from** 10% to (say) 15%. If the NPV is still positive at 15%, we might then assume that the project is both viable and reasonably safe.

Year	Cash flow £	Discount factor 15%	Present value of cash flow £
0	(40,000)	1.000	(40,000)
1-6	11,200	3.784	42,381
6	3,000	0.432	1,296
			3,677

(iii)   To allow for the **uncertainty of cash flows** in the distant future, the cash flow each year could be adjusted to a 'certainty equivalent' and an NPV could be calculated on these adjusted cash flows.

(iv)   **Risk** can be assessed by considering the worst (or best) possible outcome, and estimating the probability that this might occur.

If annual sales are only 2,000 units, there would be an annual contribution of £8,000 and an annual loss of £12,000. Similarly, if sales are 6,000 or 8,000 units, the annual profit would be £4,000 or £12,000 respectively.

		Sales 2,000		Sales 6,000		Sales 8,000	
Year	Discount factor	Cash flow	Present value	Cash flow	Present value	Cash flow	Present value
	10%	£	£	£	£	£	£
0	1.000	(40,000)	(40,000)	(40,000)	(40,000)	(40,000)	(40,000)
1-6	4.355	(12,000)	(52,260)	4,000	17,420	12,000	52,260
6	0.564	3,000	1,692	3,000	1,692	3,000	1,692
Net present value			(90,568)		(20,888)		13,952
Probability			0.1		0.25		

There is a 35% probability that the NPV will be negative. The worst possible outcome (10% probability) is that the NPV will be £(90,568).

397

(v) The **payback period** could be considered.

The non-discounted payback period, assuming annual sales of 7,800 units, is

$$\frac{40,000}{11,200} = 3.571 \text{ years.}$$

The discounted payback period is where the cumulative discount factor of £1 pa at 10% equals 3.571.

The cumulative discount factor for four years at 10% is 3.170.
The cumulative discount factor for five years at 10% is 3.791.

The discounted payback period is between four and five years.

If this payback period is too long, the project should not be undertaken.

(vi) The standard deviation of the expected cash flows each year can be calculated as follows.

Probability	Sales Units	Profit* (x) £	$(x - \bar{x})$ £	$p(x - \bar{x})^2$
0.10	2,000	(12,000)	(23,200)	53.824
0.25	6,000	4,000	(7,200)	12.960
0.40	8,000	12,000	800	0.256
0.15	10,000	20,000	8,800	11.616
0.10	14,000	36,000	24,800	61.504
EV	7,800	11,200		140.160

* Contribution of £4 per unit minus fixed costs of £20,000.

The standard deviation is $\sqrt{140,160,000} = £11,839$.

11   QW PLC

> **Tutorial note.** At first sight, this appears to be a question about interest rate swaps. In fact, swaps account for only just over 50% of the marks available. You also need to be able to explain the use of derivative products generally, and to contrast the merits of the different techniques available to hedge interest rate risk.
>
> The calculations are most easily approached by tabulating the annual interest costs under the two possible alternative arrangements, and then comparing your results.

To: Board of directors, QW plc
From: Treasurer
Date: dd.mm.yy

Re: The use of financial derivatives and interest rate swaps

Introduction

The purpose of this report is to explain the nature and function of financial derivatives, and the benefits that they could offer to QW plc. The later sections of the report deal in more detail with methods of hedging interest rate risk, and the potential benefits of negotiating an interest rate swap with ER plc.

Financial derivatives

Financial derivatives are traded products that have developed from the securities and currency markets. Examples of derivative products include futures and options in currencies and interest rates.

There are two main purposes for which these products might be used:

1 **Hedging against known risks**

This can best be explained by means of an example. The company might have a commitment to make a payment in a foreign currency on a specific date in three months' time. It knows the amount of the sum to be paid in foreign currency, but it cannot know what the exchange rate will be at that time. It therefore faces the risk that if the home currency depreciates against the foreign currency, the size of the payment in sterling will be greater than if the payment were made now. This risk could be **hedged** by using a derivative such as a **forward exchange contract**. Such a transaction would have a commission cost associated with it, but it would limit the risk faced by the company and mean that the sum that would have to be paid would be effectively **fixed** in

sterling terms. However, although the downside risk would be hedged, the company would at the same time lose the ability to take advantage of a favourable movement in exchange rates. If an **option forward exchange contract** were used instead, this would allow the company to take advantage of such a favourable movement but still be protected from downside risk. However, the commission cost is higher for this form of contract. The extent to which these products are used will therefore depend upon the company's attitude to this type of financial risk.

2   **Speculation**

Derivatives can also be used to **gamble** on expectations of movements in interest and exchange rates. For example, the investor might believe that sterling would weaken against the dollar, and therefore buy dollars forward. These dollars would then be sold on the spot market once the expected movement in rates had taken place. The transactions are made purely with the motive of **making a profit**, and are not linked to any underlying business transactions. They are therefore very risky.

Since QW plc has diversified, international interests, derivative products offer significant benefits in the management of the financial risks to which the company is exposed. The board needs to determine the level of risk that it is prepared to accept in these areas so that an integrated set of guidelines can be established for the effective management of these issues.

Hedging interest rate risk

The main techniques available to hedge this type of risk are:

1   **Forward rate agreements**

These are agreements, usually between a company and a bank, about the interest rate on future borrowing or bank deposits. The agreement will be tailored to the specific requirements of the company. For example, a company can enter into an agreement with a bank that **fixes** the **rate of interest** for borrowing at a certain time in the future. If the actual interest rate is higher than the rate agreed, the bank pays the company the difference. If the actual interest rate is lower than the rate agreed, the company pays the bank the difference.

The main advantage of forward rate agreements is that they **protect** the **borrower** from **adverse market interest rate movements**; however, the borrower will be unable to benefit from the effects of favourable market interest rate movements. A further limitation is that FRAs are **normally** restricted to loans greater than £500,000, and they are likely to be difficult to obtain for periods greater than one year.

2   **Interest rate futures**

These operate in a similar way to forward rate agreements. However, they are not negotiated directly with a bank but are **traded** on the **futures market**. Consequently, the terms, the amounts and the periods are standardised. For this reason, forward rate agreements are normally more appropriate than interest rate futures to non-financial companies such as QW plc.

3   **Interest rate options**

An interest rate option provides the **right to borrow** or to **lend** a specified amount at a guaranteed rate of interest. On the date of expiry of the option, or before, the buyer must decide whether or not to exercise the right. Thus in a borrowing situation, the option will only be exercised if **market interest rates** have **risen above the option rate**. Tailor made contracts can be purchased from major banks, while standardised contracts are traded in a similar way to interest rate futures. The cost of taking out an option is generally higher than for a forward rate agreement.

4   **Interest rate swaps**

These are transactions that **exploit different interest rates** in different markets for borrowing, to reduce interest costs for either fixed or floating rate loans. An interest rate swap is an arrangement whereby two companies, or a company and a bank, **swap interest rate commitments** with each other. In a sense, each simulates the other's borrowings, although each party to the swap retains its obligations to the original lenders. This means that the parties must accept counterparty risk.

The main benefits of a swap as compared with other hedging instruments are as follows.

- **Transaction** costs are **low**, being limited to legal fees.

- They are **flexible**, since they can be arranged in any size, and they can be reversed if necessary.

- Companies with **different credit ratings** can borrow at the best cost in the market that is most accessible to them and then swap this benefit with another company to reduce the mutual borrowing costs.

- Swaps allow **capital restructuring** by changing the nature of interest commitments without the need to redeem debt or to issue new debt, thus reducing transaction costs.

Implications of an interest rate swap with ER plc

The proposed swap would involve one company borrowing at a floating rate, and the other at a fixed rate. Each company would enter into an individual loan arrangement with the bank, and the interest rate liabilities would then be swapped. The two options are:

1   **QW borrows at 8% per annum, ER borrows at LIBOR + 0.5%**

The actual annual interest cost will depend on the actual level of LIBOR. It is assumed that ER plc is also aiming to raise £10m. If this is so, the actual costs at the various possible LIBOR rates will be as follows:

	LIBOR			
	6%	*7%*	*8%*	*9%*
QW pays per year (£'000)	800	800	800	800
ER pays per year (£'000)	650	750	850	950
Total interest cost (£'000)	1,450	1,550	1,650	1,750

2   **QW borrows at LIBOR + 0.2%, ER borrows at 9.5% per annum**

In this situation, the actual costs at the various possible LIBOR rates will be as follows:

	LIBOR			
	6%	*7%*	*8%*	*9%*
QW pays per year (£'000)	620	720	820	920
ER pays per year (£'000)	950	950	950	950
Total interest cost (£'000)	1,570	1,670	1,770	1,870

It can be seen that, regardless of the LIBOR rate, the two companies will save £120,000 per year between them as a result of exploiting QW's ability to borrow at a lower fixed rate than ER plc. In percentage terms, this is a saving of 0.6% (£120,000/£20m). Of this, the bank would take a commission of 0.2% of the benefits to the two parties, which would amount to £40,000 (£120,000 × 0.2/0.6).

It has been proposed by ER plc that the costs and gains should be split equally, leaving each company with a net benefit of £40,000 per year ((£120,000 − £40,000)/2). However, ER is effectively benefiting from the better credit rating of QW plc, and therefore QW should be able to negotiate a higher percentage of the benefits.

The main risk of entering into this agreement is that if interest rates do fall over the period, QW will benefit less from the swap than if the money was borrowed directly at a floating rate of interest.

12   OXLAKE PLC

(a)   **Receipts from export sales**

(i)   *Sales to Singapore*

The value of the sales at the spot rate is:

$$250,000 \times \text{Singapore } \$2.862 \times \frac{1}{3.1800} \text{ (W1)} = £225,000$$

If Oxlake enters into a contract to sell 250,000 × 2.862 = Singapore $715,000, delivery between two and three months,

Anticipated sterling proceeds = Singapore $715,500 ÷ 3.1592 = £226,481

Oxlake can take out a **forward option contract** to sell **Singapore dollars forward**, for delivery between two and three months. This will hopefully overcome the uncertainty surrounding the timing of the receipt from Singapore. The exchange rate used is the least favourable quoted rate for delivery during the period (in this case the three month rate).

Alternatively, Oxlake can cover its foreign exchange risk via the **money markets**, as follows.

(1) Borrow Singapore $703,194 for three months (see W2).

(2) As required, convert to sterling at spot rate of 3.18 (W1).
The proceeds will be 703,194 ÷ 3.18 = £221,130.

(3) Invest sterling in the Eurosterling market for three months at 6½% pa.
The Eurosterling deposit will grow to £224,723.

(ii) **Sales to Indonesia**

The value of the sales at the spot rate is $100,000 \times \dfrac{2246}{2481}$ = £90,528.

The first alternative is to compute the eventual proceeds using the £/US $ forward market, since payment has been offered in US dollars and no forward market exists in Rupiahs/£.

Using the US $/£ forward market, the contracted receipts from selling US $ 125,000 for delivery in three months are $\dfrac{125,000}{1.5105}$ = £82,754

The second alternative is to use the money markets, as follows.

(1) Borrow US $ 121,359 for three months (W4)

(2) Convert US $121,359 into sterling at the spot rate of US $ 1.4875/£, giving $\dfrac{121,359}{1.4875}$

= £81,586

(3) Invest the sterling proceeds of £81,586 on the Eurosterling deposit market for three months at 6½% pa, yielding £81,586 × 1.01625 = £82,912.

Conclusion. The protection should be effected through the foreign exchange market for the sale to Singapore and through the money market for the sale to Indonesia.

(b)

	Rupiahs
Sales value (100,000 × 2,246)	224,600,000
Less 5% discount	(11,230,000)
Discounted sales value	213,370,000

Proceeds of sales = $\dfrac{213,370,000}{1,667.9 \text{(W5)}}$ = $127,927

The best US $ deposit rate of interest is 8% pa in a US domestic bank.

The yield after three months is $127,927 × 1.02 = $130,486.

Converted into sterling, using the three month forward market, this is $\dfrac{\$130,486}{1.5105}$ = £86,386.

Alternatively, the US dollar proceeds could be converted immediately into sterling and then invested for three months in eurosterling. The calculation is as follows.

(i) Conversion of US $127,927 (see above) into sterling yields

$\dfrac{127,927}{1.4875}$ = £86,001

(ii)

	£
Yield of eurosterling 3 month deposit (£86,001 × 6.5%/4)	1,398
Add principal	86,001
	87,399

Conclusion. The best yield without the offer of immediate payment was £82,912. Both the forward foreign exchange market and the money market yield better returns, with the money market's £87,399 as the better of the alternatives.

Workings

W1 **Cross rates, Singapore $/£**

	Singapore $/US$	US $/£	Singapore $/£
Spot	2.1378	1.4875	3.1800
1 month forward	2.1132	1.4963	3.1620
2 months forward	2.0964	1.5047	3.1545
3 months forward	2.0915	1.5105	3.1592

W2 **Required Singapore $ borrowings**

The interest rate in Singapore $ is 7% pa or 1.75% for three months.

Thus the maximum borrowing which can be repaid from export sale proceeds is

$$\text{Singapore } \$ \ \frac{715,500}{1.0175} = 703,194$$

W3 **Eurosterling deposit**

The interest rate for three months is 1.625%.

Thus the yield on the deposit is £221,130 × 1.01625 = £224,723.

W4 **Required US $ borrowings**

US $ interest rates (eurodollars) are 12% pa or 3% for three months.

Thus, the maximum borrowing which can be repaid from the sale proceeds is

$$\frac{\$125,000}{1.03} = \$121,359$$

W5 **Cross rate, Rupiah/£**

	US $/£	Rupiah/US $	Rupiah/£
Spot	1.4875	1667.90	2,481

(c) When a company invoices sales in a currency other than its own, the amount of 'home' currency it will eventually receive is uncertain. There may be an advantage or a disadvantage, depending on changes in the exchange rate over the period between invoicing and receiving payment. With this in mind, invoicing in a foreign currency has the following advantages.

(i) The **foreign customer** will **find the deal more attractive** than a similar one in the exporter's currency, since the customer will bear no foreign exchange risk. Making a sale will therefore be that much easier.

(ii) The exporter can **take advantage** of **favourable foreign exchange movements** by selling the exchange receipts forward (for more of the home currency than would be obtained by conversion at the spot rate).

(iii) In some countries, the **importer** may find it **difficult** or even impossible to obtain the foreign exchange necessary to pay in the exporter's currency. The willingness of the exporter to sell in the importer's currency may therefore prevent the sale falling through.

The disadvantages of making export sales in foreign currency are the reverse of the advantages.

(i) The exporter (rather than the foreign customer) bears the foreign exchange risk.
(ii) If the exchange movement is unfavourable, the exporter's profit will be reduced.

13   BAILEY SMALL PLC

> **Tutorial note**. This question tests your knowledge of exchange rate hedges using fixed and option forward exchange contracts, and money market hedges. The calculations are reasonably straightforward, but as always with option contracts, you will need to think through carefully the implications of different movements in exchange rates.

(a) (i) Since both the receipts and payments are expected to occur on the same date, Bailey Small plc need only **hedge** the **net amount**, ie a receipt of $200,000 ($450,000 − $250,000). To hedge this transaction, a three-month forward contract to sell dollars will be required. The rate that will apply for this contract will be $1.6590 − $0.0077 = $1.6513/£.

The transaction cost will be paid immediately in US$. Bailey Small must therefore buy dollars now to cover this at the spot rate of $1.6540/£.

The net receipt can now be calculated:

	£
Sterling proceeds in 3 months' time: $200,000 ÷1.6513	121,117
Transaction costs: $200,000 × 0.2% ÷ 1.6540	(242)
Net receipt	120,875

(ii)   Since the company is expecting to receive dollars, to effect a money market hedge it will need to **borrow dollars** now in anticipation. The sum to be borrowed must be just enough so that the receipt in three months' time will repay the loan and the interest due for the period.

The money will be borrowed in the US at an annual rate of 6%. This equates to a three month rate of 1.5% (6%/4). The amount to be borrowed in dollars is therefore $200,000 ÷ 1.015 = $197,044. These dollars will be sold now at the spot rate of $1.6590/£ to realise £118,772.

This sterling amount can now be invested in the UK at an annual rate of 6.5%. This equates to a three-month rate of 1.625%. The value of the deposit at the end of the three month period when the dollar loan is repaid will be £118,772 × 1.01625 = £120,702.

The transaction cost will be the same as for the forward market hedge. The net receipt under this method will therefore be £120,702 – £242 = **£120,460**.

The receipts are highest if the forward market hedge is used, and this will therefore be the preferred method.

(b)   Bailey Small should consider the following factors before deciding to use a currency market hedge:

(i)   The **relative costs** of the different options

(ii)   The **ability** of the **staff** to manage the techniques, given that there is not a specialist treasury department

(iii)   The attitude of the company to **risk**

(iv)   The **size** of the transaction in relation to the company's overall operations, and therefore the scale of the risks involved

(v)   The perceived **level of risk** attached to the currencies in question

Alternative options that the company could consider to minimise risk include the following.

(i)   **Operating bank accounts** in **foreign currencies**. This is only an option if the company has regular transactions in the currencies in question.

(ii)   The use of **multilateral netting**. This will only be possible if there are a large number of foreign currency transactions.

(iii)   The company could consider the use of **swaps** and **option contracts**.

(iv)   The company could consider the cost and viability of insisting that more of its contracts are **denominated in sterling**.

(c)   A **fixed forward exchange contract** is:

(i)   An **immediately firm** and **binding contract** (for example, between a bank and its customer)

(ii)   For the **purchase or sale of a specified quantity** of a stated foreign currency

(iii)   At a **rate of exchange fixed** at the time the contract is made

(iv)   For **performance** at a **future time** which is agreed upon when making the contract

An **option forward exchange contract** has all the features of a fixed contract, except that the customer has the option to call for performance at any date from the contract being made up to a specified date in the future, or at any date between two dates both in the future.

Option contracts are attractive when:

(i)   The date on which the **transaction being hedged** will take place is uncertain

(ii)   There is **uncertainty** about the **likely movement in exchange rates** – the company can take advantage of any favourable movements in exchange rates, while continuing to hedge any unfavourable movements

The main drawbacks to option contracts are:

(i)   They are **more expensive** than fixed contracts, and the premium will have to be paid, whether or not the option is exercised

(ii)   They are **traded in standard amounts**, and therefore it is difficult to hedge exactly the sum required – in practice, the company will have to carry some of the risk itself, or use two different hedges to cover the transaction fully

Bailey Small example

The company is looking to hedge a net receipt in three months' time. It will therefore need to **buy June call options**.

The **spot rate** for selling dollars is currently $1.6590/£. If the rate falls below the current spot rate the company will benefit from the movement in rates. There is therefore no point in buying an option with an exercise price below the current spot rate. This means that the company should buy options with an exercise price of $1.70/£.

The sum to be hedged is $200,000. The number of contracts that will be needed is therefore:

($200,000 ÷ 1.70) ÷ £12,500 = 9.4 contracts.

The company should therefore take out nine contracts, and it is assumed that it will bear the remaining risk itself. The cost of this will be payable immediately, and it is assumed that dollars will be bought now at spot to cover this. The cost is:

(9 × 12,500 × $0.017) ÷ 1.6540 = £1,156

The option will only be exercised if the spot price is more than $1.70/£. If we assume that the spot rate moves to, say, $1.71/£, the net receipts would be as follows:

	£
Nine contracts of £12,500	112,500
$8,750 sold at spot (1.71)	5,116
Less premium (above)	(1,156)
	116,460

If the spot price actually moved to that predicted in the question, the option would not be exercised and the company would sell the dollars on the spot market at $1.6513/£. The net receipts would be as follows:

	£
$200,000 sold at $1.6513/£	121,116
Less premium (above)	(1,156)
	119,960

Given the **actual movement** in **exchange rates** that occurred, it is clear that Bailey Small's best decision would have been to have used a fixed forward contract rather than an option, since this would have yielded a receipt of £120,875 (greater than £119,960). However, had the dollar fallen further against sterling, for example, to $1.6385/£ or below, then the option contract would have yielded a greater receipt than the fixed contract. At this exchange rate, the receipt would be as follows:

	£
$200,000 sold at $1.6385/£	122,062
Less premium	(1,156)
	120,906

The key point is that the option contract gives the company the possibility of **benefiting** from **unexpected favourable movements** in rates, albeit at a higher premium cost. The 'correct' choice can only be made once the company has specified the degree of risk that it is willing to accept in this type of situation.

14   DINARD PLC

(a)   The **real rate of return** is the rate of return which an investment would show in the absence of inflation. For example, if a company invests £100, inflation is 0%, and the investment at the end of the year is worth £110, then the real rate of return is 10%.

In reality however, there is likely to be an element of inflation in the returns due to the change in the purchasing power of money over the period. In the example above, if inflation was running at 5%, then to show a real rate of return of 10%, the investment would need to be worth £115.50 at the end of the year. In this case the money rate of return is 15.5% which is made up of the real return of 10% and inflation at 5%.

The relationship between the nominal ('money') rate of return and the real rate of return can be expressed as follows.

(1 + nominal rate) = (1 + real rate) × (1 + inflation rate)

The rate to be used in discounting cash flows for capital project appraisal will depend on the way in which the **expected cash flows** are **calculated**. If the cash flows are expressed in terms of the actual number of pounds that will be received or paid on the various future dates, then the nominal rate must be used. If however they are expressed in terms of the value of the pound at year 0, then the real rate must be used.

(b) *Workings*

	Year 1	Year 2	Year 3	Year 4
Sales volume	25,000	25,000	25,000	25,000
Unit price (£)	80	84	88	93
Variable material cost (£)	8.00	8.32	8.65	9.00
Variable labour cost (£)	12.00	13.20	14.52	15.97
Variable overhead (£)	12.00	12.48	12.98	13.50

Notes

(i) Development costs of £480,000 are sunk costs and will be excluded from the calculations.

(ii) Depreciation does not involve any movement of cash and will be excluded from the fixed overheads (£600,000 in year 1).

(iii) All figures have been adjusted for the appropriate rate of inflation. The investment will therefore be evaluated using the WACC expressed as a nominal rate of 15%.

Evaluation of investment

(All figures £'000)

	Year 0	Year 1	Year 2	Year 3	Year 4
Capital outlay	(2,400)				
Sales		2,000	2,100	2,205	2,315
Direct costs					
Materials		(200)	(208)	(216)	(225)
Labour		(300)	(330)	(363)	(399)
Overhead		(300)	(312)	(324)	(337)
Fixed overheads		(200)	(210)	(221)	(232)
Gross cash flow	(2,400)	1,000	1,040	1,081	1,122
Discount at 15%	1.000	0.870	0.756	0.658	0.572
Present value	(2,400)	870	786	711	642
Cumulative PV	(2,400)	(1,530)	(744)	(33)	609

The investment yields a net present value at the end of four years of £608,000. In the absence of other factors such as capital rationing, production of the Rance should be undertaken.

15 ANTARES PLC

(a) The first step is to calculate the **annual contribution** from each project, together with the working capital cash flows. These cash flows, together with the initial outlay, can then be **discounted** at the **cost of capital** to arrive at the NPV of each project. Development costs already incurred are irrelevant. There are no additional administration costs associated with the projects, and depreciation is also irrelevant since it has no cash effect.

First, calculate annual contribution.

	A	B	C	D
Unit sales	150,000	75,000	80,000	120,000
	£	£	£	£
Selling price per unit	30.00	40.00	25.00	50.00
Material cost per unit	7.60	12.00	4.50	25.00
Labour cost per unit	9.80	12.00	5.00	10.00
Variable overheads per unit	6.00	7.00	2.50	10.50
	£'000	£'000	£'000	£'000
Sales per annum	4,500	3,000	2,000	6,000
Materials	1,140	900	360	3,000
Labour	1,470	900	400	1,200
Variable overheads	900	525	200	1,260
Annual contribution	990	675	1,040	540

	A	B	C	D
	£'000	£'000	£'000	£'000
Working capital requirement (20% annual sales value)	900	600	400	1,200

It is assumed that working capital will be recovered at the end of year 5. The initial outlay will be made in year 0.

The NPV of each project can now be calculated.

Cash flows

Year	A Gross £'000	A Net £'000	B Gross £'000	B Net £'000	C Gross £'000	C Net £'000	D Gross £'000	D Net £'000	Discount factor 18%
0	(3,000)	(3,000)	(2,000)	(2,000)	(2,800)	(2,800)	(1,800)	(1,800)	1.000
1	990	840	675	572	1,040	882	540	458	0.848
2	990	711	675	485	1,040	747	540	388	0.718
3	990	603	675	411	1,040	633	540	329	0.609
4	990	511	675	348	1,040	537	540	279	0.516
5	1,890	826	1,275	557	1,440	629	1,740	760	0.437
Total NPV		491		373		628		414	

(b) The **profitability** index provides a **means** of **optimising the NPV** when there are more projects available which yield a positive NPV than funds to invest in them. The profitability index measures the ratio of the present value of cash inflows to the initial outlay and represents the net present value per £1 invested.

Project	PV of inflows £'000	Initial outlay £'000	Ratio	Ranking
A	3,491	3,000	1.164	4
B	2,373	2,000	1.187	3
C	3,428	2,800	1.224	2
D	2,214	1,800	1.230	1

Project D has the highest PI ranking and is therefore the first choice for investment. On this basis the funds available should be invested as follows.

Project	Initial outlay £'000	Total NPV £'000	% taken	Cumulative outlay £'000	Actual NPV £'000
D	1,800	414	100	1,800	414
C	2,800	628	100	4,600	628
B	2,000	373	30	5,200	112
A	3,000	491	0	5,200	0
Total NPV generated					1,154

(c) The profitability index (PI) approach can be applied only if the projects under consideration fulfil certain criteria, as follows.

(i) There is **only one constraint on investment**, in this case capital. The PI ensures that maximum return per unit of scarce resource (capital) is obtained.

(ii) **Each investment** can be **accepted** or **rejected** in its entirety or alternatively accepted on a partial basis.

(iii) The NPV generated by a given project is **directly proportional** to the percentage of the investment undertaken.

(iv) Each investment can only be **made once** and not repeated.

(v) The company's aim is to **maximise overall NPV**.

(vi) If **additional funds** are **available** but at a higher cost, then the simple PI approach cannot be used since it is not possible to calculate unambiguous individual NPVs.

(vii) If certain of the projects that may be undertaken are mutually exclusive then **sub-problems** must be **defined** and **calculations made** for different combinations of projects. This can become a very lengthy process. These assumptions place limitations on the use of the ratio approach. It is not appropriate to multi-constraint situations when linear programming techniques must be used. Each project must be infinitely divisible and the company must accept that it may need to undertake a small proportion of a given project. This is frequently not possible in practice. It is also very unlikely that there is a simple linear relationship between the NPV and the proportion of the project undertaken; it is much more likely that there will be discontinuities in returns.

Possibly a more serious constraint is the assumption that the company's only concern is to **maximise NPV**. It is possible that there may be long-term strategic reasons which mean that an investment with a lower NPV should be undertaken instead of one with a higher NPV, and the ratio approach takes no account of the relative degrees of risk associated with making the different investments.

16 DA COSTA PLC

> **Tutorial note**. This question tests your ability to evaluate foreign income cash flows and the management of the risks involved.
>
> In section (b) of the question you are required to think about the specifics of the proposed investment, and not just to write about the risks and management of foreign investment in general terms.

(a) (i) In order to calculate the sterling NPV of the project it is necessary to estimate the year end US$/£ spot rates for the duration of the project. This can be done using the interest rate parity theory as follows.

	Rate at start of year $/£	Adjust by	Closing rate
Year 1	1.6000	× 1.04/1.05	1.5848
Year 2	1.5848	× 1.04/1.05	1.5697
Year 3	1.5697	× 1.04/1.05	1.5547
Year 4	1.5547	× 1.04/1.05	1.5399
Year 5	1.5399	× 1.04/1.05	1.5252

The US$ cash flow can now be converted to sterling and discounted at the sterling required rate of return (14%):

	Year 0	Year 1	Year 2	Year 3	Year 4
Cash flow in US$m	(4.50)	1.75	1.95	2.50	3.50
Closing spot rate	1.6000	1.5848	1.5697	1.5547	1.5399
Cash flow in £m	(2.813)	1.104	1.242	1.608	2.273
14% discount factors	1.000	0.877	0.769	0.675	0.592
Discounted cash flow	(2.813)	0.968	0.955	1.085	1.346

Net present value £1.542m

(ii) In order to discount the annual cash flows in US$, it is necessary to **calculate** the **appropriate discount** rate to use. This can be done by calculating the risk premium in the UK, and then applying this to the US risk-free rate.

In the UK, the risk-free rate is 5% and the required rate of return is 14%. The risk premium is therefore 1.14/1.05 = 1.0857, or 8.57%.

In the US, the risk-free rate is 4%, and the risk premium is 8.57%. The required rate of return is therefore $1.04 \times 1.0857 = 1.1291$, or 12.91%.

The discount factors at 12.91% will be:

Year 1	$1/(1 + 12.91) =$	0.886
Year 2	$1/(1 + 12.91)^2 =$	0.784
Year 3	$1/(1 + 12.91)^3 =$	0.695
Year 4	$1/(1 + 12.91)^4 =$	0.615

Note. It would be acceptable to approximate the discount rate to 13%, and take factors from tables.

The NPV calculated in US$ is as follows.

	Year 0	Year 1	Year 2	Year 3	Year 4
Cash flow in US$m	(4.50)	1.75	1.95	2.50	3.50
14% discount factors	1.000	0.886	0.784	0.695	0.615
Discounted cash flow	(4.500)	1.551	1.529	1.738	2.153

Net present value ($m)   2.471

NPV in sterling at $1.6/£   £1.544m

(b) (i) The WACC is valid for use in investment appraisal, given the following assumptions.

(1) **New investments** must be **financed** by new sources of funds.

(2) The **cost of capital** to be **applied** to project evaluation must **reflect** the **marginal cost of new capital**.

(3) The WACC **reflects** the **company's long-term future capital structure** and capital costs.

The main argument in favour of the use of the WACC in investment appraisal is that a company's capital structure changes only very slowly over time, and therefore the **marginal cost of new capital** should be **roughly equal** to the **weighted average cost of current capital.** If this is correct, then by selecting investments that offer a return above the WACC, the company will increase the market value of its ordinary shares in the long run.

The main arguments against the use of the WACC arise in the following circumstances.

(1) New investments undertaken by a company might have **different business risk characteristics** from the existing operations. In this situation, the return required by investors might go up or down as a result.

(2) The new finance raised to fund the project might significantly **change the capital structure** and the perceived financial risk of investing in the company.

(3) Where there is a significant proportion of floating rate debt, the **WACC** will be **constantly varying**, and therefore the WACC at any one point in time will only be an approximation of the true cost of capital.

In an international situation, such as that faced by DaCosta plc, the drawbacks arising from variations in risk are likely to become more significant. However, it is always difficult to quantify these types of risks objectively, and it is likely that the WACC will continue to be the most appropriate measure. Where quantifying risk is a problem, the company could use additional measures, such as sensitivity analysis, to direct attention to the key areas of concern surrounding the decision.

(ii) The main risks that are likely to be encountered by a company moving into a new international market include the following.

(1) **Foreign exchange risks**

Transaction risk. Costs and revenues may be **more volatile** than predicted due to unforeseen movements in exchange rates between the home country and that in which the investment is located. This can be managed by matching costs and revenues as far as possible, and using hedging techniques such as forward exchange contracts.

Translation risk. The valuation of the assets to be included in the consolidated balance sheet may vary due to movements in exchange rates. This is unlikely to be important in the investment decision unless the company is highly geared and close to breaching any borrowing covenants.

(2) **Economic risks**

These arise when **events occur** in the **economy** of the country that **impact** upon the **performance** of the investment. For example, a sharp rise in the level of personal taxation may cause a fall in demand for the project. This risk is unlikely to be significant in DaCosta's case, and there is little that can be done to manage such a situation.

(3) **Geographical separation**

This causes a number of problems in the areas of **communication and control**, and the recruitment of the appropriate local specialists. Since DaCosta is proposing to invest in the USA, these problems are likely to be less significant than in a more remote, less developed, non-English speaking country.

(4) **Political risk**

Where a multinational invests in another country, it may face **political risk of action** by that country's government, which restricts the multinational's freedom. An example is the import restrictions imposed by the USA on the British cashmere industry in retaliation for the EU restrictions on banana imports in 1999. This can be a risk in any country, and again there is little that the company can do to avoid it.

(iii) A company has three options when financing an overseas operation:

(1) **Export capital** from the **parent company**, either in the form of equity or debt

(2) **Raise capital** in the **currency** and country in which the investment is to take place - again, this could be in the form of equity or debt

(3) **Borrow cheaper funds** on the international markets

The main risks to be faced fall into the same main categories described above. Since DaCosta is investing in the US, political risks affecting the transfer of capital are unlikely to be significant. However, the company does face both foreign exchange risk and economic risk from the investment.

In general terms, it is a sound principle to **match costs and revenues** as far as possible. Therefore borrowing US dollars to finance the investment would help to minimise the level of transaction exposure to which the company is subjected.

Borrowing in **Euro debt is attractive** due to the low cost of the funds. However, the low rate will be based on expectations of low inflation and a strong currency. The implication of this is that when DaCosta comes to repay the debt, it could find it expensive if the Euro has strengthened significantly against the dollar.

In addition to the relative costs and risks of the different sources of finance, the company should also take into account the following factors:

- The **cost of raising the finance**.
- The **effect on the overall capital structure** and gearing of the company.
- The **ability of the treasury team** to **manage more complex forms of financing**.

17 DARON

(a)   REPORT

To: Managers of Daron
From: Company Accountant
Date: 14 December 20X6
Subject: Long-term strategic options

The purpose of this report is to evaluate the **strategic options** available to the company, namely an immediate sale of the company, continuation of existing operations, and diversification in the event of party A winning the forthcoming election.

Sale of the company. This option can be evaluated in terms of the value of the offer to the shareholders. The informal offer of $20m from the competitor compares with the current market value of the equity of $18.4m (20m × $0.92), a premium of 8.7%. However, it is perhaps more helpful to attempt a valuation of the company based on future cash flows, and figures illustrating this are included in Appendix 1 of this report. These suggest that if party A wins the election, the NPV of the future cash flows will amount to $30.3m, whereas if party B wins, the NPV will be $21.1m. Both of these are in excess of the competitor's offer, suggesting that if the shareholders do wish to sell they should seek a higher price for the company. However, these estimates are subject to a number of uncertainties which will be considered further in the next section of the report.

The shareholders will also need to consider some of the other implications of selling, such as the effect on the other stakeholders in the firm. For example, will many jobs be lost in redundancies? How will customers and the local community be affected by such a decision?

Continue existing operations. The figures contained in Appendix 1 represent a projection of performance for the ten year period up to 20Y6. However, when forecasting over such a long timescale the likelihood of inaccuracy increases, particular areas of potential error being as follows.

(i)   The assumption that the cost of capital will remain constant throughout the period

(ii)   The assumptions made about the inflation rate

(iii)   The effect on economic conditions of possible further elections beyond the one in the immediate future

(iv)   The assumption that the tax rate will remain constant at 30%

(v)   Errors in the projections of sales revenues and costs

A further major assumption built into the figures is that there will be no significant additional capital investment throughout this period. This raises a number of questions, including the following.

(i)   Will other opportunities be forgone during this period if the company starts to lag behind its competitors in technology?

(ii)   Will significant major new investment be required beyond 20Y1 to allow the company to continue operations?

(iii)   What is the realisable value of the company in 20Y1?

This final factor could also have a significant impact on the calculations in Appendix 1, and could mean that the true value of the future cash flows for the period in question is even higher than the figures suggest.

In view of the uncertainties described, it is proposed that further work needs to be done, particularly in investigating the sensitivities of the NPVs to changes in assumptions concerning the key variables.

Diversification into hotel industry. The figures relating to the diversification are contained in Appendix 2. These suggest that the project should yield a NPV of $0.56m. However, a major element in this forecast is the terminal value of $10m on disposal in 20Y1, and any variation in the amount realised is likely to have a significant effect on the projections. Again it is suggested that sensitivity analysis be undertaken to establish the impact of changes in this variable.

In addition to making the financial evaluation, Daron needs to consider the investment in the light of its strategic objectives. If the investment is essentially opportunistic with the diversification being for the benefit of the shareholders in terms of reducing their level of risk, this may be a mistaken goal. The shareholders can achieve diversification of their portfolios by themselves in their choice of other investments, and are unlikely to look to Daron to achieve this for them.

The key question is what the company strategy is to be in the face of the declining market for its core business. It may well be appropriate to seek diversification as a means for survival and growth, but the markets into which Daron seeks to diversify should be carefully chosen and should ideally be related in some way, be it technological basis or customer spread, to those in which it currently operates. The greater the departure from its existing experience, the greater the risk that the diversification will be less successful than anticipated.

Conclusions. Daron needs to consider its long-term strategic objectives and the desires of its shareholders before making any choices between the options facing it. If sale is perceived to be the best option, then the directors should seek to present the company to the market in the best possible light so as to maximise the disposal proceeds, and not just take the offer from the competitor because it is there. If continuing the existing business is desired, careful attention should be given to long-term market conditions and to the effect of alternative investment policies.

If diversification is to be pursued then products and markets should be properly evaluated to obtain the best fit with the existing business.

APPENDIX 1: ESTIMATES OF THE PRESENT VALUE OF DARON

Scenario 1: Party A wins the election

	20X7	20X8	20X9	20Y0	20Y1
	$m	$m	$m	$m	$m
Sales	28.0	29.0	26.0	22.0	19.0
Variable costs	(17.0)	(18.0)	(16.0)	(14.0)	(12.0)
Fixed costs	(3.0)	(3.0)	(3.0)	(3.0)	(3.0)
Depreciation	(4.0)	(3.0)	(3.0)	(2.0)	(1.0)
Taxable income	4.0	5.0	4.0	3.0	3.0
Tax at 30%*	(1.2)	(1.5)	(1.2)	(0.9)	(0.9)
Post tax income	2.8	3.5	2.8	2.1	2.1
Add back non-cash depreciation*	4.0	3.0	3.0	2.0	1.0
Working capital movement	—	1.0	2.0	3.0	3.0
Net cash flow	6.8	7.5	7.8	7.1	6.1
13% discount factors (see Note 1)	0.885	0.783	0.693	0.613	0.543
PV cash flow	6.0	5.9	5.4	4.4	3.3

Tutor's hint. Alternatively, depreciation can be excluded from the calculation, and two figures calculated: firstly, the tax on sales less variable and fixed costs (in 20X7: 30% × (28 − 17 − 3) = $2.4m); secondly, the tax saving on depreciation is added back (in 20X7: 30% × $4m =1.2m). The overall effect is the same.

Total PV = $25.0 million (20X7 - 20Y1)

To these figures must be added the PV cash flow for the period 20Y2-20Y6. This can be found by applying the 13% annuity value for periods 6 to 10 (5.426 −3.517=1.909) to the annual cash flows. These cash flows will be similar to those for 20Y1 excluding depreciation and working capital movements.

	$m
Sales	19.0
Variable costs	(12.0)
Fixed costs	(3.0)
Taxable income	4.0
Tax at 30%	(1.2)
Annual cash flow	2.8
Annuity value	1.909
PV cash flow	5.3

The NPV of the cash flows for the period 20X7 to 20Y6 is therefore $25.0m + $5.3m = $30.3m.

Note 1. The discount rate to be used is the cost of capital. This can be estimated by finding the cost of equity using the CAPM, and then weighting the relative costs of debt and equity on the basis of market values.

The current market value of equity is 20m × $0.92 = $18.4m. It is assumed that the balance sheet value of the debt approximates to its market value ie $14m. Its cost ($k_d$) is taken as the current bank rate of 10%. The risk free rate of return including inflation is 1 − 1.05 × 1.04 = 9.2%. The market rate of return including inflation is 1 − 1.10 × 1.05 = 15.5%.

Using the CAPM: $k_e = R_f + [R_m − R_f]\ \beta$
$= 9.2\% + [15.5\% − 9.2\%] × 1.25\% = 17.075\%$

The WACC can now be estimated.

$$\text{WACC} = k_e\left[\frac{V_E}{V_E+V_D}\right]+k_d\left[\frac{V_D}{V_E+V_D}\right]$$

$= 17.075\% × 18.4/(18.4 + 14) + 10\% × (1 − 0.3) × 14/(18.4 + 14)$

$= 12.72\%$ (approx 13%)

Scenario 2: Party B wins the election

	20X7	20X8	20X9	20Y0	20Y1
	$m	$m	$m	$m	$m
Sales	30.0	26.0	24.0	20.0	16.0
Variable costs	(18.0)	(16.0)	(15.0)	(12.0)	(11.0)
Fixed costs	(3.0)	(3.0)	(4.0)	(4.0)	(4.0)
Depreciation	(4.0)	(3.0)	(3.0)	(2.0)	(1.0)
Taxable income	5.0	4.0	2.0	2.0	0
Tax at 30% *	(1.5)	(1.2)	(0.6)	(0.6)	0
Post tax income	3.5	2.8	1.4	1.4	0
Add back non-cash depreciation*	4.0	3.0	3.0	2.0	1.0
Working capital movement	(1.0)	2.0	2.0	3.0	3.0
Net cash flow	6.5	7.8	6.4	6.4	4.0
18% discount factors (see Note 2)	0.847	0.718	0.609	0.516	0.437
PV cash flow	5.5	5.6	3.9	3.3	1.7

Tutorial note. See *Tutorial note* on Scenario 1 earlier.

Total PV = $20.1 million (20X7-20Y1)

The PV cash flow for the period 20Y2-20Y6 can be found by applying the 18% annuity value for periods 6 to 10 (4.494 − 3.127=1.367) to the annual cash flows. These cash flows will be as for 20Y1 excluding depreciation and working capital movements.

	$m
Sales	16.0
Variable costs	(11.0)
Fixed costs	(4.0)
Taxable income	1.0
Tax at 30%	(0.3)
Annual cash flow	0.7
Annuity value	1.367
PV cash flow	1.0

The NPV of the cash flows for the period 20X7 to 20Y6 is therefore $20.1m + $1.0m = $21.1m.

Note 2. The discount rate to be used is the cost of capital, which can be estimated by the same method as in Scenario 1.

The current market value of equity is again $18.4m. It is assumed that the balance sheet value of the debt approximates to its market value ie $14m, with its cost taken at the bank rate of 15.5%. The risk free rate of return including inflation is 1 − 1.04 × 1.1 = 14.4%. The market rate of return including inflation is 1 − 1.10 × 1.1 = 21.0%.

Using the CAPM:
$$k_e = R_f + [R_m - R_f]\,\beta$$
$$= 14.4\% + (21.0\% - 14.4\%) \times 1.25 = 22.65\%$$

The WACC can now be estimated.

$$\text{WACC} = k_e\left[\frac{V_E}{V_E+V_D}\right] + k_d\left[\frac{V_D}{V_E+V_D}\right]$$
$$= 22.65\% \times 18.4/(18.4 + 14) + 15.5\% \times (1 - 0.3) \times 14/(18.4 + 14)$$
$$= 17.55\% \text{ (approx 18\%)}$$

APPENDIX 2: CASH FLOW EVALUATION OF DIVERSIFICATION PROJECT

To estimate the **APV**, it is first necessary to find the **base case NPV**. This is calculated using the ungeared cost of equity. This can be found using the expression:

$$\beta_u = \beta_g\left[\frac{V_E}{V_E+V_D(1-t)}\right]$$

where:
- β_u = ungeared beta
- β_g = geared beta (1.25)
- V_E = market value of equity ($18.4m)
- V_D = market value of debt ($14.0m)
- t = tax rate (30%)

$$\beta_u = 1.25 \times \frac{18.4}{18.4 + 14(1-0.3)} = 0.82$$

The ungeared cost of equity can now be estimated using the CAPM:

$$k_u = R_f + [R_m - R_f]\,\beta$$
$$= 9.2\% + (15.5\% - 9.2\%) \times 0.82 = 14.4\% \text{ (say, approximately 14\%)}$$

This can be used to calculate the NPV of the project as if it were all equity financed.

	20X6 $m	20X7 $m	20X8 $m	20X9 $m	20Y0 $m	20Y1 $m
Turnover		9.0	10.0	11.0	12.0	13.0
Variable costs		(6.0)	(6.0)	(7.0)	(7.0)	(8.0)
Fixed costs		(2.0)	(2.0)	(2.0)	(2.0)	(2.0)
Taxable income		1.0	2.0	2.0	3.0	3.0
Tax at 30%		(0.3)	(0.6)	(0.6)	(0.9)	(0.9)
Post tax income		0.7	1.4	1.4	2.1	2.1
Purchase cost	(9.0)					
Working capital movement		(1.0)			(1.0)	
Realisable value						10.0
Cash flow	(9.0)	(0.3)	1.4	1.4	1.1	12.1
14% discount factors (see below)	1.000	0.877	0.769	0.675	0.592	0.519
PV cash flow	(9.0)	(0.3)	1.1	0.9	0.7	6.3

Total PV (base case NPV)= –$300,000

The next stage is to use the **Modigliani and Miller formula** for the relationship between the value of geared and ungeared companies to establish the effect of gearing on the value of the project. The amount to be financed by debt will be the purchase cost of the hotel plus the issue costs: $9m/98% = $9.184m.

The present value of the tax shield on the debt interest can now be found.

Annual interest charge: $9.184m × 10%	$918,400
Tax saving: 30%	$275,520
Cost of debt (pre tax)	10%
PV of tax savings at 10% for 5 years: $275,520 × 3.791 (in round $'000)	$1,044,000

The APV is the base case NPV plus the financing side effects (including issue costs):

	$'000
Base case NPV	(300)
Issue costs	(184)
PV of tax savings	1,044
APV	560

This assumes firstly that all the funds required can be raised in the form of debt ie that Daron will have sufficient debt capacity, and secondly that the coupon rate of 10% is an accurate reflection of the risk of the convertible debentures.

Index

Note: **Key Terms** and their page references are given in **bold**

REVIEW FORM & FREE PRIZE DRAW

All original review forms from the entire BPP range, completed with genuine comments, will be entered into one of two draws on 31 January 2002 and 31 July 2002. The names on the first four forms picked out on each occasion will be sent a cheque for £50.

Name: _____   Address: _____

_____

How have you used this Text?
(Tick one box only)

☐ Self study (book only)

☐ On a course: college (please state)_____

_____

☐ With 'correspondence' package

☐ Other _____

Why did you decide to purchase this Text?
(Tick one box only)

☐ Have used BPP Texts in the past

☐ Recommendation by friend/colleague

☐ Recommendation by a lecturer at college

☐ Saw advertising

☐ Other _____

During the past six months do you recall seeing/receiving any of the following?
(Tick as many boxes as are relevant)

☐ Our advertisement in CIMA *Insider*

☐ Our advertisement in *Financial Management*

☐ Our advertisement in *Pass*

☐ Our brochure with a letter through the post

☐ Our website www.bpp.com

Which (if any) aspects of our advertising do you find useful?
(Tick as many boxes as are relevant)

☐ Prices and publication dates of new editions

☐ Information on product content

☐ Facility to order books off-the-page

☐ None of the above

Which BPP products have you used?

Text ☐   Kit ☐   Passcard ☐   MCQ cards ☐   Tape ☐   Video ☐

Your ratings, comments and suggestions would be appreciated on the following areas

	Very useful	Useful	Not useful
Introductory section (Key study steps, personal study)	☐	☐	☐
Chapter introductions	☐	☐	☐
Key terms	☐	☐	☐
Quality of explanations	☐	☐	☐
Case examples and other examples	☐	☐	☐
Questions and answers in each chapter	☐	☐	☐
Chapter roundups	☐	☐	☐
Quick quizzes	☐	☐	☐
Exam focus points	☐	☐	☐
Question bank	☐	☐	☐
Answer bank	☐	☐	☐
Index	☐	☐	☐
Icons	☐	☐	☐
Mind maps	☐	☐	☐

	Excellent	Good	Adequate	Poor
Overall opinion of this Study Text	☐	☐	☐	☐

Do you intend to continue using BPP products?   ☐ Yes   ☐ No

Please note any further comments and suggestions/errors on the reverse of this page. The BPP author of this edition can be e-mailed at: nickweller@bpp.com

Please return this form to: Alison McHugh, CIMA Range Manager, BPP Publishing Ltd, FREEPOST, London, W12 8BR

REVIEW FORM & FREE PRIZE DRAW (continued)

Please note any further comments and suggestions/errors below.

FREE PRIZE DRAW RULES

1   Closing date for 31 January 2002 draw is 31 December 2001. Closing date for 31 July 2002 draw is 30 June 2002.

2   Restricted to entries with UK and Eire addresses only. BPP employees, their families and business associates are excluded.

3   No purchase necessary. Entry forms are available upon request from BPP Publishing. No more than one entry per title, per person. Draw restricted to persons aged 16 and over.

4   Winners will be notified by post and receive their cheques not later than 6 weeks after the relevant draw date.

5   The decision of the promoter in all matters is final and binding. No correspondence will be entered into.

See overleaf for information on other
BPP products and how to order

CIMA Order

To BPP Publishing Ltd, Aldine Place, London W12 8AW
Tel: 020 8740 2211. Fax: 020 8740 1184
www.bpp.com   Email publishing@bpp.com
Order online www.bpp.com

Mr/Mrs/Ms (Full name)

Daytime delivery address

Postcode

Email

Daytime Tel   Date of exam (month/year)

POSTAGE & PACKING

Study Texts

	First	Each extra
UK	£3.00	£2.00 £
Europe***	£5.00	£4.00 £
Rest of world	£20.00	£10.00 £

Kits/Passcards/Success Tapes

	First	Each extra
UK	£2.00	£1.00 £
Europe***	£2.50	£1.00 £
Rest of world	£15.00	£8.00 £

Breakthrough Videos

	First	Each extra
UK	£2.00	£2.00 £
Europe***	£2.00	£2.00 £
Rest of world	£20.00	£10.00 £
MCQ cards	£1.00	£1.00 £

Grand Total (Cheques to *BPP Publishing*) I enclose a cheque for (incl. Postage) £

Or charge to Access/Visa/Switch

Card Number

Expiry date   Start Date

Issue Number (Switch Only)

Signature

Products

	7/01 Texts	1/01 Kits	1/01 Passcards	9/00 Tapes	7/00 Videos	8/01 i-Pass / 1/02 i-Pass	1/02 i-Learn	7/01 MCQ cards
FOUNDATION								
1 Financial Accounting Fundamentals	£20.95	£10.95	£5.95	£12.95	£25.95	£24.95		£5.95
2 Management Accounting Fundamentals	£20.95	£10.95	£5.95	£12.95	£25.95	£24.95		£5.95
3A Economics for Business	£20.95	£10.95	£5.95	£12.95	£25.95	£24.95		£5.95
3B Business Law	£20.95	£10.95	£5.95	£12.95	£25.95	£24.95		£5.95
3C Business Mathematics	£20.95	£10.95	£5.95	£12.95	£25.95	£24.95		£5.95
INTERMEDIATE								
4 Finance	£20.95	£10.95	£5.95	£12.95	£25.95	£29.95	£19.95	£5.95
5 Business Tax (FA 2001)	£20.95 (9/01)	£10.95	£5.95	£12.95	£25.95	£29.95	£19.95	£5.95
6 Financial Accounting	£20.95	£10.95	£5.95	£12.95	£25.95	£29.95	£19.95	
6I Financial Accounting International	£20.95	£10.95						
7 Financial Reporting	£20.95	£10.95	£5.95	£12.95	£25.95	£29.95	£19.95	
7I Financial Reporting International	£20.95	£10.95						
8 Management Accounting - Performance Management	£20.95	£10.95	£5.95	£12.95	£25.95	£29.95		£5.95
9 Management Accounting - Decision Making	£20.95	£10.95	£5.95	£12.95	£25.95	£29.95		£5.95
10 Systems and Project Management	£20.95	£10.95	£5.95	£12.95	£25.95	£29.95	£19.95	
11 Organisational Management	£20.95	£10.95	£5.95	£12.95	£25.95	£29.95	£19.95	
FINAL								
12 Management Accounting - Business Strategy	£20.95	£10.95	£5.95	£12.95	£25.95	£29.95	£19.95	
13 Management Accounting - Financial Strategy	£20.95	£10.95	£5.95	£12.95	£25.95	£29.95	£19.95	
14 Management Accounting - Information Strategy	£20.95	£10.95	£5.95	£12.95	£25.95	£29.95	£19.95	
15 Case Study	£20.95							
(1) Workbook		£19.95		£12.95				
(2) Toolkit for 11/01 exam: available 9/01		£19.95						
(3) Toolkit for 5/02 exam: available 3/02								

Total

We aim to deliver to all UK addresses inside 5 working days. A signature will be required. Orders to all EU addresses should be delivered within 6 working days. All other orders to overseas addresses should be delivered within 8 working days.